Judgments of the Court of Criminal Appeal
1984-1989

Judgments
of the
Court of Criminal Appeal
1984-1989

Edited by

Eithne Casey

B. Soc. Sc., barrister-at-law

THE ROUND HALL PRESS

The typesetting of this book was
produced by Gilbert Gough Typesetting, Dublin
for The Round Hall Press
Kill Lane, Blackrock, Co. Dublin.

BRITISH LIBRARY CATALOGUING IN PUBLICATION DATA
Judgments of the court of criminal appeal
Vol. 3: 1984-1989
1. Ireland, Court of Criminal Appeal. Cases (Law)
I. Casey, Eithne
344. 17084

ISBN 0-947686-68-1
ISSN 0791-5373

These reports may be cited as 3 Frewen.

Printed in Ireland by
Betaprint Ltd, Dublin

Contents

Introduction

This volume, which is a continuation of the valuable work commenced by G.L. Frewen, now sadly deceased, is devoted to judgments of the Court of Criminal Appeal delivered between the years 1984 and 1989. It is divided into three parts.

Part I contains all the judgments of the Court hitherto unreported. Part II, which I hope will ease the practitioner's burden of research, is concerned with *ex tempore* judgments most of which were recorded electronically. The installation of a tape recording machine in the courtroom has been of invaluable assistance. I owe a special debt of gratitude to Geraldine Manners, Registrar of the Court of Criminal Appeal, for making available to me all such recorded judgments from the time that recording commenced in 1987. This section contains many judgments concerned with sentencing, a most important area of criminal law. Part III contains the headnotes of the judgments of the Court published in the *Irish Reports* and the *Irish Law Reports Monthly*.

My thanks are due to my colleagues who practice in the field of criminal law, in particular Patrick MacEntee S.C., Michael McDowell S.C. and Patrick Gageby, who were so generous with their time.

EITHNE CASEY,
16 May 1991

Combined Index of Applicants and Appellants

Table of Statutes (Irish and English)

Table of Constitutional Articles

Table of Statutory Instruments

Table of European Community Laws

Judges' Rules

Table of Cases Judicially Cited

Composition of the Supreme Court 1984 to 1989

1984
O'Higgins, Thomas F., Chief Justice
Walsh, Brian
Henchy, Seamus
Griffin, Frank
Hederman, Anthony J.
McCarthy, Niall St. J.

1985
O'Higgins, Thomas F., Chief
    Justice, retired 15th January
Finlay Thomas A., Chief Justice,
    appointed 16th January
Walsh, Brian
Henchy, Seamus
Griffin, Frank
Hederman, Anthony J.
McCarthy, Niall St. J.

1986 and 1987
Finlay Thomas A., Chief Justice

Walsh, Brian
Henchy, Seamus
Griffin, Frank
Hederman, Anthony J.
McCarthy, Niall St. J.

1988
Finlay Thomas A., Chief Justice
Walsh, Brian
Henchy, Seamus,
    retired 16th October 1988
Griffin, Frank
Hederman, Anthony J.
McCarthy, Niall St. J.

1989
Finlay Thomas A., Chief Justice
Walsh, Brian
Griffin, Frank
Hederman, Anthony J.
McCarthy, Niall St. J.

Composition of the High Court 1984 to 1989

1984
Finlay Thomas A., President
Gannon, John M.
Hamilton, Liam
Doyle, Thomas A., retired 13th June
McMahon, James G.
McWilliam, Herbert R.
Costello, Declan D.
D'Arcy, James A.
Keane, Ronan C.
Barrington, Donal P.
Carroll, Mella E.
O'Hanlon, Roderick J.
Barron, Henry D.
Murphy, Francis D.
Lynch, Kevin,
    appointed 24th January
Egan, Seamus F.,
    appointed 2nd July

1985
Finlay Thomas A., President,
    appointed Chief Justice 16th
    January
Hamilton, Liam, President,
    appointed 16th January
Gannon, John M.
McMahon, James G.
McWilliam, Herbert R.,
    retired 12th February
Costello, Declan D.
D'Arcy, James A.
Keane, Ronan C.

Barrington, Donal P.
Carroll, Mella E.
O'Hanlon, Roderick J.
Barron, Henry D.
Murphy, Francis D.
Lynch, Kevin
Egan, Seamus F.
Barr, Robert,
    appointed 30th January
Lardner, Gerard J.,
    appointed 7th March

1986
Hamilton, Liam, President
Gannon, John M.
McMahon, James G.,
    retired January
Costello, Declan D.
D'Arcy, James A.,
    retired 5th January
Keane, Ronan C.
Barrington, Donal P.
Carroll, Mella E.
O'Hanlon, Roderick J.
Barron, Henry D.
Murphy, Francis D.
Lynch, Kevin
Egan, Seamus F.
Barr, Robert
Lardner, Gerard J.
Blayney, John J.,
    appointed 20th January

MacKenzie, John J.P.,
    appointed 10th February

1987
Hamilton, Liam, President
Gannon, John M.
Costello, Declan D.
Keane, Ronan C.
Barrington, Donal P.
Carroll, Mella E.
O'Hanlon, Roderick J.
Barron, Henry D.
Murphy, Francis D.
Lynch, Kevin
Egan, Seamus F.
Barr, Robert
Lardner, Gerard J.
Blayney, John J.
MacKenzie, John J.P.
Johnston, Richard P.,
    appointed 19th January

1988
Hamilton, Liam, President
Gannon, John M.
Costello, Declan D.
Keane, Ronan C.
Barrington, Donal P.
Carroll, Mella E.
O'Hanlon, Roderick J.
Barron, Henry D.
Murphy, Francis D.
Lynch, Kevin
Egan, Seamus F.
Barr, Robert
Lardner, Gerard J.
Blayney, John J.
MacKenzie, John J.P.
Johnston, Richard P.

1989
Hamilton, Liam, President
Gannon, John M.
Costello, Declan D.
Keane, Ronan C.
Barrington, Donal P.,
    resigned 31st August
Carroll, Mella E.
O'Hanlon, Roderick J.
Barron, Henry D.
Murphy, Francis D.
Lynch, Kevin
Egan, Seamus F.
Barr, Robert
Lardner, Gerard J.
Blayney, John J.
MacKenzie, John J.P.
Johnston, Richard P.
Lavan, Vivian,
    appointed 20th September

Part I

UNREPORTED CASES 1984-1989

In the case of Gunner Michael Connolly, Appellant
[C.M.A.C No. 1 of 1983]

The Courts-Martial Appeal Court   20 December 1983

Military law – sentence – Defence Forces – conviction by Court Martial – appeal – severity of sentence – function of the Courts Martial Appeal Court – Courts Martial Appeals Act 1983 (No. 19)

The appellant, who was a member of the Defence Forces, was found guilty of four offences against military law, namely, deserting the Defence Forces, striking a superior officer, behaving in an insubordinate manner towards a superior officer and resisting an escort whose duty it was to apprehend him contrary to sections 135(1), 132, 133 and 134(c), respectively, of the Defence Act 1954 (No. 18). He was sentenced by a court martial to be imprisoned for four months and to be discharged with ignominy from the Defence Forces and when the said findings and sentence of the court martial were confirmed, a sentence of two months imprisonment and discharge from the Defence Forces was substituted therefor by the confirming authority. The appellant sought an order for the enlargement of time within which to appeal and lodged grounds of appeal against the severity of sentence pursuant to the Courts-Martial Appeals Act 1983.

Held by the Courts-Martial Appeal Court (Finlay P, Henchy and Hamilton JJ) in granting the enlargement of time and dismissing the appeal:

(1) That the function of the Courts-Martial Appeal Court in regard to appeals against the severity of sentence is to correct the sentence if there was an error in principle by the court martial or by the confirming officer in arriving at a decision.

(2) That the Courts Martial Appeal Court would be obliged to correct the sentence if it were satisfied that matters not relevant in law to the sentence were taken into consideration or if it were satisfied that other matters which were relevant in law were ignored. The extent or severity of the sentence could in certain cases raise an inference that this had occurred.

No cases cited in judgment

James Nicholson **for the appellant**
Erwan Mill-Arden **for the convening authority for the court martial**

Finlay P

The function of this Court in regard to appeals against the severity of sentence may be summarised as follows:

1. It is to correct the sentence if there was an error in principle by the Court-Martial or by the confirming officer in arriving at a decision concerning the sentence. Furthermore, the Court would be obliged to correct the sentence if it were satisfied that matters not relevant in law to the sentence were taken into consideration or if it were satisfied that other matters which were relevant in law were ignored. The extent or severity

1

The People (DPP) v McKeown
Finlay P

of the sentence could in certain cases raise an inference that this had occurred.

These are the only functions of this Court in regard to appeals aginst sentence. This Court cannot and does not interfere with the sentence of a Court-Martial unless one of these principles can be invoked and in particular does not seek to impose its own discretion in lieu of that of the Court-Martial.

In the instant case, the Court is satisfied that no error of the description which I have outlined has occurred and that therefore this appeal against the severity of sentence must be dismissed.

Solicitors for the appellant: *Reidy Stafford & Co.*
Solicitor for the convening authority for the court martial: *Chief State Solicitor*

Michael J. Baynes
Barrister

The People (Director of Public Prosecutions) v Sean McKeown
[C.C.A. No. 84 of 1983]

Court of Criminal Appeal   12 December 1984

Robbery – evidence – accomplice – pressure on accomplice to give evidence – trial – order of witnesses – intervention by Court of trial – whether prejudicial to accused

Special Criminal Court – composition of Court – applicant tried by two of the members of the Court on previous occasion – possiblity of prejudice – whether Court should discharge itself

The applicant was convicted by the Special Criminal Court of, *inter alia*, robbery and was sentenced to ten years imprisonment. It was argued on behalf of the applicant that the Court of trial intervened in the course of the trial in such a manner as to prejudice the accused; that the Court did not treat the evidence of an accomplice who had been tried separately and had received a suspensory sentence, and the wife of this witness, with the caution required by law; and that pressure had been put on these witnesses to give evidence. It was also argued that the Court erred in its discretion in not disqualifying itself in order that the trial be taken up before a differently constituted Special Criminal Court as the applicant had previously appeared before two members of the Court on a similar charge.

Held by the Court (Finlay P, Hederman and McWilliam JJ) in quashing the conviction and in ordering a new trial that:
(1) The interventions of the Court of trial did not prejudice the accused or cause a mistrial

as the interventions related to the admissibility of statements which were excluded, and the request by the Court to the prosecution to call witnesses in a certain order was not prejudicial to the interests of the accused.

(2) The Court of trial approached the evidence of the accomplice and his wife with the caution provided for by law and had regard to the relationship between the two witnesses and the pressure that had been put upon them to give evidence, which pressure the Court of trial had properly condemned.

(3) Having regard to the seriousness of the charges facing the applicant and the similarity of the charges on which he had been previously acquitted by two members of the Court, it could appear that there was a possibility of prejudice, and the Court of trial in referring to the lateness of the application for a differently constituted Court may have attached importance to such delay. (*People (DPP) v McMahon* 2 Frewen 162 applied). On this ground alone the Court quashed the conviction and treated the application for leave to appeal as a hearing of the appeal and directed a new trial for the applicant.

Case cited in this judgment:
    People (DPP) v McMahon 2 Frewen 162

Seamus Sorahan SC and Michael Gray **for the applicant**
Noel McDonald SC **for the respondent**

Finlay CJ

This is an application by the applicant for a certificate of leave to appeal against his conviction by the Special Criminal Court on the 23rd of June, 1983, of an offence of robbery contrary to section 23 of the Larceny Act 1916, as substituted by section 5 of the Criminal Law Jurisdiction Act 1976, in respect of which he was sentenced to 10 years, and of an offence arising out of the same facts, of carrying a firearm with intent to commit an indictable offence, namely, robbery in respect of which he was sentenced to seven years.

The applicant sought an enlargement of time for the application which was late and it was granted at the commencement of the hearing.

The grounds of appeal were five in number and were as follows:—

(1) The Court of trial erred in its discretion in not acceding to the request of counsel on behalf of the applicant to disqualify themselves from hearing the case against the applicant, two members having sat on a prior trial relating to the applicant.

(2) The Court of trial erred in not granting a separate trial to the applicant, such application having been made by counsel on behalf of the applicant at the outset of the trial.

(3) The Court of trial erred in consistently correcting, amending and advising the State on their proofs throughout the course of the trial which consequently prejudiced the applicant.

(4) The Court of trial did not treat the evidence of Gerard Ryan, an alleged accomplice, and Mary Ryan, the wife of the said Gerard Ryan, with the utmost caution having regard to the nature of the State's case against the applicant and in particular having regard to the involuntary nature of the statement made by the said Gerard Ryan and the said Mary Ryan.

(5) The evidence was by its nature insufficient to enable the Court of trial to find the applicant guilty of charges one and seven.

Counsel on behalf of the applicant conceded in the course of his submissions that the grounds upon which a separate trial had been sought did not manifest themselves during the course of the trial and that he could not therefore pursue that ground of appeal.

Counsel, with the permission of the Court, argued grounds of appeal numbers 3, 4 and 5 before he argued ground number 1 and the Court will deal with the grounds in the order in which they were argued before it.

Ground Number 3

The facts on which this submission was made consisted of a number of instances where the Court of trial either requested witnesses to be led in a particular order or indicated that if evidence which the prosecution sought to tender was to be adduced that notices of additional evidence would have to be served. This Court is satisfied that all but one of these instances related to matters which formed a trial within the trial before the Special Criminal Court and related to facts and circumstances surrounding the admission of certain alleged voluntary statements made by the applicant all of which were, in fact, ruled as inadmissible by the Special Criminal Court. The instance which did not affect the admissibility of statements was where Gerard Ryan, a witness as to certain events which occurred prior to the happening of the robbery, was called at the outset of the case and before any evidence of a robbery had been tendered and where the Court of trial suggested that it would be more appropriate that he should be called at a later time. Reliance was placed on the fact that at that time replies to two or three preliminary questions seemed to indicate that Gerard Ryan was not then going to give evidence in accordance with the statement from him contained in the book of evidence but that when called at a later time in the trial he did so.

In so far as the interventions of the Court affected the admissibility of statements which they excluded, there can be no question at all of these interventions prejudicing the accused or causing, in any way, a mistrial. The Court rejects the submission that the request by the Court to call witnesses in a certain order, which, notwithstanding the ordinary right of the prosecution to call the witnesses in the order in which leading counsel should decide, the prosecution accepted and complied with, could be prejudicial to the interests of the accused or create any form of mistrial. This ground, therefore, also fails.

Ground Number 4

The evidence of Gerard Ryan and of his wife Mary Ryan in so far as it affected this applicant constituted evidence of the arrival of the applicant to the Ryans' residence and farm on the morning of the robbery in company with another man, and of his departure shortly prior to the robbery, the farm being relatively close to the scene of the robbery; of his return at a time after the robbery had been completed; of the storing or hiding of a tin box and money identified as having been taken in the course of the robbery by Gerard Ryan at the request and with the concurrence of this applicant and of certain other matters capable of being associated with the crime.

Gerard Ryan was charged jointly with this applicant and with another person in respect of the offence of the robbery. His case came on some months prior to the hearing of this trial before the Special Criminal Court and he pleaded guilty to certain charges and a suspensory sentence was imposed on him. He was, therefore, an accomplice. Furthermore, in the course of his evidence he stated that after a suspensory sentence had been imposed on him he made the statement on which his evidence in the trial of this applicant was based and that he made that because he was told by a member of the Garda Síochána that he would have to make it and that if he did not he could be asked to serve the sentence which was imposed on him.

Mary Ryan, the wife of Gerard Ryan, gave evidence corroborative of many of the details of the evidence given by her husband. Before doing so she protested to the Court that she had, shortly before being called in evidence, been visited at night by armed men who sought to intimidate her from attending and giving evidence. The Court expressly excluded any suspicion that either of the accused before it was involved in this intimidation. She also gave evidence that she had been informed by a member or members of the Garda Síochána that, having regard to the fact that she had made a deposition in the case in the District Court, she could be charged with perjury if she gave different evidence in the trial.

These pressures put on both of these witnesses to give evidence were properly and strongly condemned by the Court of trial and with that condemnation this Court would very fully agree.

However, it is necessary to consider the way in which the Court of trial approached these two witnesses having regard:—

(a) to the fact that Gerard Ryan was an accomplice and that his wife, Mary Ryan, was his wife with an obvious interest in his welfare, and

(b) to the evidence of pressure which had been given by each of these witnesses in regard to their giving of evidence.

In the course of the verdict of the Court of trial it was stated as follows:—

> The Court is conscious of the fact that it is obliged to consider the evidence of both Mr and Mrs Ryan with the greatest care, having regard to the fact that Gerard Ryan was undoubtedly an accomplice of the accused, that Mrs Ryan is his wife and having regard to what they admitted in evidence was stated to them by members of the Garda Síochána. Having done so and having witnessed their demeanour in the box during their direct evidence and their answers in cross-examination the Court is satisfied beyond all reasonable doubt that they are truthful witnesses and accepts their evidence. Mrs Ryan was undoubtedly distressed during the earlier portion of her evidence, but subsequently gave her evidence in a clear and definite manner. Mr Ryan also gave his evidence in a clear and definite manner and both witnesses are regarded by the Court as giving a truthful account of what transpired on the morning of the 12th of February, 1982.

Dealing with the effect of the Ryans' evidence the Court continued by saying:—

> Having regard to the fact that Mr Farrell's Datsun motor car was discovered in the vicinity of Geraghtys' gateway, which is shown on

the map proved in evidence, the Court is satisfied, beyond all reasonable doubt, that those engaged in the robbery travelled from Clane in the direction of Athgoe. Accepting, as it does, the evidence of Mr and Mrs Ryan the Court is satisfied that both the accused . . . returned to the garage on Ryan's land before 11.00 a.m. Mrs Ryan's evidence that they returned while she was listening to the "Gay Byrne Hour" as it was coming to an end establishes the time of their return and on the basis of Gerard Ryan's evidence that they had, at that time in their possession, the money stolen from Mr Farrell and the gun containing ammunition and having regard to the time at which the robbery took place, the distance which they had to travel from Clane, the time involved in transferring the money from the Datsun motor car to the green Avenger, the Court is satisfied, beyond all reasonable doubt, that the two accused carried out the said robbery, one of them actually producing the gun to Mr Farrell and escaping in the Datsun car and the other escaping in a Renault car and that they were engaged in the joint enterprise. . . .

The Court of trial was entitled to accept the evidence of an accomplice whether corroborated or uncorroborated provided it approached such evidence with the caution provided for by law. The verdict of the Court, a portion of which has just been quoted, very clearly indicates the precise manner in which the Court approached the evidence of Gerard Ryan and of Mrs Ryan having regard, not only to the status of Gerard Ryan as an accomplice, but to the relationship between the two witnesses and to their statements concerning the pressures that have been put upon them. Their acceptance of the evidence of these two witnesses is expressly and specifically based upon the impression they made upon them while giving evidence in the witness box and in those circumstances, in accordance with the principles already frequently enunciated, this Court cannot and does not interfere with the finding of fact so made.

This ground of appeal, therefore, fails.

Ground Number 5
The submission made on this ground was, in effect, a repetition of the submission made on ground number 4 and depended upon the rejection by this Court on appeal of the acceptance by the Court of trial of the evidence of Gerard Ryan and Mary Ryan. Having regard to the view this

Court takes with regard to ground number 4 this ground must also fail.

Ground Number 1
At the commencement of the trial counsel on behalf of this applicant applied for an adjournment of the trial and that the trial be taken up before a differently constituted Special Criminal Court. The grounds for this application were that this applicant had, within approximately two months prior to the date of this trial, been tried on a charge of armed robbery of a bank by the Special Criminal Court, two members of which were of the Court presiding at this trial, and had been acquitted.

Upon this application being made the following dialogue took place between the Court and counsel:—

Presiding Judge: It is rather late to be making this application, Mr White, isn't it.

Mr White: Well they are my instructions.

Presiding Judge: The accused has been aware of the fact that his trial is fixed for this date for some considerable time.

Mr White: His trial has been fixed for some time, I must concede that, but I wasn't aware that the personnel had been the same until as recently as Friday.

Presiding Judge: The application could have been made on Monday, you have had ample time if there was any validity in your application to enable a separate Court to be constituted and to come in, when we are here and all the witnesses are here, to make this application is a bit late in the day.

Mr White: They are my instructions, to make the application, I should say that I only came into the case on Friday, and it was at that stage . . .

Presiding Judge: I am not criticising you at all, Mr White.

Mr White: I am not making that as an excuse either. It was only at that stage that certain matters came to my attention with regard to the matter.

Presiding Judge: The Court will refuse the application made on behalf of the accused. The Court, as constituted of experienced judges, are perfectly capable of assessing the evidence of each particular case. The case to which Mr White refers us with regard to the accused having been tried before this Court on a previous occasion, two of the members of this tribunal presided over that trial, the accused was acquitted in respect of that charge. The Court is quite satisfied that it is perfectly capable and will deal with this case purely on the evidence adduced before it and not have regard to any factors in that case.

Having regard to this portion of the transcript, counsel on behalf of the applicant submits that it is open to interpretation that one of the factors leading to the Court exercising its discretion in refusing to withdraw from the trial, and have a different Court constituted for it, was the lateness of the application and that that would not be a valid ground, whether as a sole ground or as one of many grounds, for exercising a discretion which should solely have been exercised in the interests of the justice of the trial.

Counsel on behalf of the Director of Public Prosecutions, on the other hand, contends that the words used by the presiding judge "you have had ample time, if there was any validity in your application, . . ." clearly indicate that what was in the mind of the Court was not any inconvenience arising from the lateness of the application, but a belief that the application was not *bona fide* by reason of the late time at which it was made. The question of the review on appeal of the exercise of the discretion by the Special Criminal Court to refuse an application to discharge itself from a case and constitute a different tribunal of that multiple Court, was considered by this Court in the case of *People (DPP) v Thomas McMahon* 2 Frewen 162 in which judgment was delivered on the 25th of March, 1983. In the course of that judgment which was delivered by Hederman J. it was stated as follows at p. 170:—

This Court has, of course, a right to review the conduct of the Special Criminal Court, and if it is satisfied that the Court wrongly exercised its discretion in continuing with a case after inadmissible prejudicial evidence had been elicited, it could set aside the conviction, but before so doing, the Court must be satisfied that the discretion was incorrectly used to the detriment of the accused and vitiated fair procedures.

This Court accepts that succinct statement of the principle applicable and applies it to this case.

This Court is satisfied that the members of the Special Criminal Court presiding over this trial, all of whom are experienced members of the judiciary, would in fact have no difficulty, and almost certainly had no difficulty, in excluding from their minds the evidence which they had heard in the previous trial of this applicant which resulted in his acquittal. Quite apart from the Special Criminal Court, the trial of persons necessarily takes place in the District Court on summary charges by a judge sitting without a jury, and in the Circuit Court on appeal by way of rehearing, from summary convictions by a judge sitting without a jury, on different charges at different times the particular judge being inevitably aware of a previous trial and frequently of a previous conviction. That fact could not be taken as necessarily or inevitably disqualifying the judge concerned nor vitiating the fairness of the hearing before him.

This Court has considered the interpretation which Counsel on behalf of the Director of Public Prosecutions placed on the remarks of the Court in the extract quoted above, dealing with the lateness of the application and the inconvenience caused by it being made as the trial was about to commence, and it is not satisfied that it must, inevitably, be correct. It could hardly be said that the application to seek a trial by a differently constituted tribunal on a serious charge of armed robbery on a bank, almost identical to a charge on which he had been tried by some of the members of the tribunal on a very recent occasion, was either bogus or frivolous. Having regard to the seriousness of the charges facing this applicant on his trial and the similarity of the charges on which he had shortly before been acquitted, it could be felt that there was a possibility of prejudice to the applicant on his trial. It could also be felt that there was a possibility that the Court, in referring to the time factor, had attached importance to it when exercising its discretion not to obtain a differently

constituted tribunal from amongst the membership of the Special Criminal
Court, which is a court of multiple membership.

As justice must not only be done but must be seen to be done, this
Court is of opinion that the conviction and sentence should be quashed
and, treating the application for leave to appeal as the hearing of the
appeal, so orders. Having regard to the view of this Court on the other
grounds of appeal submitted, however, this Court directs a new trial of
the applicant.

Solicitor for the applicant: *Dermot Morris and Co.*
Solicitor for the respondent: *Chief State Solicitor*

Eithne Casey
Barrister

The People (Director of Public Prosecutions) v Thomas Healy
[C.C.A. No. 65 of 1983]

Court of Criminal Appeal   12 December 1984

*Robbery – Special Criminal Court – preparation of defence – loss of documents relating to
defence – application for adjournment refused – evidence of intimidation of witnesses
for the prosecution – applicant in custody at relevant time – whether prejudicial to
accused – weight of evidence*

The applicant applied for leave to appeal against a conviction of, *inter alia*, robbery in
respect of which he was sentencd to 12 years imprisonment. The applicant was a co-accused
of one Sean McKeown who also appealed his conviction, see 3 Frewen 2.

The applicant appeared in person and stated that papers relevant to his defence were
confiscated in Portlaoise Prison; that evidence prejudicial to him was given at his trial relating
to alleged intimidation of two witnesses for the prosecution and that his conviction was
against the weight of the evidence. The applicant also adopted the arguments made by counsel
on behalf of his co-accused Sean McKeown whose application for leave to appeal was heard
prior to this application.

Held by the Court (Finlay P, Hederman and McWilliam JJ), in refusing the application:
(1) That the applicant had ample time to prepare his defence since the loss of his
documents, which the evidence suggested were mislaid, but he chose to withdraw his
instructions to his solicitor and counsel on the morning of the trial and the decision of the
Court of trial not to adjourn the hearing in those circumstances was correct.
(2) That the introduction of irrelevant evidence regarding alleged intimidation of a
witness for the prosecution did not prejudice a fair trial as the applicant was in custody at the

The People (DPP) v Healy
Finlay CJ

relevant time and the Court stated that they did not associate the applicant with the intimidation.

(3) That the conviction of the applicant was not against the weight of the evidence. The Court of trial was entitled to accept the evidence of the prosecution witnesses and there was corroboration of their evidence.

Case cited in this judgment:
People (Director of Public Prosecutions) v McKeown 3 Frewen 2

Applicant appeared in person
Names of counsel for prosecution not available

Finlay CJ

This is an application for leave to appeal against the conviction of the applicant by the Special Criminal Court on 23rd of June, 1983, of the offence of robbery in respect of which he was sentenced to 12 years imprisonment and in respect of an offence of carrying a firearm with intent to commit robbery in respect of which he was sentenced to 10 years imprisonment.

The applicant appeared in person at the trial and submitted and prosecuted his own appeal before this Court. His grounds of appeal submitted in writing were as follows:

(1) My constitutional right to prepare a proper defence was taken from me by the confiscation of my written legal instructions in Portlaoise Prison. Therefore my trial was not a fair one.

(2) During the trial, evidence was given that men armed with rifles threatened two witnesses, Mr and Mrs Ryan, in the early hours of the first day of the trial. The President of the Court said after hearing this 'that this is most prejudicial to the Accused'. The Prosecutor made known to the Court that he accepted that the other accused, Mr McKeown, had nothing to do with such threats and the Court in accepting this and giving consideration to it acted in a very unfair manner to me.

(3) I want to appeal against the conviction on the weight of the evidence. The President of the Court told me I could do this.

Upon the hearing of this application, the applicant did not develop any of these grounds of appeal to any extent but did with the permission of the Court insofar as Ground Number 3 was concerned adopt arguments and submissions which had been made by Counsel on behalf of the other applicant, Sean McKeown, who was jointly indicted with this applicant in respect of these offences and whose appeal against conviction was heard immediately prior to the hearing of this application and in the presence of this applicant.

This Court, in the judgment just delivered, has quashed the conviction and directed a retrial of this applicant's co-accused Sean McKeown on a ground which does not arise in the case of this applicant, there being no question of this applicant having previously appeared in the Special Criminal Court before any of the members of the Tribunal presiding at his trial.

Ground Number 1

Before the commencement of the trial of this applicant, which was on the 15th June, 1983, counsel and solicitor retained on his behalf, sought permission from the Court to withdraw on the grounds that their instructions had been withdrawn. The applicant stated that he had withdrawn these instructions because a note of matters pertaining to his trial which he had made whilst in Portlaoise Prison had been taken from him during the course of a search and had not been returned to him. The Court took evidence on these matters and came to the conclusion that the applicant had been returned for trial on the 29th of June, 1982; that he had been represented by counsel and solicitor on the taking of depositions including the cross-examination on his behalf of deponents in June and July, 1982, on a number of days; that in the course of a search of his cell at a time when explosives were found in Portlaoise Prison, that documents had been taken from him in March of 1983, and that one book containing notes made by him in preparation for his trial had not been returned to him. The Court was satisfied that the applicant had, since the time of the loss of this document which the evidence before it suggested was mislaid, ample time to prepare for his defence at the trial and to instruct his solicitor and counsel but had chosen instead to withdraw their instructions on the morning of the hearing. In those circumstances, the Court decided not to adjourn the trial of the applicant and with that decision this Court must agree and could not possibly interfere. This ground must therefore fail.

Ground Number 2

Mrs Mary Ryan, one of the witnesses called on behalf of the prosecution stated that she had, shortly before being called to give evidence, been intimidated by a visit from armed men who tried to prevent her from coming forward to give evidence. The Court of trial stated that this matter should not have been introduced before them but immediately stated that they did not in any way associate it with either of the accused who would have had no opportunity to take part in such intimidation, being both in custody and, upon the matter being subsequently raised by this applicant specifically stated that they did not associate him in any way with this event. There can be no question therefore that the introduction of this irrelevant evidence into the case could or did prejudice a fair trial of the applicant. This ground must also fail.

Ground Number 3

In its judgment in the case of *People (DPP) v Sean McKeown* 3 Frewen 2 the Court has already dealt with the findings as to the credibility of witnesses and the approach of the Court of trial to the evidence of Mr and Mrs Ryan having regard to the position of Mr Ryan as an accomplice. It is unnecessary to repeat these findings again. Insofar as this applicant was concerned, the evidence of Mr Ryan was to the effect that he, Mr Healy, had accompanied the applicant Sean McKeown from Ryan's premises having loaded a gun and placed it in the waistband of his trousers at a time shortly prior to the occurrence of the robbery in Clane, that he returned with McKeown to the premises again and then requested Gerard Ryan to bury money which he had in a plastic bag and which was subsequently identified as the money taken in the robbery. The evidence thus adduced and accepted by the Court of trial of the implication of this applicant in the robbery was corroborated by the fact that he was found by the Gardaí at approximately 1.00 p.m. in the shed where Ryan stated that he remained; furthermore, by the finding of firearms residue on the sleeve of his dufflecoat and furthermore, by the finding of fibres from his clothing in the car, the property of the bank official, which was taken by the robbers from the scene of the robbery. Being satisfied, as has already been indicated, that the Court of trial was entitled to accept the evidence of Gerard Ryan and of his wife Mary Ryan and being satisfied that there was corroboration of that evidence which the Court of trial was also entitled to accept, the Court must reject the submission on this ground that the conviction of the accused was against the weight of the evidence. This application for leave to appeal must therefore be dismissed.

Solicitor for the respondent: *Chief State Solicitor*

Eithne Casey
Barrister

The People (Director of Public Prosecutions) v Michael Scanlon
[C.C.A. No. 25 of 1983]

Court of Criminal Appeal   1 March 1985

Trial – rape – conduct of trial – intervention by trial judge during trial – evidence – corroboration – charge to jury – failure of trial judge to identify evidence implicating accused

The applicant was convicted in the Dublin Circuit (Criminal) Court of rape and was sentenced to ten years' penal servitude. While there was ample evidence that the injured party had been raped, the only evidence tending to incriminate the applicant was a palm print found on the window of the room in which the rape had taken place which, on the evidence of the prosecution, was identified as being that of the applicant.

Held by the Court (Finlay CJ, Carroll and Egan JJ) in quashing the conviction and in ordering a new trial:
(1) That the trial was unsatisfactory in that while the trial judge, in his charge to the jury, dealt with the general law of corroboration and the evidence adduced in the case, he failed to identify and isolate the evidence of the palm print as being the only evidence tending to incriminate the accused and this failure could have left the jury unsure of the evidence that they were entitled to accept as establishing the complicity of the accused in the crime.
(2) That the trial judge's interventions in the direct evidence and cross-examination of the technical witness proving the palm print was so extensive as to impede the proper cross-examination of the witness on behalf of the accused and constituted an unsatisfactory element in the trial.
(3) That the trial judge's extensive questioning of the accused may have conveyed to the jury a strong element of disbelief by him of the accused's evidence notwithstanding warnings that it was the exclusive right of the jury to assess the facts of the case and that when charging the jury his misrecollection of a portion of the evidence may have prejudiced the accused.

No cases cited in judgment

Sean Ryan SC and Thomas O'Connell **for the applicant**
Sean Moylan **for the respondent**

The People (DPP) v Scanlon
Finlay CJ

Finlay CJ

This is an application for leave to appeal against a conviction of the applicant of the offence of rape, the conviction being on the 17th of March, 1983, and the applicant, having been remanded for sentence, was sentenced to ten years' penal servitude on the 24th of March, 1983.

A number of grounds were put forward on behalf of the applicant and the Court having carefully considered the submissions made on his behalf and on behalf of the Director of Public Prosecutions and having carefully considered the transcript of the trial herein, has come to the conclusion that the trial was unsatisfactory and that a new trial of the applicant on this charge must be ordered.

The reasons why it has come to this decision are as follows.

1. On considering the evidence as appears in the transcript it is clear that, whereas the fact that the injured party, a young girl, was raped was amply established by her own evidence and by corroboration of that fact from other uncontested evidence, the only evidence capable of establishing that it was the accused who raped her was the evidence of identification of a palm print found on the window of the room in which the injured party was raped, which on the evidence for the prosecution was identified as being the palm print of the accused.

Although the charge of the learned trial judge to the jury dealt with the general law of corroboration and dealt extensively with the evidence which had been adduced in the case, it did not identify and isolate this evidence of palm print identification as being the only evidence tending to incriminate the accused in the commission of the crime which had undoubtedly been committed. This failure to identify and isolate this particular piece of evidence could have left the jury unsure of the evidence which they were entitled to accept as establishing the complicity of the accused in the crime.

2. Having regard to this Court's view of the supreme importance of the evidence of the identification of this palm print the Court is satisfied that it is possible that the intervention by the learned trial Judge in both the direct evidence and the cross-examination of the technical witness proving the identification of the palm print was so extensive as to impede the proper cross-examination of this witness on behalf of the accused and constituted an unsatisfactory element in the trial.

3. The accused was extensively questioned by the learned trial judge when he was giving evidence on his own behalf. The extent and nature of

this questioning was such as might have conveyed to a jury a strong element of disbelief in the trial judge of some of the evidence given by the accused, and notwithstanding proper warnings subsequently given as to the exclusive right of the jury to assess the facts in the case, could have led to an unsatisfactory element in the trial.

4. Whilst it is a detail, the learned trial judge in the course of his charge to the jury stated that the rapist was somebody who knew the family of the injured girl and who knew the names of the children in that family. He based this conclusion on a misrecollection of one portion of the evidence and there was in fact no evidence which the jury could accept as establishing that the assailant of the girl knew the names of the members of her family. Whilst this was a small detail in a case containing much evidence, having regard to the fact that the transcript records that the jury's deliberation took approximately thirteen hours, a possibility exists that the jury might have had regard to this statement in the charge of the learned trial judge to the prejudice of the accused.

For all these reasons the Court has, as I have indicated, reached a conclusion that this trial was unsatisfactory and will treat the application for leave to appeal as the appeal and will order a new trial of the accused.

Solicitor for the applicant: *Michael D. White and Co.*
Solicitor for the respondent: *Chief State Solicitor*

Margaret Stynes
Barrister

The People (Director of Public Prosections) v Mary McGing
[No. 85 of 1984]

Court of Criminal Appeal   12 November 1985

Evidence – admissibility – statement of accused – whether voluntary – oppression – lengthy interrogation by single member of Garda Síochána – discrepancies in evidence of members of Garda Síochána – Role of appellate Court regarding findings of fact – interrogation of female – whether female member of Garda Síochána should be present – Offences Against the State Act 1939 (No. 13), section 30.

The applicant was arrested pursuant to section 30 of the Offences Against the State Act 1939. She was subsequently convicted by the Special Criminal Court of harbouring and assisting three persons (by the provision of a "safe house") knowing that they had committtted a felony, and was sentenced to twelve months imprisonment. She applied for leave to appeal the conviction.

The only evidence tending to connect the applicant with the charges were certain verbal admissions alleged to have been made by her while she was in custody and a statement taken down by the interviewing detective but not signed by her.

It was argued on her behalf that there was not sufficient evidence before the Court of trial to prove that the applicant had not been subjected to oppression when she made her statement; that there were discrepancies between the evidence given by various members of the Garda Síochána; that the applicant was interrogated for lengthy periods of time by a single member of the Special Investigative Branch of the Garda Síochána; that no female member (although present in the Garda Station) was ever present at the interrogations, and that as a result the interrogations did not conform to the requirements of fairness of practices and procedures under the Constitution and accordingly there was a judicial discretion to exclude the fruits thereof and that the Court did not properly exercise such discretion in accordance with the evidence.

Held by the Court (Hederman, Keane and Barr JJ), in refusing the application:

(1) That while there were discrepancies with regard to the evidence given by two detectives as against that given by three gardaí, the existence of such discrepancies did not of itself justify the Court in interfering with the decision of the Court of trial as to the credibility of the witnesses concerned, and having accepted the evidence of the detectives as truthful there was ample evidence to justify a finding that there had been no oppression as alleged by the applicant. (*Northern Bank Finance Corp. Ltd v Charlton* [1979] I.R. 149 and *People (DPP) v Kelly (No. 2)* [1983] I.R. 1 applied.)

(2) That it is undesirable for persons detained under section 30 of the Act of 1939 to be interviewed for lengthy periods by a single member of the Gardaí, and where practicable it was desirable that a Ban Garda should be physically present in the interview room while a female was being interrogated. However, the Court of trial was entitled to take into account all the evidence of the circumstances of the interrogation and to conclude, on a review of all the evidence, that the interrogation was not conducted in a manner so oppressive as to render the statement made as a result thereof inadmissible.

Cases cited in this judgment:
Northern Bank Finance Corp. Ltd v Charlton [1979] I.R. 149
People (Director of Public Prosecutions) v Kelly (No. 2) [1983] I.R. 1;
    [1983] ILRM 271

Patrick MacEntee SC and Gregory Murphy **for the applicant**
Noel MacDonald SC and Denis Vaughan-Buckley **for the respondent**

Hederman J

The applicant was arrested on the 21st of December, 1983, under section 30 of the Offences Against the State Act 1939, and brought to Castlebar Garda Station. She remained in Garda custody until the 23rd of December, 1983, when she was brought before the District Court at Balla. She was there charged with having on the 20th and 21st of December, 1983, in County Mayo harboured and assisted three persons, not then arrested, knowing that they had committed a felony, *i.e.*, possession of a firearm with intent to endanger life. She was subsequently charged with a further offence that on the 20th of December, 1983, in County Mayo, she harboured and assisted three persons, not then arrested, knowing that they had committed a felony, *i.e.*, false imprisonment. The applicant was tried on both these counts by the Special Criminal Court on the 1st, 2nd, 6th and 7th of November, 1984. She was convicted on the first count and sentenced to imprisonment for twelve months and acquitted on the second count. Having been refused leave by the Court to appeal, she has now applied to this Court for such leave.

Evidence was given at the trial that on the 20th of December, 1983, three members of the Gardaí in uniform were on duty at Ballaveeney Bridge, Ballycroy, Co. Mayo at about 9.15 p.m. They signalled a motor car coming from the Mulrany direction to stop. There were five people in the car, one of whom was carrying a gun, which appeared to one of the Gardaí to be a machine gun. The three Gardaí were forced at gunpoint to lie down on the roadway and were tied up. The Garda car was driven up a laneway by one of the occupants of the car which had been intercepted; and the latter car was then driven off at speed towards Mulrany. It was accepted at the trial, and at the hearing of this application, that the only evidence tending to connect the applicant with these events were certain verbal admissions alleged to have been made by her while she was in custody in Castlebar Garda Station and a statement reduced to writing, but not signed by her, which she was alleged to have made while in such custody.

In the course of the alleged statement, the applicant said that on the 20th of December, 1983, she was approached by a person whose identity she did not wish to disclose to help in the transportation of three people from Charlestown to Ballycroy. She gave an account of having been driven with three men who were unknown to her, by a Mrs McIntyre, with the object of leaving the men at a house there. The alleged statement goes on to describe the halting of the car at a Garda checkpoint on the Ballycroy road, the production by the three men of guns and the driving of the Garda car up a side road. It says that one of the three men then took over the driving of Mrs McIntyre's car and that she (the applicant) was asked where she could get another house for them. The statement says that she (the applicant) knew that Colm O'Raghallaigh from Claremorris had a new house built just outside the town and that she decided to take the three men there, which she did. In the course of the alleged statement, the applicant also said that she was a member of Sinn Féin for the past 18 months and that she assumed that the three men were members of "the Republican movement".

The alleged statement begins with the words:—

> I have been cautioned that I need not make a statement unless I wish to do so but any statement I do make will be taken down in writing and may be used in evidence.

It ends with the words:—

> This statement has been read over to me and it is correct, except for one point we did not reverse up the side road past the checkpoint, we drove up it. I have no other additions or alterations to make in it.

The whole of the alleged statement is in the handwriting of Detective Garda Patrick Tuohy, who was attached to Castlebar Garda Station. The written statement is followed by the words "Miss McGing declined to sign the statement", underneath which are the signatures of Sergeant Tuohy and Detective Garda Patrick Walsh, a member of the Criminal Investigation Section of the Garda Technical Bureau, at Garda Headquarters.

The evidence as to the taking of this statement, and the making of the alleged verbal admissions which preceded it, may be summarised as follows. Sergeant Tuohy said that he arrested the applicant under section 30 of the Offences Against the State Act at 9.45 p.m. on the 21st of December at a house in Castlebar because he believed that she was a member of an unlawful organisation, namely, the Irish Republican Army. He then had her conveyed to Castlebar Garda Station. He said that on the following day he went with Detective Garda Walsh to the Detective Branch Office in Castlebar Garda Station at approximately 6.15 p.m. Mr Patrick Moran, solicitor, had just left at that stage. He said that the applicant was in the office alone and that Garda Walsh cautioned her that she was not obliged to say anything unless she wished to do so but that anything she would say would be taken down in writing and might be used in evidence. He said that Garda Walsh then told her that the Gardaí were satisfied that she had left three armed men at the home of Colman O'Raghallaigh in Claremorris on the night of the 20th and that the Gardaí believed that those three men had earlier been involved in the armed robbery and false imprisonment of three Gardaí at Ballycroy. He said that the applicant replied:—

"Yes, they were the men, but, as I have told you already, we did not expect to meet any Guards".

Sergeant Tuohy said he then asked the applicant to tell them about her involvement in the incident at Ballycroy and that she replied:—

"Yes, I'll tell you my part. Colman O'Raghallaigh has told you his. Tommy Devereux is here in the station and he can speak for himself".

Sergeant Tuohy said he then asked her if she wished to make a statement and that she said she did. He said that he cautioned her that she was not obliged to make a statement unless she wished to do so but that any statement she made would be taken down in writing and might be used in evidence. He said that she then dictated a statement which he took down in writing. He said that when the statement was concluded, he told her he was going to read it over to her and she could make any additions or alterations she wished. He said that he then read the statement over to her and that she made one alteration and one addition. He said that she initialled the addition and also initialled the bottom of page one. She then said the statement was correct and he noted that in the statement. He said that he invited her to sign it but she declined.

Sergeant Tuohy in cross-examination denied that while the applicant was being interviewed there was a good deal of noise coming from another office where somebody else was being interviewed. He also denied that there was an intimidating atmosphere in the Garda Station. It was also suggested to him that, while the applicant was being interviewed by Garda Walsh on the evening she was brought to the station, he (the witness) entered the room and found that she had been required by Garda Walsh to take her shoes off, and that he (the witness) said to him "this is not Castlereagh, it's Castlebar." This suggestion was denied by the witness, as was the suggestion also put to him that the alleged statement was taken in the form of questions and answers.

Garda Walsh said that he took the applicant to the Detective Branch Office in the station at 10 p.m. on the 21st of December. He told her that he was investigating the armed robbery and false imprisonment at Ballycroy and cautioned her that she was not obliged to say anything unless she wished to do so but that anything she did say would be taken down in writing and might be given in evidence. He said that he asked her if she understood the caution and that she made no reply. He said that he asked her some general questions about herself, but she again made no answer. He then told her that she had been arrested under the Offences Against the State Act and asked her to account for her movements from 5 p.m. on the previous night until her arrest on that night. He said that she again made no reply and that he asked her again to account for her movements. He said that on this occasion she replied:—

"I know all about it. This is not the first time I was arrested".

He said that he then asked her to account for her movements and she replied:—

"Yer looking for more powers and the law is already on your side".

He said that he asked her what she meant by that and that she said:—

"I open my mouth I am in trouble and I say nothing — that says I'm in trouble".

He said that he then got Ban Gharda Rush, who was on duty in the station, to get the applicant and himself some tea and biscuits and that he then had further discussion with her. He said that as this stage she was speaking freely. He told her that Colman O'Raghallaigh had made a statement that she (the applicant) had left three armed men in his house in Claremorris on the previous night and said that she asked if she could see the statement. He said that he then showed her the statement, that she read it and that when she had finished reading it she sat back for a minute and said:

"He has told ye all".

Garda Walsh said that he then asked the applicant to tell him her part of what had happened and that, in answer, she said that she did not mean the Gardaí any harm and that she was only taking people from A to B. He said that she stated it was a pity they hadn't been an hour earlier as they wouldn't have met any Gardaí.

Garda Walsh said that at this stage the applicant's solicitor, Mr Patrick Moran, arrived and that he (the witness) left the applicant alone with Mr Moran. He said that when Mr Moran had finished his interview with the applicant, he (the witness) returned to the room where she was and read over the notes he had taken of his earlier interview with her. He said that he cautioned her that she was not obliged to say anything unless she wished to do so but that anything she did say would be taken down in writing and might be given in evidence. He said he then asked the applicant if the notes were correct and that she replied "I say nothing". He said that he then invited her to sign the notes and that she said she would sign nothing. He said that thereupon she was placed in a cell by the station orderly.

Garda Walsh said that he next saw the applicant at 10 a.m. on the following morning when he brought her to the Detective Branch Office again and spoke to her. He said that she had her breakfast on that occasion and that he stayed with her until she had finished her breakfast when he placed her back in the cell at 10.30 a.m. He said that at 2 p.m. on that day he again brought her to the office and cautioned her that she was not obliged to say anything unless she wished to do so but that anything she did say would be taken down in writing and might be given in evidence. He said that before that she was served with lunch but had not eaten it. He said that he again questioned her about the incident at Ballaveeney Bridge but that she wouldn't discuss it. She said that she was expecting her solicitor to call back to her that day and that she would not say anything about it until she had spoken to him. He said that he had a general discussion with her then about various topics. Mr Moran called again at about 5.30 p.m. and was with the applicant until about 6.15 p.m. He said that he then went into the office with Sergeant Tuohy and again cautioned her in the same terms. He said that he suggested to her that she was involved with the men at Ballaveeney Bridge who had tied up the Gardaí and robbed them and that she then brought those men to Colman O'Raghallaigh's house in Claremorris. He said that the applicant replied:—

> "Okay, they were the men . . . but as I have told you we didn't expect to meet any Guards".

He said that these were her exact words and that he had noted them at the time. He gave evidence to the same effect as Sergeant Tuohy as to the making of the statement by the applicant.

Garda Walsh in cross-examination denied that, at their first meeting, he had made the applicant take off her shoes and stand in her stockinged feet for a while. He said that Sergeant Tuohy was not presente in the interview room at any time until the following day.

Ban Gharda Rush said that she was on duty in the station on the 21st of December, 1983, when the applicant arrived there and remained on duty until 9.30 a.m. the following day. She said that she saw the applicant twice in the interview room at 11.30 p.m. and 12.30 a.m., that she placed her in the cell at 2 a.m. and that she visited her at hourly intervals thereafter until 5 a.m. She said that everything seemed to be in order and that the applicant made no complaints to her. In cross-examination, she said that she recalled bringing a glass of water to the applicant while she was in the interview room and that she thought there were three people there, the applicant and two detectives.

Garda John Melvin, the station orderly, said that he was on duty from 6 a.m. on the 22nd of December and he identified entries made by him in the C.84 Form kept, in accordance with the relevant regulations, in relation to the custody of the applicant. These recorded the applicant as having been questioned between the hours of 10 a.m. and 2 p.m., at which stage she was served with lunch but refused it. Garda Melvin said that the Garda questioning her during this time was Garda Walsh. Ban Gharda Brett said that she was on duty in the station from 9.30 a.m. on the 22nd of December until 5.30 p.m. and served breakfast to the applicant at 11.30 a.m. She recalled two men in plain clothes being in the room with the applicant at that time, but could not identify them.

Garda Walsh was recalled and said that at 11.30 a.m. on the morning of the 22nd of December, he was out in the country with Sergeant Tuohy who arrested another man at that stage and brought him to the Garda Station.

At the close of the State's evidence in relation to the taking of the statement and the making of the alleged admissions, an application was made for a direction on behalf of the applicant. The Court refused this application and, thereupon, the applicant gave evidence as to the taking of the statement and the alleged admissions. She said that at the beginning of her interview with Garda Walsh, he asked her to look at him in the face, which she did not do, and that he then caught her head and turned it around, forcing her to look into his face. She said that he then pulled her out of the chair she was sitting in and told her to stand up and take off her shoes, which she did. She said that he then started to question her and that after about ten minutes Sergeant Tuohy came in and seemed surprised to see her standing in her stockinged feet. He said something to the effect that this was Castlebar, not Castlereagh, and told her to put on her shoes and sit down, which she did. She said that both Gardaí then started to question her and that this went on for about an hour, at which stage her solicitor arrived and she had a consultation with him. This lasted for about 15 minutes and Garda Walsh then returned and continued to question her in a manner which she described as "very aggressive". She denied that she made the statements during the course of this questioning attributed to her by Garda Walsh. She said that the following morning she was in the Detective Branch Office from the time she had her breakfast onwards and that Garda Walsh was with her most of the time questioning her. As a result, she was worried and frightened and wasn't able to eat her lunch. She denied that during the course of this questioning she made the statements attributed to her by Garda Walsh. She said that when Sergeant Tuohy came in later in the afternoon he produced some yellow foolscap sheets on which there was what she now knew to be the caution written on top. He said that he asked her to account for her movements and that she decided to do so because her solicitor had advised her that under the Offences Against the State Act she was obliged to give such an account of her movements. She said she was afraid not to give such an account, because for a number of hours the previous evening and again on the morning of the 22nd she could hear very loud noises up the corridor coming from what she assumed to be the room where the other prisoner was being questioned. She said there was banging and shouting coming from the room and that Garda Walsh seemed to become more aggressive as time passed. She said that the statement was entirely the result of questions put to her. She also said that she initialled the written statement in certain places at the suggestion of Sergeant Tuohy.

Mr Patrick Moran said that he was a solicitor and had visited the station on the 21st of December at about 11 o'clock where he saw the applicant. He said that he returned the following afternoon to see her at about 3 o'clock in the afternoon. On that occasion he also saw another person who was in custody, Mr Devereaux, and that the latter was being questioned in an aggressive manner by two detectives. He said that he saw the applicant again later the same afternoon at which stage he had come to the conclusion that, because of a conflict of interest, he could not act for her and advised her accordingly. The only noises that he heard in the station were the loud shouting when he was with Mr Devereaux. He was not with her for more than about ten to fifteen minutes on the third occasion. He said that he had no reason to complain to anybody about the treatment of the applicant. Mr Tom Devereaux, who was also in custody in the station on the 21st and the 22nd of December, gave evidence of having been interviewed in an aggressive manner by two detective Gardaí from Dublin, who shouted and screamed at him over a period of time and also kicked the filing cabinet.

The Court, having heard the evidence of which a summary has been given, ruled that the statement reduced to writing was admissible. Having heard further evidence of a largely formal nature and further submissions on behalf of the applicant and the State, the Court convicted the applicant on the first count and acquitted her on the second count.

Mr MacEntee SC on behalf of the applicant argued in this Court that the Court of trial had erred in admitting the statement and advanced a number of grounds in support of this submission which were summarised by him as follows:—

> (i) There was no or no sufficient evidence before the Court of trial to allow that Court to decide (applying the appropriate onus and

burden of proof) that the applicant had not, at the time of making her statement, been subjected to oppression and that the making of the statement had not resulted from, or was not materially contributed to, by such pressure. Alternatively, the state of the prosecution's evidence was such as to preclude any such determination being properly made.

(ii) The mere fact that the Court accepted the evidence of Detective Garda Walsh and Detective Sergeant Tuohy as being truthful does not adequately dispose of the difficulties presented by the incompatible evidence of Ban Gharda Rush, Ban Gharda Brett, Garda Melvin, by the contents of the C.84 Form and by the additional matter contained in paragraph (iii) (a) and (b) below.

(iii) There is nothing in the ruling of the Court of trial to show that the Court took into account and/or gave adequate weight to

(a) the fact that, on the findings of the Court, the applicant was interrogated for lengthy periods of indeterminate length by a single member of the Special Investigative Branch of the Garda Síochána, *i.e.* Garda Walsh and/or

(b) the fact that at such interrogations (however long they may have been) no female member of the Garda Síochána was ever present (other than as a messenger) although the evidence established that Ban Ghardaí were present on duty in sufficient numbers at Castlebar Garda Station throughout the applicant's interrogation and there was no evidence before the Court of any circumstances precluding the reasonable attendance of such Ban Ghardaí at such interrogations for even limited periods.

(iv) The interrogation of the applicant carried out under the circumstances aforesaid did not conform to the requirements of fairness of practices and procedures under the Constitution and accordingly gave rise to a judicial discretion to exclude the fruits of such interrogations analogous to the discretion to exclude confessional material obtained in breach of the Judges' Rules.

(v) There is nothing in the rulings of the Court of trial to indicate that the Court exercised any such discretion or that it exercised it in accordance with the evidence or upon a proper basis.

The People (DPP) v McGing
Hederman J

The first and second of these grounds may be conveniently considered together. There were undoubtedly discrepancies between the evidence given by Detective Garda Walsh and Detective Sergeant Tuohy on the one hand and Ban Gharda Rush, Ban Gharda Brett and Garda Melvin on the other hand. It is also clear that, if Garda Walsh's account of the periods during which he interrogated the applicant was correct, they were not accurately recorded in the C.84 Form. These discrepancies were, however, strenuously relied on in the Court of trial and there is no reason to suppose that they were not taken into account by that Court in deciding whether or not to accept the evidence of Garda Walsh and Sergeant Tuohy as truthful. The existence of such discrepancies does not of itself justify this Court in interfering with the decision of the Court of trial as to the credibility of the witnesses concerned. The limitations of an appellate Court's capacity to interfere with such findings were made clear in the judgment of O'Higgins CJ in *Northern Bank Finance Corp. Ltd v Charlton* [1979] I.R. 149 at p. 180:

> A judge's findings on fact can and will be reviewed on appeal. Such findings will be subjected to the normal tests as to whether they are supported by the evidence given at the trial. If such findings are firmly based on the sworn testimony of witnesses seen and heard and accepted by the judge, then the court of appeal, recognising this to be the area of credibility, will not interfere.

In *People (DPP) v Kelly (No. 2)* [1983] I.R. 1, the Supreme Court again reaffirmed that this is the approach which must be adopted by this Court so far as the credibility of witnesses is concerned. In the present case, the Court of trial having accepted the evidence of Garda Walsh and Sergeant Tuohy as truthful, there was ample evidence to justify a determination that there had been no such oppression as was alleged by the applicant.

The grounds set out in paragraphs (iii), (iv) and (v) above may also be conveniently considered together. The evidence undoubtedly established that the applicant had been interrogated for periods of significant length by a single member of the Special Investigative Branch of the Garda Síochána. Nor was any Ban Gharda present during the course of the interrogation, although a Ban Gharda was at all times present in the Garda Station while the applicant was being interviewed, as required by the Garda regulations. The evidence also established that the Ban Gharda on duty at the relevant time visited the interview room in which the interrogation was taking place from time to time and also looked into the cell in which the applicant was being detained from time to time.

It is undesirable and, in the experience of the Court, contrary to normal Garda practice for persons detained under section 30 of the Offences Against the State Act 1939, to be interviewed for lengthy periods by a single member of the Gardaí. Moreover, while strict adherence to the regulations requires no more than the presence of a Ban Gharda in the station, it is obviously desirable where it is practicable (as undoubtedly it was in this case) that a Ban Gharda should be physically present in the interview room while a female is being interrogated. The Court cannot, however, accept the submission of Mr MacEntee that these facts of themselves necessitated a conclusion by the Court of trial that the interrogations did not conform with the constitutional requirements of fairness of practices and procedures. In arriving at a conclusion as to whether those requirements had been observed, the Court of trial was entitled to taken into account all the evidence as to the circumstances of the interrogation and not only the factors relied on by Mr MacEntee. In particular, the Court was entitled to give such weight as it thought proper to the fact that during the course of what was alleged to be an unfair and oppressive interrogation, the applicant was visited on three separate occasions by a solicitor acting on her behalf (and who did not cease to act on her behalf until the third interview) and that there was no evidence that the applicant complained at any time of the manner in which she was being treated either to her solicitor, to any other member of the Gardaí present in the station or to her parents who visited her in the station on the night of the 22nd of December. It was, in the view of this Court, entirely open to the Court of trial to come to the conclusion on a review of all the evidence that the interrogation of the applicant in the present case was not conducted in a manner so oppressive as to render the statement made by her as a result thereof inadmissible.

The submission advanced by Mr MacEntee that an interrogation carried out in the circumstances alleged gives rise to a judicial discretion to exclude the fruits of such an interrogation analogous to the discretion arising in the case of a breach of the Judges' Rules is not supported by any authority opened to this Court. It is not, however, necessary to express any opinion as to its validity. The matters relied upon on behalf of the applicant in this Court were drawn to the attention of the Court of trial on several occasions during the course of the trial and that Court gave a careful and considered ruling on the admissibility of the impugned statement. This Court is satisfied that the Court of trial was perfectly entitled on the materials before them to come to the conclusion that, whether or not the circumstances alleged can be equated to a breach of the Judges' Rules, they had not resulted in any essential want of fairness which required the exclusion of the statement in question.

The grounds of appeal relied on, accordingly, fail and the Court refuses the application for leave to appeal.

Solicitor for the applicant: *Michael Moran and Co.*
Solicitor for the respondent: *Chief State Solicitor*

Eithne Casey
Barrister

The People (Director of Public Prosecutions) v John Lawless
[C.C.A. No. 69 of 1984]

Court of Criminal Appeal   28 November 1985

Evidence – possession of controlled drug – defective warrant – unlawful entry into and search of premises – whether breach of constitutional rights – admissibility of evidence – Misuse of Drugs Act 1977 (No. 12) sections 3, 15, 26

The applicant was convicted in the Dublin Circuit Court of two offences relating to drugs contrary to sections 3 and 15 of the Misuse of Drugs Act 1977. A search warrant was obtained by a member of An Garda Síochána pursuant to section 26, subsection 1(a) of the said Act to enter and search the relevant premises. However, the information sworn to obtain the warrant, which was based on a standard form then in use in the District Court, did not correspond with the wording required by section 26, subsection 1(a) of the Acts of 1977.

It was argued on behalf of the applicant, *inter alia*, that, as the warrant was defective, the entry into and search of the premises was unlawful; further that it was in breach of the applicant's constitutional rights and that the applicant's conversation with Garda Rafter whilst in custody and prior to being brought before a court was inadmissible in evidence. In addition it was submitted that the presumption under section 15, subsection 2 of the Act of 1977 did not arise on the evidence as the amount of drugs found was less than a day's intake for an addict.

Held by the Court (McCarthy, Keane and O'Hanlon JJ), in dismissing the application:
(1) That the omission of the necessary statutory foundation for the issue of the search warrant was an oversight, and whereas the act of entering the premises was a deliberate act,

there was no evidence of deliberate deceit or illegality and no policy to disregard the provisions of the Constitution.

(2) That the production of an exhibit, in this case of packets of drugs, to the accused while awaiting arrangements to bring him before a court was not a breach of the duty of a Garda officer to bring an arrested person before a court as soon as was reasonably possible. (*Dunne v Clinton* [1930] I.R. 366 considered.)

(3) That there was compelling evidence that an offence under section 15 of the 1977 Act had been committed.

Per curiam: Even if a conscious and deliberate violation of a constitutional right in respect of the inviolability of the home had occurred, the rights of the applicant had not been violated as the dwelling entered was not his, consequently he was not entitled to rely on such a violation for the purposes of having evidence excluded.

Cases cited in this judgment:
Dunne v Clinton [1930] I.R. 366; 64 I.L.T.R. 136
People (Attorney General) v O'Brien [1965] I.R. 142
People (Director of Public Prosecutions) v Higgins, Supreme Court, 22nd November, 1985, unreported
People (Director of Public Prosecutions) v O'Loughlin [1979] I.R. 85; 113 I.L.T.R.109
People (Director of Public Prosecutions) v Walsh [1980] I.R. 294

Barry White SC **for the applicant**
Peter Charleton **for the respondent**

McCarthy J

Following a trial before the President of the Circuit Court, on the 25th of July, 1984, the applicant was convicted by a jury of

(a) possession of a controlled drug, contrary to section 3 of the Misuse of Drugs Act 1977 and

(b) possession of a controlled drug for the purpose of unlawfully supplying it to another contrary to section 15(1) of the Act.

The drug in question was heroin. On the 4th of October, 1983, Detective Sergeant John G. O'Malley swore an information before a Peace Commissioner that "I have reasonable ground for suspecting from information which I have in my possession that a controlled drug namely Diamorphine (Heroin) a forged prescription, or a duly issued prescription which has been wrongfully altered will be found at the premises No. 60 Rathland Flats, Dublin 12, in the said District" (sic) and sought a warrant to enter and search such premises, which warrant, on the same date, was granted by a Peace Commissioner being "satisfied on the Information on Oath of Detective Sergeant John O'Malley of An Garda Síochána, that there is (sic) reasonable grounds for suspecting that a controlled drug to which the Misuse of Drugs Act 1977, applies namely:—

Diamorphine (Heroin) or any pipe, document, utensil, forged prescription, or a duly issued prescription which has been wrongfully altered, is, in contravention of the said Act or Regulation made thereunder in the possession or under the control of any person in the premises 60 Rathland Flats, Dublin 12 in the said District.

In reliance on the warrant, Detective Sergeant O'Malley and other Gardaí went to the premises at 60 Rathland Road (sic) Flats, Dublin 12 and, using such force as was necessary, made their way into a flat where the applicant and another man, Ryan, were present. At the time of the forced entry, the applicant was in the lavatory and the noise of a flushing W.C. was heard. Detective Garda Byrne had waited at what was established to be the manhole being fed from the lavatory in question and found seventeen small white packets each of which contained heroin in quantities from 5 to 10 milligrammes. Sergeant O'Malley and Detective Garda Byrne, by experiment, established the fact of discharge from the lavatory in which the applicant was found to the manhole where the heroin was found.

This application for leave to appeal has been founded upon four grounds:—

1. The refusal of the learned trial Judge to discharge the jury following an allegedly inflammatory opening address by counsel for the prosecution. There is no requirement that such an address be transcribed, no more than that of counsel for the accused; from, however, such portions of the address as are to be found in the application for a discharge of the jury, the Court is satisfied that there was no impropriety or, indeed, anything of an inflammatory nature in such address.

2. That the information sworn by Detective Sergeant O'Malley did not comply with the requirements of section 26 of the Act of 1977 and that, consequently, evidence of the search or any fruits thereof should have been excluded. Section 26 requires:—

> "information on Oath of a member of the Garda Síochána that there is reasonable ground for suspecting that — (a) a person is in possession in contravention of this Act on any premises of a controlled drug, a forged prescription or a duly issued prescription which has been wrongfully altered and that such drug or prescription is on a particular premises" (the remainder is not relevant to the present application).

It is clear and, indeed, it appears to have been conceded by counsel for the prosecution at the trial as he did in this Court, that the information did not correspond in terms with the wording required by section 26, subsection (1)(a) of the Act of 1977. The learned trial judge declined, incorrectly in the view of this Court, to go behind the warrant, and admitted the evidence, although counsel for the prosecution had argued for its admission, not on the legality of the search, but rather on the basis that the illegality could properly be excused. Neither at the trial nor in this Court was any point taken about the misdescription of the premises in the information and warrant (60 Rathland Flats, Dublin 12), and the address given by the Gardaí in evidence (60 Rathland Road Flats, Dublin 12). Such a point was superfluous.

The warrant being defective, because of the defective information, the entry into and search of the premises was unlawful. It is argued, further, that it was in breach of a constitutional right; if it was, such was not the right of the applicant but of the tenant of the flat in question and persons residing with him. On his own evidence, the applicant was not the tenant but had been asked by Noel Foy, "the owner of 60" to wait there for his, the applicant's brother. The arrest there carried out of the applicant was an interference with his constitutional right to personal freedom, but no illegality attached to it; the Court is not satisfied that there was any breach of the constitutional rights of the applicant. Even if, however, there were such a breach in respect of inviolability of the home, or personal liberty, the Court is satisfied that there was no conscious violation of any consti-tutional right of the applicant. The act of Detective Sergeant O'Malley and his colleagues in entering the premises was, of course, a deliberate act. The omission of the necessary statutory foundation for the issue of the search warrant was a pure oversight; there was no evidence of deliberate deceit or illegality, no policy to disregard the provisions of the Constitution or to conduct searches without a warrant (see the obser-vations of Kingsmill Moore J. at p. 161 in *People (Attorney General) v O'Brien* [1965] I.R. 14. Even if there were a deliberate and conscious violation of the constitutional rights of an accused person, in the instant case there are "extraordinary excusing circumstances" — the need to prevent the imminent destruction of vital evidence. (See observations of Walsh J. at p. 170 in *O'Brien's* case, cited with approval by Kingsmill Moore J. at p. 162).

It is true that in this case the learned trial judge did not reach the stage of exercising a discretion to overlook an illegality or, *a fortiori*, the conscious breach of constitutional rights, but the Court is satisfied that if had done so, his discretion could only have been exercised in one way, to admit the evidence.

3. That the accused's conversation with Garda Rafter, whilst in custody, was not admissible in evidence. Garda Rafter arrested the accused between 5 and 6 p.m. on the 14th of October, and took him to Terenure Garda Station where he showed him the packets that Detective Garda Byrne had found in the manhole; the accused said that he had nothing to say and followed it by saying "I was on top of the stairs when the police came to the door, I was about to come down the stairs." The Court is at a loss to know what significance is to be attached to this statement; indeed, the learned trial judge whilst reciting it as part of the evidence made no comment on it. In any event, the Court cannot identify any principle making such evidence inadmissible. It was argued that, in some fashion, there had been a breach of the duty commonly depended upon the authority of *Dunne v Clinton* [1930] I.R. 366. It need scarcely be stated that the duty of a Garda Officer who has arrested and charged a citizen is, as soon as is reasonably possible, to bring the accused before a court or a judicial officer: *People (DPP) v O'Loughlin* [1979] I.R. 85; *People (DPP) v Walsh* [1980] I.R. 294; *DPP v Higgins* Supreme Court, unreported, 22 November 1985. The mere production of an exhibit, indeed of the critical incriminating articles found in or about the premises where the accused was arrested, whilst awaiting arrangements to bring him before a court or a judicial officer is in no way a breach of that duty; it might forcefully be suggested that it would be unfair to the accused not to produce these incriminating articles to him at the earliest possible opportunity. There is no true basis for this ground of appeal.

4. That the learned trial judge should have directed the jury to enter a verdict of not guilty on count 2. This ground of appeal was, finally, limited to an argument based upon the construction of section 15 of the 1977 Act which provides by subsection (2):—

> . . . where it is proved that a person was in possession of a controlled drug and that the court, having regard to the quantity of the controlled drug which the person possessed or to such other matter as the court considers relevant, is satisfied that it is reasonable to assume that the controlled drug was not intended for the immediate personal

use of the person, he shall be presumed, until the court is satisfied to the contrary, to have been in possession of the controlled drug for the purpose of selling or otherwise supplying it to another in contravention of regulations under section 5 of this Act.

The quantity found — the total of the seventeen packets — was 161 milligrammes of Diamorphine (heroin); there was also found on the floor in the living-room of the flat, close to the left foot of the other person (Ryan) sitting beside the accused, a small plastic package wrapped in tinfoil and which contained 5 milligrammes of brown powder which itself contained Diamorphine (heroin). The evidence of Dr. MacDermott permitted the view that the total amount found was less than a lethal dose and significantly less than what might be a day's intake for an addict. Thus, it is argued, the presumption under section 15, subsection (2) did not arise. This argument overlooked the fact that there was no evidence that the accused was, at the relevant time, a drug addict at all, a person who required it "for — immediate personal use" and further the highly incriminating circumstances of there being seventeen separate packets and of the attempted destruction or disposition of them. In the view of the Court, there was ample, virtually compelling, evidence of guilt.

In respect of the error in the information sworn by the Detective Sergeant, the Court would wish to make it clear that this arose because of the content of the printed form then in use in the Dublin District Court and for no other reason.

Solicitor for the applicant: not available
Solicitor for the respondent: *Chief State Solicitor*

Eithne Casey
Barrister

The People (Director of Public Prosecutions) v Thomas Eccles, Patrick McPhillips and Brian McShane
[C.C.A. Nos. 30, 31 and 32 of 1985]

Court of Criminal Appeal   10 February 1986

*Special Criminal Court – jurisdiction – applicants charged with non-scheduled offence –
certificate of Director of Public Prosecutions that ordinary courts inadequate to secure
proper administration of justice – Prosecution of Offences Act 1974 (No. 22), section
4*

*Detention – extension of initial period of detention – bona fide suspicion of involvement in
original offence for which arrested – source of information – whether privileged –
Offences Against the State Act 1939, section 30(3)*

*Statute – interpretation – whether, upon arrest under section 30 of the Offences Against the
State Act 1939, interrogation must be confined to the matters specified in section 52 of
the said Act*

*Capital murder – Mens rea – common design – accessory – murder occurring prior to
applicant's arrival at scene – whether part of joint venture – Offences Against the State
Act 1939 (No. 13), sections 30, 47, 52*

The three applicants, having been arrested pursuant to section 30 of the Offences
Against the State Act 1939, were convicted in the Special Criminal Court of the capital
murder of a member of the Garda Síochána, and were sentenced to death. The only evidence
grounding their convictions were certain verbal and written statements allegedly made by
the applicants while in custody.

Section 47, subsection (2) of the 1939 Act provides that before the Special Criminal
Court can have jurisdiction to try a person charged with a non-scheduled offence, the Director
of Public Prosecutions must certify that the ordinary courts are inadequate in the circumstances to secure the effective administration of justice. In an application seeking leave to
appeal against their convictions, the applicants submitted that proof of the issuing of the
certificate should have been given to the Court at the time when the applicants were first
brought before it, and since this had not been done at that stage, the Court had no jurisdiction
to embark upon a trial.

With regard to a direction given by a Chief Superintendent of the Gardaí that the
applicants' period of detention under section 30 of the 1939 Act should be extended for a
further twenty-four hours, the applicants submitted, *inter alia*, that it was premature, having
been given some six hours prior to the expiration of the first period. It was also submitted
that the Court had erred in allowing the Chief Superintendent to claim privilege in respect
of the information upon which one of the extension orders was based.

The applicants' next submission related to their interrogation while in custody, in
relation to which they claimed that, once they had been arrested pursuant to section 30 of
the 1939 Act, they could be questioned only in regard to the matters specified in section 52
thereof. Other submissions related to alleged unfair, abusive and oppressive treatment of the
applicants while in custody, which they alleged to have been a deliberate and conscious

36

violation of their constitutional rights, which rendered their detention unlawful and their statements inadmissible. Finally, the applicants submitted that it was not sufficient, in order to convict them of capital murder, to show that they had adhered to a common design which included even the risk of death or serious injury to a Garda, and that there was insufficient evidence to show that they knew the deceased to have been a member of the Gardaí acting in the course of his duty.

Held by the Court (Hederman, Keane and Barron JJ) in refusing leave to appeal:

(1) The fact that a certificate had been issued by the Director of Public Prosecutions pursuant to section 47(2) of the 1939 Act may be proved at any time before the close of the prosecution's case.

(2) The invoking of section 52 of the 1939 Act simply adds a statutory power to require the giving of information, and does not limit the power of interrogation already existing. (*People (DPP) v Kelly (No. 2)* [1983] I.R. 1 followed).

(3) On a correct interpretation of section 30(3) of the 1939 Act a Chief Superintendent, or superintendent if authorised, may direct that a person may be detained for a further period of 24 hours provided that when he did so the detainee was *bona fide* suspected by him of being involved in the offence for which he was originally arrested. An extension order may be made at any time during the initial period of 24 hours, and must be made before the expiration of that period.

(4) Although a member of the Gardaí cannot normally claim privilege in respect of information received from a fellow-member of the force simply by virtue of its being such a communication, in the circumstances of the instant case, where privilege was claimed on the ground that it would be dangerous to identify the source of information received, privilege had been properly accorded.

(5) Since the conclusions of the Court of trial as to the admissibility of the applicants' statements were based on the sworn evidence of witnesses seen, heard and accepted by that Court, such conclusions could not be disturbed upon appeal (*Northern Bank Finance v Charlton* [1979] I.R. 149 and *People (DPP) v Kelly (No. 2)* [1983] I.R. 1 followed.)

(6) Evidence showed that the applicants knew in advance that members of the Gardaí would be present at the scene of the proposed crime, and once the applicants were aware (as evidence showed they were) that any prospective resistance by the Gardaí would be met with the use of firearms, they would be guilty of whatever offence arose from the actual use of firearms by those with whom they acted in concert.

Cases cited in this judgment:

Murphy v Dublin Corporation [1972] I.R. 215; 107 I.L.T.R. 65
Northern Bank Finance Corporation Ltd v Charlton [1979] I.R. 149
People (Attorney General) v Cummins [1972] I.R. 312; 108 I.L.T.R. 5
People (DPP) v Higgins, Supreme Court, 22 November 1985 (unreported)
People (DPP) v Kelly (No. 2) [1983] I.R. 1; [1983] ILRM 271
People (DPP) v Lynch [1982] I.R. 64; [1981] ILRM 389
People (DPP) v Madden [1977] I.R. 336; 111 I.L.T.R. 117
People (DPP) v Murray [1977] I.R. 360; 111 I.L.T.R. 65
People (DPP) v Pringle, McCann and O'Shea 2 Frewen 57
People (DPP) v Shaw [1982] I.R. 1
People (DPP) v Walsh [1980] I.R. 294
R. v Anderson (1966) 50 Cr. App. R. 216

Seamus Sorahan SC, Rex Mackey SC and Paul Coffey **for the first applicant**
James Carroll SC and Roger Sweetman **for the second applicant**
Sean McBride SC, Barry White SC and Patrick Gageby **for the third applicant**
Name of counsel for the respondent not available

Hederman J

On the 28th of March, 1985, the Special Criminal Court after a lengthy trial convicted the three applicants, Thomas Gerard Noel Eccles, Patrick McPhillips, and Brian McShane, of the capital murder of Garda Francis Hand on the 10th day of August, 1984, at Drumree Post Office in the County of Meath. The applicants were also convicted of robbery contrary to section 23 of the Larceny Act 1916, as inserted by section 5 of the Criminal Law (Jurisdiction) Act 1976.

After conviction all three applicants applied, on specific grounds, for certificates of leave to appeal. The Court refused the applications.

The Facts of the Commission of the Crimes

On the morning of the 10th of August, 1984, Detective Garda Michael Dowd and Detective Garda Francis Hand left the Special Detective Unit at Harcourt Square, Dublin, in a Fiat Mirafiori car before 7 a.m. on escort duty in relation to post office deliveries. Detective/Garda Dowd was the observer and Detective Garda Hand the driver. Both were in plain clothes. Before leaving the Detective Unit Garda Dowd placed a loaded Uzi sub-machine gun in the front seat beside him. He had a spare magazine on the floor. Detective Garda Hand was armed with a gun and a walkie-talkie set to maintain radio communications.

At approximately 7.20 a.m. the post office van driven by Joseph Bell with his helper, Donald Brady, left the G.P.O. Dublin with the Garda escort car following it. The post office van made a delivery at Dunboyne at approximately 7.43 a.m. and at Batterstown some few minutes later. At Batterstown Detective Garda Hand accompanied the post office official into the post office with the bag to be delivered. The next point of delivery was at Drumree Post Office, also in County Meath. Mr Bell stopped the post office van outside the post office. As the escort car was pulling in behind the van Detective Garda Dowd looked over his left shoulder. He saw two men in blue boiler suits and black balaclava helmets coming through a garden gate beside the post office. The first man had a sub-machine gun and the second man appeared to be armed. The man with the machine gun ran straight for the Garda car window and the second man took up a position directly behind Detective Garda Dowd and started firing into the patrol car while the first man pointed the sub-machine gun at the garda. He then moved to the front of the vehicle, took aim and fired a burst of machine gun fire through the front windscreen of the patrol car at both gardaí. At that time the second raider was at the passenger door of the garda vehicle. Detective Garda Dowd felt a stinging in the left upper portion of his head and was jerked to his right hand side. He put his hands up to his head and the sub-machine gun fell from his hands. As he was getting back up he saw Detective Garda Hand backing out of the car with his gun in his left hand. Detective Garda Hand had both feet on the ground. At that stage Detective Garda Dowd was caught by the left upper arm and pulled to the ground. He was told to get down on the ground and not to move. A gun was put to his head and he was told to stretch out on his belly. Within about 10 seconds Detective Garda Dowd heard a car coming at a very high speed. It appeared out of control and skidded to a halt. It was an Opel car and as it was stopping one or two shots were fired, followed by a burst of sub-machine gunfire.

Mr Brady had taken bags from the front of the van and gone to the post office door. As Mr Brady was about to step into the post office Mr Bell heard a scuffling sound behind him. He looked in the rear view mirror and saw two men. One had a machine gun and the other a small gun. They were dressed as described by Detective Garda Dowd. There were short bursts of gunfire. When the firing stopped one of the raiders told Mr Bell to turn off his ignition and get out of the van. Mr Bell was then told to open the back of the van, which he did. He was then told to stand against the wall and put his hands behind his back. He was then told to get down on the ground on his face. Cars then arrived. One of the witnesses recognised as an Opel car by the insignia. The money was transferred from the van to one of the vehicles. A raider then approached Mr Bell, the keys were kicked from under him, a gun was put to the back of his neck and he was told "If you move, son, you are fucking dead". Meanwhile Detective Garda Dowd saw the legs of the raiders at the back of the van, at least eight raiders. A second car arrived and parked in front of the mail van. One of the men moving the bags appeared to have a pistol similar to the one taken from the witness. The moving of the mail bags took between two to three minutes. As the cars drove away the witness observed that one of the cars was beige-coloured — a Ford Sierra or Opel — and the second and third letters of the number plate were ZG.

Detective Garda Dowd looked around and saw Mr Bell lying on the ground. Later he looked under the patrol car and saw Detective Garda Hand lying face down, with both hands out by his side. When he ran round to Detective Garda Hand he saw a large pool of blood under his head. The raiders had pulled the radio out of the garda car but Detective Garda Dowd summoned assistance on a walkie-talkie set. All the Garda weapons had been taken by the raiders. Detective Garda Hand had been shot dead.

Mr Michael Gilsenan who lived in Drumree Post Office got his mother to ring 999 during the raid. When he went upstairs he saw a big red car up above the mail van. Its registration number was TZN 370. It drove off in the direction of Trim. Mr James Gorman who lives about 50 yards from the post office heard a number of shots at approximately 7.55 a.m. When he went out he saw the bright coloured car parked behind the post office van. He saw two or three of the raiders. One was in front of the car in a crouched position. After ringing 999 and reporting the raid he went out again to get further information and saw a large, dark-red coloured car pulled up beside the mail van. The Opel car and red car drove away towards Trim with the raiders and £202,900 in money.

The case for the prosecution

The prosecution contended that this particular robbery was well planned in the manner of a military type operation. Prior to the commission of the crimes, all three applicants were at two meetings planning the commission of the offences. To ensure the success of the operation the perpetrators had stolen a red Mercedes and an Opel car, had armed themselves with a variety of lethal weapons, which, with the cars, had been hidden on Mr Duffy's property. Further, each person involved in the actual raid had a particular role in the execution of the crime. To co-ordinate the overall plan, the raiders were in constant communication with each other by radio.

The only evidence implicating the three applicants were certain verbal and written admissions alleged to have been made to members of the Garda Síochána while they were in custody in Navan Garda Station.

The first-named applicant, Thomas Eccles, was arrested by Sergeant McGee at his home at 9 Grange Drive, Muirhevenamore, Dundalk, Co. Louth, at 6.20 a.m. on the 22nd of August, 1984, under section 30 of the Offences Against the State Act 1939, on suspicion of having committed a scheduled offence under the Act, to wit, unlawful possession of firearms at Drumree Post Office on the 10th of August, 1984. He was brought to the Garda Station in Navan where Station Orderly, Garda Joseph Keogh, booked him in as a prisoner. At 8.30 a.m. Detective Sergeant Joseph Shelly and Detective Garda James B. Hanley took the applicant to an interview room where he was cautioned by Detective Sergeant Shelly in the following terms: "you are not obliged to say anything, but anything you do say will be taken down in writing and may be used in evidence." The applicant remained in Navan Garda Station and an extension order, made by Chief Superintendent John T. Moore, was read over to him in his cell at 12.10 a.m. on the morning of the 23rd of August, 1984, by Detective Sergeant Michael A. Finnegan. On the night of the 23rd of August, 1984, the applicant was brought to the Special Criminal Court and charged with the offences for which he was convicted.

The following are the statements alleged by the prosecution to have been made by the applicant in such circumstances as to render them admissible at the trial.

(a) **A written statement alleged to have been made and signed by the first-named applicant in the presence of Detective Sergeant Joseph Shelly and Detective Sergeant James Hanley between 7.15 p.m. and 9.50 p.m. on the 23rd of August, 1984**
The following is the alleged statement:

On a Friday at the end of July this year it was either the 20th or the 27th I went to Newry to collect a Mercedes motor car. I had been asked the day before by a man to collect it. I was given the registered number which as far as I can remember was WCC. I cannot recall the figures but it had a V registration. I was given directions as to where I would find this car, it was to be parked on a road where the Cupid nightclub is. I found this car parked on the side of the road about 100 yards from the Club. It was a wine Mercedes. The keys were in the ignition as I had been told. I drove this car to Pat Duffy's yard in Dundalk. Pat Duffy told me to take it to Annagassa Village and leave it at O'Neill's pub. I drove it there and parked it behind a wall at O'Neill's pub. A fellow driving my own car, a blue Hillman Hunter, registered number BZY 359, picked me up there and brought me back to Dundalk. On Sunday the 5th of August, 1984, I was told by a fellow, I do not wish to mention any names, that there was a job on on a Friday and he asked me if I would go on it. I say 'Aye'. He said that it was to be a robbery, he didn't tell me where. This man called to my house on the following Thursday and told me that I was to pick a man up and the two of us were to go down to Drumree where a security van was to be robbed. He said to go down and have a look at it and sus it out. This was around dinner time. I picked up this other man in Dundalk and drove to Drumree in my own car. We picked up another man in Navan and he showed us a route to take after the robbery on the following morning. We drove a couple of hundred yards from the Post Office at Drumree and it was pointed out to us where it was. I was then told to drive back the way I came, I travelled along bye-roads and across a main road into other smaller roads until I was shown a field. I was told that this was the place I was to drop the money off the following morning and the fellow we picked up in Navan said he would meet us there. Before I was shown this route I was taken up another lane two or three miles from the Post Office at Drumree, there were sheds at the end of this lane and we were told that we would stay there that night. When we had been shown all these places we travelled along back roads and the man from Navan got out somewhere then the man I picked up in Dundalk and I travelled back to Dundalk. I drove to my own house and got my tea. I left my home again at around 8 p.m. I went to collect the wine Mercedes at another place where I knew it was. I drove it to Duffy's yard, after a while a cream coloured Ascona motor car arrived. I do not know the registration number but it was a Free State one. I was in the caravan with Pat Duffy's wife when it arrived. I wish to say that when I went to collect the Mercedes I drove my own car there I also had the man that was in Drumree with me that evening, and when I collected the Mercedes this man drove my car to Duffy's also. When the Ascona arrived a number of people began to load guns into the Ascona, these were in a bag. There were walkie-talkies in a small bag there too and these were put into the Ascona. When this was done we began to move out, the Ascona went in front of me. I was in the Mercedes on my own. There were two in the lane which I had been shown earlier. There were other men at the sheds when we got there. The bag of guns was taken out of the Ascona.

There were a few rifles and I think only one machine gun and small guns. One man was given a rifle and he acted as a look out. There were eight or nine men there at this stage. Three of these were called aside and there was a discussion amongst them. After a while one of the fellows came to the rest of us and said that there would be two Guards with the van in the morning and that they would be taken care of. He told us to go about 7.55 a.m. to the Post Office at Drumree. I was told that the money and guns would be put in my car. I was given a walkie-talkie and I was told to drive towards the Post Office at 7.55 a.m. and I would get the call on my radio to move into the Post Office. I put on a pair of my own overalls and I got into the car and fell asleep. I was awake in the morning about 7 a.m. Two of the other fellows got into the Mercedes with me and we waited until 7.55 a.m., then I moved out and the Ascona followed me. I drove as far as the Post Office at Drumree, as I was passing it I could see the top of a Post Office van outside the Post Office. The Ascona was behind me. I looked in the drive-way of the Post Office and I saw a masked man with a gun. I think it was a rifle pointed towards the ground. I assumed that he had a man lying on the ground. I continued on for about 100 yards and I turned the Merc. in the gate-way on the left hand side. I travelled back to the Post Office. I then saw the Ascona had driven into the first entry towards the Post Office, I continued to the next entry a few yards further on and drove in. The Post Office van was facing me, the two fellows with me jumped out. They had a rifle and a hand-gun. I turned the Mercedes and had the boot next to the front of the van. I got out and opened the boot and the other men began to load mailbags into it. I saw a man lying on the ground near the Post Office van and a fellow standing over him pointing a gun at him. I helped to stack the bags in the boot. When all the bags were in, they put the guns into the boot of the Merc. too. I closed the boot and got into the driver's seat. Two other fellows got in with me and we drove away. I drove onto the main road and turned right and one of the men in the car gave me the directions to go to the field where I had been the evening before. When I arrived at this field a yellow car was waiting there for us. I cannot say what make it was, everything was a blur at this stage. We loaded the mailbags and the guns into the boot of the yellow car. There was one fellow there with the yellow car. He was the man I had picked up in Navan the evening before. One of the fellows got a plastic container and threw petrol over the Mercedes and threw a match into it and the car took fire. The three of us then got into a blue Mark IV Cortina in which there was a driver and we drove away. I didn't notice the yellow car leave at all. We drove off along bye-roads until we eventually arrived at the new bridge in Drogheda. We had got lost on the back roads. The driver asked us to get out of the car at the new bridge, he said he wouldn't take us any further because there would be checkpoints out. Three of us got out there and we split. I walked into the town and bought a peach in a shop in a street near the big chapel, St. Oliver Plunketts. I ate the peach while I was walking and I went into the chapel and I thanked God that I had got away. I then walked away out the Dundalk road and started to thumb. I got a lift from a woman driving a blue Datsun or Toyota Corolla. She had a girl of about six of seven years with her. She said she was going to Dundalk. She drove me to the Dublin bridge. I got out there, and I went to Seamus McGrane's shop at the Laurels so that I would be seen. I asked him if he had any work for me and he said he would give me a few days and to start the following morning. I left him and got a taxi home. It cost me £1.80. I think the taxi driver was a Mrs Dempsey. She told me there was after being a robbery and that there was a guard shot dead. I knew that this was the robbery I had been on, I felt sick. On the night before the robbery while we were at the sheds we were told that two men had gone to the Post Office and would have things in control when we got there. I took this to mean that the two men who had gone would have the way clear for us and we were told to collect the guard's guns and bring them with us. This statement has been read over to me and it is correct.

Signed: T. Eccles

Witness: Detective Garda James B. Hanley

Witness: Joseph O. Shelly, Detective Sergeant

(b) **Verbal statements alleged to have been made to Detective Sergeant Shelly and Detective Garda Hanley, earlier than the written statement, between 1.30 p.m. and 7.15 p.m. on the afternoon of the 23rd of August, 1984, and written down as follows:—**

Caution — Detective Sergeant Shelley.

1.30 p.m. Dinner. Well looked after. Didn't believe that he told us the truth in his account of movements. Account time. You know I was in McGrane's. Were you ever asked to do robbery by Greene or Duffy. They wouldn't discuss things with me. Somebody has told you the story about it. I wouldn't shoot a guard. Tell me the truth what would a fellow be charged with if he only drove the car in that robbery. Detective Sergeant Shelley — Up to the DPP. Names of fellows from Navan. Seamus Lynch, Joseph Gargan. Description. Somebody has told the story. I had my mind made up that I would not make a statement, go to jail for 40 years rather than have it said in Portlaoise I made a statement. Tell the truth. Will tell truth, things to think about.

Returned after solicitor. Caution. Will confess to my part, no names. I will ask you something, laugh at it. Do you know what I did when I knew the guard was shot. Not hard man you know, you might think I am bullshitting you. I went into a church, said prayer for detective that morning after robbery. Only for wife and kids would have skipped it.

Notes read over, cautioned. Advised to make any changes or additions. That's how it happened. It's all in the statement I have signed for you. Can I see my wife before I go to Court.

Signed: Refused to sign.
Witness: James B. Hanley, Detective Garda.
Witness: Joseph O. Shelley, Detective Sergeant.

(c) **Verbal statement alleged to have been made to Detective Garda Mulvey and Detective Sergeant Michael Finnegan shortly after 9.50 p.m. on the 23rd of August, 1984, including a sketch alleged to have been made by the applicant, written down by Detective Sergeant Mulvey as follows:—**

Navan 23/8/84. 9.50 p.m. I/V T. Eccles. Sorry didn't tell you, cautioned by me, should have told today. M.F. came and cautioned by him. Sketch drawn of D/Ree and initialled. I told the truth to the lads, I went there on the date with two other fellows, one I think had a h/gun one had rifle. There was a walkie-talkie in the car. Got a lift to Drogheda in a Cortina from the field where I left the Merc, the bags of money put in Escort car. I didn't go to the Post Office in the dark. It was daylight at the Post Office. These notes have been read over to me and is correct.

TE.
T. Mulvey Detective Garda, witness
Witness Michael Finnegan Detective Sergeant
23/8/84.

(d) Verbal statement as follows alleged to have been made by applicant to Detective Garda Sullivan and Detective Garda M. O. Lennon while being transported from Navan to the Special Criminal Court on the evening of the 23rd of August, 1984, after caution

He told me he was sorry for not telling the truth when I was there with him earlier that day. He told me he was on the job, that he drove the red Mercedes and that he collected it the night before in Duffy's yard at about 9 p.m. He drove it to a house near Drumree and he collected two armed men. He also said he got lost on the way. The day before the robbery a man took him to the post office at Drumree and told him that they were to do the post office van. He drove a dummy run there in his own car, which was a blue Hunter car, to the field where the Mercedes was burned and he also said they took the money from the Mercedes into a yellow car. He also stated there was up to eight or nine men on the robbery.

(e) A verbal statement alleged to have been made by the accused to Detective Garda John Maunsell, after the accused had been charged in the Special Criminal Court, at 11.55 p.m. on the 23rd of August, 1984, written down as follows:—

"Look what I've been charged with, I didn't do the shooting. I only drove the Merc." Cautioned. "I already made a statement what I told the lads is true. I didn't do the shooting".

On the 13th of November 1984 at 10.30 a.m. I saw Thomas Eccles of 9 Grange Drive, Muirhavnamore, Dundalk, Co. Louth in a room at the Special Criminal Court, Green St., Dublin. I introduced myself to him and he said he remembered me. I told him that I had noted the conversation that I had with him on the night of the 23rd of August 1984 and that I wished to read them over to him. I read over the above notes to him and cautioned him as follows: "You are not obliged to say anything unless you wish to do so but anything you do say will be taken down in writing and may be given in evidence". I invited him to make any alterations and he replied "no". I asked him if he wished to sign the above notes and he replied "no".

The second-named applicant, Patrick McPhillips, was arrested at his home in Dundalk at 6.25 a.m. on the morning of the 29th of August, 1984, by Sergeant McGee of Navan Garda Station under section 30 of the Offences Against the State Act 1939, on suspicion of having committed a scheduled offence under the Act, to wit, unlawful possession of firearms at Drumree Post Office on the 10th of August, 1984. At 7.50 a.m. after being booked in as a prisoner he was placed in a cell at Navan Garda Station. At 8.05 a.m. he was taken to an interview room by Detective Garda Hanley and Detective Garda Healy where he was cautioned by Detective Garda Hanley in the presence of Detective Garda Healy. He remained in custody in Navan Garda Station and an extension order, made by Chief Superintendent John Moore, was read over to him by Detective Sergeant Finnegan at 12.38 a.m. on the morning of the 30th of August, 1984, and at approximately 5 p.m. on the evening of the 30th of August, he was charged with the offences for which he was subsequently convicted.

The following are the statements alleged by the prosecution to have been made by the applicant in such circumstances as to render them admissible at the trial.

(a) An unwritten statement alleged to have been made by the applicant to Detective Inspector Culhane and Detective Sergeant O'Carroll after 2 p.m. on the 29th of August, after a statement alleged to have been made by one Noel McCabe had been read over to him by Detective Inspector Culhane at the applicant's request

The applicant was alleged to have said: "he has incriminated me in his statement. Ye know the part I played in the robbery but I did not shoot the guard." Detective Sergeant Carroll made notes of this statement and cautioned the applicant. The garda read the note over to the applicant who replied "that's fair enough" but refused to sign the statement.

(b) An unsigned statement as follows alleged to have been made by the second-named applicant to Detective Garda Hanley and

Detective Garda Healy and to have been written down by Detective Garda Hanley between 3.30 p.m. and 4.05 p.m. on the 29th of August, 1984:

"all I want to say is that you already know the story of the robbery at Drumree on Friday the 10th of August, 1984, others have told you. My part in that robbery is just what McCabe has told you. I drove the Ascona from Dundalk to Dunshaughlin on the Thursday night, there were others with me. We stayed near Dunshaughlin that night. I knew that a Post Office van was to be robbed on Friday morning. This was discussed, we knew that there would be armed guards with this van. Certain people got the job of looking after that part of it, I was not any of these. On Friday morning I travelled to Drumree Post Office in the red Mercedes with others. We were in radio contact with the people at the post office. My job was to load the bags of money into the Mercedes and bring it to a place where we would be met. When I got to the post office, I took mailbags from a post office van and put them into the red Mercedes. I saw a number of people lying on the ground. The Ascona was there too and another car, it was the police car. When the bags were in the Mercedes the guns were put in also the radios. I knew there was a guard shot, there was no shooting while I was there, I did not fire my gun, I travelled in the Mercedes again to the place where we were to be met. There were to be two cars waiting there, one to take the money and guns and the other car was to bring us back to Dundalk. The Mercedes was driven into a field, I left it there and went to the other car which was waiting for us. The driver of this car then drove us along back roads we took a wrong turn somewhere. The map shown to me by Detective Garda Healy is the map that I was using to direct us back to Dundalk. I threw it out the window because I was afraid of being stopped by the guards. I wish to say that I did not tell you where this map was. I got out of the car before we got to Drogheda and I made my own way home. I got a lift. On Thursday night it was discussed that there might be resistance from the guards with the Post Office van. We were to get the call when our fellows had things in hand. I now regret being involved in this robbery. This statement has been read over to me and it is correct, I have nothing further to say".

The third-named applicant, Brian McShane, was arrested at approximately 6.20 a.m. on the 29th of August, 1984, at his home by Detective Sergeant Corrigan under section 30 of the Offences Against the State Act 1939, on suspicion of having committed a scheduled offence under the Act, to wit, unlawful possession of firearms at Drumree Post Office on the 10th of August, 1984. At 7 a.m. he was booked in as a prisoner by Garda Cunningham at Navan Garda Station. At 8.10 p.m. he was brought to an interview room by Detective Sergeant Lynagh and Detective Sergeant Carty where he was cautioned by Detective Sergeant Carty at 12 noon. He was interviewed by Detective Garda Tim Mulvey, Detective Garda Martin Sullivan, Detective Sergeant Lynagh and Detective Sergeant Carty after again being cautioned. The applicant was served with an extension order made by Chief Superintendent Moore and read over to him by Detective Sergeant Finnegan at 12.30 p.m. on the 30th of August, 1984.

The following are the statements alleged by the prosecution to have been made by the applicant in such circumstances as to render them admissible at the trial.

(a) A written statement alleged to have been made by the third-named applicant to Detective Sergeant Carty and Detective Sergeant Lynagh at 10.30 p.m. in the following circumstances:

At 10.30 p.m. Detective/Sergeant Carty cautioned the applicant and Detective Sergeant Lynagh commenced to write the statement. At 11.30 p.m. approximately the statement was completed. After it had been read to the applicant, he replied, "It is correct. I am signing nothing on the instructions of my solicitor." The alleged statement is as follows:—

Statement of Brian Paul Martin McShane, D.O.B. 26.2.64. A labourer of 99 Oaklawn Park, Dundalk, Co. Louth made to Detective Sergeant Kevin Carty and Patrick Lynagh at Navan Garda Station on the 29th of August 1984 after having been cautioned as follows by Detective Sergeant Carty: 'You are not obliged to say anything unless you wish to do so, but anything you do say will be taken down in writing and may be given in evidence'.

I was told to go to Paddy Duffy's on the night before the robbery. There was other fellows there. The guns were brought to Duffy's yard and we put them into a car that was going on the job. I was driven in that car to a place near the Post Office. There was a man at this place and he gave the orders. He told us that a Post Office van would be at Drumree Post Office at 8 o'clock the next morning. He said that there would be Special Branch with the van. He handed out guns to us and gave each of us our orders. He said that there was a couple of boys at the Post Office already staking out the place. The man told us that if the Branch went for their guns that we knew what to do. We stayed at the place for the night. The next morning we left and went where we were told to go. I was in a car near the Post Office. We got a call on the radio. I had to move in. We went to the Post Office and the van and Branch car was there. The other boys were there before us and they had the place held up. We helped to load the bags into the car. Somebody shouted an order and we moved out. That's my part in the job and I'm not saying any more about it. My conscience is clear. I didn't shoot the guard. This statement has been read over to me and it is correct. I am signing nothing on the instructions of my solicitor.

Signed: Refused to sign. B. McS.
Witness: Kevin Carty, Detective Sergeant.
Witness: P. Lynagh, Detective Sergeant.
29/8/84.

3.05 p.m. 30/8/84 — Cautioned
The Guard was dead before we arrived at the scene.
B. McS.

Witness: Kevin Carty, Detective Sergeant.
Witness: P. Lynagh, Detective Sergeant.

(b) **At 3.05 a.m. on the 30th of August the applicant said to Detective Sergeant Carty in the presence of Detective Sergeant Lynagh after caution: "the guard was dead before we arrived at the scene."**

This latter statement was initialled by the applicant and is incorporated in Exhibit 314.

(c) **A statement alleged to have been made by the applicant to**

Detective Garda Mulvey and Garda Sullivan at approximately 10
a.m. on the 30th of August, 1984, after being cautioned by Detective
Garda Mulvey.

The applicant said "I said it all last night." When asked if he signed
notes or a statement the applicant said: "they read the stuff once to me. I
can't sign them. I am afraid to sign them. What I told them is true."

(d) **In the car on the way to the Court in the presence of Detective
Garda Kennedy, Detective Garda Maunsell and Detective Garda
Lennon the applicant having been cautioned by Detective Garda
Kennedy stated "I made a statement back in Navan Garda Station.
It is the truth. I had to tell the truth, sure they knew already".**

All three applicants challenged the above, referred to alleged statements and admissions, gave evidence and called witnesses.

The Court of trial admitted all the alleged statements and admissions
of the first and second-named applicants in a full and reasoned judgment
and also admitted the alleged statements and admissions of the third-
named applicant in a separate full and reasoned judgment.

The evidence for the defence

The applicants in evidence denied that they made any verbal or written
admissions of complicity in the crime and challenged the veracity of the
evidence of the prosecution. They also gave evidence denying any
involvement in the robbery and shooting and stated they were in their
respective homes at the time of the commission of the offences.

Mrs Eccles, the wife of the first-named applicant, gave evidence that
on the morning of the robbery she was sleeping in the same room as her
husband, the twins and a little girl. She and the children got up at about 8
a.m. She left the applicant sleeping in bed. She called him at 8.30 a.m. and
he came down and joined the family for breakfast. He left the house at
about 9.30 a.m. to see a Mr McGrane about a job and returned about
mid-day.

Mrs McPhillips said she was at home on the morning of the 10th of
August, 1984, and so was her husband, the second-named applicant.

Mrs McDaniels said that on the morning of the 10th of August, 1984,
the second-named applicant, was at his home between 10 a.m. and 10.30
a.m. and paid the milk bill.

Mrs McShane, the mother of the third-named applicant, swore that on the night of the 9th of August, 1984, the applicant was in the house until 8.30 to 9 p.m. when he left to go fishing and that he was back in the house about 11.30 p.m. On the morning of the 10th of August, the applicant was in bed until she called him at about 10 a.m. He came down, took his breakfast, and went into town to get fishing gear.

Counsel then submitted to the Court that all three should be acquitted of each offence. The Court rejected the submissions on behalf of the defence.

In its judgment the Court said that it was satisfied beyond all reasonable doubt that the evidence of both the first-named applicant and his wife was untrue and rejected same. The Court was further satisfied beyond all reasonable doubt that the statements made by the applicant were true. The Court was satisfied that the admissions of the applicant established beyond all reasonable doubt the following facts:

1. The applicant was a member of the group that carried out the robbery at Drumree Post Office on the morning of the 10th of August, 1984.

2. The applicant and other members of the group were, on the night prior to the robbery, informed that there would be two guards with the van and that they would be taken care of.

3. The applicant was aware of the fact that guns had been distributed to the members of the group and would be used in the course of the robbery.

4. The applicant was further aware that the taking care of the guards would involve, if necessary, the use of such guns against the gardaí to kill or cause serious injury to them.

5. It was part of the common agreement or design between the parties, including the applicant, to do all things necessary to execute the robbery and effect their escape and to shoot a member of the Garda Síochána acting in the course of his duty, should that be necessary.

6. In pursuance of this common design, Detective Garda Hand was murdered in the execution of his duty as a member of the Garda Síochána.

7. The action of the person concerned who shot at and killed Detective Garda Hand was not outside the scope of the common design or agreement.

In the case of the second-named applicant the Court was satisfied beyond all reasonable doubt that the evidence of the second-named applicant and his wife was untrue and rejected same. The Court was further satisfied beyond all reasonable doubt that the statements made by the applicants were true. The Court was satisfied that the admissions of the applicant established beyond all reasonable doubt the following facts.

1. The applicant was part of the group which was engaged in the planning and execution of the robbery at Drumree.

2. On the night before, namely, the 9th of August, 1984, he drove an Ascona car to a rendezvous near Dunshaughlin.

3. He stayed there with others during the night.

4. He knew that a post office van was to be robbed on the following morning.

5. He knew that gardaí would be with the van.

6. He knew that certain people "got the job of looking after that part of it".

7. On the morning of the robbery he travelled to Drumree Post Office in a red Mercedes.

8. His job was to load money in the red Mercedes and escape therewith to the agreed rendezvous.

9. At Drumree he loaded the money from the van into the Mercedes.

10. He escaped to the agreed rendezvous, when the money was transferred from the Mercedes.

11. He was armed at the time of the robbery and must have been aware that the others would be armed.

12. It was part of the common design or agreement between the parties, including the applicant, to the robbery to do all things necessary to execute the robbery and to shoot a member of the Garda Síochána acting in the couse of his duty should such be necessary.

13. He knew that "looking after the armed guards" would involve the use of guns against the gardaí to kill or cause serious injury to them.

14. In pursuance of this common design or agreement, Detective Garda Hand was murdered in the execution of his duty as a menber of the Garda Síochána.

15. The action of the person who shot at and killed Garda Hand was not outside the scope of the common agreement or design.

In the case of the third-named applicant the Court was satisfied beyond all reasonable doubt that the evidence of both the applicant and his mother was untrue and rejected same.

The Court was further satisfied beyond all reasonable doubt that the statements made by the applicant were true. The Court was further satisfied that the admissions of the applicant established beyond all reasonable doubt the following facts.

1. The applicant was one of the group that carried out the robbery at Drumree Post Office on the morning of the 10th of August, 1984.

2. On the night before the robbery he and others were informed that there would be "Special Branch" with the van.

3. The leader of the group handed out guns and orders.

4. He and the others were told that if the Branch went for their guns, "they knew what to do".

5. He was informed that the Post Office was already "staked out".

6. It was part of the common design or plan, to which the applicant was a party, to do all things necessary to execute the robbery and to shoot a member of the Garda Síochána in the execution of his duty, should such be necessary.

7. In pursuance of this common design Detective Garda Hand was murdered in the execution of his duty as a member of the Garda Síochána.

8. The action of the person who shot at and killed Detective Garda Hand was not outside the scope of the common design or agreement.

The Grounds of Appeal

In the case of the second and third named applicants, one of the grounds of appeal put forward was that the Court of trial erred in law and in fact in holding that a certificate signed by Simon P. O'Leary and an oral statement made to the Court by Charles Moran, Solicitor, on the 30th of August, 1984, complied with section 47, subsection (2) of the Offences Against the State Act 1939, and section 4, subection (1)(a) and section 4, subsection (3)(b) of the Prosecution of Offences Act 1974, so as to confer jurisdiction on them to try the applicants.

Section 47, subsection (2) of the Offences Against the State Act 1939, as amended, provides that:

"Whenever it is intended to charge a person with an offence which is not a scheduled offence and the Director of Public Prosecutions certifies that the ordinary Courts are, in his opinion, inadequate to secure the effective administration of justice and the preservation of public peace and order in relation to the trial of such person on such charge, the foregoing (subsection (1)) of this section shall apply and have effect as if the offence with which such person is so intended to be charged were a scheduled offence".

Section 47, subsection (1) empowers the Director of Public Prosecutions, if he thinks proper, to direct that a person, whom it is intended to charge with a scheduled offence, be brought before a Special Criminal Court and there charged with such offence, whereupon the Special Criminal Court has jurisdiction to try that person on that charge.

Section 4, subsection (1)(a) of the Prosecution of Offences Act 1974 provides that:

> "A law officer may direct any of his professional officers to perform of his behalf and in accordance with his instructions any particular function of the law officer in relation to a particular case or cases in all cases in which that function falls to be performed".

Section 4, subsection (3) provides that:

> "The fact that a function of a law officer has been performed by him (whether it has been so performed personally or by virtue of subsection (1) of this section) may be be established, without further proof, in any proceedings by a statement of that fact made —
>
> (a) in writing and signed by the law officer, or
> (b) orally to the court concerned by a person appearing on behalf of or prosecuting in the name of the law officer".

Since each of the applicants was charged with a non-scheduled offence, *i.e.* capital murder, the Court of trial had no jurisdiction to try either of them unless the Director of Public Prosecutions, or a professional officer discharging the function on his behalf, issued a certificate in accordance with section 47, subsection (2) of the Offences Against the State Act 1939. Such a certificate was produced to the Court of trial signed by Simon P. O'Leary who was described therein as a professional officer of the Director of Public Prosecutions. At the hearing before the Court of trial, counsel for the Director of Public Prosecutions stated orally to the Court that the relevant function of the Director of Public Prosecutions in relation to the giving of such a certificate had been performed on his behalf by Simon P. O'Leary.

It was submitted on behalf of the second and third-named applicants that, since the issuing of a certificate by the Director of Public Prosecutions under section 47, subsection 2 of the 1939 Act was an essential precondition to the exercise by that court of any jurisdiction to try either of the applicants, the necessary proof of the issuing of the certificate should have been given to the Court of trial when the applicants were first brought before it. As this had not been done, it was submitted that the Court of trial thereafter had no jurisdiction to embark on the trial of either of the applicants.

It is clear that unless the Director of Public Prosecutions has issued a certificate in accordance with section 47, subsection (2) of the 1939 Act, the Special Criminal Court has no jurisdiction to try any person on a non-scheduled offence. Section 4, subsection (3)(a) of the 1974 Act provides for a method of proof of the fact that this certifying function has been performed on the Director's behalf by one of his professional officers. The submission advanced to the Court of trial, and again in this Court, that this proof must be tendered at the stage when the accused persons are brought before the Court for the first time is, in the opinion of this Court, erroneous. While the issuing of the appropriate certificate by the Director, or a professional officer on his behalf, is undoubtedly a necessary precondition to the exercise by the Special Criminal Court of its jurisdiction to try any persons on a scheduled or non-scheduled offence, the fact that the certificate has been given may be proved in the manner described by section 4 of the 1974 Act at any time before the close of the prosecution's case. In this respect it is no different from any other proof which may be necessary to establish that a particular court has jurisdiction to try a particular offence. This ground of appeal accordingly fails.

The next ground of appeal was submitted on behalf of all three applicants. While each applicant had incorporated a number of grounds touching on this aspect of the application for leave to appeal, it was agreed that a submission worded as follows would embrace all the points on behalf of all the applicants:

"Where a person has been arrested and detained pursuant to section 30 of the Offences Against the State Act 1939, and in the course of such detention a determination has been made not to rely upon, and/or waive such powers of interrogation, or of demanding of information as are conferred by the said Act, then the subsequent subjection of the detaineee to a protracted interrogation, or to any interrogation, calculated to incriminate him, constitutes such a deliberate and conscious violation of his constitutional rights as to render any statement by such detainee made as a result of and/or in the course of such interrogation inadmissible upon the trial of such person.

The submissions on behalf of all the applicants were made by counsel appearing for the first-named applicant.

Counsel submitted that the evidence established that, on the night of 21 August, 1984, there was a conference at Garda Headquarters, Phoenix Park. It was decided at the conference to send Detective Sergeant Shelly and Detective Garda Hanley to Navan Garda Station. This decision was made before the applicant was arrested and at a time when the Gardaí had no evidence implicating him in the crime. Counsel further submitted that the evidence also established that Detective Sergeant Shelly and Detective Garda Hanley did not go to the scene of the crime at Drumree but went, on the morning of the 22nd of August, to Navan Garda Station to interview a prisoner (the first-named applicant) who had been arrested under section 30 of the 1939 Act.

Counsel submitted that in so far as the cases of *People (DPP) v Madden* [1977] I.R. 336, and *People (DPP) v Kelly (No. 2)* [1983] I.R. 1, held that section 30 of the Offences Against the State Act 1939, or section 52 of that Act, or the combined effect of the said two sections read together, authorised interrogation by the Garda Síochána of a person detained in custody under the said section 30 and that members of the Garda Síochána were not confined, in relation to a person arrested under the said section 30, after arrest and during detention, only to require such detained person to give an account of his movements or information as provided for in the said section 52, the said cases and each of them were wrongly decided.

It was further submitted that the evidence established that, on the morning of the 22nd of August, 1984, at the first interview with Detective Sergeant Shelly and Detective Garda Hanley the applicant was cautioned. Because he was arrested under section 30, counsel submitted that once the applicant was cautioned before questioning he ceased to be a person in custody under section 30 and was now being interrogated as an ordinary prisoner under common law.

It was submitted that once the applicant was arrested under section 30 of the Act he could only be questioned under section 52 of the Act. Once a caution was administered the custodians of the prisoner had abdicated their powers under section 52.

It was also submitted that, from the time of the caution being given, when the applicant refused to make a statement he should have been brought before a court or released and, as at that time there was no adequate evidence to warrant a charge, he should have been released.

Counsel further submitted that the applicant was arrested for the purpose of being interrogated and that such a motive for arresting a person under section 30 of the 1939 Act should not be tolerated by the courts.

It was further submitted that the detention from the time of the giving of the caution in the circumstances of the applicant's case was unlawful as he was denied the ordinary constitutional protection and rules applying to common law prisoners. Counsel referred to *People (DPP) v Walsh* ([1980] I.R. 294 and *People (DPP) v Higgins*, Supreme Court, 22 November 1985; *Maxwell on Statutes* (12th edition) and *Bingham on Statutory Interpretation* (1984), pp. 609 *et seq.* to 629. As the other applicants were immediately cautioned before being interrogated in Navan Garda Station, counsel on their behalf adopted the submissions made on behalf of the first-named applicant. Counsel for the prosecutor, in reply, relied on the judgment in *People (DPP) v Madden* [1977] I.R. 336 and, in particular, pp. 336 to 353 and also the judgment of the Court of Criminal Appeal and the Supreme Court in *People (DPP) v Kelly (No. 2)* [1983] I.R. 1 *et seq.* Counsel referred to *People (DPP) v Pringle, McCann and O'Shea*, 2 Frewen 57 and submitted that in the instant case the Judges' Rules were at all times complied with. (The Judges' Rules are set out in *People v Cummins* [1972] I.R. 312). It was further submitted that the giving of a caution to a person in custody cannot change the nature of the custody. It was also contended that fair procedures were adopted in this case in respect of the custody and questioning of all the applicants. A caution can never be an abandonment of either the powers of arrest under section 30 of the Act or of a subsequent right to invoke the powers under section 30 of the Act. Finally, counsel for the prosecution submitted that under section 30, subsection (1) of the 1939 Act

> "a member of the Garda Síochána . . . may without warrant . . . arrest . . . any person . . . whom he suspects of being in possession of information relating to the commission or intended commission of

any such offence as aforesaid".

Section 30 of the Offences Against the State Act 1939 is always in force while the Act remains on the Statute Book. However, section 30 of the Act only applies to scheduled offences when and only for as long as Part V of the Act is brought into force and remains in force in accordance with the provisions of Part V of the Act.

Section 52 is contained in Part V of the Act and therefore the power to examine detained persons by virtue of the provisions of that section is operative only when Part V is in force.

The powers given to arrest and interrogate persons under section 30 of the Act are always in force in respect of offences under the Act itself as distinct from scheduled offences. These powers of arrest and interrogation which are always in force are subject to the Judges' Rules and the invoking of section 52 in the appropriate circumstances simply adds a statutory power to require the giving of the prescribed information and in no way limits the powers of interrogation already existing. The operation of Part V of the Act extends the pre-existing powers under section 30 of the Act to scheduled offences.

Therefore the Court is satisfied that the applicants' submissions on this point are not well founded and the Court follows the reasoning of the Supreme Court in *People (DPP) v Kelly* [1983] I.R. 1.

Counsel on behalf of the second and third-named applicants contested the validity of the extension order under section 30, subsection (3) of the Act. Counsel for the second-named applicant contended

(a) that the Court of trial erred in law in holding that Chief Superintendent John J. Moore had given a valid direction to Sergeant Finnegan for the continued detention of the applicant after 6.25 a.m. on the 30th of August, 1984.

(b) that the Chief Superintendent should not have been allowed to claim privilege against the disclosure of the source of the information on which he decided to order the further detention of the applicant.

Counsel on behalf of the third-named applicant submitted that the Court was perverse in holding that a lawful direction for the further detention of the applicant had been given at 9 p.m. by Chief Superintendent Moore.

Counsel for the second-named applicant submitted that the evidence established that the direction for an extension of the twenty-four hour period by Chief Superintendent Moore to Sergeant Finnegan was Exhibit No. 298. It was contended that on the evidence the filling up of the contents of the document and its subsequent signature by the Chief Superintendent was irreconcilable with the uncontroverted evidence of Mr Terry Carlin, a typographical expert, that three different typewriters had been employed to make various insertions in the standard form of order which could not therefore have come into existence in the manner sworn to by Chief Superintendent Moore. Because Mr. Carlin's evidence was not challenged, at least a doubt must have existed and the applicant should have been given the benefit of that doubt. It was further contended that before giving a direction to extend the twenty-four hour period of detention, the officer giving such a direction must, at the appropriate time, have a *bona fide* belief that the direction to detain for a further period is necessary in all the circumstances of the case. It was contended that when challenged as to the source from which he got the information on which he decided to make the extension order, the Chief Superintendent refused to say whether it was from sources within or outside the Garda force. Counsel contended that if the source of the information was from within the Garda force, he might have been asked what facts were so communicated to him.

Counsel for the third-named applicant adopted the same arguments and further submitted that the making of the extension order was premature, being made over 6 hours before the termination of the original twenty-four hour period of detention at 6.25 a.m. on 30 August, 1984.

In relation to Exhibit No. 298 and Exhibit No. 300 (the relevant extension orders) Chief Superintendent John Moore denied that he signed the documents in blank or that only portions were typed in on each of them.

Sergeant Finnegan also gave evidence as to the orders. He said that he read over to the third-named applicant at 12.30 a.m. on the 30th of August, 1984 at Navan Garda Station the extension order directing his detention for a further period of twenty-four hours commencing at 6.25 a.m. on the 30th of August, 1984, and expiring at 6.25 a.m. on the 31st of August, 1984. It was signed by Chief Superintendent Moore and was given to him by the Chief Superintendent at 9 p.m. on the 29th of August, 1984.

He further gave evidence that at 12.28 a.m. on the 30th of August, 1984, at Navan Garda Station he read over an extension order to the second-named applicant, given by Chief Superintendent Moore, directing his detention in custody for a further period from 6.25 a.m. on the 30th of August, and expiring at 6.25 a.m. on the 31st of August, 1984. On cross-examination he said he received the order from Chief Superintendent Moore at Navan Garda Station at 9 p.m. on the 29th of August.

Mr Carlin gave evidence as a typographical expert that three different typewriters were used in the typing on both Exhibits 298 and 300 and counsel for the second-named applicant contended that this evidence, not being challenged, should have been accepted by the Court of trial, in which event the evidence of Chief Superintendent Moore could not have been acceptable beyond all reasonable doubt.

It was further contended for the applicants that the Court of trial erred in allowing Chief Superintendent Moore to claim privilege in respect of the information he alleged satisfied him that there was a suspicion against the second-named applicant warranting the issuing of an extension order. Counsel submitted that on the authority of *Murphy v Dublin Corporation* [1972] I.R. 215 a member of the Gardaí could not plead privilege when questioned about information he might have received from other members of the force.

Lastly, it was submitted that an extension order could not be issued prematurely. In the case of the second-named applicant the extension order was read over to him while there was still six hours unexpired of the original period of detention under section 30. Chief Superintendent Moore, when cross-examined by counsel for the second-named applicant, agreed that he gave the order for the further detention of the second-named applicant and pointed out that it did not need to be in writing. He said he gave the order because he believed that the applicant had committed a scheduled offence. Later he stated that he had quite a lot of information of a confidential nature that the applicant was involved in this crime.

The Chief Superintendent also said he was satisfied in his own mind that it was necessary to hold the applicant for a further period of twenty-four hours. He had formed the opinion earlier in the day but gave the direction at 9 p.m. He said that he based this opinion on confidential information of a sensitive nature. When asked whether somebody other than a garda gave him information which suggested that he should detain the applicant for longer than twenty-four hours the Chief Superintendent replied:—

It was confidential, my lords, confidential information. I don't think it would be fair to distinguish between persons who gave me confidential information.

He was then asked: "does this mean someone other than a policeman?", and he replied:— "If I answer that, I am distinguishing the person." He also said that he believed he could claim privilege in respect of his source of information if it was from a policeman and confidential. The witness refused to differentiate between a policeman and somebody else.

He was then asked by the presiding Judge: "Are you claiming privilege?", and replied:

"I am claiming privilege, my lords, yes. It would be dangerous to differentiate in cases such as this between one person and another and I am claiming privilege."

The Court held that the answer to counsel's question was privileged.

Earlier, Chief Superintendent Moore had been cross-examined by counsel for the third-named applicant. In reply to counsel's questions, he said that he was in possession of confidential information that a scheduled offence under the Offences Against the State Act, 1939, had been committed. He said that he obtained this confidential information from a source other than a police officer. He stated that he obtained this information that evening in Trim. He agreed that he issued the detention order so that the applicant could be further questioned and went on to say

"Well, he was being interrogated in relation to this scheduled offence and if he had made an admission, naturally, of course, it would be used in evidence against him. If he did make a voluntary confession it would be used in evidence against him".

Section 30 of the Act is as follows:—

"Whenever a person is arrested under this section, he may be removed to and detained in custody in a Garda Síochána Station, a prison or some other convenient place for a period of twenty-four hours from the time of his arrest and may, if an official of the Garda Síochána not below the rank of Chief Superintendent so directs, be detained for a further period of twenty-four hours".

The Court is satisfied that on the evidence before it the Court of trial was entitled to accept beyond reasonable doubt the evidence of Chief

Superintendent Moore as to the manner and circumstances in which he decided to extend the period of detention and signed the forms in the case of both applicants and to conclude beyond reasonable doubt that at the time of extending the period of detention he suspected both applicants of being involved in the commission of the scheduled offence for which they were originally arrested.

The Court is also satisfied that in the circumstances of this case the Court of trial was entitled to hold that Chief Superintendent Moore was entitled to claim privilege in respect of both the source, and the nature of the source, of the sensitive, confidential information he received in respect of the applicant. Normally, a member of the Garda Síochána cannot claim privilege in respect of information received from a fellow member of the force simply by virtue of its being such a communication. The circumstances in this case were, however, exceptional. As already indicated, when replying to counsel for the second-named applicant, the witness had no hesitation in telling the Court that the information he received of a confidential nature which caused him to extend the period of detention did come from a source other than a garda officer. In the case of the second- named applicant, however, he claimed privilege on the ground that

> "in a case such as this it would be dangerous to identify whether the source was civilian or police".

This he was clearly entitled to do.

Finally, the Court is satisfied that on a correct interpretation of section 30, subsection 3 of the Offences Against the State Act 1939, any officer not below the rank of Chief Superintendent (or a Superintendent if authorised by section 3 of the Act) may direct that a person arrested under section 30 of the Act may be detained for a further period of 24 hours from the expiration of the first period of 24 hours provided that when he does so the detainee is *bona fide* suspected by him of being involved in the offence for which he was originally arrested. This direction may be given at any time during the initial 24 hours and must be given before the expiration thereof. For these reasons, these grounds of appeal also fail.

In the case of the first-named applicant, grounds 3, 4 and 5 of the Notice of Appeal were that:

1. The procedures adopted by the Gardaí while the applicant was in

custody were unfair and unreasonable, entailed threats both physical and psychological, were unduly protracted and oppressive, and were calculated so to break down the mental resistance of the applicant as to render involuntary and inadmissible the alleged oral and written statements.

2. By reason of the deliberate and conscious disregard of the applicant's constitutional rights by reason *inter alia* of the matters referred to in paragraph 1 below, the applicant was in unlawful custody at the time of the alleged making of the said alleged oral and written statements and each of them so as to render them inadmissible in evidence.

3. The Court of trial in making its findings adverse to the applicant failed to have any, or any sufficient, regard to the principle of the presumption of innocence and/or the principle of reasonable doubt and in each such finding accepted unquestioningly the evidence of the prosecution and rejected the evidence tendered by the defence in consistent disregard of the said principles.

4. In rejecting the evidence given by and on behalf of the applicant the Court of trial took into account evidence irrelevant to his trial, namely, the evidence of Daniel McDonald.

In the case of the second-named applicant the first, fourth, fifth and sixth grounds of appeal were as follows:

1. The Court of trial failed to pay any regard or attend to the evidence given by and on behalf of the applicant and found the evidence of Daniel McDonald as being given in relation to the first-named applicant instead of the second-named applicant, as was the case, and in so far as it purported to alter, on 29 March, 1985, the terms of the judgment delivered on 28 March, 1985, was not lawfully entitled to do so and was *functus officio*.

2. The Court of trial was wrong in law in preferring on the issue as to whether the applicants made the alleged verbal statements the evidence of Garda witnesses who were shown to be evasive and untruthful to the otherwise uncontradicted evidence of the applicant.

3. Even if the Court of trial was entitled to act on the Garda evidence it was wrong in law in admitting any of the alleged verbal admissions on the grounds that:

(1) All of the said admissions were obtained as a result of conscious and deliberate violations of the applicant's constitutional right to liberty and bodily integrity and access to and by his solictor.

(2) None of the said admissions was made voluntarily and there was no evidence on which the Court of trial could have held that they were

although the same were not induced by violence, threats and inducements and as a result of excessively prolonged and oppressive questioning without any or any adequate opportunity for rest or refreshment or that the procedures employed throughout his interrogation while under arrest were not unfair and unconstitutional.

(3) Having accepted the evidence of Mr Frank McDonnell that he believed he had telephoned Navan Garda Station in the early afternoon on the 30th of August 1984, and having found that there was doubt as to which Garda Station he telephoned, the Court of trial failed to resolve the doubt in favour of the applicant.

In the case of the third-named applicant, the third, fourth, fifth, sixth, seventh, ninth, tenth and eleventh grounds of appeal were as follows:

1. The procedures adopted by the Gardai on the 29th and the 30th of August, 1984 were unfair and unreasonable, entailed threats both physical and psychological, were unduly protracted and oppressive, and were calculated so to break down the mental resistance of the applicant as to render involuntary and inadmissible the said alleged oral and written statements.

2. By reason of the deliberate and conscious disregard of the applicant's constitutional rights by reason, *inter alia*, of the matters set out in the preceding paragraph the applicant was in unlawful custody at the times of the alleged making of the alleged oral and written statements and each of them so as to render them inadmissible in evidence.

3. The Court of trial in making its findings adverse to the applicant failed to have any, or any sufficient regard, to the principle of the presumption of innocence and/or the principle of reasonable doubt, and in each such finding accepted unquestioningly the evidence of the prosecution and rejected the evidence tendered by the defence in consistent disregard of the said principles.

4. The statements alleged to have been made by the applicant should not have been admitted in evidence for the reasons advanced in the course of the trial on the issue as to their admissibility.

5. The findings of fact made by the Court of trial in relation to the issue as to admissibility of the statements allegedly made by the accused were contrary to the evidence and to the weight of the evidence and were contrary to the observations expressed by the Court to counsel for the prosecution after it had called upon him to reply to submissions made by counsel for the applicant.

6. The Court of trial should have granted the application for a direction made at the close of the prosecution case.

7. The Court of trial in rejecting the evidence of the applicant and his mother failed to have regard to the fact that the evidence was not seriously challenged nor was the entirety or any portion of the prosecution case put to the applicant in his evidence and in the circumstances the Court should have entertained a reasonable doubt and thereby acquitted the accused.

8. The Court of trial failed to pay any or any sufficient attention to the evidence adduced on behalf of the accused.

While some of the grounds of appeal set out above are relevant only to the cases of individual applicants, the principles of law which this Court is obliged to apply in respect of each of them are the same in relation to all the grounds and they may therefore be conveniently considered together.

In the case of the first-named applicant, the evidence established that he was arrested by Sergeant McGee on 22 August, 1984, at 6.20 a.m. at his home and brought to Navan Garda Station where he arrived at 7.15 a.m. He was then given into the charge of the station orderly, Garda Keogh, and put by him in a cell. At 8.30 a.m. on the same morning, Detective Sergeant Joseph Shelly and Detective Garda James Hanley, who were both members of the Investigation Section of the Garda Technical Bureau, Phoenix Park, Dublin, arrived at 8.30 a.m. and, having introduced themselves, began to interview the applicant. Detective Sergeant Shelly said that the applicant was then cautioned and asked to account for his movements between 6.00 a.m. on the morning of 10 August, 1984 and 12 noon on the same day. He said that the applicant gave an account of his movements and that Garda Hanley then put it to him that he (the applicant) could help them with their enquiries into the armed robbery and the murder of Detective Garda Hand. He replied that he was not there and that he knew nothing about it. The witness then asked him if he had any knowledge of a red Mercedes motor car (registration number WCC 267B) and the applicant denied knowing anything about the car. The witness then asked him about Paddy Duffy from Drumeskin and he told him that he knew Duffy. At approximately 10.30 a.m. he was served a breakfast of bacon, egg and sausage, tea, bread and butter, which he was allowed to eat without interruption. Detective Sergeant Shelly said that he and Detective Garda Hanley did not speak to the applicant while he was eating. They then had a further general conversation with him and at about 11.35 he was taken to another room to be fingerprinted. At that stage, Detective Garda Kennedy started to interview the applicant and the witness and Detective Garda Hanley left.

They next saw him at 2.45 p.m. in the same interview room. Gardaí Maunsell and Kennedy were with him at the time and left as soon as the witness and Detective Garda Hanley went in. Detective Garda Hanley cautioned him again and he and the witness put it to the applicant that he had not given a true account of his movements. The applicant denied this and the witness and Detective Garda Hanley then questioned him further about his movements, and in particular about his statement that he had collected the dole of Thursday, which they said was a peculiar day on which to collect it. He then told them about his financial problems and the witness and Detective Garda Hanley discussed his friends with him, and in particular friends from Northern Ireland whom the applicant said he thought were Republicans. The witness and Garda Hanley asked him if he was involved in politics and the applicant replied that he had no interest in politics. At around 3.50 p.m. he was served fish and chips, tea and bread and butter, and he ate that meal. The witness and Garda Hanley questioned him further about his possible involvement in the armed robbery at Drumree after this meal and the applicant said he did not want to say more about it. Around 4.40, Detective Garda Maguire from the photographic section came into the room and photographed the accused. Detective Garda Hanley left at that time.

Detective Garda Hanley returned when Detective Garda Maguire left at approximately 4.45 p.m. and at that stage the witness and Detective Garda Hanley resumed their interview with the applicant. They again suggested to him that he was not telling the truth and the applicant replied that he did not want to say any more about it. Detective Sergeant Shelly said that he and Detective Garda Hanley spoke generally to him and that the applicant spoke quite openly to them. He said that the applicant remained silent for periods. At around 5.30 p.m. he and Detective Garda Hanley were informed that a doctor had called to the station to examine the applicant and he was taken to a room to be examined. He said that at approximately 5.45 p.m. the applicant was allowed a visit to his wife who had called to the station, and that they had a private meeting which lasted approximately 15 minutes. At 6.00 p.m. they again went back to the interview room and the applicant told them that he was being treated "O.K." and that he was glad to be able to see his wife. He also said to them that they had Duffy and Greene there and asked Garda Hanley what gear was found in Duffy's place that morning. Detective Garda Hanley told him there were a number of guns and forged money found on the premises. They asked the applicant if he knew anything about this as he was always round Duffy's place and he denied knowing anything about it. The interview finished at around 6.10 p.m. and Detective Gardaí Kennedy and Maunsell then came into the room and commenced interviewing the applicant.

Detective Sergeant Shelly said that at 9.00 p.m. that night he and Detective Garda Hanley resumed interviewing the applicant. At the outset, the witness cautioned him in the usual manner and they again proceeded to ask him about the events of the 9th and the 10th of August, and in particular about the use that might have been made of his car on those days. The witness said that he put it to the applicant that they believed the car was observed in the Kentstown area of Navan on the evening of Thursday night and that he remained silent for some time and then said "the less I say the better". At that stage he requested a drink of water and Detective Garda Hanley left the room and when he came back in gave him a full cup of water. They then asked him what he meant by this remark and he said "look lads, I'm a married man with a family", and asked them "what would these fellows get if they were caught?". The witness told him that that would be entirely a matter that would depend first, on what they were charged with and, secondly, on how the Courts would deal with the matter. They then had further discussions with the applicant about another motor car, a bronze Opel Ascona, registration number OZG 66. At approxi- mately 12 midnight, Detective Garda Hanley read over the notes which he had been taking of the interview and asked him if they were correct. The applicant asked him to read over the notes again, which Detective Garda Hanley did. He then said that the notes were "O.K.", but that he wasn't signing them. At approximately 12.10 a.m. on the morning of the 23rd of August, they handed the applicant over to the station orderly who was on duty and he was placed in the cell.

Detective Sergeant Shelly said that he next saw the applicant at 1.30 p.m. on the following day, the witness being accompanied on this occasion by Detective Garda Sullivan and Detective Garda Mulvey. He was having his dinner at that time which he continued eating until approximately 2.15 p.m. The witness then cautioned him in the same terms and the applicant initially told them that he was putting on weight and was being well looked after. They again told him that they did not believe he was telling them the truth about his movements and there was a further discussion about what he had been doing on the morning of the 10th of August, and as to whether Duffy had been charged yet. They told him that that had not been decided and he then asked them if Duffy had made a statement and they told him that he had. He also asked them about Greene and they told him that they did not know the decision about Greene. There was a further discussion about Greene and he was again asked to give an account of his movements for the 9th and the 10th of August, and he gave the same account as previously. He was asked about the activities in Duffy's yard and whether he was there the night before the robbery when the guns were being loaded into the cars. He remained silent for some time and then said "someone has told you the story, I wouldn't shoot a Guard." After a further period of silence, he asked the witness "what would a fellow get if he only drove a car on the job?" A solicitor called to see the applicant at 5.15 p.m. and remined with him until about 5.30 p.m. Neither the witness nor Garda Hanley were present while the applicant was seeing his solicitor.

When he and Garda Hanley returned to the interview room, the latter cautioned him again and they then asked him had he now considered his position. The applicant then said that he would tell them the truth but that he would not mention any names. The witness said that he told him at that point that the solicitor had told him that his wife had been arrested. He (the witness) had not been aware of that fact until then and they informed the applicant of it. He asked them if he could have a visit from his wife and Detective Garda Hanley then left the room to see if this could be done. Detective Garda Hanley returned after some minutes and the witness asked the applicant if he would make a written statement about the part he played in the affair and he said he would. At that stage Detective Superintendent Hubert Reynolds, who was also from the Garda Technical Bureau, came into the room and the latter asked the applicant if he wanted to see him. The applicant said to him that if it was possible at a later stage he would like to see his wife and Superintendent Reynolds confirmed that she was detained and told him that if it was decided that she was going to be released he would certainly see to it that he had a visit from her. The witness said that the Superintendent reminded the applicant that this was not an inducement or a promise to him in any way. After that the applicant proceeded to dictate the statement. While it was being taken a meal was supplied to the applicant, of fish and chips and a glass of milk. The meal was brought in at approximately 9 o'clock and he was given 15 or 20 minutes to eat it. The taking of the statement was resumed after the meal had been finished and when it was finished, it was read over to the applicant who was invited to make any alterations or additions that he deemed necessary. He was also invited to correct any mistakes which were made in it. He asked Detective Garda Hanley to change the colour of the Mercedes from red to wine. He also initialled it and then signed the statement. The statement was also signed by Detective Garda Hanley and himself and was completed at 9.50 p.m. on the 23rd of August. Twenty minutes after the taking of the statement, the applicant was again seen by a doctor.

Detective Sergeant Shelly's evidence as to the interviewing of the applicant and the taking of the statement was in general corroborated by Detective Garda Hanley.

Detective Garda Maunsell said that he and Detective Garda Kennedy began interviewing the applicant at about 11.50 a.m. on the 22rd of August. They had a discussion with him about his ownership of a car and his ability to pay for it, which was interrupted by the arrival of the applicant's solicitor from Dundalk. The applicant had an interview with his solicitor lasting about eight minutes and the interviewing of the applicant was then resumed by the witness and Detective Garda Kennedy, the witness first being cautioned again. There were further discussions about the applicant's motor car and the access of other people to it, followed by a general conversation about the applicant's family. The interview came to an end at 2.15 p.m., when Detective Sergeant Shelly and Detective Garda Hanley re-entered the room. They saw him again later that day at 6.10 p.m. when they questioned him further about his movements. This interview came to an end at 9.00 p.m., the applicant having been served tea at 8.30 p.m. He saw the applicant no more that day, but at 8.10 p.m. on the following morning, he brought him from the cell to the interview room accompanied by Detective Garda Kennedy who cautioned him again in the same terms. He was asked further about Duffy's yard and the car and the interview ended at approximately 10.00 a.m. Detective Garda Maunsell's account of these interviews was corroborated by Detective Garda Kennedy.

Detective Garda Sullivan said that he saw the applicant, accompanied by Detective Garda Mulvey, at 10.00 a.m. on the 23rd of August. Detective Garda Mulvey told the applicant that they were investigating the armed robbery at Drumree and that they believed that the applicant could help them with their enquiries. He was cautioned in the usual terms and asked to tell the truth about the matter. He denied knowing anything about the robbery. At 10.15 a.m. he was served with a breakfast, consisting of bacon and egg, tea, bread and butter. He ate the meal provided and the witness and Detective Garda Mulvey did not ask him any questions while he was having them. He asked to be brought to the wash-room after his breakfast and this was done. They again put it to him that he should tell them the truth about his involvement in the robbery and the applicant denied any knowledge of it. He had a visit at about 11.10 a.m. from his solicitor, Mr Rogers, and was left alone with the latter until 11.30 a.m. He was further interviewed about his involvement in the robbery at Drumree at 11.30 and the applicant again denied any knowledge of it. He was given a change of clothing at approximately 12.20 p.m. after which they had a general conversation with him. At 1.30 p.m. he was served his dinner and Detective Sergeant Shelly and Detective/Garda Hanley then came into the room. Detective Garda Sullivan's evidence in relation to this was in general corroborated by Detective Garda Jim Mulvey.

The applicant then gave evidence. He said that he was never cautioned at any stage during his interview with Detective Sergeant Shelly and Detective Garda Hanley. He said that he was treated very badly by both Gardaí, who used abusive and obscene language to him. He said that Detective Garda Hanley grabbed him by the throat and called him a liar. He said that a request by him for a solicitor was rejected in an obscene and abusive manner and that both Gardaí kept shouting at him and banging the table. He said that the only breakfast he had was a piece of bread and a cup of tea. He said that the two detectives who replaced Detective Sergeant Shelly and Detective Garda Hanley were polite but kept insisting that the applicant should give them an account of his movements and that he kept insisting that he should see a solicitor. He said that they told him they could not get him any cigarettes. They then had a further conversation about his possible involvement in the robbery and murder.

When Detective Sergeant Shelly and Detective Garda Hanley returned, the atmosphere changed completely and he was again subjected to verbal abuse by them and was told that he would be going to Portlaoise. He said that he was seen by a person whom he did not know, in the afternoon, who described himself as a solicitor. He said that he (the applicant) was suspicious of him and thought he might be a detective and, accordingly, made no complaints of ill-treatment to him. He asked if he could be seen by a doctor and the solicitor said he would look after that. The interviewing then resumed and he said that it was conducted in the same aggressive manner as before. He said that he only had one cigarette, although he was a heavy smoker, during the time that he was detained in the Garda Station. When he attempted to re-light that cigarette, he was told in a rude fashion by Detective Garda Shelly and Detective Garda Hanley to put it out. During the course of the first day Detective Garda Hanley also spat in his face several times. He also told him to stand up against a wall where he kept digging him in the ribs, pulling him by the hair, spitting into his face and calling him a murdering bastard. He said that he saw his wife during that night and was given an ample opportunity to talk to her. She asked him if he was alright and he said that he was and that she was not to worry.

He was put in the cell that night, where there was a horrible smell and where the bed clothes were dirty. He slept for only 2 hours that night and felt tired and hungry the next morning when the interviewing resumed. He had seen his solicitor twice the previous day. The questioning by Detective Gardaí Maunsell and Kennedy on the second morning was polite at the outset, but their manner changed at a later stage and they began to abuse him verbally. He said that Detective Garda Kennedy pulled out a hand gun and pointed it at him and said he would blow his f------- head off and that he (the witness) had murdered Frank Hand and that he (Garda Kennedy) was at his wedding six weeks ago. He said that this scared the life out of him. He said that during the course of the interviewing on the 23rd, Detective Garda Hanley kicked him on the behind and on his legs. He made no complaints about these assaults to any of the three doctors who visited him while he was detained in the Garda Station. He said that while he was provided with meals during the day, he didn't eat them as they were mainly fish and chips and they were "rotten". He said that during the course of the interviewing, Detective Garda Hanley pulled him by the hair, made him get out of a chair, put him up against the wall and kept forcing him down onto the ground until he was on both knees. He kept spitting into his face while doing this and calling him a f------- murdering bastard who was going to Portlaoise. He kept insisting that he (the witness) had killed Garda Hand and had committed the robbery. He said that Detective Sergeant Shelly and Detective Garda Hanley continued to question him and that at one stage they went "pure mad". He said that just before he saw his solicitor at 5.15 on that day, the Gardaí kept telling him that "a whole pile" had been found in his house and that they were going to charge his wife with having explosive substances in her possession. He said that they said she would be sent to Mountjoy jail where she would be with the prostitutes and drug addicts, that their children would be taken off them and put into a home and that, if he did not agree to sign the statement, he would be in Portlaoise as well and the whole family would be destroyed. He said that Detective Garda Hanley wrote out a statement and told him to sign it and that when he (the witness) refused to sign it, Garda Hanley grabbed him by the hair, put a pen into his hand and tried to make him sign it. He said that he thought they were bluffing when they told him his wife had been arrested. He said that he told his solicitor that he was being ill-treated and that the solicitor told him his wife had been arrested. He said he was "shattered" by this information. When the interviewing with Sergeant Shelly and Garda Hanley resumed, he told them his solicitor had informed him that his wife had been arrested and that they told him in abusive language that when he went home neither his wife nor his children would be there. He said that he told Garda Hanley that he would do anything as long as his wife was allowed go home and that Garda Hanley said "right, sign this statement". He said that he did not dictate any part of the statement and that he simply signed it where Garda Hanley indicated.

Mr Rogers, the applicant's solicitor, gave evidence of having had three interviews with him in Navan Garda Station when he was being detained there. He said that the applicant had complained of being ill-treated by the Gardaí and that at the third interview, he seemed shocked when the witness told him that his wife had been detained.

In the case of the second-named applicant the evidence established that he was brought to Navan Garda Station at 7.50 a.m. on the 29th of August, 1984. Detective Garda Hanley gave evidence that he began to interview the applicant at approximately 8.05 a.m. on that morning in an interview room in Navan Garda Station. He was accompanied by Detective Garda Healy. They told him that they were investigating the armed robbery at Drumree and cautioned him in the usual terms. He said that the applicant replied that he knew nothing about it and that Garda Healy told him that they had information that he was involved in the robbery and to tell the truth. He said that the applicant continued to deny having had anything to do with it and he was then asked for an account of his movements on the 10th of August, 1984. After some further discussion about his movements on that day, Dr Kiernan arrived at 9.45 a.m. to examine the applicant and the witness and Detective Garda Healy left the room. They went back into the room after fifteen minutes and at 10.10 a.m. the applicant's fingerprints were taken and he was examined again by Garda doctor, Dr Hayes, at 10.25. At 10.40 a.m. they returned to the interview room and breakfast was served to the applicant which he refused to take. A solicitor, Mr Frank McDonnell, arrived to see him at 12.30 p.m. and Detective Garda Healy and the witness left the room. He thought that the interview with Mr McDonnell lasted about half an hour. They returned to the interview room and resumed their interviewing of the applicant, who again said that he had nothing further to say. At 1.15 p.m., Detective Sergeant O'Carroll came to the interview room and the witness and Detective Garda Healy left.

He saw the applicant later that day at 5.45 p.m. in the interview room, again accompanied by Detective Garda Healy. He said that he cautioned the applicant again and that the latter continued to deny any involvement in the killing of the Guard. They had a further discussion with him and at 7.20 a meal was supplied to him of salad which he ate. They did not question him while he was having the meal, which took him about twenty minutes to eat. They resumed questioning him at that stage and at 9.30 p.m., the witness read over the notes of the interview to him and cautioned him again. The applicant refused to sign the notes when asked to do so.

The witness did not see the applicant again until the following day at 8.00 a.m. when he was again cautioned and questioned about the robbery and the shooting of Garda Hand. The applicant again said that he did not wish to discuss it and there was a further discussion of a general nature. At 9.45 a.m. breakfast was served to the applicant, which he took about half an hour to eat, during which time he was not questioned. That interview lasted until 11.15 a.m. when Detective Sergeant O'Carroll entered the room and the witness and Garda Healy left.

They saw him again at 2.25 p.m. in the interview room when he was again cautioned and then asked "what was happening to McCabe", another person who was suspected of involvement in the robbery and killing. The witness told him that McCabe was being charged with the armed robbery and he replied "I wouldn't like to be him going to Portlaoise when they hear the names he dropped in the statement." The witness told him that the third-named applicant had also made a statement and he asked if the third-named applicant had mentioned him in that statement. The witness told him that he had not read the third-named applicant's statement but he was satisfied that he had not mentioned the second-named applicant's name in it. At the applicant's request, a copy of this statement was then read to him. He was then shown a map which had been found by a Garda search party in the Julianstown area. After further discussion about the circumstances in which this map had been found, the applicant said:

> "You know well that that's the map. Look, everybody else has told their part in it. I will tell my part. You know it already anyway".

The witness then wrote down the statement as dictated by the applicant who, however, refused to sign it. At 5.50 p.m., he was taken to another room where he was examined by Dr Hayes. Neither he nor his colleagues had used any physical force during the course of any of the interviews, nor had they threatened him or held out any inducements to him. Detective Garda Healy gave evidence to the same effect.

Detective/Sergeant O'Carroll and Detective Inspector Culhane gave evidence of having interviewed the applicant between 1.15 p.m. and 5.45 p.m. on the 29th of August. At approximately 2.45 p.m. he was supplied with a meal which he took about half an hour to eat. Detective Sergeant O'Carroll saw him again the following day at 11.15 a.m. and was with him until 12.45 p.m. Detective Inspector Culhane and Detective Sergeant O'Carroll said that during the course of the interview they did not use any physical violence or threaten or abuse the applicant in any way or make any promises to him in order to get him to make a statement.

The applicant said in evidence that during the course of the interview on the 29th of August, Detective Sergeant Healy constantly thumped the table and used bad language towards him. At one stage he walked round the room with a piece of stick about two feet long, tapping it off his hand and saying that he was going to kill the witness if he did not make a statement. At one stage Garda Healy lunged forward and caught the witness by the throat and pushed him against the wall and slapped his face. Detective Garda Hanley at that stage said "don't hit Paddy, Paddy is not a bad man". He said thereafter the mood changed slightly. He had a consultation during the morning with his solicitor and told him of being slapped. His solicitor said he would make a complaint about this matter and advised the witness that he had the right to remain silent. As soon as he left, Detective Gardaí Healy and Hanley returned and the former said that he (the witness) had reported him for hitting him. Detective Garda Healy was using bad language again and said that the witness "hadn't seen anything yet". The witness told him that he hadn't anything to say and that he had seen his solicitor. He said that they continued shouting at him, slapping the table and making threats.

Some time later, Detective Sergeant O'Carroll told him that a statement had been made by Noel McCabe that had incriminated him and the witness told him that he had never heard of Noel McCabe and wasn't involved in any crime. He was also told by the Gardaí that his wife was going to be brought into custody and charged if he (the witness) did not sign a document. He said that at one stage Detective Sergeant O'Carroll wrote out a statement and said that if the witness signed it, he would get 15 years. He had said he was signing nothing and Detective Sergeant O'Carroll then said it would be 40 years and that that was the best he could do for him. He was also using abusive language to the witnesses. He was questioned all the time he was having a meal and had never been cautioned by any of them. Detective Garda Murray at one stage stood in front of the witness, twiddling some bullets in his fingers, and said that some dark night he would come up behind the witness and would kill him. He was eventually put in a cell and tried to sleep but the door was rattled at intervals and woke up the witness.

He had no breakfast the next day and was again interviewed by Gardaí Healy and Hanley who said that his wife was in custody and that if he didn't make a statement and sign one she would be charged with the murder. He was then taken to another room and Detective Sergeant O'Carroll rushed across the room to him, gripped him by the ears and shook the chair. He told the witness that his wife wasn't there when he went to arrest her that morning and that he would murder the witness if he didn't make a statement and sign one. He said that Detective Garda Hanley and Detective Sergeant O'Carroll kept pushing a statement across the table which they said had been made by the third-named applicant and kept insisting that the witness should make a statement. He denied ever having made any statement himself.

Mr Frank McDonnell, the second-named applicant's solicitor, gave evidence that he saw his client in Navan Garda Station at 12.30 p.m. on the 29th of August. He said that the applicant told him that he had been interrogated continuously since he arrived in the Garda Station and that one of the Gardaí interviewing him had taken a piece of wood, approximately two feet long, from a nearby press and had tapped this on his hands for some time and walked about. He said that the applicant also told him that the Guard had grabbed him by the throat or the top of his shirt and lifted him out of his seat and slapped him. He also told the witness that immediately this incident occurred the other Guard had told his companion to stop. The witness advised him of the nature of his detention, that he was not obliged to answer any questions other than to give his name and address and if called upon to do so, to account for his movements and also advised him that he was obliged to submit to certain forensic tests. He further advised him that at the expiry of the first 24 hours the gardaí had power to detain him for a further 24 hour period and that he should be aware if an extension order was read out to him that that was what it meant. The witness transmitted the applicant's complaint to Garda Robinson, gave the latter his office number and home number and asked him if it could be seen to that he would be 'phoned in the event of his client being charged. He said that Garda Robinson agreed that he would look after that. The following day he decided to ring Navan Garda Station and, since he did not know the telephone numbers from memory, took out a telephone directory and looked up the listing "for the Gardaí in County Meath". He said that he dialled a number which he did not now remember and a man identified himself as a member of the Gardaí. He said that he identified himself to this person and said that he was a solicitor from Dundalk and was "enquiring about Paddy McPhillips". The person to whom he was talking said "I don't know anything about him". The witness then said that he had been over to see him yesterday and asked "Is he not there anymore?" The person on the line then said "Well, if he was, he's not here now". The witness then said to him "I take it he has been released" and was told 'He must be", or words to that effect. It came as a complete surprise to him to learn at 5.30 p.m. that evening from Mrs McPhillips that her husband was being charged before the Special Criminal Court.

In the case of the third-named applicant, the evidence established that he was brought to Navan at 7.00 a.m. on the 29th of August, 1984. Detective Sergeant Carty said that at 8.10 a.m. on that morning he brought him to an interview room. He was accompanied by Detective Sergeant Lynagh. He informed the applicant that they were investigating an armed robbery at Drumree in the course of which Detective Garda Hand had been shot dead, and then cautioned him. The applicant denied that he was involved in the robbery and they then had a general conversation. At 10.10 a.m. the applicant was served with breakfast in the interview room which he declined to eat, saying that he wasn't hungry. At 10.30 a.m. he was taken to be fingerprinted and photographed and returned at 10.45 a.m. when Detective Sergeant Lynagh and the witness resumed the interview. The former asked the applicant if he would give them an account of his movements for the 9th and the 10th of August, 1984. Having thought for a while, the applicant gave an account of his movements, which the witness wrote down. At 12 noon, Detective Gardaí Mulvey and Sullivan entered the room and Detective Sergeant Lynagh and the witness left.

During the course of the same afternoon, the witness met a Mr Lavery, a solicitor, in the public office area of the station. Mr Lavery told him that he was there to see the applicant, and the witness told him that he had already been seen by Mr Rogers at around 2.30 p.m. Mr Lavery then asked the witness to ask the applicant if he would see him. The witness went to the interview room where the applicant was being interviewed by Detective Gardaí Sullivan and Mulvey and told him there was a solicitor called Mr Lavery from Dundalk in the building and asked if he wished to consult with him. The applicant told him he had already seen a solicitor and that he was "O.K." He then returned to the public office area, spoke to Mr Lavery and told him this. Mr Lavery said that he would go and have a drink and would return to the station later. He asked the witness to enquire from the applicant if he would see him when he returned after a short time. The witness went back to the interview room and asked the applicant whether he would see Mr Lavery on his return and the applicant replied that that would "do the best". He then returned to Mr Lavery and told him this, and Mr Lavery left the station.

Detective Sergeant Carty said that at 5.00 p.m. he and Detective Sergeant Lynagh returned to the interview room and that he (the witness) cautioned the applicant in the usual terms. In response to a query from Detective/Sergeant Lynagh, the witness said that he was "O.K.", that he had seen his solicitor and his mother and had been examined by the doctor. They had a conversation with him for a time and then at 5.35 p.m. he was taken to be examined by another doctor. He returned to the interview room at 5.45 p.m. and Detective Sergeant Lynagh and he had a conversation with him until 6.15 p.m. when his colleague took the applicant to meet his solicitor, Mr Lavery. At 6.45 p.m., Detective Sergeant Lynagh and the

applicant returned to the interview room. At 7.20 p.m., the applicant was
served with tea and sandwiches in the interview room, which he ate.
Between 6.45 p.m. and 7.20 p.m., there was a general conversation at the
end of which Detective Sergeant Lynagh told him that he did not believe
the account he had given of his movements and he (the witness) asked the
applicant to tell the truth. He asked for time to think things over and they
agreed to this request. After a time the applicant said that there were other
men arrested in connection with the robbery and that he was afraid of them
and could not tell them everything but would tell his part as he wanted to
get it off his mind. At that stage the witness cautioned the applicant in the
usual terms and asked him if he wished to make a written statement, which
he agree to do. This was at approximately 10.30 p.m. The witness then
wrote down the statement as dictated to him by the applicant. When it was
completed, he read it over and asked him if it was correct. He told him
that he could change anything in the statement that he wanted or that he
could add anything he wanted. The applicant said that the statement was
correct and that he did not want to change it. The witness then asked him
to sign it and he refused, saying that his solicitor had told him not to sign
anything.

Detective Sergeant Carty said that he saw the applicant again at about
3.00 p.m. on the 30th of August. He spoke to him and said that Garda
Mulvey had informed him (the witness) that the applicant wished to see
him. The applicant said he wanted him to read the statement to him again,
which the witness did. The applicant then said "You told me last night
that I could add anything to that statement that I wanted to". The witness
agreed that was correct and the applicant then said "I want you to write
something else at the bottom of the statement". At this stage, the witness
cautioned him and then wrote down what the applicant had said, read it
over to him and asked him if it was correct. The applicant said it was
correct and that was all he wished to add to the statement. The witness
asked him to sign it, which he refused to do but said that he would initial
it, which he did.

Detective Sergeant Lynagh gave evidence confirming Detective
Sergeant Carty's account of these interviews.

Detective Garda Timothy Mulvey gave evidence that at about 12
noon, accompanied by Detective Garda Martin Sullivan, he interviewed
the applicant. He said that he cautioned the applicant in the usual manner
and asked him to tell the truth about his involvement in the crime. The

applicant denied any involvement and they then asked him to account for his movements on the 9th and 10th of August, 1984. He said that he had accounted for his movements and that he was at home on the on the night of the 9th and 10th of August. They again asked him to tell the truth about his involvement and he denied being involved, saying that he was exercising his right to remain silent. When they asked him about it again, he said "What did the other fellows say my part was in it?" They asked him what fellows was he talking about and he made no reply. He remained silent for most of the time. At about 2.15 p.m., he had a visit from his solicitor, which lasted until approximately 2.30 p.m. They then resumed interviewing him and cautioned him again. They again asked him to tell the truth and he replied that his solicitor had told him not to say anything and not to admit to any involvement in the robbery. He went on to say that if he admitted any part in the robbery "he could be done for capital murder". He also went on to say that he could not admit it because of fear, not for himself, but for his family. The witness took notes during the interview of these remarks.

At 2.45 p.m. a meal was supplied to the applicant, which he did not eat. He asked for water which was given to him. At 2.55 p.m. he was photographed and at 3.10 p.m. he had a visit from his mother and sister which lasted until about 3.30 p.m. The witness and Detective Garda Sullivan returned to the interview room when that visit had ended. They again asked him to tell the truth about his involvement and he made no reply. Dr Coleman visited him at about 4.40 p.m. and spent a couple of minutes with him. Shortly after the conversation between Detective Sergeant Carty and the applicant as to the presence of Mr Lavery in the station, the witness read over the notes he had made of the interviews to the applicant. He cautioned him in the usual manner and asked him if he had anything to say about the notes. The applicant said that he had nothing to say and the witness noted his reply, and invited him to sign the notes which he declined to do.

He saw the applicant again the following day at 10 o'clock and he cautioned him again and asked him how he was. The applicant said he had no more to say, that he had said it all the previous night and that what he had said was the truth. The witness asked him had he signed anything and he said that he had not because of fear. The witness noted this conversation and again asked the applicant to tell the truth. He cautioned him again at 11.30 a.m., having read the notes over to him, and asked him to sign the notes, which he declined to do. He brought the applicant to the interview room for the purpose of having an interview with Mr Rogers but could not say whether Mr Rogers had actually seen him. At 1.15 p.m., the applicant was placed in the cell and the witness did not see him until approximately 2.40 p.m. He and Detective Garda Sullivan then saw him again in the interview room and he cautioned him again in the same terms. He asked him a few questions, to which he made no replies. At about 2.50 p.m., Detective Sergeant Corrigan informed the applicant that he was being brought before the Special Criminal Court to be charged. The witness said that at no stage during any of the interviews did he or his colleague use any physical violence or touch or assault the applicant in any way, nor did they threaten him in any way or issue any threats in regard to his family or friends. They had not given him any promises or other inducements to make him say any of the things that he had said.

Detective Garda Sullivan gave evidence confirming Garda Mulvey's account of the interviews.

The applicant said in evidence that, until he saw Mr Lavery at 6.15 p.m. on the 29th of August, he had never been told that the latter had called to see him. He had never at any stage told the Gardaí that he (the witness) did not want to see Mr Lavery. He said that Mr Lavery told him that the best thing was not to answer any more questions and he agreed with that. He said that when the questioning resumed, Detective Sergeant Lynagh made him stare at autopsy photographs of the Garda. He said that both Gardaí then started issuing threats to the witness and members of his family. They told him that his mother would be walking down the street one day and that a car would come and kill her and no more would be said about it. One of the Gardaí said that they would take him out the back of the station and shoot him and make it look as if he was escaping, if he did not admit to the robbery. Both Detective Sergeant Lynagh and Detective Sergeant Carty got hold of his arms, stretched them out and started twisting them for long periods of time. the former thumped him in the stomach. This went on for about 20 minutes. After that Detective Sergeant Lynagh made him stand in the middle of the room. He then switched off the light and banged something on the table at which stage Detective Sergeant Carty tripped him. This happened three or four times. They also told him that McCabe had made a fifteen-page statement and that he was prepared to go into the witness box and say that he (the witness) was in the car and did the robbery. He was made to sit in the chair again and the two Gardaí then asked him if he was prepared to make a statement. He again said that he was not involved and that Detective Sergeant Carty then said he would make a statement for him and began writing the statement. He would write a few lines and then show it to the witness and ask him if it was correct. The witness kept telling him that he did not want to have anything to do with it and that it was not his statement. He took about 20 minutes to write it and then asked the witness to sign it. The witness told him it was his own statement and he could sign his own name to it. They said it would be their word against his and that if the two of them went into the witness box and gave evidence against him they would be believed instead of the witness.

The applicant further said that the following morning he was interviewed by Detective Sergeant Mulvey and Detective Garda Sullivan. He said that he told them the statement was written out in his presence the night before by Detective Sergeant Carty and he denied that he told them that he had been afraid to sign it. He said that he was not cautioned at any stage by either Detective Sergeant Mulvey of Detective/Garda Sullivan. He saw Mr Rogers at about 2.00 p.m. that day and told him how he had been thumped and slapped and had his arm twisted. He said that shortly afterwards Detective Garda Corrigan told him that he was being taken before the Special Criminal Court to be charged. Following this, Detective Sergeant Mulvey and Detective Garda Sullivan kept telling him that he would have to sign the statement or he would be charged with murder. He told them he would not sign any statement. He said that Detective Sergeant Carty then took a statement out of his coat pocket and put it in front of him and asked him to sign it. The witness told him he would not sign it. Detective Sergeant Carty then wrote something on to the statement and said "That's the best I can do for you, everybody knows you had nothing to do with the murder of the Guard". He then asked the witness to sign it and the witness declined. The witness told Detective Sergeant Carty that he would initial the fact that he was not going to sign the statement.

Mr Rogers said that he saw the applicant at 2.20 p.m. on the 29th of August. The applicant told him that he had given an account of his movements over a specified period. He said that he had not been threatened but that he would like to be seen by a doctor. He said that he had been told that a statement had been made implicating him in the armed robbery. The witness advised him that if this were correct he would be involved in a murder charge. He also advised him that he was not obliged to make any statement or to answer any questions and that he had given the statutory information required. He saw the applicant again the following day at 2.20 p.m. when the latter told him that he had been interrogated until 12.30 a.m. that morning. The applicant told him that at about 11.30 the previous night a detective had written a statement in his presence and had read it over to him, but that he (the applicant) told the detective that he did not want to have anything to do with the statement and he refused to sign it. He said that before the statement was written he was put standing against the wall by two detectives with his arms outstretched, that his arms were twisted and that he was slapped in the face by one of these men. He also said that he had got at thump in the stomach as well.

Mr Lavery gave evidence that when he went to Navan Garda Station on the 29th of August, he was accompanied by his colleague, Mr Roger McGinley. Detective Sergeant Carty told him (the witness) that in his case they (the Gardaí) did not think it was reasonable for him to see the applicant again so soon, as he had already seen another solicitor. The witness said to him that he thought it was not unreasonable since the applicant had been in custody since 6.00 o'clock and that in any event he was his solicitor and wanted to see him. Detective Sergeant Carty then said: "he is all right, he does not want to see anybody. He has seen a solicitor". The witness then said he would like Detective Sergeant Carty to tell the applicant that he was there and to ask him would he see him. He said that Detective Sergeant Carty went inside again for a very brief period, came out and said: "He doesn't wish to see you and he has never heard of of you". The witness again indicated his desire to see the applicant, but Detective Sergeant Carty was unwilling to do this and eventually said: "however, things may be different in an hour. Come back in an hour, you can see him". The witness went away and came back in about an hour and was then shown into a room where the applicant was. The applicant told him that the first he had heard of his presence was ten minutes ago. He gave general advice to the applicant as to his rights. Mr McGinley gave evidence confirming Mr Lavery's account of his interview with Detective Sergeant Carty when they first arrived at the garda station.

On the 15th day of the trial, the Court, having heard legal submissions, ruled that, in the case of the first and second-named applicants, the statements made were voluntary statements and were admissible. At the beginning of its ruling, the Court referred to the statement of the law by Griffin J. in *People (DPP) v Shaw* [1982] I.R. 1 at p. 60 as to the admissibility of such statements. The Court also referred to the statement of the law by Walsh J. in *People (DPP) v Lynch* [1982] I.R. 64 at p. 84 and p. 87. It has not been submitted to this Court that the Court of trial in any way erred in treating these as the principles of law applicable to the issues as to the admissibility of the statements.

In the case of each of the applicants, the Court of trial concluded that the Garda witnesses had given truthful evidence as to the events in Navan Garda Station during the period of the applicants' detention, and as to the subsequent admissions by the applicants, prior to their being brought before that Court. The Court further rejected the evidence of the applicants as to these events. The Court was, accordingly, satisfied beyond reasonable doubt that, in the case of each of the applicants the interrogation conducted by the various members of the Gardaí was conducted in a fair and reasonable manner, was not of such a nature as would render any reply thereto as other than voluntary and was not, at any time, accompanied by threats, abuse, assault or any physical or psychological pressure. In the case of the second-named applicant, the Court said it was satisfied beyond reasonable doubt that he had dictated the statement in question to Detective Gardaí Hanley and Healy and made the statements to Detective Inspector Culhane and Detective Sergeant O'Carroll, of which they gave evidence.

The Court also said that it was satisfied beyond reasonable doubt that, in the case of each of the applicants, he was at all times afforded his right of reasonable access to his solicitor. In the case of the telephone call made by Mr Frank McDonnell, the solicitor for the second-named applicant, in the course of which he was told that his client had left the Garda Station at a stage when he was in fact still being detained, the Court said it was satisfied that Mr McDonnell had dialled the number of a Garda Station in Meath other than the Navan station. The Court also said that, in the case of each of these applicants, it was satisfied that the Judges' Rules had been observed and that the applicants had been properly cautioned in accordance with the requirements of those rules.

On the 16th day of the trial, the Court gave its ruling on the admissibility of the statements alleged to have been made by the third-named applicant. Having again referred to the legal principles applicable to the admissibility of the statements, the Court said that it accepted the evidence of the Garda witnesses as to the events in Navan Garda Station during the period of the applicant's detention as truthful and rejected the evidence given by the applicant as to these events. The Court then said that it was satisfied beyond reasonable doubt that the interrogation of the applicant was conduced by the Gardaí in a fair and reasonable manner, was not of such a nature as to render any reply thereto as other than voluntary and was not accompanied by threats, abuse, assault or physical or psychological pressure of any kind. The Court also said that it was satisfied beyond reasonable doubt that the applicant had adequate rest and nourishment. The Court also said it was satisfied beyond reasonable doubt that the applicant dictated the statements to Detective Sergeants Carty and Lynagh and made the verbal statements referred to in the evidence to other members of the Gardaí. The Court also found that the requirements of the Judges' Rules in regard to each of the statements had been complied with. The Court accordingly ruled that the statements made by the applicant were admissible in accordance with the legal principles already referred to.

It is, accordingly, clear that, in the case of each of the three applicants, the conclusions of the Court of trial as to the admissibility of the statements were based on the sworn testimony of witnesses seen, heard and accepted by the Court of trial. These conclusions are manifestly beyond the reach of an appellate court to disturb, having regard to the following statement of the law by O'Higgins CJ in *Northern Bank Finance Corporation Ltd v Charlton* [1979] I.R. 149 at p. 180:

"A judge's findings on fact can and will be reviewed on appeal. Such findings will be subjected to the normal tests as to whether they are supported by the evidence given at the trial. If such findings are firmly based on the sworn testimony of witnesses seen and heard and accepted by the judge, then the court of appeal, recognising this to be the area of credibility, will not interfere".

In *People (DPP) v Kelly (No. 2)* [1983] I.R. 1 at p. 24, O'Higgins CJ reaffirmed this statement of law, on this occasion with particular reference to the functions of this Court:

"It is submitted on this appeal that the principles laid down in *People (DPP) v Madden* [1977] I.R. 366 impose too rigid a restriction on the powers of the Court of Criminal Appeal and that the court, on an examination of the evidence as disclosed in the transcript, should have felt free to come to a conclusion different from that of the court of trial upon the facts. Necessarily involved in this submission is the assertion that, from a reading of the transcript, the Court of Criminal Appeal could have, and should have, concluded that the various garda witnesses involved in the allegations of ill-treatment had committed perjury in their denials of the appellant's allegations and that, contrary to the conclusion reached by the court of trial, the evidence given by the appellant was true in substance and in fact. If this submission were well-founded and were accepted, we would be required to hold that this drastic conclusion should have been drawn by a court which neither saw nor heard any of the witnesses involved but which, nevertheless, was at liberty to brand as untruthful those witnesses who, by their manner, demeanour and evidence, had satisfied experienced judges at the trial that they were telling the truth. If such were truly within the powers of a court of appeal in our jurisprudence, one wonders what would be the function of a court of trial.

And again at p. 25:

"In these circumstances I am quite satisfied that the principles set out in *The People v Madden* (and referred to in the judgments of this Court in *Northern Bank Finance v Charlton*) apply and that the Court of Criminal Appeal was correct in regarding the decision of the Court of trial on the issue of the facts surrounding the making of the various statements as one which should not be disturbed. . .".

The same considerations apply to the rejection by the Court of trial of the evidence of the various witnesses as to the movements of the applicants on the day of the commission of the crime.

Particular stress was laid by counsel for third-named applicant on the fact that the Court of trial accepted as truthful the evidence of the two solicitors, Mr Lavery and Mr McGinley, as to what transpired in the course of the interview with Detective Sergeant Carty. He submitted that this necessarily involved a finding by the Court of trial that the evidence of Detective Sergeant Carty on this matter was untruthful and that accordingly the Court of trial could not reasonably conclude that this testimony afforded a reliable basis for the admission of his client's statements. The essential conflict of evidence, however, which the Court of trial had to resolve was between the evidence of the Garda witnesses and the applicant and not between Detective Sergeant Carty and the two solicitors. The discrepancies between the evidence of Detective Sergeant Carty and the solicitors was only one of a number of matters which the Court of trial was entitled to take into account in resolving this conflict. Even if their finding on this particular topic justified the inference that Detective Sergeant Carty was not telling the truth in relation to it (and this Court is by no means satisfied that that is a necessary inference from this finding), that would not necessitate a conclusion that the evidence of all the Garda witnesses as to the events in the Garda Station should be rejected as untruthful or unreliable. On the contrary, the fact that such a finding was made indicates no more than that the Court of trial addressed themselves expressly to this matter before reaching their conclusions as to the weight which should be given, respectively, to the Garda evidence and that of the applicant. For the reasons already stated, that conclusion is beyond the reach of this Court to disturb.

Similar considerations also apply to the observations of the Court of trial during the course of submissions by counsel for the Director of Public Prosecutions on the reference by the third-named applicant in his evidence to a fifteen-page statement made by Noel McCabe. The Court of trial drew counsel's attention to the fact that, although the Garda witnesses had denied producing this statement to the third-named applicant, he had accurately identified the number of pages in it. This again was one of a number of factors which the Court of trial was entitled to take into account in assessing the credibility of the Garda witnesses on the one hand and the applicant on the other, and again the fact that they referred to it during the course of counsel's submissions indicates no more than that they expressly addressed their minds to that matter before reaching their conclusions.

The Court is, accordingly, satisfied that each of these grounds of appeal fails.

In the case of the second-named applicant, a further ground of appeal was that the Court of appeal failed to have any regard to the evidence given by and on behalf of the applicant and found the evidence of Danny McDonnell as being given in relation to the first-named applicant instead of the second-named applicant as was the case, and that in so far as it purported to alter on the 19th of March, 1985, the terms of the judgment delivered on the 28th of March, 1985, it was not lawfully entitled to do so and was *functus officio*.

This ground of appeal refers to the fact that in the course of the judgment delivered in this case by the Court of trial, reference was made to the evidence of Daniel (or Danny) McDonnell. This witness was called on behalf of the second-named applicant and gave evidence that he had spoken to the latter at his home between 10.00 a.m. and 10.30 a.m. on the morning of the commission of the offences with which he was charged. In its judgment, the Court referred to this evidence when dealing with the case against the first-named applicant. The apparent error was drawn to the attention of the Court who made it clear that they had considered the evidence in relation to the case against the second-named applicant only, but had in error referred to it in the context of the case against the first-named applicant. This Court is satisfied that in these circumstances the mistake in ascribing this evidence to the case against the first-named applicant affords no ground for a successful appeal on behalf of these applicants. This ground of appeal accordingly also fails.

The final grounds of appeal on behalf of the first and second-named applicants were:

(i) That there was no or no sufficient evidence adduced by the prosecution to entitle the Court to hold that the applicants knew that Garda Hand was a mamber of the Garda Síochána acting in the course of his duty when killed.

(ii) That the Court erred in law in holding that the *mens rea* of capital murder is constituted by adherence to a common design which includes even a risk of causing death or serious injury to a guard.

(iii) That there was no or no sufficient evidence on the part of the prosecution to prove that either of the applicants intended to kill or cause serious injury to any person and in particular Garda Francis Hand, and that therefore the Court was not entitled to find any of the applicants guilty of capital murder.

(iv) That the Court of trial erred in law in holding that it was entitled to find either of the applicants guilty of murder.

It was submitted on behalf of the first-named applicant that on the prosecution's case Garda Hand had been shot before he arrived on the scene. A similar submission was made on behalf of the second-named applicant. It was further submitted that the shooting of the guard was outside the common design to rob the Post Office van. It was also submitted on behalf of both applicants that it was outside the common design of robbery to kill or seriously injure anyone in the robbery.

Counsel on behalf of the first-named applicant referred this Court to the submissions in Book D1 on the 27th of March, in the transcript and adopted them before this Court. He submitted that the evidence against the first-named applicant was his knowledge that "the guards will be taken care of" did not establish that the first-named applicant knew or could have known that the guns would be used to kill or cause grievous bodily harm to anyone and in particular to a member of the Garda Síochána on duty. Counsel referred to *R v Anderson* (1966) 50 Cr. App. R. 216 and submitted that the killing in the circumstances of this case was not part of a joint enterprise in which the applicant was engaged.

It was submitted on behalf of the second-named applicant that there were only two passages in the verbal admissions relating to guards: "We knew there would be armed Guards" and, on the second page, "might be resistance from the guards". Counsel submitted that the capital letter "g" in "Guards" was written down by the guard taking the note to imply, wrongly, that the applicant was referring to the Gardaí as distinct from security guards.

This Court is satisfied that the Court of trial, adopting the majority decision of the Supreme Court in *People (DPP) v Murray* [1977] I.R. 360 correctly held that to prove capital murder in the present case the Court would have to be satisfied beyond all reasonable doubt that the participants in the crime

(1) had to have prior knowledge that the Post Office van would be escorted by members of the Garda Síochána,

(2) knew of the arrangements made and outlined at the meeting of the raiders after they had left Mr Duffy's house,

(3) were aware that certain members of the raiders were allocated to render ineffective the members of the Garda Síochána, necessarily involving the use of firearms if the situation arose.

In the first-named applicant's statement he set out in detail his part in the planned robbery, including the route he was to take from Drumree Post Office after the robbery and where he was to drop the money. He also stated that when the operation commenced a number of guns and walkie-talkies were loaded into the Ascona at Mr Duffy's yard. They then moved out of Duffy's and stopped in a lane. The statement continues:

"The bag of guns was taken out of the Ascona. There were a few rifles and I think only one machine gun and small guns. One man was given a rifle and he acted as a look out. There were eight or nine men there. Three of them were called aside and there was a discussion amongst them. After a while one of the fellows came to the rest of us and said that there would be two guards with the van in the morning and that they would be taken care of. . . . I was to get a call on my radio to move into the Post Office".

And later in the same statement:

"On the night before the robbery while we were at the meeting we were told that two men had gone to the Post Office and would have things in control when we got there. I took this to mean that the two men who had gone would have the way clear for us and we were told to collect the guards guns and bring them with us".

In his statement to Garda Sullivan he stated: . . . the day before the robbery a man took him to the Post Office at Drumree and told him they were to do the Post Office van.
And to Garda Maunsell:

"Look what I have been charged with. I didn't do the shooting. I only drove the Merc".

The applicant told Detective Inspector Culhane and Detective Sergeant O'Carroll: ". . . ye know the part I played in the robbery but I did not shoot the guard". In the course of the written statement made to Garda Hanley and Garda Healy, the applicant said:—

"I knew that a Post Office van was to be robbed on Friday morning. This was discussed, we knew that there would be armed guards with this van. Certain people got the job of looking after that part of it. I was not one of these. . . . I knew there was a guard shot, there was no shooting while I was there. I did not fire my gun. . . . On Thursday night it was discussed that there might be resistance from the guards with the Post Office van. We were to get the call when our fellows had things in hand".

The Court has already referred to the seven reasons given by the Court of trial for convicting the first-named applicant of the capital murder of Detective/Garda Hand and the nine reasons for convicting the second-named applicant of the same offence.

The Court is satisfied that on this evidence the Court of trial was entitled to convict both applicants of capital murder and that in reaching their decision they applied the correct principles of law. Both applicants voluntarily participated in an expedition to carry out the armed robbery. They had prior knowledge that the Post Office van, the subject of the robbery, would be escorted by guards. They were also informed that "there might be resistance from the guards" and that "the guards would be taken care of", that is to say, overcome with the use of firearms by the raiders. As this was a robbery planned on a Post Office van, of monies the property of the State, the only reasonable inference is that the "guards" that were anticipated would be members of the Garda Síochána (or as popularly referred to, "the guards". There was no evidence to suggest that this was not the correct inference to draw from all the circumstances of the case. Once the applicants were aware that any prospective resistance by the Gardaí would be overcome by the use of firearms they are guilty of whatever offence arises from the actual use of firearms by those with whom they were acting in concert.

For these reasons this ground of appeal also fails. The Court therefore, refuses leave to appeal in respect of all three applicants.

Solicitors for the first applicant: *Johnson Lavery McGahan*
Solicitors for the second applicant: *Ahern and McDonnell*
Solicitor for the third applicant: *Anne B. Rowland and Co.*
Solictor for the prosecution: *Chief State Solictor*

Noreen Mackey
Barrister

The People (Director of Public Prosecutions) v Dominic Burke and John O'Leary
[C.C.A. Nos. 98/99 of 1984]

Court of Criminal Appeal   10 March 1986

Trial – joint trial – convictions – each accused making statements incriminating the other – separate trials refused – whether discretion of trial judge properly exercised – whether refusal resulted in miscarriage of justice – Judges' Rules – inducements – whether jury properly charged that statement of one accused is not evidence against the other accused – Judges' Rules, rule 8

Rule 8 of the Judges' Rules states that when two or more persons are charged with the same offence and their statements are taken separately, the police should not read these statements to the other person charged, but each of such persons should be given by the police a copy of such statements and nothing should be said or done by the police to invite a reply. If the person charged desires to make a statement in reply the usual caution should be administered.

The appellants were tried jointly in the Central Criminal Court (Egan J and jury) for the murder of one Patrick Deasy and for burglary contrary to section 23(1)(a) of the Larceny Act 1916, as inserted by section 6 of the Criminal Law (Jurisdiction) Act 1976. Each of the accused had applied to the trial judge for a separate trial, on the ground that while in custody both accused made statements which implicated the other. The applications for separate trials were refused. It was submitted that they should have been granted because while a co-accused's statement was not evidence against the other it would have been impossible for the jury to exclude such statement from their minds when considering the admissible evidence against the other. Furthermore, while the questions as to alleged inducements were left to the jury to decide in the trial within the trial, other questions should also have been left regarding, *inter alia*, whether or not the gardaí told the second applicant that they had found his fingerprints at the scene and that they had a witness who could identify him.

On O'Leary's behalf it was also submitted that his statement was taken in breach of Rule 8 of the Judges' Rules.

The trial judge granted a certificate that the case was a fit one for appeal.

Held by the Court (Finlay CJ, Gannon and Lynch JJ) in dismissing both appeals:

(1) That the fact that one or both of two co-accused make statements incriminating the other was not of itself a reason why separate trials should be ordered and that on the facts, the refusal of the trial judge to grant separate trials was within his discretion and no miscarriage of justice occurred. *People (Attorney General) v Murtagh* [1966] I.R. 361; *Attorney General v Joyce and Walsh* [1929] I.R. 526; *People (Attorney General) v Carney and Another* [1955] I.R. 324 followed.

(2) That the statements of each of the accused was admissible only against himself and not the other, and the trial judge gave an emphatic warning to that effect in his charge to the jury.

(3) That the allegations made against the gardaí, even if substantiated, would amount to the gardaí having obtained evidence by means of a relatively minor trick or subterfuge

92

without any actual illegality, therefore such allegations could not constitute grounds for excluding the statements.

(4) That the statement of the second accused was voluntary and that there had been no breach of Rule 8 of the Judges' Rules.

Cases cited in this judgment:

Attorney General v Joyce and Walsh [1929] I.R. 526
People (Attorney General) v Carney [1955] I.R. 324
People (Attorney General) v Murtagh [1966] I.R. 361; 102 I.L.T.R. 146
People (DPP) v Conroy [1986] I.R. 64; [1988] ILRM 4
People (DPP) v Lynch [1982] I.R. 64; [1981] ILRM 389

Patrick MacEntee SC and Paul Sreenan **for the first appellant**
Barry White SC and Blaise O'Carroll **for the second appellant**
N.K. Macdonald SC and Peter Charleton **for the respondent**

Lynch J

The Court will deal first with the appeal of the accused John O'Leary.

The first ground of his appeal is that "the learned trial judge erred in law or alternatively in the exercise of his judicial discretion in failing to grant separate trials herein".

The main argument advanced in support of this ground of appeal is that the accused Dominic Burke made a number of confessions which implicated the accused John O'Leary. It is correctly submitted that Dominic Burke's statements are not evidence against John O'Leary and it is further submitted that it would be impossible for the jury to have excluded such statements of Dominic Burke from their minds when considering the admissible evidence against John O'Leary.

It is well settled law that the fact that one or both of two accused make statements incriminating the other accused is not of itself a reason why separate trials must be ordered: *People (Attorney General) v Murtagh* [1966] I.R. 361; *Attorney General v Joyce and Walsh* [1929] I.R. 526; *People (Attorney General) v Carney* [1955] I.R. 324. It was therefore clearly within the learned trial judge's discretion to refuse the application for separate trials, as in fact he did, and this Court sees nothing wrong in his exercise of his discretion in so refusing. However, this Court is of the view that it should also consider whether in fact the refusal of separate trials has operated in such a way as might have given rise to a miscarriage of justice as the trial actually ran. There was ample evidence admitted at the trial to justify the verdict of the jury against John O'Leary. The learned trial judge give a very clear explanation and emphatic warning to the jury to the effect that the statements of each accused were evidence only against himself and were not in any way evidence against the other accused. This Court is accordingly satisfied that this ground of appeal fails.

The second ground of appeal is:

> The learned trial judge erred in law in failing to formulate or leave to the jury on the trial within a trial herein separate questions in respect of each and all of the issues of fact raised by the accused.

This ground of appeal raises questions as to how the trial within the trial regarding the admissibility of the statements made by John O'Leary should have been conducted. The Court was referred to the decisions of the Supreme Court in *People v Lynch* [1982] I.R. 64 and a judgment of the Court of Criminal Appeal in *People v Conroy* [1988] ILRM 4.

John O'Leary alleged that he was promised that he would be charged with a lesser offence and would be given bail if he made the statements which are the subject of this ground of appeal. If these allegations were not proved to be untrue then the statements would be inadmissible in evidence as having been obtained by an inducement. John O'Leary also made a number of subsidiary allegations to the effect that he was untruly told that the gardaí had found his fingerprints at the scene of the crime: that they had a witness who knew him for some eleven years and could identify him as having been at the scene of the crime on the day of the crime and further that he was refused an identification parade and was told that the gardaí had got convictions on less evidence than they had against him.

The learned trial judge left appropriate questions to the jury on the issue as to whether John O'Leary was promised bail and promised that he would be charged with a lesser offence than murder and the jury brought in a verdict for the prosecution on these issues. It is submitted on behalf of John O'Leary that questions should also have been left to the jury regarding the issues as to whether the gardaí had told John O'Leary that they had found his fingerprints at the scene of the crime and had told him that they had a witness who could identify him as having been at the scene of the crime and had refused him an identification parade.

It would seem to this Court that these allegations even if substantiated would at most amount to the gardaí having obtained evidence by means of a relatively minor trick or subterfuge without any actual illegality. There being no actual illegality these complaints could not in themselves constitute grounds for excluding the statements of John O'Leary. It is clear to this Court that this was the view taken by the learned trial judge and accordingly this ground of appeal fails.

This Court does not decide whether or not it was necessary for the learnd trial judge to submit for the verdict of the jury the questions which he did submit to them or whether he might not have tried these questions himself.

The third ground of appeal is:

> The learned trial judge erred in law in holding that Sergeant Lynagh was not in breach of the Judges' Rules in telling the accused that another person had made a statement implicating him in the crime.

What is referred to in this ground of appeal is Rule 8 of the Judges' Rules which apply in this State. Unfortunately, while John O'Leary can write his name he is otherwise illiterate and therefore no purpose would have been served by the Gardaí leaving a copy of the statement of Dominic Burke for the benefit of John O'Leary. If, on the other hand, the gardaí had read the statements of Dominic Burke to John O'Leary because he was illiterate that would appear to be in breach of the express terms of the rule.

There is no suggestion by John O'Leary that the gardaí read to him extracts from the statements of Dominic Burke or asked him questions about the statements. The only thing that John O'Leary alleges is that he was told that the gardaí had a statement from another person implicating him in the crime.

This Court is satisfied that there was no breach of the spirit of Rule 8 of the Judges' Rules. Moreover, counsel for the prosecution in his submissions pointed out that the rule applies only when two or more persons "are charged" with the same offence and at the time of the alleged statement by the gardaí to John O'Leary he had not been charged. That being so there was no breach of the letter of the rule any more than a breach of the spirit of the rule. There is therefore no substance in this ground of appeal which fails.

The fourth and fifth grounds of appeal can be taken together:

> (4) The learned trial judge erred in law in failing to properly or

adequately put to the jury the accused's defence.

(5) The learned trial judge erred in law in failing to recharge the jury on each of the matters raised by counsel for the accused on his requisitions on the learned trial judge's charge to the jury.

When it came to his substantive defence in this case John O'Leary relied on an alibi. His defence was that he was never at the scene of the crime on the occasion when the crime was committed and it was emphasised by the learned trial judge that unless the jury were satisfied beyond reasonable doubt that John O'Leary was present at the scene of the crime when the crime was being committed then he could be guilty of nothing.

The trial commenced on the 26th of November, 1984 and continued on the 27th, 28th, 29th and 30th of November and the 3rd and 4th of December, 1984. John O'Leary's evidence commenced on the afternoon of the 30th of November and continued into the 3rd of December and his wife Mrs Mary O'Leary gave evidence on the 3rd of December supporting his alibi. On the 4th of December another witness a Mr Hyde gave evidence also supporting John O'Leary's alibi and this evidence was then followed by speeches from counsel and the learned trial judge's charge and the verdict of the jury, all taking place on the 4th of December, 1984.

In charging the jury the learned trial judge did not re-read his note of the evidence in the case. As already pointed out, however, he emphasised that John O'Leary could be guilty of no offence unless he was present at the scene of the crime and that there was no onus on him to establish that he was not present; that the onus was on the prosecution to prove that he was present.

The fact that the learned trial judge did not read extracts of the evidence given by the witnesses if anything favoured the accused John O'Leary because his witnesses were most recently in the minds of the jury. While this Court agrees that both the case for the prosecution and the case for the defence must be fairly left by the trial judge for consideration this Court is of the opinion that this requisition was satisfied in this case and accordingly these grounds of appeal fail.

The last ground of appeal of the accused John O'Leary is that the trial was unsatisfactory. This Court is satisfied that there is no substance in this ground and accordingly the appeal of John O'Leary wholly fails.

The Court now turns to the appeal of Dominic Burke. The main ground of this appeal is the refusal of the learned trial judge to order separate trials.

As this Court has already pointed out it was within the learned trial judge's discretion to refuse the application for a separate trial and there was no wrong exercise of his discretion at the time when he made his order refusing the separate trial. As in the case of John O'Leary, however, this Court is of the opinion that it must now consider whether in fact in the case of Dominic Burke the refusal of separate trials operated in such a way as might have given rise to a miscarriage of justice as the trial of Dominic Burke actually ran. In the case of Dominic Burke also there was ample evidence admitted at the trial to justify the verdict of the jury. The Court has already referred to the learned trial judge's very clear explanation and emphatic warning to the jury as to the statements of each accused being evidence only against himself and not against the other accused. The Court is accordingly satisfied that this ground of appeal fails.

Dominic Burke also appeals on the basis that the verdict of the jury was perverse and against the weight of the evidence and such that no reasonable jury could have arrived at. As the Court has already said there was ample evidence from the statements of Dominic Burke himself, the evidence of Dr Harbison and the evidence of John J. O'Leary, nephew of John O'Leary upon which the jury could arrive at their verdict. There is therefore no substance in this ground of appeal and accordingly the appeal of Dominic Burke also fails.

Solicitors for the first appellant: *Fleming & Taaffe*
Solicitors for the second appellant: *Daly, Derham & Co*
Solicitor for the respondent: *Chief State Solicitor*

Darina O'Sullivan
Barrister

The People (Director of Public Prosecutions) v Noel Callan
[C.C.A. No. 112 of 1985]

Court of Criminal Appeal   14 May 1986

Evidence – admissibility – unsigned statements made by the accused – Judges' Rules –
inferences drawn by Court of trial – capital murder – killing of uniformed garda –
Criminal Justice Act 1964 (No. 5), section 1 – Larceny Act 1916 (ch. 50), section 23 –
Criminal Law (Jurisdiction) Act 1976 (No. 14), section 5 – Judges' Rules, rule 9

Rule 9 of the Judges' Rules states that any statement made in accordance with Rules 1-8 should, whenever possible, be taken down in writing and signed by the person making it after it has been read to him and he has been invited to make any corrections he may wish.

The applicant was tried and convicted jointly with one Michael McHugh in the Special Criminal Court (Hamilton P, Judge Fawsitt and District Justice Ó Floinn) for the capital murder of Sergeant Patrick Morrissey contrary to section 1, subsection 1 of the Criminal Justice Act 1964, and robbery contrary to s. 23 of the Larceny Act 1916, as inserted by section 5 of the Criminal Law (Jurisdiction) Act 1976. He was sentenced to death and twelve years imprisonment on the respective charges.

The applicant took part in an armed robbery of the Social Welfare Office in Ardee, County Louth. During the police chase which followed, Sergeant Morrissey was shot dead. The applicant was found wounded in a nearby field. On the way to hospital the applicant made incriminating verbal statements to the accompanying garda who recorded them in writing but this record was never signed due to the applicant's state of apparent semi-consciousness while in hospital. A second incriminating verbal statement was made by the applicant while travelling to court. This statement was recorded in writing but the applicant refused to sign it. At the trial the applicant denied making the statements.

During the trial evidence was admitted of these incriminating statements although they were not signed by the applicant as required by Rule 9 of the Judges' Rules. The applicant's clothing was subjected to forensic testing with negative results. An application for a certificate of leave to appeal having been refused by the Court of trial, application was made to the Court of Criminal Appeal for leave to appeal conviction and sentence.

Counsel for the applicant argued that the applicant's statements had been taken in breach of Rule 9 of the Judges' Rules and ought not to have been admitted at the trial; that even if the statements were admissible they should have been rejected on the basis of the applicant's denial that he made them; that the meaning of the statements was wrongly interpreted by the Court and that there was no forensic evidence to support the applicant's involvement in the shooting and that the evidence adduced was insufficient to support the verdict.

Held by the Court (Finlay CJ, Barron and Blayney JJ), in refusing the application:

(1) That there was no injustice in the admission of the verbal statements into evidence, and that the inferences drawn by the Court of trial from those statements were reasonable. The Court could not interfere with the resolution of the issues of fact made by the Court of trial.

(2) That there was no error by the Court of trial in the exercise of its discretion under Rule 9 of the Judges' Rules.

(3) That the absence of forensic evidence connecting the applicant with the offence did

98

not vitiate the Court's finding, based on his verbal admissions, that he had participated in the robbery.

(4) That there was sufficient evidence to justify a conviction of capital murder.

No cases cited in this judgment

Patrick MacEntee SC and Roger Sweetman **for the applicant**
Kevin Haugh SC and Fergal Foley **for the respondent**

Finlay CJ

This is an application for a certificate of leave to appeal against a conviction by the Special Criminal Court on the 3rd of December, 1985 on count No. 1 for the capital murder of Sergeant Patrick Morrissey on the 27th of June, 1985, he then being a member of the Garda Síochána acting in the course of his duty, and on count No. 2 for a robbery contrary to section 23 of the Larceny Act 1916, as inserted by section 5 of the Criminal Law (Jurisdiction) Act 1976, from Sean Boyle of approximately £25,000 in cash.

The uncontested facts as to what occurred at the Labour Exchange at Ardee where the robbery occurred and thereafter prior to the shooting of Sergeant Morrissey were thus set out in the verdict of the Special Criminal Court and are a convenient description of the events out of which these charges arose.

1. At 9.55 a.m., approximately, on the 27th day of June, 1985, Sean Boyle, the Manager of the Social Welfare Office at Dundalk Road, Ardee in the County of Louth was robbed of the sum of £25,000 in notes and a quantity of silver amounting to £250 approximately.

2. The robbery was executed by two men wearing combat jackets of a different type, balaclavas, and carrying firearms which were used during the execution of the robbery.

3. The two men took possession of Mr Boyle's car, a Stanza motor vehicle, registration No. RZY 777, made good their escape from Ardee, travelling first in the Dunleer direction and then back in the direction of the Drogheda Road.

4. While the robbery was in progress an official garda car being driven by Garda Long in which Garda Brendan Flynn was travelling as a passenger and both of them were in garda uniform, came to the scene.

5. They slowed down as they approached the Social Welfare Office and noticed a man wearing a balaclava and a camouflage jacket and carrying a shotgun, emerge from behind Mr Boyle's car.

6. The car then accelerated in the direction of Dunleer and as it was doing so two shots were fired in its direction by one of the raiders, the raider wearing the balaclava and the multi-coloured camouflage jacket.

7. The Stanza car sped in the direction of Dunleer and as it did so Mr Cluskey threw a stone through the passenger window, shattering the glass therein.

8. Garda Long and Garda Flynn turned the patrol car at Dawson Demesne and returned to the Social Welfare Office and then proceeded to Castle Street where they collected the late Sergeant Patrick Morrissey who was in full garda uniform, and they then travelled in the direction of Tallanstown where they set up a roadblock.

9. The raiders abandoned Mr Boyle's car at or in Farrell's Field, Pepperstown, Ardee, where it and a black tin containing £25,000 which had been taken from Mr Boyle's car were subsequently discovered.

10. Shortly after setting up the roadblock, a motorcycle approached and turned right at the junction on the incorrect side of the traffic island.

11. Garda Long noticed that the driver of the motorcycle was wearing a camouflage jacket similar to that worn by the raider who had shot at the car in Ardee, and that the pillion passenger was wearing a combat jacket.

12. Sergeant Morrissey, Garda Long and Garda Flynn got back into the patrol car and followed the motorcycle in the direction of Rathbrist Cross.

13. They had the motorcycle in view from a distance of approximately 200 yards until it rounded the left-hand bend at Rathbrist Cross.

14. When they rounded the bend Garda Long and Garda Flynn saw the same two men who were on the motorcycle running across the road and going into the main entrance to McDermott's house.

15. The motorcycle had crashed into a motor vehicle registered No. 346 TZU, the property of Mrs Mallon.

16. In the immediate vicinity of the scene of the crash was found:

(a) a green carrier bag containing a sawn-off shotgun and a sawn-off rifle similar to the guns used in the execution of the robbery at Ardee

(b) a bag containing coins

(c) a blue balaclava

(d) a black glove

(e) considerable quantities of broken glass and a black glove of knitted material.

There was further uncontested evidence of the subsequent events. Two of the occupants of Rathbrist House, Sean Pierre McDermott and Mary Kindlon, heard a shot being fired and Mr McDermott then saw one of the persons who had been on the motorcycle standing over Sergeant Morrissey on the avenue, close to the house, and firing a second shot which killed him. Almost at the same moment Mr McDermott saw the second man at the front of the house walking in the direction of where Sergeant Morrissey was, and so in a position from which he must have seen the shooting. This second man appeared to have blood on one of his hands which he held over his head.

Evidence was then given of a trail of blood from Rathbrist House through fields, lanes and roads, which eventually led to a barley field some distance away where the applicant was found in a ditch, partly covered by grass and other vegetation, in an injured condition, bleeding from the hand. Another man who was the co-accused with the applicant, Michael McHugh, was found in the same field. In the field, not far from the applicant, was found the gun established to have been used in the shooting of Sergeant Morrissey, and a balaclava helmet. The applicant was arrested and taken from the ditch by a number of members of the Garda Síochána. As he was being escorted from the field and being linked by the gardaí, he asked: "Is the guard dead?", and was informed that he was. He was then cautioned by Detective Sergeant Finnegan.

The evidence was that the applicant then said: "Why did he follow us, didn't he know that he would be shot?" The applicant became weak in crossing the field to get to the garda car and was subsequently carried to that car and driven straight to the casualty department of the Louth County Hospital.

Sergeant Finnegan on arrival at the hospital made a note of the conversation which it is alleged the applicant had while crossing the field, signed it himself but did not submit it to the applicant to be signed as the applicant was then apparently in a semi-conscious condition, or in a coma. The Sergeant did not at any time proffer the note to be signed by the applicant.

On a later date, when travelling to the Special Criminal Court in Dublin the applicant was accompanied by a number of members of the Garda Síochána and on travelling through the town of Ardee it was alleged that the applicant stated: "It was a bad day we ever came to this town. The Sergeant would be alive only for us". The evidence was that that conversation was taken down almost immediately by Detective Garda Hanley and, on arrival at Dublin, at the end of the journey, was proffered to be signed by the applicant who, though he had previously acknowledged that it was correct, refused to sign it.

The applicant gave evidence in his own defence. He stated that he had been asked some days before the robbery was committed, by a person whom he knew to be in the Republican Movement to do a job for him which consisted of taking a motorcycle and going to a field at Pepperstown near Ardee and collecting a bag or parcel that would be given to him there on the morning of the 27th of June. The applicant states that he was not informed as to what was in the parcel or what the purpose of the operation was, but he was merely to bring it home with him where it would be collected. He was given a motorcycle for that purpose. He stated in evidence that he drove to Pepperstown on the morning in question and that when he got to the field he observed another motorcycle already parked at the far end of it, so he rode up to it and waited there and that after a relatively short time a car arrived in a great rush; two men got out of it; one of them handed him a bag and that he did not know what was in it, but it was heavy and green, and told him to get up on the pillion of one of the motorcycles which this man drove away. The other man get up on the second motorcycle and drove away. He stated that he was on the pillion of this motorcycle when it crashed into Mrs Mallon's car; that he dropped the bag but he still didn't know what it contained; that he was very dazed and staggered up the avenue; that he did not hear a shot; that he did not see Sergeant Morrissey being shot, but after a time continued in a dazed condition with the assistance of the other man who was beside him and eventually collapsed into the ditch where he was arrested. He denied making the statement on arrest which were tendered in evidence and he denied making the statement in the car travelling through the town of Ardee. He stated that whilst he thought it likely that it was guns he was going to collect on that morning, he was not aware of what was going on and was unaware of any robbery. He said that he did not know a Sergeant had been shot until he came to in the hospital some days after he was arrested.

Grounds of Appeal

In all, seven grounds of appeal were submitted, but they may be grouped into certain main headings.

1. It was submitted that the Court erred in law in admitting into evidence the statements made by the applicant in the field immediately after arrest, on the grounds that the Court should not have been satisfied with the explanation given as to the failure to comply with Rule 9 of the Judges' Rules. This point was not taken at the hearing before the Court and no submission seems to have been made to the effect that the non-compliance made this evidence inadmissible, nor was any enquiry made, as was the basis of the argument before this Court, as to the next available opportunity which the Sergeant might have had of presenting it after the applicant had recovered from his apparent coma. Medical evidence strongly supported the view that the applicant, after being treated on immediate arrival in hospital, for a number of days maintained a condition of feigned semi-consciousness or unconsciousness, not related to his physical injuries. The Court is satisfied that there was no injustice in the admission of these verbal statements into evidence, and that there was no error by the Court of trial in the exercise of its discretion under Rule 9.

It was further contended that even if these statements were admissible that what was described as a desire to protect the applicant against the planted verbal admission should have led the Court of trial to reject the statements on the basis of the applicant's denial that he made them. This Court can not interfere with the resolution by the Court of trial of the issue which arose between the members of the gardaí who swore that these statements were made by the applicant, and the applicant who swore that he did not make them. There was evidence on which the Court of trial would have been entitled to decide that issue in either direction and once it does so that cannot be disturbed by this Court on appeal.

It was further contended that the statement: "Why did he follow us, didn't he know that he would be shot?", was wrongly interpreted by the Court in that it should have been interpreted as indicating that the applicant, even assuming he did make that statement, was referring to the fact that he had discovered for the first time when he saw his companion shoot Sergeant Morrissey, that his companion was a ruthless or desperate man, and was merely reflecting on the fact that the Sergeant in following such a man was doing something perilous.

Such an inference appears to this Court to be strained in the extreme, and the inference which was put by the Court of trial on this statement, seems not only a justifiable one but the only reasonable one, and that was to the general effect that the applicant must be taken from that statement to have been aware that he was engaged at that time in an enterprise in which if he or his companion were being thwarted or likely to be caught, they were prepared to shoot their pursuers, including the gardaí, so as to avoid being arrested.

With regard to the statement alleged to have been made by the applicant while driving with the gardaí through the town of Ardee, it is firstly submitted that because three gardaí gave a different version of the part of the lengthy Main Street of Ardee which the car was travelling through at the time when the statement was made, that the Court was bound to reject the truth of the garda evidence that the statement was made, and was bound to give the benefit of the doubt to the applicant's evidence in which he denied the making of the statement. This Court is not satisfied that it can impose upon the Court of trial any such requirement or standard. The Court listened to and heard the evidence of the three gardaí who swore to the making of this statement, and they heard the evidence of the applicant who denied it, and their resolution of that issue of fact must remain undisturbed by this Court on appeal.

It was contended further, however, that the inference which the Court of trial drew from this statement, namely, that the applicant was involved in Ardee in the actual robbery on the 27th of June, of the Labour Exchange, was an incorrect inference or construction and that the proper construction which should have been put on it, as being the one more favourable to the applicant, was that he was referring to a gang of persons of whom he was one, by the plural "we" and that it was consistent with his evidence that he had not been in the town of Ardee at all on the 27th of June, but that it was merely a statement that his companions had.

Again this Court is not satisfied that there is any warrant for putting such a construction on this statement, and is satisfied that the inference which the Court of trial drew from this statement, once it was satisfied that it had been made, is the correct inference and was inevitably to lead to the conclusion that the applicant was admitting that he was in Ardee on the day of the robbery and of the murder and that, therefore, he took part in the entire enterprise. It was clear from the activities in which the raiders took part in Ardee and, in particular, from the firing at the garda car in that town, that this was an enterprise in which they were prepared to shoot their way out of trouble, irrespective of whether civilians or gardaí were the victims of their shooting.

The other grounds of appeal were to the effect that whereas in relation to Michael McHugh, evidence was given of the finding of firearm residue on a glove in the pocket of his clothes, and evidence was given of the finding of glass similar to the glass in the window of Mr Boyle's car, in his clothes, that neither of these two findings was made in the examination of the clothes of the applicant.

It is said that this negative finding is inconsistent with the applicant's presence in Ardee and his participation in the raid on the Labour Exchange. It is clear from the verdict of the Court of trial that the point was put to it and that it considered this point. This evidence, was, however, neutral. It was not a necessary consequence of the applicant being in Ardee that he should have had firearm residue on his clothing or glass from the window of Boyle's car. The absence of any firearm residue could be accounted for by such residue being dissipated while he was on the motorcycle and travelling through the countryside, and the absence of any glass could be accounted for by his not having been sitting beside the window of the car which was broken. The presence of firearm residue on the glove in the pocket of the co-acused, McHugh, could be accounted for by the firing, which the evidence indicated, he did at Rathbrist House.

Once the Court of trial was satisfied that the verbal admissions, which have been dealt with in this judgment, were made by the applicant and once it put upon those the construction or inference it did, there was no inconsistency, having regard to this evidence of the absence of findings of glass or firearm residue, in the Court's conclusion that the applicant was in Ardee and participated in the robbery.

Lastly, it was urged on this Court that the Court of trial did not appear to pay sufficient regard to the applicant's sworn testimony in his defence.

In referring to the evidence of the applicant the Court of trial stated as follows:

> "The Court has considered the entire of his evidence with the greatest of care and in the light of the evidence adduced by the prosecution and in the light of submissions made by counsel on his behalf for the purpose of determining whether it or any relevant portion thereof could possibly be true, because if the Court had any doubt, the accused is entitled to the benefit of such doubt as of right.
>
> Relevant to the consideration of this evidence are the statements made by the accused to different members of the Garda Síochána".

The Court subsequently went on, having dealt with various details of the evidence, to state that having carefully considered the evidence of the accused with regard to his non-involvement in the robbery in Ardee on the morning of the 27th of June, that it was satisfied beyond all reasonable doubt that the evidence in this regard was untrue and must be rejected by the Court.

This Court is satisfied that that was a conclusion on the evidence which was open to the Court of trial to reach and which was well supported by the evidence adduced.

In these circumstances, this Court is satisfied that none of the grounds of appeal urged on behalf of the applicant have been made out, and on an examination of the entire of the trial, the evidence and the verdict of the Court of trial, it is satisfied that the trial was a satisfactory and just one and that the verdict of the Court was one supported by the evidence before it. This application for leave to appeal must, therefore, be refused. The Court, accordingly, orders pursuant to section 6, subsection 2 of the Courts of Justice Act 1928, that the sentence of death pronounced at the trial of the said Noel Callan shall have effect as if for the day therein mentioned, the 30th day of May, 1986 was substituted and that meanwhile the said Noel Callan be detained in a lawful prison and be taken thence to a place of execution.

Solicitors for the applicant: *Patrick Quin & Co.*
Solicitor for the respondent: *Chief State Solicitor*

Darina O'Sullivan
Barrister

The People (Director of Public Prosecutions) v William Anthony Ryan
[C.C.A. No. 3 of 1986]

Court of Criminal Appeal   7 July 1986

Charges of attempting to obtain money by false pretences – state funds – application for recoupment of expenses – intend to defraud – intent to deceive – whether error in trial judge's charge to the jury

The applicant was convicted in the Cork Circuit (Criminal) Court of attempting to obtain £443 by false pretences from State funds and was sentenced to a term of imprisonment of one year, suspended for three years. The facts were that the applicant was a member of the Garda Síochána and he was transferred to another area. He was entitled to be recouped by the State for his removal expenses, provided he submitted to the authorities three tenders from licensed hauliers and, after receiving approval from the authorities for one of these tenders, he was obliged to have that firm carry out the removal.

The applicant obtained estimates from two hauliers, he had a discussion with a third and obtained a blank billhead from them upon which he was to list the items to be moved and the cost would then be estimated. However the third haulier was not interested in the job. The applicant then typed out on the billhead an estimate for £443.80 and submitted the three estimates to the authorities. The third estimate was sanctioned.

However, the applicant had his brother-in-law carry out the removal. He then submitted a claim for recoupment. A query arose within the Garda Síochána regarding the genuineness of the application leading to the putting of two charges of forgery (on which he was found not guilty by direction) and a charge of attempting to obtain money by false pretences on which he was convicted. He applied to the Court of Criminal Appeal for leave to appeal that conviction.

It was argued on behalf of the applicant that the case should have been withdrawn from the jury as there was no evidence of an intent to defraud, though there was evidence of an intent to deceive; if there was evidence of an intent to defraud the trial judge failed adequately to charge the jury with regard to the meaning of fraud in the context of the facts of the case and that by reason of the absence from the application form of the signature of the relevant superior officer, without which the application could not be considered by the appropriate authorities, there was, therefore, no evidence of a sufficiently proximate act to justify a conviction for attempt.

Held by the Court (Finlay CJ, Lynch and Barr JJ), in quashing the conviction and in ordering a re-trial:

(1) That the central issue was whether there was an intent to defraud as distinct from an intent to deceive and there was a risk that the jury was inadequately charged by the trial judge on the distinction between deceit and fraud in the context of the particular facts of the case. A deceit which induced a course of action which was not to a person's injury or disadvantage would not be to defraud. (*In re London and Globe Finance Corporation Ltd* [1903] 1 Ch. 728 approved.)

(2) That there was evidence of an intent to defraud on the part of the applicant and the trial judge was correct when he refused an application for a direction on that ground.

(3) That there was evidence of a sufficiently proximate act to establish an attempt. (*Attorney General v Sullivan* [1964] I.R. 169 considered.)

Per curiam: Notwithstanding the general principle that, where there was a complaint of a deficiency or error in the trial judge's charge to the jury, the Court will pay particular regard to the run of the trial and whether counsel saw the fault as bearing on the justice of the case and made a requisition for its correction, the Court must, however, in discharge of its obligation to see justice done, fully consider any such complaint even in the absence of a requisition at the trial.

Cases cited in this judgment:
Attorney General v Sullivan [1964] I.R. 169
In re London and Globe Finance Corporation [1903] W.N. 54; [1903] 1 Ch. 728

Hugh O'Flaherty SC and Uinsin MacGruairc **for the applicant**
Edward Ryan **for the respondent**

Finlay CJ

This is an application for leave to appeal against a conviction for the offence of attempting to obtain £443.80 by false pretences from State funds which was recorded against the applicant on the 31st of January, 1986, in the Cork Circuit (Criminal) Court.

The applicant is a sergeant in the Garda Síochána, and in June, 1984, was transferred from Timoleague, Co. Cork to Rosscarbery, Co. Cork. Under the regulations governing such transfer, the applicant was entitled to be recouped by the State the amount which he expended in removing his furniture and other belongings from his residence at Timoleague to the residence which he was obtaining in Roscarbery.

Apparently the procedure for recovering the amount of such cost of removal was that the member of the force concerned was required to submit to the authorities not less than three separate tenders from licensed hauliers for the removal of the furniture and other effects and upon receiving approval of the authorities for one of these tenders, was obliged to have the removal carried out by that firm. On the completion of the removal and the payment to the furniture remover by the member, he was entitled to recoupment from State funds.

On the evidence, which was not contested at the trial, the applicant obtained an estimate for the removal of his furniture from CIE and from Nat Ross Limited. In addition he had a discussion with one William Kirby who was a licensed haulier and asked him if he would like to tender for the job. Kirby expressed an interest and gave to the applicant or his wife two billheads without any particulars or writing entered on them, the purpose, apparently, being that the applicant should fill in on one of these billheads a list of the furniture and effects to be removed, and upon looking at that, Kirby would be in a position to make an estimate of the cost of the job. The applicant did not fill in a list of the goods to be removed on either of the billheads, but on a further discussion with Kirby it became clear that Kirby was not anxious to undertake the job. The applicant then typed out on one of the billheads an estimate in the sum of £443.80 which was less than the lower of the other two estimates, and submitted these estimates; one from CIE, one from Nat Ross, and one purporting to be from William Kirby, to the authorities. The authorities sanctioned the employment of William Kirby. The applicant had the furniture and effects removed by his brother-in-law who was not a licensed haulier but had an appropriate conveyance to bring the articles and who had in fact quoted to him the figure of £443.80. He did not pay his brother-in-law that amount, but then submitted to the authorities a claim for recoupment, supported, *inter alia*, by a receipt purporting to have been signed by Wiliam Kirby for the sum of £443.80 entered on the second of the pieces of notepaper which the applicant had obtained from him. The application for recoupment having been received required a further signature from one of the officers superior to the applicant in his own district before it could be considered and apparently before such signature was obtained, a query arose in the administration section of the Garda Síochána with regard to the genuineness of the application and an investigation was commenced leading to the putting of two charges of fraud and a charge of attempting to obtain the money by false pretences.

At the trial the learned trial judge directed the jury to find the applicant not guilty on the two charges of forgery but left to them the charge of attempting to obtain the money by false pretences, and on this charge he was convicted.

Grounds of Appeal

Though a number of grounds of appeal were submitted reliance was placed on three only. It was firstly submitted that there was at the conclusion of the evidence for the prosecution no evidence of an intent to defraud on the part of the applicant, though there was evidence of an intent to deceive, and that accordingly the case should have been withdrawn from the jury and a verdict of *not guilty* directed on this count as well as on the other two counts of forgery. Secondly, and in the alternative, it was submitted that if there was evidence to go to the jury of an intention to defraud, that the learned trial judge failed adequately to charge the jury with regard to the meaning of fraud in the context of the facts of the case and that accordingly the trial was unsatisfactory.

Thirdly, and in the alternative, it was submitted that by reason of the absence from the application form for the money of the signature of the superior officer required, and by reason of the fact that without such signature the application could not be considered on its merits by the appropriate higher authorities that there was no evidence of a sufficiently proximate act to justify conviction for attempt or, in the further alternative, that the learned trial judge failed adequately or at all to direct the jury as to the issue of proximity arising on the facts of the case.

On these submissions the Court has come to the following conclusions. The Court would adopt with approval the definition of an intent to defraud contained in the judgment of Buckley J in *In re London & Globe Finance Corporation Ltd* [1903] 1 Ch. 728, where, at p. 732 of the report, he stated as follows:

> To deceive is, I apprehend, to induce a man to believe that a thing is true which is false, and which the person practising the deceit knows or believes to be false. To defraud is to deprive by deceit: it is by deceit to induce a man to act to his injury. More tersely it may be put, that to deceive is by falsehood to induce a state of mind; to defraud is by deceit to induce a course of action.

In the context of the charge with which the Court is concerned, of course, a deceit inducing a course of action which was not to a person's injury or disadvantage would not be to defraud.

Having regard to that definition, it was, in the view of the Court clearly open to a jury properly charged on the evidence led by the prosecution to come to the conclusion that what was being attempted by the applicant was to obtain from State funds a payment of £443.80 by falsely pretending that his goods had been transported by a licensed haulier, William Kirby, a deceit the falseness of which he was aware and that the authorities controlling the payment from State funds concerned would not have made the payment to the decrease of the funds had they been aware of the true fact that an unlicensed haulier had carried out the transaction. Once such a view was open on the evidence, though of course it is not necessarily the only view of the evidence open to the jury, the learned trial judge was correct in refusing to give a direction on this count and the first ground of appeal must fail.

With regard to the second ground of appeal, the position in relation to the charge of the learned trial judge is as follows.

In the couse of his charge the learned trial judge made very clear indeed to the jury both the onus of proof which was on the prosecution and the fact that the central issue in the trial now was as to whether there was an intent to defraud as distinct from an intent to deceive. He did not, however, in any way define what an intent to defraud was, either in general or in the context of and with relevance to the facts of this case. At the conclusion of his charge he was not requisitioned by counsel on behalf of the accused to give any further directions concerning the question, though he was requisitioned on another matter.

After the appropriate period the jury returned and were informed by the judge of their right to enter a majority verdict. Having been so informed, the foreman of the jury raised a question in the following manner:

> Foreman of the jury: Your honour, we would like clarification of the actual point of the law that we are. . . .

> Judge: Well, it is not a question of law, at all, it is a question of fact for you whether this man. . . .

> Foreman of the jury: May I speak?

Judge: Of course. I did not mean to interrupt you.

Foreman of the jury: The matter of defrauding the State or fraudulent means of obtaining the money. . . .

Judge: That is a question of fact for you. It is a question of — he is attempting to obtain money by false pretences. He did not get it — that is out. Did he attempt to obtain money by false pretences, the false pretence being that Mr Kirby had done the job for him and was charging him £443.80 with intent to defraud? In other words, he set out to do it and, of course, gentlemen, the overwhelming proposition in the matter is this: if you have any doubt about the case, he is entitled to the benefit of it. Now, does that satisfy you? (The jury indicated that it did).

There was again no requisition by counsel on behalf of the accused for any further direction or charge on the part of the learned trial judge. After the jury had entered a verdict of guilty, the foreman, according to the transcript, volunteered the information that the jury found it very difficult to come to a decision.

In the ordinary way, this Court pays particular regard to the run of a trial in a criminal case, and therefore, where there is a complaint of a deficiency or error in the charge of the trial judge, looks usually to the question as to whether counsel for the accused has at the hearing seen the omission or fault as bearing on the justice of the case and made a requisition for its correction. Notwithstanding this general principle, the Court must, however, in discharge of its obligation to see justice done, fully consider any complaint with regard to the inadequacy of a charge, even made in the absence of a requisition at the trial.

Having regard to the nature of the original charge, and more particularly to the reply to the specific query made by the jury for directions on this point, this Court is satisfied that there is a risk that the jury was inadequately charged on the distinction between deceit and fraud in the context of the particular facts of this case. Having reached that conclusion the Court is satisfied that the applicant's application should be treated as an appeal and that the conviction should be quashed and a retrial ordered.

It is not necessary for the Court for the purpose of the decision in this case to decide the last ground with regard to the question of proximity and attempt. In so far, however, as a retrial has been ordered, it feels it should express its view that there were on the evidence no grounds for granting a direction to the accused on the basis that the evidence failed to establish an attempt. Furthermore, although the general proposition of law is correctly stated to be that the judge must direct the jury to make findings of fact concerning the question of proximity in a charge of an attempt, on the transcript of the previous trial at least, there does not appear to have been any contested issue of fact which it was necessary for the jury to determine in dealing with this. The facts simply were that if the jury believed the witnesses, the accused had done everything which he was required to do in order to submit his application to the appropriate authorities and, if they passed it, to obtain from them a payment of the monies sought. The only matter remaining to be done was to be done by another agency than him, namely, an officer superior to him in his district.

Having regard to the principles laid down in particular in the judgment of Walsh J in *Attorney General v Sullivan* [1964] I.R. 169, the Court is satisfied that if the jury accepted the evidence with regard to the steps which the accused is alleged to have taken in the submission of this claim, and accepted the evidence with regard to what was necessary to bring the claim for determination by the appropriate authorities in the Garda Síochána, that there was no room for any question specially to be left to them or their minds to be directed in a special way to any issue arising with regard to proximity and the evidence they should have been told in a charge, would amount to an attempt if they were satisfied of its truth.

Solicitors for the applicant: *Collins Brooks and Associates*
Solicitor for the respondent: *Chief State Solicitor*

Eithne Casey
Barrister

The People (Director of Public Prosecutions) v Martin Ferris, John Crawley and Michael Brown
[C.C.A. Nos. 100-102 of 1984]

Court of Criminal Appeal   15 December 1986

Arrest – arrest pursuant to section 30 of Act of 1939 – reason – accused informed by arresting garda that arrest was made on suspicion that scheduled offence had been committed, namely, possession of firearms – Possession of firearms simpliciter not an offence – whether arrest lawful – Offences Against the State Act 1939 (No. 13), section 30

Special Criminal Court – whether certificate of Director of Public Prosecutions pursuant to section 7, subsection 1 of the Explosive Substances Act 1883, necessary where persons are charged with offence under the Act before the Special Criminal Court – Explosive Substances Act 1883, (Ch. 3) section 7(1)

Arrest at sea – whether applicants arrested within territorial waters of the State – Admissibility of admiralty charts – admissibility of evidence of location of arrest – Maritime Jurisdiction Act 1959 (No. 22), section 13 – Maritime Jurisdiction Act 1959, (Charts) Order, 1959 (S.I. No. 174 of 1959)

European community – reference of question to European Court of Justice – whether question posed fell within the terms of Article 177 of the Treaty of Rome 1957 – Council Directive 80/181 EEC, Articles 1, 2 – European Communities (Units of Measurement) Regulations 1983 (S.I. No. 235 of 1983) – Maritime Jurisdiction Act 1959 (No. 22), section 13

The applicants, who were the crew of a motor vessel, were arrested at sea pursuant to section 30 of the Offences Against the State Act 1939, on suspicion of possession of firearms. A large quantity of firearms, ammunition and explosive substances were found on board the vessel at the time of arrest. They were subsequently convicted before the Special Criminal Court of, *inter alia*, possession of firearms with intent to enable other persons to endanger life.

Having been refused leave to appeal by the Special Criminal Court, the applicants applied for leave to appeal to the Court of Criminal Appeal. The grounds of their appeal were first that the applicants had not been properly informed of the reasons for their arrest under section 30 of the Act of 1939, in that the reason given was "suspicion of having committed a scheduled offence, namely, possession of firearms". Secondly, it was submitted that possession of firearms, *simpliciter*, was not a scheduled offence, that the certificate of the Director of Public Prosecutions required by section 7 subsection 1 of the Explosive Substances Act 1883 had not been furnished to the Special Criminal Court, and thirdly, that the principal Admiralty chart used in evidence to show that the vessel had been within the territorial waters of the State when it was stopped did not comply with the requirements of the Maritime Jurisdiction Act 1959 (Charts) Order 1959, which provided that such charts should be "published at the Admiralty, London". The relevant chart bore upon its face the legend "Published in Taunton". It was argued that it was not a chart admissible in evidence by virtue of the 1959 Order and accordingly there was no proof of the extent of the territorial

114

seas of the State. The applicants submitted that the 1959 Act should be the subject of strict construction appropriate to a penal statute. A further submission related to the validity of the term "nautical mile". The applicants submitted that such unit of measurement could not be used as the basis on which to calculate the outer limits of the extent of the territorial seas of the State having regard to the fact that the European Communities (Units of Measurement) Regulations (S.I. No. 235 of 1983), made pursuant to Council Directive 80/181 EEC, prohibit the use of such unit of measurement for economic, public health, public safety and administrative purposes, and prescribed that the metrical equivalent of a nautical mile should be used which was 1,853 metres. It was submitted that the term nautical mile was no longer a legal unit of measurement and therefore the extent of the territorial seas of the State had not been properly proved. The applicants requested that a reference be made to the European Court of Justice under Article 177 of the Treaty of Rome as to whether the term "nautical mile" was compatible with the 1980 Directive.

Held by the Court (McCarthy, Barron and Barr JJ), in dismissing the applications and in refusing to make a reference to the Court of Justice of the European Communities:—

(1) That the authority to make an arrest under section 30 of the Act of 1939 arises from the suspicion formed by a member of the Garda Síochána. The arrested person must be informed of the offence of which he is suspected unless he already has that information. It was the unlawful nature of the possession that was the essence of the offence. The vessel in which the applicants were arrested contained a large quantity of arms, ammunition and explosives. Consequently, it could not reasonably be said, once possession of firearms had been mentioned, that the applicants were unaware of the reason for their arrest. *People (DPP) v Quilligan* [1986] I.R. 495 followed.

(2) That the requirements of section 7 subsection 1 of the Act of 1883 related to persons charged before a Justice. It did not apply to persons charged before the Special Criminal Court where such persons were brought before that Court at first instance. *R. v Bates* [1911] 1 K.B. 964 considered.

(3) That the ordinary meaning of the phrase "published at the Admiralty, London" was that the chart was issued with the authority of the Admiralty, London, and as such came within the kind prescribed in the Statutory Instrument.

(4) That the purpose of the Council Directive 80/181 EEC was to harmonise the laws relating to units of measurement. It did not make illegal the use of any form of measurement. The territorial seas of the State were properly defined, and the delineation of the outer limits of the territorial seas was a political act whereas the directive was concerned with units of measurement for economic, public health, public safety or administrative purposes. The questions sought to be referred to the European Court of Justice, as to whether the term nautical mile was compatible with EEC law was not a question that came within the meaning of Article 177 of the Treaty of Rome.

Cases cited in this judgment
People (DPP) v Quilligan and O'Reilly [1986] I.R. 495; [1987] ILRM 606
People (DPP) v Walsh [1980] I.R. 294
R. v Bates [1911] 1 K.B. 964; (1911) 6 Cr. App. R. 153
The State (Healy) v Donoghue [1976] I.R. 325; (1978) 112 I.L.T.R. 37

Additional cases cited in argument
Browne v Donegal County Council [1980] I.R. 132

Christie and Anor. v Leachinsky [1947] A.C. 573; 63 T.L.R. 231; [1947] 1 All E.R. 567
The People (Attorney General) v McDermott and Others 2 Frewen 211
Myers v DPP [1965] A.C. 1001; [1964] 3 W.L.R. 145; [1964] 2 All E.R. 881

Seamus Sorahan SC and Michael Gray **for the first applicant**
Paul Carney SC and Patrick Gageby **for the second applicant**
Frank Clarke SC and Martin Giblin **for the third applicant**
Kevin Haugh SC and Fergal Foley **for the respondent**

McCarthy J

On the 29th of September, 1984, units of the Naval Service intercepted a motor vessel, the Marita Ann, in the waters off the Great Skellig, called on the vessel by megaphone to halt and fired tracer rounds; the vessel was stopped and boarded by a party, including Garda Inspector Ryan and Detective Garda McGillicuddy who were on board L/E Emer; the Marita Ann was escorted to Haulbowline in Cork Harbour. At the time it was stopped, there was on board the Marita Ann a large quantity of firearms, ammunition and explosives. The three applicants and two other men were all on board the Marita Ann at the time she was stopped and taken under escort to Haulbowline. All of those on board were charged before the Special Criminal Court with offences under the Explosive Substances Act 1883, and the Firearms Act 1925, as amended by the Firearms Acts 1964-1971, and the Criminal Law (Jurisdiction) Act 1976. All the accused were found guilty of

(a) possession of explosive substances contrary to section 4 of the Act of 1883

(b) possession of firearms and ammunition with intent to enable other persons to endanger life

(c) possession of an F.N. rifle and an M1 carbine, and ammunition therefor, with intent to endanger life.

They were acquitted of a charge of possession with intent to endanger life of the entire quantity of firearms and ammunition, the distinction being that the two weapons specified had been prepared for use and had clips of ammunition nearby.

Each of the accused was, at the trial, represented by senior and junior counsel and, having been refused leave to appeal by the Special Criminal Court, served notice of application to this Court for such leave and, in support of such application filed elaborate grounds of appeal, numbering

47 in the case of Martin Ferris, 47 in the case of John P. Crawley and 17 in the case of Michael Brown.

At the commencement of the hearing, in the case of Martin Ferris, it was stated that the grounds relied upon were numbers 4 to 14, dealing with the admiralty charts, and 27 to 29, dealing with the search of the vessel and the arrest of the applicant. It later transpired that this applicant wished to rely also upon grounds 1, 15-19 and 30-33.

Counsel for Michael Brown confined his argument to grounds 4 and 5, the admissibility of the charts, and 15, which rested upon an observation made by the President of the Special Criminal Court at the commencement of the trial. Counsel for John P. Crawley confined himself to grounds 37 and 38, which rested upon the same argument as ground 15 of Michael Brown. On the second day of the hearing counsel for Michael Brown and John P. Crawley stated that they were expressly instructed to adopt all the arguments advanced on behalf of all of the applicants; the Court invited counsel for the Director of Public Prosecutions to deal with all of these argued grounds of appeal, save one, but his arguments did not evoke a response on behalf of any of the applicants. The task of this Court has not been helped by this method of presentation of these applications; the task is, however, untrammelled by any consideration of merit. The guilt of each of the applicants is clear beyond question; the issue is whether or not there were technical defects in the proof of that guilt.

The Court is satisfied that there were not and the applications for leave to appeal will be dismissed. It is necessary, however, to deal with each of the matters advanced in argument, in so far as the Court can appreciate the nature of the argument. Since each of the applicants, through his counsel, adopted the arguments of his fellows, it is unnecessary to distinguish between any of the applicants in respect of any of these arguments which, themselves, being entirely of a legal and technical nature are the responsibility of those presenting the arguments.

1. That the certificate of the Director of Public Prosecutions required by section 7 subsection 1 of the Explosive Substances Act 1883 had not been furnished to the Special Criminal Court.

Section 7 subsection 1 applies where a person is charged before a Justice; these applicants were charged before the Special Criminal Court. In fact, counsel for the Director expressly conveyed to the Court the consent of the Director to the charge under the Explosive Substances Act being disposed of in the Special Criminal Court (Book I, p. 26). The powers of the Attorney General for Ireland were conferred upon the Attorney General of Saorstát Eireann by section 6 of the Ministers and Secretaries Act 1924, and thence on the Attorney General established by the Constitution, all of whose functions capable of being performed in relation to criminal matters are, pursuant to section 3 of the Prosecution of Offences Act 1974, to be performed by the Director of Public Prosecutions. Section 4 subsection 3 of the 1974 Act provides that the fact that the function of a law officer has been performed by him . . . may be established, without further proof, in any proceedings by a statement of that fact made . . . orally to the Court concerned by a person appearing on behalf of or prosecuting in the name of the law officer. The requirement of section 7 subsection 1 of the 1883 Act, by definition, cannot apply to a prosecution before the Special Criminal Court, where, as in the instant case, those charged were brought before the Special Criminal Court in the first instance. It is only the Attorney General and the Director of Public Prosecutions who can bring proceedings in the Special Criminal Court; the weakness of this ground of appeal is all too apparent. When the argument was advanced at the trial, counsel for John P. Crawley referred to *R. v Bates* [1911] 1 K.B. 964. It was a case where the accused, prosecuted by the King in the first instance, was brought before a Justice; it has nothing to do with this case.

2. *The admissibility of the admiralty charts.*

The offences were charged to have been committed "off the Great Skellig Rock, within the State". Evidence was, accordingly, led to establish that this particular area, where the vessel was stopped and the applicants arrested, is within the territorial seas being part of the national territory as defined by Article 2 of the Constitution. The territorial seas of the State, for the purposes of the Maritime Jurisdiction Act 1959, are that portion of the sea which lies between the baseline and the outer limit of the territorial seas (sections 2, 3 and 4); the outer limit is a line every point of which is at a distance of 3 nautical miles from the nearest point of the baseline. A nautical mile means the length of one minute of an arc of a meridian of longitude. Accordingly, it was necessary to prove that the area around the Great Skellig Rock is within the outer limit. Section 13 of the Act of 1959 provides:—

The Government may by order prescribe the charts which may be used for the purpose of establishing low-water mark, or the existence and position of any low-tide elevation, or any other matter in reference to the internal waters, the territorial seas, the exclusive fishery limits or a fishery conservation area, and any chart purporting to be a copy of a chart of a kind or description so prescribed shall, unless the contrary is proved, be received in evidence as being a prescribed chart without further proof.

By Statutory Instrument No. 174 of 1959 — Maritime Jurisdiction Act 1959 (Charts) Order 1959:—

The Government, in exercise of the power conferred on them by section 13 of the Maritime Jurisdiction Act, 1959 (No. 22 of 1959), hereby order as follows:—

. . . (2) Charts published at the Admiralty, London, shall be charts for the purposes of section 13 of the Maritime Jurisdiction Act, 1959.

In the course of trial extensive evidence was given by naval personnel as to the use of charts for the purpose of plotting a "fix" on the position of the Marita Ann at relevant times so as to establish that she was within the outer limit. The most important of these charts, that used on L.E. Emer and produced in Court bore upon it the words "published at Taunton". Taunton was identified in evidence as being in Somerset in England. The applicants submitted that the charts "published at the Admiralty, London" specified in the statutory instrument could not and did not include the chart in question which expressed itself to be "published at Taunton". It was submitted, as a foundation for this argument, that the Act of 1959 should be the subject of the strict construction appropriate to penal statutes. The Act of 1959 made provision in respect of the territorial seas and the exclusive fishery limits of the State but did also prescribe for jurisdiction and procedure in respect of the infliction of penalties; whilst section 13 is not limited to use in the prosecution of offences, it can, as in this case, be used for that purpose and sections 9, 10 and 11 are clearly penal in application; the Court is satisfied, accordingly, that section 13 should be strictly construed. The rule of strict construction arises if and when there is a doubt or ambiguity as to the meaning of the provision being construed; for example, if there is an interpretation open which would avoid the imposition of penalty, then that is the interpretation that should be applied. The first test is to look at the provision in its ordinary natural meaning. If examination reveals a doubt, then that doubt must be resolved in favour of a person accused. Essentially, the issue raised in the instant case is whether or not the chart (exhibit 9) is a chart within the terms of the statutory instrument; it is not a question of whether or not the statutory instrument is within the terms of the section. Accordingly, the rule of strict construction of penal statutes has no application to this ground of appeal. The power given to the Government under section 13 is to prescribe charts which may be used for particular purposes, which the Government has done by prescribing "charts published at the Admiralty, London" and the issue is whether or not the particular chart purported to be a copy of a chart of a kind or description so prescribed. Whilst the particular chart produced contains the legend "published at Taunton" the evidence clearly established through Mr Mount that it was a chart emanating from the Admiralty, London. The word "published" in its ordinary meaning means made publicly or generally available and in a specialised meaning, to issue or cause to be issued for sale to the public (Oxford English Dictionary). In context, however, it means no more than issued with the authority of the Admiralty, London. It would be nonsense to suggest that if the printing of such charts and their initial production were to be changed from one venue within the United Kingdom to another or, indeed, to a venue outside the United Kindgom, that this would require consequent fresh statutory instruments to be made. The Court is quite satisfied that the chart relied upon came within the kind or description prescribed in the statutory instrument.

3. *Admiralty Charts — second ground*
Council Directive 80/181/EEC made on the 20th of December, 1979, made provision for the approximation of the laws of the Member States relating to units of measurement. It required that Member States should adopt and publish before the 1st of July, 1981, the laws, regulations and administrative provisions necessary to comply with the directive. The directive prescribed legal units of measurement under three separate chapter headings and included in Chapter III legal units of measurement referred to in Article 1(c) which permitted the continued use of the Chapter III units in certain Member States until a date not later than the 31st of December, 1989. Article 2 provided that the obligations under article 1

"relate to measuring instruments used, measurements made and indications of quantity expressed in units of measurements, for economic, public health, public safety or administrative purposes". This provision is echoed in Statutory Instrument No. 235 of 1983 which, clearly, was made in compliance with the EEC directive and prescribed the metrical equivalent of a wide variety of measurement, including "nautical mile (U.K.)" at 1,853 metres. The nautical mile as defined in the Act of 1959 means "the length of one minute of an arc of a meridian of longitude". It was, apparently seriously, contended that because of the EEC directive the term "nautical mile" could not legally be used and, it followed, that the prescription of the outer limit of the territorial seas in section 3 of the 1959 Act was invalid with the consequences that the territorial seas of this State are either undefined or are without limit.

It is clear beyond peradventure that the purpose of the directive was to achieve what is called the approximation or harmonization of the laws of the Member States relating to units of measurement; in no sense does this make illegal the use of any form or expression of measurement but, as an examination of the directive reveals, demands that along with the older form of measurement, in the instances prescribed by Article 2(a) the units of measurement set out in the directive must be used. In the view of the Court the prescribing of the outer limit of the territorial seas of the State does not fall within "economic, public health, public safety or administrative purposes"; the prescription or delineation of the outer limit of territorial seas is a political act which may have consequences in a variety of ways. This ground of appeal is rejected.

4. *Application for reference.*
In the course of argument, Mr Gray, on behalf of Martin Ferris, applied to the Court, as had been done on behalf of one of the other accused, not an applicant to this Court, in the Special Criminal Court, to refer to the Court of Justice of the European Economic Community the question as to whether the term "nautical mile" contained in the 1959 Act is compatible with EEC directive No. 80/181 of the 20th of December, 1979.
Article 177 of the Treaty of Rome provides:—

> The Court of Justice shall have jurisdiction to give preliminary rulings concerning:

(a) the interpretation of this Treaty;
(b) the validity and interpretation of acts of the institutions of the Community;
(c)the interpretation of the statutes of bodies established by an act of the Council, where those statutes so provide.

Where such a question is raised before any Court or tribunal of a Member State, that court or tribunal may, if it considers that a decision on the question is necessary to enable it to give judgment, request the Court of Justice to give a ruling thereon.

Where any such question is raised in a case pending before a court or tribunal of a Member State, against whose decisions there is no judicial remedy under national law, that court or tribunal shall bring the matter before the Court of Justice.

Assuming, without deciding that this Court is a court against whose decisions there is no judicial remedy under national law within the meaning of the last paragraph of Article 177; that, although this Court or the Attorney General may certify an appeal to the Supreme Court in a matter that has been decided by this Court, the ordinary reading of the paragraph indicates a judicial remedy that does not require special leave, the Court is satisfied that the question posed is not a question within sub-paragraphs (a), (b) or (c) of Article 177.

5. *Search and arrest*

Inspector Ryan of the Garda Síochána on stopping the Marita Ann was one of the first boarding party of four persons who went by rubber dinghy to the Marita Ann and boarded it. He went to the after deck, was in full uniform, and informed the five men, later to be identified as all of the persons accused in the Special Criminal Court and including the three present applicants, who he was and that he was arresting them under section 30 of the Offences Against the State Act 1939, because "I suspected they were engaged in the commission of a scheduled offence under that Act, namely, possession of firearms." He told them to turn around and to face down on the deck which they did; Inspector Ryan requested the naval personnel to secure the prisoners and accompanied by Detective Garda Michael McGillicuddy and two naval officers searched the Marita Ann.

Inspector Ryan did not have a warrant; if he had, section 29 of the 1939 Act, as inserted by section 2 of the Criminal Justice Act 1976, would have been ample authority for the officers of the naval service acting on their own. The search and arrest are challenged on the grounds that the wording used by Inspector Ryan was not in compliance with the standard requirement of a valid arrest in that there is no such offence as possession of firearms, *simpliciter*. There are a variety of offences that can arise from the possession of firearms, ranging from mere possession without a firearms certificate to possession with intent to endanger life; there is an incidental power (under section 21 of the Firearms Act 1925) for any member of the Garda Síochána at all reasonable times to enter upon and to have free access to the interior of any ship or other vessel used for the conveyance of goods. Where a vessel is being used for the importation of a large variety of arms and ammunition, any time is a reasonable time for access by the Garda Síochána. As to the information regarding the offence upon which the arrest was being made, it is apt to quote a passage from the judgment of Walsh J in *The People (Director of Public Prosecutions) v Quilligan and O'Reilly* [1986] I.R. 495 at p. 508:—

> When a person is arrested under section 30 as in any other arrest he must be informed of which of the many possible offences he is suspected unless he already has that information, see *People (DPP) v Walsh* [1980] I.R. 294.

It is important to emphasise that the authority to arrest under section 30 springs from a suspicion held by a member of the Garda Síochána that an individual has committed or is about to commit or is or has been concerned in the commission of an offence under any section or subsection of the 1939 Act or an offence which is for the time being a scheduled offence or otherwise as provided in subsection 1. There may well be circumstances in which the arresting Garda may not have sufficient information at the time of arrest to specify in detail which of several possible scheduled offences the person arrested is suspected of having committed. This is particularly so in respect of offences under the Firearms Act; essentially, it is the unlawful nature of the possession that is the gravamen of the offence. Where the crew of a vessel at sea have in their possession the large stock of arms, ammunition and explosives as found in Marita Ann and are told by an Inspector of the Gardaí that they are being arrested for possession of firearms, it can scarcely be intelligently argued that they have not the information as to the offence or offences of which they are suspected when, as here, Inspector Ryan spoke of possession of firearms. In any event, even assuming the arrest was unlawful and, consequently, a breach of the constitutional rights of the applicants, it is nothing to the point. They did not make inculpatory statements and it does not bear upon the search. The search was authorised by section 30 of the Offences Against the State Act 1939, apart from section 21 of the Firearms Act 1925. The complaint in respect of the search is that it was not carried out by the Gardaí only but also by members of the Naval Service. This is so. It is not to the point. As was held in the Special Criminal Court, the Gardaí are entitled to call upon the assistance of the Defence Forces in support of the civil power; it would be ludicrous if it were otherwise.

6. Notices of further evidence

An argument was advanced on the contention that the trial had been unfair in that there was what was called a stream of notices of further evidence; this is just not so. Four notices of further evidence were furnished, some well in advance of the date of trial which itself lasted four days. On being questioned in the course of argument, Mr Gray agreed that there was no basis on which it could be said that the service of these notices prejudiced the conduct of the defence. The Court refrains from further comment on this ground.

7. The preliminary observation of the President of the Court

McMahon J at the very beginning of the trial referred to the public knowledge that a vessel loaded with arms and ammunition had been found and it was said that the persons charged were those on it. The complaint is made that this was in contravention of what are said to be the principles in *State (Healy) v Donoghue* [1976] I.R. 325, in that the particular applicant would feel that he was not getting a fair trial. The Court considers this a quite unsustainable ground of appeal. It is fortifed in this belief by the very fact that no objection was taken at the trial on behalf of any of the accused until the very end of the trial when the matter was first mentioned on behalf of the accused John P. Crawley, this despite the fact that each of the five accused was represented by senior and junior counsel. Being a member of the judiciary does not preclude the reading of newspapers, listening to the radio or watching television. The observation of the President of the Court was made in the context of a totally unsustainable objection to the form of the indictment in respect of the particulars; it is being taken out of context and used or sought to be used in a manner which the Court considers quite improper and unwarranted.

As already stated, these applications for leave to appeal are dismissed.

Solicitors for the applicants: *S. Pierse O'Sullivan and Co.*
Solicitor for the respondent: *Chief State Solicitor*

Noreen Mackey
Barrister

The People (Director of Public Prosecutions) v Edward Doran
[C.C.A. No. 105 of 1986]

Court of Criminal Appeal   7 December 1987

Murder – defence of self-defence – pre-trial statements of accused – sworn testimony giving different account – charge to jury – whether duty of trial judge to advance an alternative factual base for defence of self-defence based on statements – whether judge's charge unduly favourable to prosecution

The applicant broke into a house, the home of a couple with three children, ran out of the house and was pursued by the householder who was carrying a golf club. The householder caught the applicant and struck him several times with the golf stick whereupon the applicant stabbed the householder with a knife and killed him.

The applicant was tried in the Central Criminal Court (O'Hanlon J and jury) for murder and other counts relating to burglary and larceny. He was convicted of murder to which he had pleaded not guilty and was sentenced to penal servitude for life with concurrent sentences of imprisonment of ten years and three years on the other counts to which he had pleaded guilty. He applied for leave to appeal against the conviction for murder.

The applicant had made a number of written statements to the gardaí which he had signed and while the admissibility of these statements was not contested at the trial, it was stated that in significant details they were untrue. The accused gave a different account in his sworn evidence and the defence put forward was one of self-defence.

It was submitted on behalf of the applicant that even if the jury rejected the applicant's account in the witness box of what happened immediately before the fatal blow, they might return to the account given in the written statements where they could find an intermediate story and that the trial judge never put the statements to the jury as also constituting an alternative factual base for the defence of self-defence. It was also argued that the charge of the trial judge was unduly favourable to the prosecution.

Held by the Court (McCarthy, Barron and Egan JJ) in refusing the application:

(1) It was not open to an accused to make a case in which he denies on oath the facts set out in a written statement to then ask a jury, if they reject his sworn testimony, to uphold his defence based on such written statement and that in any event the applicant's statements did not constitute an answer in self-defence. (*R v Porritt* (1961) 45 Cr. App. R. 348 distinguished.)

(2) The judge's charge to the jury must be looked upon as a whole, and while the judge expressed clear views of his own he left it to the jury in the clearest terms to come to the conclusion of fact on the critical issue as to whether, despite the account given by the applicant, they were satisfied that murder had been committed.

Cases cited in this judgment:
  R. v Bullard [1957] A.C. 635; [1957] 3 W.L.R. 656; (1957) 42 Cr. App. R. 1
  R. v Porritt [1961] 1 W.L.R. 1372; [1961] 3 All E.R. 463; 45 Cr. App. R. 348

Seamus Sorahan SC and Patrick Marrinan **for the applicant**
Kevin Haugh SC and Michael McDowell SC **for the respondent**

McCarthy J

Early in the morning of the 22nd of May 1986, the accused broke into a house at 66 Dollymount Park, Dublin, where there lived James and Pauline Wall and their three young daughters. The intruder was disturbed and ran out the back door of the house after some scuffle with Mr Wall who had obtained a golf club from under a bed. The only eye witness account of what happened afterwards came from the accused who made two written statements, both admitted at the trial, and from his sworn testimony upon trial for the murder of Mr Wall.

The trial took place before O'Hanlon J and a jury at the Central Criminal Court, the trial judge stating that;

> "... essentially, your task is to determine whether a defence arises on the basis of self-defence and the prosecution have to satisfy you that the defence does not exist in this case and that the accused should not be given the benefit of the defence. The onus is never on the accused to prove that he committed the killing in lawful self-defence. The onus remains at all times on the prosecution to satisfy the jury, to convince them, that no defence arises on the basis of self-defence".

The prosecution put in evidence a series of exhibited statements. In each statement the accused described running from the house and then:

> "I fell on the roadway. When I fell on the roadway the man struck me behind with the golf stick on the back. I jumped up and he kept

swinging the golf stick at me. I tried to get away from the man but he struck me again with the golf stick in the lower part of my back. I then pulled out my knife which I had on my belt. There was a loop on this knife to carry on a belt. I hit him with the knife in the belly first but he kept coming at me and I stuck the knife then in his chest. I think I got him a few times in the chest with the knife and he fell on the roadway near the church railings. It happened so quick I don't know how many times I stabbed him with the knife. At the time I thought it was him or me the way he was coming at me with the golf club. ..."
(Exhibit 36)

"... I was trying to get into another room from the kitchen when a man appeared from another door with a golf club. I ran from the kitchen and out the back. I jumped over the gardens on my left and then over a back wall onto a laneway at the rear. I then ran into the church yard. I looked behind me and he was still after me. I got a belt of the golf club over the back. It was starting to get bright. I ran out the roadway at the side of St. Gabriel's Church and while I was looking behind I fell on the roadway. He came up behind me and broke the golf stick on my back. I lost my temper and stabbed him with a knife I had in my belt. He fell to the ground. . . . I then went down to the slipway near the carpark opposite the yacht club and buried the knife which I used to stab the man in the sand under the slipway with the pair of gloves I wore on the night. I'm sorry I killed him but it was either him or me. ..." (Exhibit 40).

Both of these written and signed statements were made on the 22nd of May. The admissibility of these statements was not contested at the trial but it was alleged that in significant details they were untrue.

The accused gave evidence and testified that he was running away, that he had thrown a chisel at the pursuing Mr Wall, that when he reached the barbed wire at the gap beside the road he was hit with the golf stick in the back and that he was grabbed with the golf stick first up around the shoulder and then around the throat.

"... I just automatically went for the knife then; I was striking blows at the deceased's hands and body, when he released his grip on me I turned around and struck out at him with the knife — in the upper part of the body; he grabbed the blade of the knife. . . ."

In cross-examination much of the questioning was directed as to where the alleged struggle took place (Book E at p. 37) and the conduct alleged of Mr Wall that he tried to choke the accused with the golf club. Further questioning was related to the number of knife wounds sustained by Mr Wall (nine in all) as described by the pathologist, including one which the accused regarded as the fatal blow, that in which Mr Wall grasped the knife.

Whilst the learned trial judge made a number of references in the course of his charge to the written statements, essentially he posed the real issue to the jury, with a very stringent direction on the onus of proof, as to whether or not, despite the account given by the accused in the witness box, the jury were satisfied that murder had been committed, that there was no valid answer in self defence. It is quite apparent from the requisitions made to the trial judge at the end of his charge that no other case was made to the jury in the closing address of counsel for the defence and the only reference to any possible other case is contained in the following abstract from Mr Sorahan's concluding submission (Book H, p. 30):

"... even if the jury were not (satisfied) or had doubts about the verdict or the story about the struggle at the barbed wire that on the statements such as they were given to the police by my client undoubtedly that discloses *prima facie* and goes a long way towards establishing a basis or bases for the defence of self-defence. ..."

No such point is taken in the grounds of appeal served in advance of this hearing nor was it advanced by leading counsel for the accused. Mr Marrinan, however, junior counsel who had suggested the requisition at the trial, sought to enlarge upon it before this court, while acknowledging that no such case had been made during the trial itself, to wit, that even if the jury rejected the accused's account of what took place immediately before the fatal blow, the jury might return to the account given in the written statements which I have sought to cite in short form in this judgment. He submitted, in effect, that there was an intermediate story contained in the statements made to the gardaí, in particular exhibit 36, and that the trial judge never put those statements to the jury as constituting an answer in self-defence. Counsel cited, in support of this proposition, *R. v Porritt* (1961) 45 Cr. App.R. 348 where Ashworth J at p. 356, quoted the judgment in *R. v Bullard* [1957] A.C. 635:

"... it has long been settled law that if on the evidence, whether of the prosecution or of the defence, there is any evidence of provocation fit to be left to a jury, and whether or not this issue has been specifically raised at the trial by counsel for the defence and whether or not the accused had said in terms that he was provoked, it is the duty of the judge, after a proper direction, to leave it open to the jury to return a verdict of manslaughter if they are not satisfied beyond reasonable doubt that the killing was unprovoked".

There is no necessary inconsistency in a defence primarily based on self-defence but with a fall back on manslaughter; no such defence was, however, advanced in the instant case at the trial or on the appeal. The complaint is that the learned trial judge did not advance an alternative factual base for self-defence, nor a defence of provocation. Having examined in detail the several written statements and compared them with the sworn testimony of the accused and the description of the wounds, the Court is satisfied that it would have been to no purpose to ask the jury to consider the detail set out in the written statements as was suggested in the argument in this appeal, which the Court permitted despite the fact that none such had been advanced in the Court below. That is not to say that it is open to an accused to make a case in which he denies on oath the facts set out in a written statement and asks the jury, if they reject his sworn testimony, to uphold his defence based on such a written statement.

As to the other ground of appeal, that the charge of the learned trial judge was unduly favourable to the prosecution, it is not suggested that the trial judge may not properly comment on such matters of fact which appear to him to be worthy of comment whilst taking care to caution the jury to disregard such comments if they do not appeal to them. In any transcript of the charge by a trial judge it is possible to seek out and find some isolated matter of complaint; such is the case here but that is not the correct way of looking at a charge; rather this Court, as the jury did, must look upon it as a whole. In the view of the Court, the learned trial judge, whilst expressing clear views of his own, gave a most painstaking and accurate charge to the jury, leaving it, in the clearest terms, to the jury to come to the conclusion of fact on the critical issue.

The application for leave to appeal is dismissed.

Solicitors for the applicant: *Dermot Morris & Co.*
Solicitor for the respondent: *Chief State Solicitor*

Eithne Casey
Barrister

The People (Director of Public Prosecutions) v Sean Howley
[C.C.A. No. 70 of 1986]

Court of Criminal Appeal   4 March 1988

Criminal Law – arrest – evidence – admissibility – statements of accused – whether arrest and subsequent detention pursuant to section 30 of the Offences Against the State Act 1939 lawful – arrest on suspicion of having committed scheduled offence of cattle maiming – applicant interrogated in respect of unconnected crime of murder – scheduled offence occuring sixteen months prior to murder – predominant motive for arrest – whether arrest was a colourable device in order to question the applicant about the crime of murder – validity of extension order permitting detention for further period of twenty-four hours – whether chief superintendent must be informed of desire to interrogate in respect of non-scheduled offence – Offences Against the State Act 1939, section 30, section 30(3)

The applicant was convicted of murder and he applied for leave to appeal his conviction. It was argued on his behalf that the arrest, pursuant to section 30 of the 1939 Act was a mere colourable device and that the predominant motive of the arrest was to enable the gardaí to question the applicant about the crime of murder while he was in custody, and consequently that all of the statements allegedly made by the applicant were inadmissible in law having been obtained in conscious and deliberate violation of the applicant's legal and constitutional rights.

The facts were that a tenant of the applicant disappeared and her body was subsequently found in a lake some ten days later. Subsequently the applicant was arrested pursuant to section 30 of the Act of 1939 on suspicion of having committed a scheduled offence namely the maiming of cattle it being an offence under the Malicious Damage Act 1861 and which had occurred some sixteen months earlier. Part of the interrogation of the applicant was directed to the incident of the maiming of the cattle and at other times directed to the disappearance of the deceased. The applicant's period of detention was extended pursuant to an extension order signed by the chief superintendent. It was during the second period of detention that he was alleged to have made an admission to the crime of murder. At the trial the applicant denied that the alleged statements were his and denied complicity in the crime.

Held by the Court (Finlay CJ, Gannon and Barrington JJ):
(1) That the arrest pursuant to section 30 of the Act of 1939 was a genuine arrest *bona fide* carried out on a suspicion held of complicity by the applicant in a real scheduled offence and statements made during the ensuing detention which otherwise could not be objected to were admissible in evidence. There was no requirement that an arrest under section 30 of the Act must be predominantly motivated by a desire to investigate a scheduled offence.

(2) The extension of the period of detention by the chief superintendnet was lawful once the chief superintendent making the order *bona fide* suspected the detained person of being involved in the offence for which he was originally arrested. The fact that the chief superintendent was not informed that in addition to the interrogation with regard to the scheduled offence an interrogation was also being conducted concerning the disappearance of the deceased was not relevant. The information laid before the chief superintendent which concerned the subject matter of the actual arrest was the relevant information and once he

came to a *bona fide* decision on that information the Court could not set aside that decision.

Cases cited in this judgment:
> *The People (DPP) v Quilligan* [1986] I.R. 495; [1987] ILRM 606
> *The People (DPP) v Walsh* [1986] I.R. 722

Additional cases cited in legal argument:
> *Cassidy v Minister for Industry and Commerce* [1978] I.R. 297
> *East Donegal Co-Operative Livestock Meats Ltd v Attorney General* [1970] I.R. 317;
> 104 I.L.T.R. 81
> *People (DPP) v Eccles*, 3 Frewen 36

On the application of counsel for the applicant the Court granted a certificate pursuant to section 29 of the Courts of Justice Act 1924, and certified that its decision involved two points of law of exceptional public importance and that it was desirable in the public interest that an appeal should be taken to the Supreme Court on those points namely:

> (a) Whether, notwithstanding the finding made by the learned trial judge that the arrest of the accused pursuant to section 30 of the Offences Against the State Act 1939, was an arrest in respect of a genuine offence based upon a genuine belief that the accused might have committed such an offence, the arrest was unlawful unless on behalf of the prosecution it was established beyond a reasonable doubt that the predominant or primary motive for the arrest of the accused was the necessity to investigate the offence of maiming cattle, and
> (b) A question of law as to whether, even if the arrest of the accused pursuant to section 30 of the Offences Against the State Act 1939 was lawful, the extension of his detention for a further twenty-four hours ordered by Chief superintendent O'Connor was unlawful by reason of the fact that he was not informed of the desire of members of the Garda Síochána interviewing the accused to interview him not only in respect of the offence of maiming cattle but also in respect of a suspicion of an offence of murder.

The Supreme Court in a judgment delivered on 29 July 1988, dismissed the appeal and confirmed the conviction. The headnote of the judgment of the Supreme Court appears in Part III at p. 300, below.

David Butler SC and Patrick Gageby **for the appellant**
Hugh O'Flaherty SC and Fergal Foley **for the DPP**

FINLAY CJ

This is an application for leave to appeal against a conviction for murder entered in the central Criminal Court on the 18th of July 1986 on an indictment charging the applicant that on a date unknown between the 29th of May 1985 and the 9th of June 1985 within the County of Mayo he murdered Lily Ormsby.

The grounds of appeal are two in number and are confined to a ruling made by the learned trial judge, Barron J, in the absence of the jury, admitting in evidence oral statements and statements in writing alleged to have been made by the accused of an incriminatory nature, on the 27th of June 1985 while he was in custody in the garda station in Ballina.

The facts

The deceased, who resided as a tenant or lodger, in a house the property of the accused, in Ballina, was last seen alive in that house on the evening of Wednesday, the 29th of May 1985. Her body was subsequently discovered in a lake some distance outside Ballina on the 9th of June 1985, and she obviously had been dead for a considerable time. The cause of death was found to be drowning.

At 11.30 a.m. on the 26th of June 1985 the applicant was arrested by a member of the Garda Síochána pursuant to section 30 of the Offences Against the State Act 1939 on suspicion of having committed a scheduled offence, namely the maiming of cattle at Ballina in the County of Mayo on the 12th of February 1984. During the day of the 26th of June, the applicant was interrogated by a number of members of the Garda Síochána, part of the interrogation concerning the incident of the maiming of the cattle and at other times the interrogation concerning the disappearance of the deceased. The applicant went to bed shortly after midnight on the evening of Wednesday, the 26th of June, and was again interrogated in the morning. At approximately half past ten, Chief Superintendent O'Connor signed an extension order extending the detention of the applicant under section 30 for a further twenty-four hours and this was read over to the applicant at approximately 11.20 a.m. Shortly after noon on the 27th of June the applicant is alleged to have made an admission of the crime of murdering Lily Ormsby. It was taken down in writing and purports to have been signed by him. He made further statements and visited the area in the lake where the body of the deceased was found. The applicant at the trial and on oath in his evidence denied that the statement was his or that he made it and denied complicity in the crime.

From the time of the discovery of the body of the deceased the applicant was, on the admission of the Garda Síochána, a suspect in the event of it being established that her death was a murder. He was interviewed by members of the Garda Síochána on two occasions and denied any knowledge concerning her disappearance or death.

On the 12th of Feraury 1984 a complaint was made to the Garda Síochána in Ballina by one Sean Geraghty, a number of whose cattle having strayed from land on which they were being grazed had apparently been maimed and some of them had died. This complaint was extensively investigated by the Gardaí after it was made to them, and suspicion rested on the applicant and his brother who owned a farm of land, near to the complainant, upon which the cattle were apparently trespassing before being discovered to be injured. An internal garda file on this apparent crime was opened and was put in evidence at the hearing of this trial. It indicates that investigations were continued from time to time and that the superintendent in charge at the time of the Ballina Garda Station and the chief superintendent stationed in Castlebar both took an active interest in the crime which they considered to be one of considerable importance and seriousness. On the file it appears that the suggestion was made on a number of occasions that the applicant and his brother should be arrested pursuant to section 30 of the Offences Against the State Act 1939 and should be interrogated with regard to the suspicion concerning this crime. Comments occurred of difficulties with regard to staffing which made this inopportune at various times and also the comment occurs on the file that they would be unlikely to make admissions unless interviewed over a period. No concrete evidence from other witnesses against them appears to have been obtained by the Garda Síochána. The last entry on this file was that of Chief Superintendent O'Connor of Castlebar, entered on the 23th of May 1985, which directed that the enquiries into the crime were to continue and that a further report was to be made to him in three months, or sooner if necessary.

The challenge to the admissibility of the statements alleged to have been made by the applicant while in custody made at the trial was the same as the issues arising on this appeal.

It was contended on behalf of the applicant that in order to make admissible statements concerning the disappearance of the deceased made by the applicant whilst under detention pursuant to his arrest under section 30 it would have been necessary for the prosecution to establish beyond a reasonable doubt that the predominant or primary motive for the arrest of the accused was the necessity to investigate the offence of maiming the cattle and that the prosecution had failed to do so. It was asserted that having regard to the relative seriousness of the crime of murder compared to the crime of maiming the cattle and to the importance, from the Garda Síochána point of view, in investigating the crime of murder to have an opportunity of interrogating this applicant, that a desire to solve the offence of maiming the cattle, which was then sixteen months old, could not have been the predominant or primary motive for the arrest.

Having reviewed the authorities submitted to him, the learned trial judge ruled that the arrest was lawful, as also was the extension of the further twenty-four hours and that that being the only challenge to the admissibility of the statements, admitted the statements in evidence. The terms of his ruling are as follows:

> The test is: was the arrest in respect of a genuine offence? If it was, then the detention was lawful. The motive of the arresting officer is not queried. Accordingly it is not necessary to consider what was the predominant or primary motive for the arrest, nor to consider whether or not the arrest would have been affected if there had been no murder investigation in being.
>
> The sole test is: was the arrest in respect of a real offence and was there a genuine belief that the person arrested might have committed such offence? In the present case the answer to both questions is Yes.
>
> Counsel further makes the point that the extension order must be generally made in like circumstances. He contends it was made solely to enable the murder investigation to continue. Again the test is the same. Clearly the offence continued to be a real offence. Further, there was no suggestion that there was no longer a genuine belief that the accused committed such offence. This contention fails.

An issue close to this precise issue came before the Supreme Court in the case of *The People (DPP) v Patrick Lynch* [1986] I.R. 722, the case being a reference to that Court by the Court of Criminal Appeal pursuant to section 29 of the Courts of Justice Act 1924. The facts of that case were that a lady residing in Kerry and having a shop in her house was murdered by a person or persons who in order to gain access to the room in which she was and where she was killed broke a pane of glass in the door between the shop premises and the dwelling premises, and also damaged a heavy iron pot which was thought to be the murder weapon. The applicant in that case was arrested pursuant to section 30 of the Offences Against the State Act, on suspicion of being involved in the breaking of the glass window in the door and of the iron pot, and, on being interrogated made admissions with regard to the crime of murder. In the course of his judgment Walsh J stated as follows on p. 731 of the report:

The facts of this case disclose unquestionably that the alleged offence of malicious damage was very insignificant in comparison with the offence of murder. The fact also disclose, notwithstanding the difference in the seriousness between the two offences, that there was a connection between them in that the case of the prosecution was and is that it was sufficient to establish a case fit to go to a jury that the malicious damage was caused in the course of and as part of the incident which led to the fatal assault upon the deceased. The facts of the case also disclose that the members of the Garda Síochána were generally concerned to ascertain the author of the malicious damage in question because it was manifestly clear that the damage and the death were so connected that the author of the malicious damage, more than likely, was in some way connected with the death of the deceased.

The fact that there was a great disproportion between the nature of the offences in question, and that the greater concentration of police effort was on the investigation into the more serious of them, namely, the murder charge, is not in itself sufficient to establish as a reasonable probability that the arrest in respect of the malicious damage charge was simply a colourable device to hold the accused in custody for an ulterior purpose on an alleged offence in which the guards had no real interest. The real question in this case is whether, on the evidence, there resided in the minds of the Garda Síochána a genuine interest in the malicious damage and a desire to pursue it. All the evidence in the case indicates the answer to this is in the affirmative. That being so, I am satisfied that the learned trial judge was warranted in holding that the arrest under section 30 of the Offences Against the State 1939, in respect of the scheduled offence of malicious damage was *bona fide*, and genuinely motivated an arrest on the suspicion of having committed that offence.

In the case of *The People (DPP) v Quilligan* [1986] I.R. 495 which was appealed by the DPP from a decision of the Central Criminal Court acquitting the accused by direction, the Supreme Court held that an arrest of the applicant under section 30 was lawful where he was suspected to have been invovled with others in the murder of a man in his own home, the motive apparently being robbery, and where the entry into the home involved the damaging of a bolt on one door and the receiving lock on another, and where in the course of a struggle within the home and the ransacking of it for money and valuables certain items of furniture had been damaged. Consideration of the judgments in that case, which dealt with other matters not here arising, would again indicate that the test which the Court applied was whether there was a genuine suspicion on the part of the gardaí that the applicant had been guilty of being involved in these offences of malicious damage, which were scheduled offences, and once having concluded that there was such a *bona fide* suspicion, the Court ruled that the arrest was lawful and that statements taken during it to which there was no other objection were admissible, even though the importance of that offence was very slight indeed in relation to the offence of murder which the gardaí were investigating. In that case it was also clearly laid down that where a person has been arrested under section 30 of the Offences Against the State Act 1939 it is lawful and proper for members of the Garda Síochána duing the period of his detention to interrogate him about matters other than those on the suspicion of which he was arrested, though of course he has no obligation to answer such questions and, of course, such interrogation must be conducted in accordance with the Judges' Rules and with the fair procedures which have been laid down.

In the present case, the learned trial judge's ruling that the garda had a genuine suspicion of the applicant as being involved in the maiming of the cattle and had a genuine interest in seeking to have that crime solved was well supported by the evidence and is not contested by the applicant on this appeal. It is clear on the evidence which was accepted with regard to this ruling that the applicant was, during the period of his detention frequently and persistently interrogated about the maiming of the cattle as well as being interrogated about the disappearance of the deceased. There can, of course, be no question but that the guards must have been more concerned with solving the apparent crime involving the death of the deceased than they were in solving the crime of the maiming of the cattle. Chief Superintendent O'Connor gave evidence which the learned trial judge accepted, however, that the question of maiming cattle, particularly in a rural area, remained a very serious crime indeed, and one he would be anxious to see solved.

If this Court were to apply the test contended for on behalf of the applicant, namely, of a predominant or primary motive for the arrest of the applicant, it would, in the view of this Court, be introducing two wholly new and unsupported principles into the consideration of this question. The first would be that the motive or intention of the arresting officer as distinct from the *bona fide* could be the determining factor for the rights of members of the Garda Síochána interrogating the person detained and for the rights of the person detained and the admissibility of evidence obtained from such interrogations. The second would be that a person who was arrested on a *bona fide* suspicion of the commission of a scheduled offence and detained under section 30 of the Offences Against the State Act would, if he were under suspicion for a significantly more serious crime at the same time, be in some way immune from questioning on that serious crime.

The Court is satisfied that the true construction of the cases to which it has referred and of other authorities which were submitted in the course of the argument must be that the test remains as it was stated to be in *The People (DPP) v Walsh* [1986] I.R. 722 and *The People (DPP) v Quilligan* [1986] I.R. 495, and that is that the Court must ascertain whether the arrest under section 30 is a genuine arrest *bona fide* carried out on a suspicion actually held of complicity by the applicant in a real scheduled offence. If it is, then the arrest is and remains lawful and statements made which otherwise cannot be objected to on grounds of fairness or the form of questioning with regard to any matter must be admissible in evidence. If, on the other hand, the arrest is made as a device to secure the detention of a person who is not really under a *bona fide* suspicion with regard to the commission of a real scheduled offence but whom the gardaí wish to interview with regard to murder which is not a scheduled offence then the position is different.

The Court is, therefore, satisfied that the first ground of appeal, namely, that the arrest of the applicant was unlawful, must fail. The statements which were tendered in evidence and which are the incriminatory statements were all alleged to be made after the time when the first twenty-four hours of the applicant's detention had expired and he was being detained pursuant to the purported extension for a further twenty-four hours. It is, therefore, contended on behalf of the applicant that even if the arrest was lawful that the evidence did not support a finding made by the learned trial judge that the extension was also lawful. On the evidence given, Chief Superintendent O'Connor made the extension order stated that he was informed by Inspector McCallion who was in charge of the Ballina Station, of the desire of the Inspector, partly based on recent information obtained, to have the applicant interrogated with regard to the maiming of the cattle. He was further informed coming to the end of the first twenty-four hours that a further period of twenty-four hours of the following day would be necessary to complete these investigations. He was not informed that parallel with this interrogation interrogation was being conducted concerning the disappearance of the deceased. The learned trial judge held that the information which was laid before the chief superintendent which concerned the charge of the subject matter of the actual arrest under section 30 was the relevant information and that once he came to a *bona fide* decision on that information that the Court could not set aside that decision or find it to be invalid. This Court is satisfied that that is the true and correct ruling to have made. The Court cannot put itself in the position of exercising the discretion which is granted to the chief superintendent by the terms of the section, and there is not any evidence which was before the trial judge which would have permitted him to reach a conclusion that the chief superintendent's decision was based on some erroneous principle or that he failed to have regard to some matter which would have been relevant. In these circumstances, the application for leave to appeal must be dismissed.

Solicitor for the applicant: *Adrian P. Bourke & Co.*
Solicitor for the respondent: *Chief State Solicitor*

Eithne Casey
Barrister

The People (Director of Public Prosecutions) v Yvonne Donaghy
[C.C.A. No. 50 of 1987]

Court of Criminal Appeal   25 July 1988

Arrest – validity – purpose of arrest – detention after arrest – improper motive – desire to obtain evidence – additional purpose of arrest to bring person before a court – court appearance – identification of suspect by injured party – breach of constitutional rights

The appellant was tried on counts of robbery and assault by the Dublin Circuit Court. She was convicted and sentenced to two years imprisonment.

The facts of the case were that a pedestrian had been attacked and robbed by three youths and a girl. The appellant was subsequently arrested by a garda who had reliable information, but no admissible evidence, that she had been involved in the attack. She was brought to a garda station and charged and was then brought to the Children's Court, where it was expected that the injured party would be present. The appellant was then identified by the injured party as one of the persons who had attacked him.

At the trial, the arresting garda agreed that after arrest his purpose was to have her at the Court at a time when the injured party would be present to see if he could identify her and that he also had the purpose of bringing the appellant before a Court as soon as reasonably practicable.

On application to the Court of Criminal Appeal, the appellant was granted leave to appeal and bail pending her appeal.

It was argued on her behalf that the purpose of the arrest was to secure evidence; that when the appellant was brought to the Children's Court, the arresting garda had no admissible evidence in law and that if a positive identification had not been obtained outside the Children's Court that would have been the end of the case.

Held by the Court (McCarthy, Egan and Blayney JJ) in allowing the appeal, that the arrest was unlawful, because the conduct of the gardaí was tainted by an ulterior motive and that the evidence of identification was obtained by illegal means and involved a breach of the constitutional rights of the appellant and must be rejected. (*People (DPP) v Walsh* [1980] I.R. 294 applied; *People (Attorney General) v O'Brien* [1965] I.R. 142 considered.)

Cases cited in this judgment:
People (Attorney General) v O'Brien [1965] I.R. 142
People (DPP) v Walsh [1980] I.R. 294

Bruce Antoniotti **for the appellant**
Donal O'Donnell **for the respondent**

McCarthy J

On Sunday, 5 October 1986, shortly after 2 a.m., Vincent Kavanagh, while walking down Griffith Avenue Extension in the City of Dublin, was engaged in conversation by a group of three young men and a girl who walked with him for a few minutes down the road. They then assaulted and robbed him; the girl took a chain off his neck and spat in his face. This appeal concerns the conviction of Yvonne Donaghy, whom Mr Kavanagh subsequently identified as the girl who had assaulted and robbed him. After a trial in the Dublin Circuit Court she was convicted on 3 April 1987, on counts of robbery and assault, for which she was sentenced to two years imprisonment. On application to this Court on 11 May 1987, she was granted leave to appeal and bail pending appeal. Having heard argument on 16 May 1988, this Court allowed the appeal and quashed the convictions; it now states its reasons.

The issue at the trial was that of identification. Vincent Kavanagh identified the appellant when he saw her in the vicinity of the Children's Court at Smithfield, Dublin on 13 October 1986. The quality of the

identification, having regard to its circumstances, was challenged but that
is not relevant now. The appellant was arrested at 6.30 a.m. on 13 October
by Garda McIntyre. It is common case that the warrant, issued by a peace
commissioner, was, for reasons not relevant, invalid and, consequently,
the arrest was unlawful. There is no suggestion that the defects in procedure were other than accidental; there was no conscious impropriety on
the part of Garda McIntyre. After arrest, the appellant was brought to and
charged at Finglas Garda Station and, then, to the Children's Court
building at Smithfield, where it was known that another accused, David
Kearns, who was a minor, would be appearing on remand charged with
offences arising out of the same incident. Garda McIntyre had reliable
information that the appellant was the girl involved, but had no admissible
evidence to that effect. Garda McIntyre whilst stating that he had the
additional purpose of bringing the appellant before a Court as soon as
reasonably practicable after arrest agreed that his purpose was to have her
at the particular Court at a time when Vincent Kavanagh would be present
to see if he would identify her.

In *People (DPP) v Walsh* [1980] I.R. 294 at p. 300 O'Higgins CJ said:

> However, such an arrest and subsequent detention is only justified
> at common law if it is exercised for the purpose of which the right
> exists, which is the bringing of an arrested person to justice before a
> court. If it appears that the arresting gardaí have no evidence on which
> to charge the person arrested, or cannot justify the suspicion on which
> he was arrested, he must be released. He cannot be detained while
> investigations are carried out. Reasonable expedition is required but
> more than this cannot be demanded. Regard must be had to the
> circumstances and to the time of the arrest. If a person is arrested late
> at night, it scarcely seems unreasonable if he is held overnight and
> charged before a court the following morning. The important thing is
> that his detention after arrest must be only for the purpose of bringing
> him before a District Justice or a peace commissioner with reasonable
> expedition so that a court can decide whether he is to remain in custody
> or to be released on bail.

If evidence is obtained by illegal means, involving a breach of
constitutional rights, it is difficult to see how that may not, of itself, lead
to the rejection of the evidence. When this is combined with an ulterior,

if not improper, motive or purpose, the trial court must reject such evidence. If the District Justice, in the present case, had asked Garda McIntyre if he had any evidence to connect the appellant with the crime he would have been forced to answer "not yet but I hope to have it if the victim arrives in time to identify her here in Court or outside Court"; the District Justice would have been bound to direct her immediate discharge. So also is the court of trial. It is unnecessary to consider the further argument on behalf of the Director to the effect that the reasoning of *People (Attorney General) v O'Brien* [1965] I.R. 142 excusing the illegality of breach of constitutional rights could be applied in the instant appeal. Suffice it to say that in *O'Brien's* case the conduct of the gardaí was not tainted by any ulterior motive; it was a case of a typing error.

Solicitor for the appellant: *Dermot Morris & Co.*
Solicitor for the respondent: *Chief State Solicitor*

Eithne Casey
Barrister

The People (Director of Public Prosecutions) v J.T.
(Attorney General, Notice Party)
[C.C.A. No. 106 of 1986]

Court of Criminal Appeal   27 July 1988

Evidence – sexual offences – incest – wife called as witness for the prosecution – whether competent to testify against husband – Criminal Justice (Evidence) Act 1924 (No. 37), section 1 – whether carried over by Article 50 of the Constitution

Complainant – mental handicap – whether competent to give sworn evidence – use of anatomical dolls at trial

Corroboration – complaint – credibility – remoteness

Constitution – rights of the family – personal rights of individuals within the family – violation of bodily integrity of child by parent – whether spouse permitted to give evidence against an accused spouse – whether also compellable – common law rule preventing spouses testifying against each other in a criminal prosecution – whether rule carried over by Article 50 of the Constitution – Constitution of Ireland 1937, Articles 40, 41 and 50

Section 1 of the Criminal Justice (Evidence) Act 1924 provides *inter alia* that:—

(c) The wife or husband of the person charged shall not, save as in this Act mentioned, be called as a witness in pursuance of this Act except upon the application of the person so charged.

The applicant was tried by a jury at the Dublin Circuit (Criminal) Court and found guilty on five counts of sexual offences against his daughter. The offences concerned incest, buggery and indecent assault. The offences were alleged to have been committed on dates unknown between September 1977 and June 1985. The applicant was sentenced to three years penal servitude in respect of buggery and indecent assault and to five years penal servitude on each of the counts of incest. All sentences were to run concurrently.

The applicant's daughter, the victim of the offences which were alleged to have taken place between the ages of 11 and 19, suffered from Downs Syndrome. After examination by the trial judge as to her understanding of the oath, she was permitted to give sworn evidence. She was aged 20 at the date of the trial.

The applicant insisted on representing himself at the trial despite the advice of the trial judge. During his cross-examination of witnesses for the prosecution he elicited information prejudicial to his own case on matters that had not been referred to by the prosecution in spite of a warning by the trial judge that he should confine his cross-examination to what the witness had said in examination-in-chief.

The daughter had some difficulty and embarrassment in giving her evidence. She was permitted to have her mother sit beside her near the witness box. The trial judge permitted to be introduced anatomical dolls, which show the parts of the human body, to assist the daughter because of her limited use of language in giving her evidence after she had described in a general way penetration by her father's penis into her own body.

The wife of the applicant gave evidence of the relationship of herself, the child and her husband as a witness for the prosecution. The issue of the competence of the wife to give evidence against her husband in respect of the counts of buggery and incest was not adverted to by either side or by the judge at the trial.

The applicant was refused liberty to appeal by the trial judge. He appealed this refusal to the Court of Criminal Appeal. He obtained legal representation and the grounds of appeal are set out in the judgment. The principal grounds of appeal argued before the Court were an additional two grounds which counsel for the applicant obtained leave of the Court to adduce namely:—

1. The trial judge erred in allowing the daughter to be sworn and to give evidence on oath without the Court satisfying itself that she understood the concept and meaning of an "oath" and "truth" or without making any satisfactory enquiry that she was competent to give sworn evidence.

2. The trial judge erred in allowing the prosecution to adduce evidence from the wife of the accused when she was not a competent witness.

Counsel for the applicant argued that at common law there was a general rule that the spouse of a party in a criminal trial was not competent to testify against the other spouse. He relied also on the provisions of the Act of 1924, and said that the statutory exceptions to the common law rule did not apply to incest or buggery. Counsel for the Director of Public Prosecutions argued that if there was such a rule, it was inconsistent with the provisions of Article 41 of the Constitution. He further argued that a mother may be in a particularly good position to give corroborative evidence in cases such as this. He said that if a child was incompetent to take the oath a mother's evidence may be the only evidence available. He argued that the Constitution guarded the family in a particular way and that incest strikes at the fundamental premise upon which the family was built and that each member of the family had a right to be protected from unjust attack which occurred from within the family.

The Court directed, pursuant to O. 60, r. 2 of the Rules of the Superior Courts, 1986, that notice should be served on the Attorney General to enable him to appear or be represented. On the resumption of the application on 7 March, 1988 the Attorney General was represented and counsel on his behalf supported all the submissions in respect of the constitutional aspect of the case put forward by counsel for the Director of Public Prosecutions.

Held by the Court (Walsh, Costello and Barron JJ) in refusing the application:

(1) That having regard to the run of the case, the complainant could not be regarded as an unreliable witness by reason of her handicap, she was able to understand the nature of the evidence she gave and her recollection could be relied upon. Furthermore the trial judge was justified in allowing her to be sworn and the transcript indicated that she understood the nature of an oath and what was meant by truth.

(2) That in the circumstances of the case the trial judge was justified in allowing the daughter to use the anatomical dolls to assist her in giving evidence after she had given general evidence of sexual contact between herself and her father.

(3) That the trial judge warned the jury of the danger of acting upon the uncorroborated evidence of complainants in sexual cases; however there was evidence elicited by the applicant in his cross-examination of the witnesses which, if its truth was accepted, amounted to corroboration.

(4) That in the circumstances of the case the evidence of the complaint, which goes to support of the credibility of the complainant, was not too remote and was rightly admitted.

(5) That the trial judge discharged his duty to protect the interests of the applicant having regard to the difficulties he encountered in giving good advice to him.

(6) That where a husband was indicted for assaults on his child the wife was a competent witness. If she was not willing to give evidence, she could be compelled to do so. (*McGonagle v McGonagle* [1951] I.R. 123 considered. *Hoskyn v Metropolitan Police Commissioner* [1979] A.C. 474 and *Leach v Rex* [1912] A.C. 305 not followed.)

(7) The evidence of the wife in this case which, apart from that which proved the birth and paternity of the daughter, was elicited by the applicant, and was admissible and relevant and the common law rule that she was not a competent or compellable witness against her husband, with regard to offences which injured the family, and any provision of the Criminal Justice (Evidence) Act 1924 which provides that she was not competent, was inconsistent with the Constitution and could not be deemed to have been carried over into law by Article 50 of the Constitution. (*The State (Browne) v Feran* [1967] I.R. 147 followed.

(8) Every individual within the family had personal rights which must be vindicated in the case of injustice done and all necessary relevant evidence on which that vindication depends must be available in Court. The public had a right to every person's evidence except those who were privileged and the judicial power did not admit any other body of persons to decide whether or not certain evidence would be produced in Court. The sole power of resolving any conflict of interest involved in the non-disclosure of evidence resided in the courts. In so far as there might be a conflict between the individual within the family and the rights of the family as a unit which was protected by Article 41 of the Constitution, sexual

offences committed by a spouse on a child were subversive of family life itself, and could not be concealed and permitted to go unpunished.

Cases cited in this judgment
    Hawkins v United States (1958) 358 U.S. 74
    Hoskyn v Metropolitan Police Commissioner [1979] A.C. 474; [1978] 2 W.L.R. 695;
        [1978] 2 All E.R. 136; 67 Cr. App. R. 88
    Lady Ivy's Trial (1684) 10 St. Tr. 555
    Leach v Rex [1912] A.C. 305
    Lord Audley's Trial (1631) Hut. 115; 1 Hale 629; 3 St. Tr. 401
    McGonagle v McGonagle [1951] I.R. 123; [1952] Ir. Jur. Rep. 13
    Murphy v Attorney General [1982] I.R. 241
    Murphy v Dublin Corporation [1972] I.R. 215; 107 I.L.T.R. 65
    O'Kelly, In re (1974) 108 I.L.T.R. 97
    People (DPP) v Tiernan [1988] I.R. 250; [1989] ILRM 149
    Rex v Wasson (1796) 1 Cr. & Dix, C.C. 197
    Ryan v Attorney General [1965] I.R. 294
    State (Browne) v Feran [1967] I.R. 147
    State (Nicolaou) v An Bord Uchtála [1966] I.R. 567; 102 I.L.T.R. 1

Kevin Haugh SC and Gregory Murphy **for the applicant**
Peter Charleton **for the respondent**
Aindrias O Caoimh **for the notice party**

Walsh J

On 11 November 1986, the applicant was tried and convicted by a jury at the Circuit Court in Dublin. He had been indicted on six counts of sexual offences against his daughter and had been found guilty on five of them. On one of the counts, namely a charge of indecent assault as provided for by section 10, subsection (1) of the Criminal Law (Rape) Act 1981, he was acquitted by direction of the trial judge. The offences of which he was found guilty were:

(a) buggery contrary to section 61 of the Offences Against the Person Act 1861;

(b) indecent assault as provided for by section 10, subsection (1) of the Criminal Law (Rape) Act 1981;

(c) incest contrary to section 1 of the Punishment of Incest Act 1908;

(d) incest contrary to the same statutory provision; and

(e) incest also contrary to the same statutory provision.

The first offence was alleged to have been committed on a date unknown between 19 September 1977 and 1 June 1985 in the county of the city of Dublin. All of the other offences were laid as having been committed also on a date unknown between the same dates. The first count of incest was laid as having been committed within the county of the city of Dublin and the second and third counts of incest were laid as having been committed within the State.

In respect of the count of buggery he was sentenced to three years penal servitude, in respect of the count of indecent assault he was also sentenced to three years penal servitude and in respect of the three counts of incest he was sentenced to five years penal servitude on each of them. It was directed that all five sentences should run concurrently.

Immediately after the sentencing the applicant applied to the trial judge for liberty to appeal and this was refused. The judge told him he might apply to this Court. On 20 November 1986, the applicant served a notice of application for leave to appeal in which he indicated that he desired to appeal against the conviction and sentences. The notice of application for leave to appeal contained no grounds, but a statement of the grounds was filed with this Court on 19 January 1988. The grounds of appeal as stated in that document were as follows:—

·1. That the evidence of his wife was unreliable and that insufficient warning as to its unreliability was given by the trial judge to the jury.

2. That there was no adequate corroboration.

3. That the evidence of complaint was too remote and should not have been admitted.

4. That the learned trial judge failed in his duty to protect the interests of the accused in the particular circumstances of the case.

5. That the trial judge should have intervened at the end of the case for the prosecution on the basis that the applicant would have been entitled to a direction for an acquittal and that there was no case to answer.

The applicant also asked for the costs of the application for leave to appeal and of the appeal. At this stage the applicant, who had defended himself at his trial, was already represented by counsel for the purpose of this application.

When the present application came on for hearing before this Court on 18 February 1988, counsel on behalf of the applicant asked permission to serve additional grounds of appeal. In view of the importance of the issues raised in the additional grounds of appeal the Court allowed this application to file additional grounds of appeal.

The additional grounds of appeal were as follows:—

1. The trial judge erred in allowing the daughter (the alleged victim

of the offences) to be sworn and to give evidence on oath without the Court satisfying itself that she understood the concept and meaning of an "oath" and "truth" or without making any satisfactory enquiry that she was competent to give sworn evidence.

2. That the trial judge erred in allowing the prosecution to adduce evidence from the wife of the accused when "she was not a competent witness".

At the commencement of the trial counsel for the prosecution drew the trial judge's attention to the provisions of section 20 of the Criminal Justice Act 1951, and invited him to exercise his discretion to exclude from the Court all persons except the witnesses in the case. The judge having inquired of the accused if he had any objection to this and upon being assured that the accused had no objection agreed, though somewhat reluctantly, to exercise his discretion to exclude members of the public who were not witnesses in the trial. The judge's reluctance to do so was entirely due to his desire to uphold the principle, which is enshrined in Article 34, subsection 1 of the Constitution that justice shall be administered in public. The applicant insisted on representing himself. He was twice queried by the trial judge on this attitude and his attention was drawn to the existence of the free legal aid scheme although it did not appear that the applicant's desire to represent himself was due to want of means. Counsel for the prosecution, very properly, in view of the fact that the applicant was defending himself, drew the attention of the trial judge to the fact that most of the contents of the book of evidence served upon the applicant was not admissible in law, and that he would only lead the portions of it which were relevant and admissible. Counsel for the prosecution also invited the applicant to indicate if there was anything he, the applicant, would object to being referred to by counsel for the prosecution in his opening address to the jury. On the suggestion of the judge, because the nature of the case, counsel for the prosecution agreed that it was desirable that the opening address should be a very short one. It does not appear that the applicant indicated any matter which he did not wish to be referred to in the opening address. At the date of the trial the daughter, who is the alleged victim of the offences charged, was 20 years old. Therefore, the period of time within which the alleged offences were said to have been committed ranged from when she was approximately 11 years old up to the time she was approximately 19 years old. Although the girl was 20 years old at the date of the trial, nevertheless because of some degree of handicap she was alleged to suffer, and which had been outlined to the jury by the prosecuting counsel in his opening address, the judge asked her certain questions to ascertain if she understood the meaning of the word "oath" to which she replied she did. She was then asked if she understood what it meant to tell the truth and she said she did. At that the judge expressed himself satisfied and did not further question her and she was duly sworn.

It emerged from her evidence that she lived at home with her mother and one of her sisters, but that formerly three other sisters had lived at home. Two of them had since left home, at least one of them being married. The applicant and his wife had been living apart for eight years prior to the date of the trial. During that period the applicant had lived in at least two, if not more, different addresses in Dublin. During that period of separation the applicant often visited his daughter at the mother's home, apparently every week. It would appear that so far as the visits to the home were concerned they took place during weekends. During this period, or most of this period, the daughter was attending a residential school in Cabra in Dublin which specially catered for handicapped people, but she spent each weekend in her family home. It appeared also from her evidence that her father visited her on at least one occasion at the school in Cabra.

On the occasions of his visits the applicant used to bring his daughter for drives in a motor-car. It appears from the transcript of the evidence that the daughter had some difficulty, and indeed embarrassment, in giving her evidence. At one stage she asked, and was permitted, to have her mother sit beside her near the witness box. It appeared from her general evidence that the girl knew what constituted male and female genital and sexual organs and her genital area generally, and described in a general way penetration by her father's penis into her own body at various times. The judge permitted to be introduced, and used to assist her in giving her evidence, objects which are called anatomical dolls such as are used in the Sexual Assault unit in the Rotunda Hospital. These dolls were explained as being correctly structured to show the parts of the human body. The application on behalf of the prosecution was to permit the girl to demonstrate what occurred between herself and her father with the assistance of these dolls because of her limited use of language. The initial application was refused by the judge until the evidence had developed somewhat but when the girl had given the general evidence of sexual contact between herself and her father and of some form of sexual penetration the judge acceded to a further application to allow anatomical dolls to be used. On the basis of her evidence given with the assistance of these dolls it is abundantly clear, that if her evidence was accepted, both carnal knowledge and buggery were established. Her general evidence also, if accepted, would be sufficient to sustain a charge of indecent assault. It should be added that in the course of giving evidence the girl used anatomical dolls which represented both the female body and the male body. The incidents complained of were alleged to have occurred in the applicant's flat and also in his motor-car. The girl was cross-examined by the applicant. The general object of the cross-examination was apparently to demonstrate the improbability of the event, if not the actual difficulty or impossibility, of the incidents alleged to have occurred in the motor-car. The applicant's cross-examination of his daughter also consisted of some questions which themselves contained information of a character prejudicial to the applicant himself. This was in reference to matters which had not been hitherto referred to in the case and the total effect of which must have been quite damaging to the applicant in the eyes of the jury.

The prosecution also called as a witness, Dr Maura Woods, who works in the Sexual Assault Unit of the Rotunda Hospital and who had interviewed and examined the girl on 10 September 1985, and who gave evidence of what was found upon physical examination. It is unnecessary to go into the details of her evidence but the effect of it was that the condition in which she found the girl's vagina and her rectum were consistent with abusive dilation. The cross-examination of Dr Woods by the applicant was also of a nature which could only be regarded as prejudicial to the applicant's own case. At one stage the judge warned the accused that it was in his own interest to confine his cross-examination to what the witness had said in the witness box and not to introduce a lot of other prejudicial matter. The Court is of the opinion that the applicant, in refusing to heed the judge's warning, undoubtedly damaged his case in the eyes of the jury.

The prosecution called the applicant's wife as a witness. The first question she was asked was to give the date of the birth of the daughter, which she gave as 10 April 1966. She also identified the applicant as the girl's father and that they had all lived together as a family in the same house until the father and mother separated some eight years before the date of the trial. The witness' attention was then directed to a specific date, namely, 9 September 1985, when she and the daughter in question were looking at a television programme in their home. The television programme was one of a well-known police series known as "Cagney and Lacey" and the particular programme was a story dealing with the investigation of a case of incest. Apparently in that programme the culprit, the father, was brought to justice. The mother of the complainant gave evidence to the effect that on seeing the programme the daughter expressed her satisfaction that the father in the film had been apprehended. That was the sum total of the witness' evidence until the applicant began to cross-examine her. As a result of that cross-examination it emerged that the daughter had told her mother that the applicant had done similar things to her as those illustrated in the television programme. There was some dispute as to the actual date of the programme between the applicant and his wife as he was cross-examining her. Furthermore, some very damaging evidence emerged in the cross-examination including an answer from the wife that the only pornographic books she has ever seen were those of the applicant. It also emerged in cross-examination that the daughter complained to the mother on 3 September 1985 about sexual misbehaviour on the applicant's part with the daughter. It further emerged in the cross-examination that many years earlier the wife had complained to the applicant that he had interfered with the daughter sexually though not in the form of having sexual intercouse with her. Several other matters of a highly prejudicial character emerged as a result of the applicant's persistent cross-examination of his wife and which it is unnecessary to detail here.

Another witness called for the prosecution was the girl's sister. The total effect of her evidence in direct examination was that she did not live in the family home. She was then cross-examined at some length by her father and this again elicited a great deal of material which was prejudicial to the applicant's case. The effect of this was to have the witness repeat to the Court the somewhat detailed complaints which had been made to her by the girl of what she claimed to have suffered at the hands of her father. Another sister of the girl, a married sister, was also called to testify for the prosecution. The sum total of her evidence was to describe the different addresses at which the girl lived and the fact that her father would come on occasions to take the girl out for a drive, and that the period they were away would last several hours. She also gave evidence of the fact that on one occasion her father had been in Tramore with the girl and that the girl had spoken to her on the telephone in what appeared to be a very distressed condition and that during that telephone conversation she could hear the applicant's voice in the distance and that he made an exclamation and took the telephone from the girl and spoke to the sister giving evidence. She had asked him to bring the girl to her as she appeared to be obviously distressed but he said "No" and said that the girl would be alright. Once again the applicant's persistent cross-examination of this witness elicited more material damaging to the applicant's case.

The applicant put in evidence tape recordings he had made on various occasions he had been with his daughter and these were played to the jury. The contents of these tapes were not transcribed on the transcript of the evidence given to this Court. However the purpose of the tapes apparently was to show that on the occasions on which the recordings were made the relationship between the father and the daughter appeared to have been a very happy one. This is the point made by the accused when addressing the jury. In his address the applicant also referred to the possibility of sexual interference by some unknown person with occurring his daughter while she was in the home in Cabra. Perhaps the best description comes from the judge's reference to this matter in his charge to the jury. The following quotation from the transcript of the judge's words indicates the general nature of the tapes:

"The accused, himself, gave evidence in relation to the tapes. I think you should consider the tapes carefully, or the tape. It was hard to hear but it was . . . the impression I got from it — I give it to you for what it is worth — it is that it was a very normal family conversation. It was a happy conversation. The accused was singing and his daughter was laughing happily on a number of occasions and she gave a description of her going out in Tramore, a point that was made play of by the other witness. She said she planned to go out. She went to the amusement park. 'I was watching at the amusements' and she said in a very human way what every child has said when they are being interrogated by their parents about doing something like that 'there was nothing wrong in that'. He described going in search of her and he said he was so relieved when she saw him, 'I remember you kissing me'. It was, as I say, a happy tape, something you have got to take into account. In this regard you should also I think take into account the evidence of Mr Mitchel Fleming, the psychologist, who was called by the prosecution. He gave evidence of examining the daughter in 1983 and of finding her a normal happy child, within the limit of her disability at that stage".

So far as the original grounds of appeal are concerned the Court is quite satisfied that on the run of the case it is apparent that the girl in question could not be regarded as an unreliable witness by reason of her handicap, particularly in the way she was able to cope with the cross-examination and even though, as appears in the evidence, she was to some extent afflicted by Downes Syndrome, there is nothing in the case to suggest that she was unable to understand the nature of the evidence she gave or indeed that her recollection could not be relied upon. It is undoubtedly true that while at times she was embarrassed and found some difficulty in explaining herself, in the circumstances the Court is of opinion that the judge was quite justified in admitting the use in evidence of the anatomical dolls, in view of the ground work that had already been laid with regard to the witness' own testimony. In view of the type of material which was elicited by the applicant in the cross-examination of the complainant and of other witnesses called for the prosecution, the Court is satisfied that, if the jury accepted the truth of the evidence which was given, there was corroboration of the girl's testimony. The learned trial judge warned the jury on the danger of acting upon the un-corroborated evidence of complaintants in cases such as this.

It has been objected that on the evidence the complaint the girl made to her mother was too remote and should not have been admitted. In all the circumstances of the case the Court is of opinion that it would not be regarded as being too remote but however the Court is satisfied that a complaint as such does not amount to corroboration but it does support the credibility of the girl. Corroboration must be some piece of independent testimony which tends to support the truth of what is alleged by the complainant. However the other evidence in the case, in the view of the Court, if its truth is accepted does amount to material which the jury would be justified in regarding as corroboration.

The learned trial judge did his best in the circumstances, having regard to the difficulties encountered by him in trying to give good advice to the applicant, to do his duty and protect the interests of the applicant and the Court is satisfied that the judge cannot be faulted under this heading. The

Court is also of the opinion that the trial judge would not have been justified in directing the jury to acquit the applicant on the grounds that there was no case to answer. If that was all that was in the case the Court would have had to reject this application for leave to appeal.

However, the additional grounds of appeal lodged raised two important matters, the second of which is vital to the present case. The Court is satisfied that the trial judge was justified in allowing the complainant to be sworn and that the transcript indicates clearly that she did understand the nature of an oath and what was meant by "truth" and the run of the case indicates that she was quite competent to give sworn evidence.

It is the second point which is of the utmost importance. That arises from the fact that the wife of the accused gave evidence in this case as a witness for the prosecution. This was a point which was never adverted to throughout the trial by either side or by the judge and raises a point of fundamental importance.

In common law there was a general rule that a spouse of a party was not competent to testify for or against the other spouse. In this case the Court is concerned only with the question of whether or not the wife is a competent witness in the case against her husband.

The Criminal Justice (Evidence) Act 1924 at section 1 provides:

"Every person charged with an offence, and the wife or husband, as the case may be, of the person so charged, shall be a competent witness for the defence at every stage of the proceedings, whether the person so charged is charged solely or jointly with any other person: Provided as follows:—

(a) a person so charged shall not be called as a witness in pursuance of this Act except upon his own application;

(b) the failure of any person charged with an offence, or of the wife or husband, as the case may be, of the person so charged, to give evidence shall not be made the subject of any comment by the prosecution;

(c) the wife or husband of the person charged shall not, save as in this Act mentioned, be called as a witness in pursuance of this Act except upon the application of the person so charged".

In the decision of the former Supreme Court of Justice in *McGonagle v McGonagle* [1951] I.R. 123 it was held that the wife or husband of a person charged with the offence of wilful neglect of a child contrary to section 12 of the Children Act 1908, was competent, by virtue of section 133, subsection 28 of the said Act, notwithstanding the omission of that statute from the Schedule to the Criminal Justice (Evidence) Act 1924. The Court held that the general rule of construction that a prior statute is held to be repealed, by implication, or by a subsequent statute which is inconsistent with it and repugnant to it does not apply where "as in the present case the prior statute is special and the subsequent statute general. In such a case the Court applies the doctrine *generalia specialibus non derogant*. The effect of that decision was that the enactments set out in the Schedule to the 1924 Act were not deemed to have the effect of excluding "special acts". This decision is to be contrasted with a decision on a similar point which arose in England in *Leach v Rex* [1912] A.C. 305. In *McGonagle v McGonagle* [1951] I.R. 123 the argument had been that when section 5 of the Act of 1924 provided that "this Act shall apply to all criminal proceedings" that had the effect that a wife could be a competent witness only in offences in the statutory provisions set out in the Schedule.

There are many statutory provisions prior to 1924 which provide that a wife may be a competent and even a compellable witness for the prosecution under those particular statutory provisions. In the decision in *McGonagle v McGonagle* the effect would appear to be that all such special provisions remain intact notwithstanding the Act of 1924. However all of these are statutory exceptions to a common law rule. Thus the statutory exceptions would have permitted the wife to be a competent witness in the present case insofar as a charge of indecent assault was concerned but did not touch the question of calling her in respect of the other charges. As all of the counts on the indictment were heard together there can be little doubt that if the wife can not be held to be a competent witness in respect of the other charges, the effect must be that her evidence was so prejudicial to the accused that the trial would have to be set aside. While it is true that the part in which she was called by the prosecution did not relate to anything other than the formalities of establishing the relationship of herself, the child and her husband, none the less as a witness she was called by the prosecution and as a result of the imprudent type of cross-examination indulged in by the applicant her evidence could only have been most damaging to the applicant.

Counsel for the applicant in the present case relied upon the provisions of the Act of 1924 and in particular the provisions of section 1 thereof. While accepting the decision in *McGonagle v McGonagle* [1951] I.R. 123, the applicant's counsel made the point that the statutory offences laid in the indictment other than the indecent assault contained no special provisions relating to the competence or compellability of a spouse and therefore must be governed by the common law. Counsel for the Director of Public Prosecutions in effect said that there was no rule of common law whereby a wife was incompetent as a witness against her husband on a charge of incest or of buggery and secondly that even if there had been any such rule, it was one so inimical to, and inconsistent with, the provisions of Article 41 of the Constitution, that any such common law rule must be deemed not to have been carried over by Article 50 of the Constitution. Because of the far-reaching nature of this second submission the Court, pursuant to the Rules of the Superior Courts 1986, directed that notice should be served on the Attorney General pursuant to O. 60, r. 2 of the said rules and adjourned the hearing until 7 March 1988, to enable the Attorney General to appear or be represented as he wished. On the resumption of the hearing the Attorney General was represented and his counsel supported and endorsed all the submissions put forward in respect of the constitutional aspect of the case by counsel for the Director of Public Prosecutions.

It is first necessary to look at the rule itself and the history of it apart from any constitutional context.

It is commonly believed that in common law trials of any sort, spouses were not permitted to be witnesses for or against each other. This rule was based upon different types of reasoning which were not mutually consistent. On the one hand, it was thought that it would be impossible for the testimony of spouses to be impartial or indifferent in any matter affecting the other spouse. Secondly, it was thought that because of the "union of the person" that if they were admitted as witnesses for each other they would contradict another maxim of the law namely, that no one should be a witness in his own cause and, if against each other, that they would contradict another maxim namely that no one is bound to incriminate himself. The rule is not to be confused with the question of the privilege which may attach to confidential communications between husband and wife.

Wigmore on Evidence (3rd Ed. 1940 and 1964 Supplement) offers the view that possibly the true explanation for the disqualification of a spouse from giving evidence against the other was that a natural and strong repugnance was felt, especially in the days of close family unity and rigid paternal authority, to condemning a person by admitting as a witness against a husband a member of his family — a view which derived from Roman law and ecclesiastical law. Those who lived under his roof shared the secrets of his domestic life, depended on him for sustenance and were almost numbered among his chattels. However at common law this exclusion was not adopted in respect of members of the family or servants in the house. The disqualification first appears in the common law in *Coke's Commentary upon Littleton*, Lib 1 Sect 1 6b n6 published in 1628, in which he coupled both privilege and disqualification but with regard to the latter he noted that "it hath been resolved by the justices, that a wife cannot be produced either against or for her husband, *quia sunt duae animae in carne una*; and it might be a cause of implacable discord and dissention between the husband and wife, and a means of great inconvenience, but in some cases women are by law wholly excluded to beare testimony; as to prove a man to be a villeine . . .". Despite the absolute terms of that statement it was already understood that there were exceptions in some types of criminal cases. A statute of Henry VII, Abduction Act 1487 (3 Hen 7. Ch. 2), provided that in any case if a woman had been forcibly taken away and married she could be a witness against her husband in order to convict him of the felony. The justification put forward for that was that as she could not be properly regarded as being his wife because the main ingredient of marriage, namely her consent, was wanting therefore the question of the union of the person did not arise. There was also another maxim of the law that no man should be allowed to take advantage of his own wrong, and that would have been the case if a ravisher could by forcibly marrying a woman prevent her from being a witness, and perhaps the only witness, to that very fact. In *Lord Audley's Trial* (1631) 3 St. Tr. 401 the judges resolved, at p. 402, that a wife might be a witness against her husband for rape upon her instigated by him "for she was the party wronged; otherwise she might be abused". It goes on to say at p. 414 "in civil cases the wife may not (be a witness against him); but in a criminal cause of this nature, where the wife is the party grieved, and on whom the crime is committed, she is to be admitted as a witness against her husband". It appears clear from the case that the privilege or the disqualification was denied for criminal cases in general where the crime was against the wife. In *Lady Ivy's Trial* (1684) 10 St. Tr. 555 the Lord Chief Justice Jeffreys said:—

> "By the law the husband cannot be a witness against his wife, nor a wife against her husband, to charge them with anything criminal; except only in cases of high treason. This is so known a common rule, that I thought it could never have borne any question or debate".

It could be strongly argued that this rule should no longer be sustained because of the fact that, in the modern age with the inde- pendence of women, married or otherwise, and the recognition of the equality of men and women, both within and out of marriage, such a distinction could only be regarded as outmoded and unreal. Yet as recently as 1958 the United States Supreme Court held in the case of *Hawkins v United States* 358 US 74, *per* Black J at p. 77:—

> "While the rule forbidding testimony of one spouse *for* the other must be supported by reasons which time and changing legal practices had undermined, we are not prepared to say the same about the rule barring testimony of one spouse *against* the other. The basic reason the law has refused to pit wife against husband or husband against wife in a trial where life or liberty is at stake was a belief that such a policy is necessary to foster family peace, not only for the benefit of husband, wife and children but for the benefit of the public as well. Such a belief has never been unreasonable and is not now.

He went on to add that to have one spouse give evidence against the other was calculated to break up the relationship.

Husband and wife at common law were disqualified to testify on behalf of each other and could not testify against the other nor be testified against by the other. Yet it seems certain that in all causes involving assault or battery or other corporal violence to the wife or husband committed by the other, the spouse alleged to be injured could not be excluded. So an attempt by one spouse to kill another by poison is clearly within the exception. As *Lord Audley's Trial* 3 St. Tr. 401 indicated, the rape of the wife committed by the husband or at his instigation was an offence of corporal violence although this ruling has several times been doubted. In the Irish case of *Rex v Wasson* (1796) 1 Cr & Dix, C.C. 197 all the Irish judges decided that the wife could be admitted as a witness in a case where the accused was charged with administering poison to her.

Another line of thought which underlay the doctrine was one which could not possibly be sustained under our present view of the law and the purpose of the law and in particular the provisions of the Constitution itself. That view was that by marriage the husband and wife became one person in law in the result that the very being or legal existence of the woman was suspended during the marriage, or, at the very least, incorporated and consolidated into that of the husband under whose wing, protection and cover, she does everything.

Insofar as the rule may be thought to have been based upon, or is even still based upon, the suggestion that because marriage is to be regarded as "a union of person" it obviously could not be applicable by its own very definition to cases where one spouse has abandoned the other or where by mutual consent they were living apart in what is more graphically described in the French civil code as "*la séparation de corps*". In the present case the husband and wife were living apart, and it matters little whether they were living apart by mutual consent or by reason of the abandonment or desertion of one by the other. Here it would appear that the separation was due to the effect of a barring order which had been obtained some years ago by virtue of the provisions of the Family Law (Maintenance of Spouses and Children) Act 1976. In effect a barring order amounts to a finding of constructive desertion at the very least.

Article 41 of the Constitution recognises the family as the fundamental unit group of society and clearly establishes that the family as such unit has its own special rights. The Constitution however also makes it clear in its various provisions that every member of the family, as an individual, has his own personal rights also guaranteed by the Constitution. One of these is the guarantee contained in Article 40, section 3 of the Constitution wherein the State undertakes to vindicate the personal rights of the person, and to vindicate the rights of such persons in the case of any injustice done. On the assumption, which this Court is satisfied is correct, that the applicant committed the acts alleged against his daughter, it is beyond argument that she suffered a very grave injustice. The State, in the exercise of its judicial power, is bound by the Constitution to vindicate her right to have justice done within the sphere of operation of the judicial power of government. In this case, it was claimed, that can only be done by enabling her mother to give evidence at least in the most essential details such as proving the birth of the child, and the relationship of the child to the applicant. There is however another aspect of the case also. Insofar as the law requires a judge to inform a jury that in a case such as this it would be unsafe to convict in the absence of corroboration there may be cases where a mother's evidence may be the only way to supply the corroboration which is desirable in a case in which the husband is being prosecuted for violating the bodily integrity and human rights of his own child — a concept which was most recently recognised by the Supreme Court in the case of *The People v Tiernan* [1988] I.R. 250. It has been urged by counsel on behalf of the applicant in the present case that to permit or to compel a spouse to give evidence against an accused spouse would be a violation of the protection of the family guaranteed by the Constitution. It can be validly claimed that the constitutional provision is intended to be for the protection and benefit of the family and for the defence of the family and is not intended to be used to permit to be concealed a criminal assault on one of the members of the family by another member of the family or to permit any rule to obstruct the vindication of the right to protection which the members of that family may invoke under the Constitution.

Insofar as it may be thought that there is a competing interest between this latter and the unity of husband and wife, which is brought about by marriage, it is a consideration to be taken into account in examining Article 41 of the Constitution. It should be stressed that the unity which is in question in the Constitution is a union of spouses who are considered to be equals and not a union in which the personality, whether legal or otherwise of the one, being completely subsumed or incorporated in the other. If, as the Court believes to be the case, the common law never envisaged any such prohibition on the competence or compellability of a wife in case of attacks upon her by her husband, the members of the family, as envisaged by the Constitution, can have no lesser claim to have the right to justice vindicated by ensuring that all necessary relevant evidence on which that vindication will depend is available to the courts.

In viewing the case in the light of Article 41 of the Constitution dealing with the protection of the family it could possibly be argued that such a rule is justifiable for the sake of avoiding injury to the family as a unit which is held to be the fundamental unit group of society. But where the act alleged is itself a violation of the rights of that unit such as an assault by one spouse upon the other or an assault by either spouse upon the children of the family, particularly assaults as serious as the charges in the present case, other considerations must be taken into account. It is to be noted that no other family relationship disqualifies a witness; so therefore an assault, or other serious crime, committed against one of the children of the family whether it be an adult or one under age does not disqualify that person from giving evidence against the parent who is alleged to have committed the offence. It is only as between husband and wife that the privilege is claimed and would only apply when the spouse in question is the lawful spouse of the other party. Thus parties to a bigamous union or a void union are not covered by the common law rule.

The present case is not concerned with considering the effect or the justification of the rule in respect of criminal offences which do not injure the family. The view of the Director of Public Prosecutions, which is supported by the Attorney General, is that it would be an obstacle to the protection of the family guaranteed by the Constitution if one member of the family could be prevented from giving evidence against another member of the family where an injury has been done to members of the family. As the rule only applies to cases of spouses it is very narrow indeed. The Constitution gives special recognition and protection and safeguards to the parents of a family in relation to their children, but it must follow that each and every right so given carries with it correlative obligations. It has been held by the Supreme Court in the case of *Ryan v Attorney General* [1965] I.R. 394 that a parent has no right to endanger the health of his or her child. In the criminal law it is quite clear that no parent has any right to injure his own child and the obligation of safeguarding the family and protecting the family is as much an obligation on the members of that family as upon other parties. This has already been recognised to some extent by the statute law which renders both competent and compellable a spouse as a witness in respect of a complaint to the effect that one spouse has been assaulted or injured by the other or where a spouse has been charged with cruelty to his or her child.

The Constitution places upon the courts the obligation to enforce the protection given to the family and family life by the Constitution itself. That must necessarily include an obligation to enforce these protective provisions even against members of the family who are guilty or alleged to be guilty of injuries to members of the family.

It would be difficult to consider or to imagine any matter which would be more subversive of family life than sexual offences committed against his child by a spouse of the nature alleged in the present case particularly when the child in question is less than fully normal. It is obviously the duty of one spouse to protect the child or children against the other in cases of any such abuse, and it would completely frustrate the obligation placed upon the State to protect the family if the very person upon whom the obligation is said to rest should be prevented or inhibited from testifying in a prosecution against the offending spouse. This is particularly so in the circumstances where a spouse whose testimony it is sought to introduce is a vital witness. Insofar as the justification sought for the existence of the rule is the prevention of family dissension, it can quite clearly have no validity in a situation where the application of the rule is so far from preventing family dissension, is assisting in concealing in effect, and thus permitting to go unpunished, a serious offence committed upon members of the family by other members of the family, particularly sexual offences by a father upon his own daughter. In view of the sense of obligation placed upon this Court to assist insofar as it can in the protection of the family the Court must take the view that the maintenance of the common law rule relied on in this case would be a failure to comply with the obligations imposed by the Constitution. This is all the more so in cases of assault upon the children of the family by the parents. Such a case should not be more hampered in its proof by the existence or the enforcement of the rule than in the case of an assault by the husband upon the wife.

Attention should also be drawn to the fact that the administration of justice itself requires that the public has a right to every man's evidence except for those persons who are privileged in that respect by the provisions of the Constitution itself "or other established and recognised privilege". (See the judgment of this Court in *In re Kevin O'Kelly* (1974) 108 I.L.T.R. 97.) It was pointed out by the Supreme Court in the case of *Murphy v Dublin Corporation and the Minister for Local Government* [1972] I.R. 215 that it would be impossible for the judicial power under the Constitution, in the proper exercise of its functions, to admit any other body of persons to decide for it whether or not certain evidence should or would be disclosed or produced in Court. In the last resort the decision lies with the Courts so long as they have seisin of the case. The exercise of the judicial power carries with it the power to compel the attendance of witnesses, the production of evidence and, *a fortiori*, the answering of questions by the witnesses. This is the ultimate safeguard of justice in the

State, whether it be in pursuit of the guilty or in vindication of the innocent. It was pointed out in that case that there may be occasions when different aspects of the public interest may require a resolution of a conflict of interest which may be involved in the non-disclosure of evidence but that if there is such a conflict then the sole power of resolving it resides in the courts.

In the form of a common law rule the law has recognised a rule to the effect that one spouse may not give evidence against the other in a criminal prosecution. Insofar as that may be based upon the view that it would tend to rupture family relationships it must be set against the public interest in the vindication of the innocent who have been subjected to injustice. As both may be said to fall within the provisions of Article 41 of the Constitution it is the view of the Court that the interest of the child must prevail because what is alleged against the applicant is an attack of a particularly unpleasant kind upon his own child and therefore an attack upon the very fabric of the family itself and the bodily integrity of a member of that family.

The effect of the decision of the Supreme Court in *State (Brown) v Feran* [1967] I.R. 147 was to hold that Article 50 of the Constitution encompasses not merely all prior statutory rules but also all prior common law judge-made rules. In the present case there has been no suggestion that the wife was not a willing witness so the Court is not being specifically asked to rule upon whether if it is of opinion that she is a competent witness she should also be regarded as a compellable witness. It does, however, follow from the logic of the Court's approach to the constitutional question in this case that if the judicial power is to vindicate the victim of an injustice it is obvious that such a witness must be a compellable one. Therefore if the mother had not been willing to testify she could have been compelled rightly to do so. The attention of the Court has been directed to the decision of the House of Lords in *Hoskyn v Metropolitan Police Commissioner* [1979] A.C. 474. This court is not concerned to consider whether that case was rightly or wrongly decided upon English law or upon the particular facts of that case. It is sufficient to say that the decision would not be compatible with the principles of constitutional law which have been stated by this Court in this judgment. This Court is not concerned to offer any view on what ought to be the policy of the law so far as the competence or compellability (insofar as they are at all distinguishable) ought to be in the case of a spouse who is in a position to give evidence against another spouse, in a criminal prosecution, for an offence other than one which constitutes an attack upon a member of the family. It is right however to point out that even in the latter case if the family happens to be one which, in ordinary parlance is such, even though not based on marriage and therefore not within the provisions of Article 41, it is within the provisions of Article 40, as was stated by the Supreme Court in *In re Nicolaou* [1966] I.R. 567 and yet no problem would arise as to the competence or compellability of one of the parents of a child in a case of any such offence committed by the other parent on the child. Proof of marriage of the parents of a child is not a necessary proof in establishing incest nor is it in anyway relevant to the establishment of the offence of buggery against such child. The family based on marriage may not be placed in a less advantageous position or receive less protection from the law than the one not based on marriage. See the decision of the Supreme Court in *Murphy v Attorney General* [1982] I.R. 241.

For the reasons given the Court is of the opinion that the evidence given by the wife in the present case, although mostly elicited by the applicant, was admissible and relevant and the common law rule that she was not a competent or compellable witness against her husband must be deemed not to be applicable in this case and any provision of the Criminal Justice (Evidence) Act 1924 which purports to provide that she was not such must be deemed to be inconsistent with the Constitution and by Article 50 to be deemed not to have been carried over into law. The application for leave to appeal will therefore be refused.

Solicitors for the applicant: *Garrett Sheehan & Co.*
Solicitor for the respondent: *Chief State Solicitor*

Eithne Casey
Barrister

The People (Director of Public Prosecutions) v Donal O'Leary
[C.C.A. No. 137 of 1987]

Court of Criminal Appeal   29 July 1988

Membership of unlawful organisation – possession of incriminating documents – burden of proof – Offences Against the State Act 1939 (No. 13), section 24

Search warrant – validity – whether warrant unrestricted – belief of superintendent grounding issue of warrant – whether satisfied – Offences Against the State Act 1939 (No. 13), section 29

Sentence – extraneous factors taken into account – whether error in principle

The Offences Against the State Act 1939, section 29 as substituted for by section 5 of the Criminal Law Act 1976, provides:

(1) Where a member of the Garda Síochána not below the rank of superintendent is satisfied that there is reasonable ground for believing that evidence of or relating to the commission or intended commission of an offence under this Act, or the Criminal Law Act, 1976, or an offence which is for the time being a scheduled offence for the purposes of Part V of this Act, or evidence relating to the commission or intended commission of treason, is to be found in any building . . . or in any other place whatsoever, he may issue to a member of the Garda Síochána not below the rank of sergeant a search warrant under this section in relation to such place.

Section 24 of the Act of 1939 provides:

On the trial of a person charged with the offence of being a member of an unlawful organisation, proof to the satisfaction of the court that an incriminating document relating to the said organisation was found on such person or in his possession or on lands or in premises owned or occupied by him, or under his control shall, without more, be evidence until the contrary is proved that such person was a member of the said organisation at the time alleged in the said charge.

The applicant was convicted in the Special Criminal Court of membership of an unlawful organisation, contrary to section 21 of the Act of 1939, and of possession of incriminating documents contrary to section 12 of that Act. He was sentenced to terms of imprisonment of five years and three months respectively. He applied for leave to appeal both conviction and sentence.

At his trial the applicant swore that he was not a member of any unlawful organisation, but that he was a member of a lawful political party, namely, the Sinn Féin party. The evidence of the prosecution included the sworn evidence of a Chief Superintendent of the Garda Síochána that it was his belief that on the relevant date the applicant was a member of an unlawful organisation. Premises occupied by the applicant had been searched pursuant to a search warrant issued under section 29 of the Act of 1939. Thirty-seven copies of a poster were found on the premises which showed a man in a paramilitary uniform holding a rifle and with the words "IRA call the shots" alongside the picture. The Court of trial took the view that the applicant was disseminating the posters to

163

young people as part of a campaign of recruitment for the IRA. The gounds of appeal are set out in the judgment.

Held by the Court (McCarthy, Carroll and Murphy JJ), in dismissing the application for leave to appeal against conviction and in granting the application for leave to appeal against sentence:

(1) That section 29 of the Act of 1939 states a variety of circumstances under which a search warrant may validly be issued, the warrant in the instant case accorded with the wording of the section and was in accordance with law.

(2) That there was no basis for challenging the opinion of the Superintendent who stated that he had been satisfied, when issuing the warrant, that there was reasonable ground for believing that evidence of an offence under the Act of 1939 would be found on the premises occupied by the applicant.

(3) That is was not disputed that the poster found on the applicant's premises was an incriminating document within the meaning of section 24 of the Act of 1939; however the applicant failed to displace the *prima facie* evidence of membership of an illegal organisation furnished by the possession of the poster and there was nothing to indicate that the Court of trial imposed an incorrect burden of proof of beyond a reasonable doubt on the applicant to prove the contrary.

(4) That the Court of trial erred in principle when, in imposing sentence, it took into account an allegation of wrongdoing which in itself constituted an offence and with which the applicant had not been charged and accordingly the Court reduced the sentence of imprisonment to one of four years.

Case cited in this judgment:
People (Attorney General) v O'Brien [1965] I.R. 142

Feargus Flood SC and Patrick Gageby **for the applicant**
Fergal Foley **for the respondent**

McCarthy J

The applicant was convicted in the Special Criminal Court on 19 November 1987, on an indictment containing two charges, membership of an unlawful organisation, contrary to section 21 of the Offences Against the State Act 1939, as amended by section 2 of the Criminal Law Act 1976, and possession of incriminating documents contrary to section 12 of the Offences Against the State Act 1939, both offences alleged to have taken place on 18 April 1987. He was sentenced to 5 years imprisonment on the first count and 3 months imprisonment on the second.

The evidence upon which he was convicted may be summarised as follows:

(a) Chief Superintendent McKeon, the Chief Superintendent in charge of the Garda Division of Cork East Riding who swore as to his belief that on 18 April 1987, the applicant was a member of an unlawful organisation known as the IRA, Irish Republican Army, or Óglaigh na hÉireann. This was challenged in cross examination of the Chief Superintendent who further asserted his belief that the applicant, at the time of the trial, was a member of a subversive organisation. Such evidence, pursuant to section 3, subsection 2 of the Offences Against the State (Amendment) Act 1972, is evidence that the person concerned was then such a member.

(b) The finding by the Gardaí in the applicant's home of 37 copies of a poster showing an action picture of a man in paramilitary uniform brandishing a rifle and with the words prominently displayed "IRA call the shots" alongside the picture.

The applicant, Mr O'Leary, gave evidence at the trial in the Special Criminal Court and swore that he was not a member of the Irish Republican Army on the date alleged or at any time but was, as the Court accepted, and had been for some years an active member of the Sinn Féin Party, a lawful political organisation in the State, and that he had stood for election to Dáil Éireann on behalf of that party.

The challenge to the conviction is based, broadly, upon two contentions:

1. That the search warrant under whose authority the Gardaí obtained entry to and searched the applicant's home, finding the posters there, was an invalid search warrant, and that the fruits of the search were inadmissible in evidence.

2. On that premise, since the finding of the Court on the membership charge was founded, in part, on the presumption created by section 24 of the Offences Against the State Act 1939, the conviction could not stand.

3. *A fortiori* the possession charge could not stand.

4. As an alternative, if reliance was sought to be placed solely upon the evidence of the Chief Superintendent as to membership, where the accused had made a sworn denial that he was a member of the illegal organisation, such virtually automatically rebutted the evidence of the Chief Superintendent.

5. Further, it was contended that the judgment of the Special Criminal Court did not identify, in terms, the burden of proof placed upon the person charged to prove the contrary within the meaning of section 24 of the 1939 Act and, accordingly, the Court must have applied an excessive test of beyond a reasonable doubt.

The search warrant
Section 5 of the Criminal Law Act 1976, substituted for section 29 of the Act of 1939, the following provision:

> 29.–(1) Where a member of the Garda Síochána not below the rank of superintendent is satisfied that there is reasonable ground for believing that evidence of or relating to the commission or intended commission of an offence under this Act, or the Criminal Law Act 1976, or an offence which is for the time being a scheduled offence for the purposes of Part V of this Act, or evidence relating to the commission or intended commission of treason, is to be found in any building or part of a building or in any vehicle, vessel, aircraft or hovercraft or in any other place whatsoever, he may issue to a member of the Garda Síochána not below the rank of sergeant a search warrant under this section in relation to such place.

> (2) A search warrant under this section shall operate to authorise the member of the Garda Síochána named in the warrant, accompanied by any members of the Garda Síochána or the Defence Forces, to enter, within one week from the date of the warrant, and if necessary by the use of force, any building or part of a building or any vehicle, vessel, aircraft or hovercraft or any other place named in the warrant, and to search it and any person found there, and to seize anything found there or on such person.

The warrant is a printed form which allows for the insertion of the name of the authorising officer, the address of the premises to be searched, the officer authorised to search, the description of the property and the name of the individual to be searched with a provision for signature, rank and dating. The offences envisaged are under the Act of 1939, the Criminal Law Act 1976, the schedules of offences provided for under Part V of the Act of 1939, and the offence of treason. This may cover a range of hundreds of offences. The applicant argues that such an unrestricted form of warrant has too broad a sweep, that it is a warrant "at large". No authority in support of this proposition was cited to the Court save to point by analogy to the more limited form of warrant that is permitted to be issued under a variety of statutes as, for example, the Larceny Act 1916, or the Misuse of Drugs Act 1984. These, however, are what may be termed judicial warrants as compared with the executive warrant permitted under the 1939 Act and, for example, the Firearms Act 1925, section 24. Article 40.5 of the Constitution states that the dwelling of every citizen is inviolable and shall not be forcibly entered save in accordance with law. This is not a guarantee against forcible entry only; the dwelling is inviolable save for entry as permitted by law: (see judgment of Walsh J in *People (Attorney General) v O'Brien* [1965] I.R. 142). Section 29 of the 1939 Act, as cited, does permit entry under a valid warrant; the section states a variety of circumstances under which the appropriate garda officer may validly issue a search warrant; there may be circumstances under which offences under all of the several categories are suspected; the warrant accords with the wording of the section and the entry of the dwelling was, thus, in accordance with law.

The second attack on the warrant was to the effect that the evidence showed that Superintendent Glavin could not have been satisfied within the meaning of the section which requires that he "is satisfied that there is reasonable ground for believing etc." In every case there must be proof that the relevant officer was satisfied as required by the Act. In this case there was no basis for challenging the opinion of Superintendent Glavin as expressed in the warrant and testified in Court.

In the opinion of the Court, the warrant was valid and provided full authority for the search and seizure carried out by the Gardaí.

The membership charge

Section 24 of the 1939 Act states:—

> On the trial of a person charged with the offence of being a member of an unlawful organisation, proof to the satisfaction of the court that an incriminating document relating to the said organisation was found on such person or in his possession or on lands or in premises owned or occupied by him or under his control shall, without more, be evidence until the contrary is proved that such person was a member of the said organisation at the time alleged in the said charge.

It is not an issue but that the Special Criminal Court, as it did, was entitled to hold that the poster as described was an incriminating document within the definition in section 24 of the Act, was found in the applicant's home and, consequently, without more, was evidence, until the contrary were proved, that he was a member of the IRA. In the judgment of the Special Criminal Court it was stated:—

However, the Court is not satisfied that the ascused's explanation as to his possession of the posters is sufficient to displace the presumption that such documents are evidence of his membership of the unlawful organisation in question.

And later:

. . . the Court is satisfied that in having such posters in his possession for the purpose of sale to the public, whether for the financial benefit of the Sinn Féin Party or not, the accused was well aware that he was thereby publicising in laudatory terms the terrorist activities of the IRA. In taking that course he was not merely indicating a sympathy with the IRA, he was participating actively in the promotion of their aims and unlawful activities. Bearing that in mind this Court rejects his denial of membership of that organisation and accepts the evidence of Chief Superintendent McKeon as to his belief that the accused was in fact a member of the IRA on the date alleged. The nature and content of the posters, the obvious purpose and the explanation of the accused that he had them in his possession for the purpose of disseminating them to the public amply corroborated the Chief Superintendent's opinion.

There is nothing to indicate that the trial Court imposed on the applicant a burden of proof such as was argued.

In the result, this court is satisfied that the applicant has failed to make out any case for which leave to appeal against conviction should be granted and dismisses the application.

Sentence

The applicant seeks to leave to appeal against the sentence of five years imprisonment imposed on the membership charge.

When section 21 of the Act of 1939 was passed the maximum penalty was one of imprisonment for a term not exceeding two years. In 1976 the Oireachtas increased the level of maximum penalty from two to seven years and, since then, it would appear that sentences of two, three, four and five years have been imposed. In the course of sentencing the applicant the Special Criminal Court stated:—

The Court also accepts the evidence of Inspector Brennan that the accused was disseminating such posters to young people as part of a campaign on his part — as part of a campaign conducted by him to recruit new young members for the Irish Republican Army. The Court must regard such conduct as being most reprehensible and grievously wrong.

The applicant was not charged with any offence under section 3 of the Criminal Law Act, 1976.

The Court should not have been influenced, as it clearly was, by an allegation of wrongdoing with which the applicant was never charged or convicted. The Court, therefore, erred in principle. The application for leave to appeal severity of sentence will be granted and the sentence reduced to 4 years imprisonment.

Solicitor for the applicant: *Ann B. Rowland & Co.*
Solicitor for the respondent: *Chief State Solicitor*

Eithne Casey
Barrister

The People (Director of Public Prosecutions) v Mark Kenny
[C.C.A. No. 44 of 1987]

Court of Criminal Appeal   15 June 1989
                                                 30 November 1989

Evidence – search warrrant – validity – possession of controlled drug – suspicion – swearing of information by garda – information grounding garda suspicion not specified – requirement that peace commissioner be satisfied by information on oath of reasonable grounds for suspecting that an offence has been committed – whether warrant validly issued – Misuse of Drugs Act 1977 (No. 12), s. 26

Constitution – inviolability of dwelling house – domiciliary search on foot of invalid search warrant – standard procedure followed for obtaining warrant – whether deliberate and conscious violation of accused's constitutional rights – admissibility of evidence consequent on unlawful search – judicial discretion

Section 26, subsection 1 of the Misuse of Drugs Act 1977, as amended by section 13 of the Misuse of Drugs Act 1984, provides, *inter alia*:—

(1) If a Justice of the District Court or a Peace Commissioner is satisfied by information on oath of a member of the Garda Síochána that there is reasonable ground for suspecting that —

(a) A person is in possession in contravention of this Act on any premises of a controlled drug . . . and that such drug . . . is on a particular premises . . . such Justice or Commissioner may issue a search warrant mentioned in subsection (2) of this section.

The appellant's flat was searched by Garda C pursuant to a search warrant issued under section 26 of the Act of 1977 and samples of heroin were found. The admissibility of Garda C's evidence concerning the search turned on the validity of the search warrant. Garda C swore an information before a Peace Commissioner that:—

. . . I suspect, on the basis of information within my possession, that (a) a person is in possession on the premises . . . of a controlled drug, namely Diamorphine or Cannabis resin. . . . I hereby apply for a warrant to search for and seize the articles named above.

The warrant to search stated, *inter alia*:—

Whereas I, the undersigned Peace Commissioner, being satisfied on the information on Oath of Garda C. . . .

There was no evidence that any enquiry was made by the Peace Commissioner as to the basis of the Garda's suspicion.

Held by the Court of Criminal Appeal (McCarthy, O'Hanlon and Lardner JJ) in allowing the challenge to the validity of the search warrant, that the warrant was invalid because there was no evidence that the Peace Commissioner enquired into the basis of the Garda's suspicion. He failed to exercise any judicial discretion and failed therefore to carry out his function under the Act. *Byrne v Grey* [1988] I.R. 31 applied.

The Court granted leave to appeal and required further argument as to whether the deliberate and conscious act of forcing admission into the appellant's home was a violation of his constitutional rights with the result that the fruits of the search were inadmissible in evidence.

Held by the Court, in its second judgment, in dismissing the appeal on the ground that no miscarriage of justice occurred:
(1) That while the procedure for obtaining the search warrant was found to be invalid, and the consequent entry onto the premises unlawful, there was no deliberate and conscious violation of the appellant's constitutional rights, that Garda C took all steps believed to be necessary for obtaining the search warrant, and it was issued by the Peace Commissioner on the basis that there was compliance with the requirements of the Act of 1977.
(2) The admissibility of the evidence obtained on foot of the invalid search warrant was a matter for the discretion of the Court. In the circumstances of this case the correct decision for a trial judge would have been to admit the evidence. While the evidence was admitted by the trial judge on an incorrect basis, no miscarriage of justice occurred.
Semble: The concept of "extraordinary excusing circumstances" had only to be considered when the Court was of the view that a deliberate and conscious violation of constitutional rights had taken place, otherwise the admissibility of the evidence was a matter for the Court's discretion.

Dicta of Walsh J in *People v Walsh* [1980] I.R. 294 at p. 317 and *People v Shaw* [1982] I.R. 1 at p. 32 not followed.

Cases cited in both judgments
Byrne v Grey [1988] I.R. 31
Reg. v I.R.C., Ex P. Rossminister [1980] A.C. 952; [1980] 2 W.L.R. 1; [1979] 3 All E.R. 385; [1980] 1 All E.R. 80; 70 Cr. App. R. 157
People (Attorney General) v O'Brien [1965] I.R. 142
People (DPP) v Farrell [1978] I.R. 13
People (DPP) v Madden [1977] I.R. 336; 111 I.L.T.R. 117
People (DPP) v O'Loughlin [1979] I.R. 85; 113 I.L.T.R. 109
People (DPP) v Quilligan [1986] I.R. 495; [1987] ILRM 606
People (DPP) v Shaw [1982] I.R. 1
People (DPP) v Walsh [1980] I.R. 294
State (Quinn) v Ryan [1965] I.R. 70; 100 I.L.T.R. 105
United States v Leon (1984) 468 U.S. 897

Additional cases cited in legal argument
Berkeley v Edwards & Others High Court, 9 October 1987 (unreported)
People (DPP) v Conroy [1988] I.R. 641; [1988] ILRM 4
People (DPP) v Lynch [1982] I.R. 64; [1981] ILRM 389

The application for leave to appeal was heard on 8 May 1989 and judgment was delivered on 15 June 1989. The appeal on the constitutional issue was heard on 17 July 1989, judgment was delivered on 30 November 1989, and the appeal was dismissed.

Counsel for the appellant applied for and was granted a certificate pursuant to section 29 of the Courts of Justice Act 1924, and the Court certified that its decision involved a point of law of exceptional importance, namely:—

> Whether the forcible entry of the appellant's home by members of An Garda Síochána on foot of an invalid search warrant constituted a deliberate and conscious violation of the appellant's constitutional rights such as to render any evidence obtained by the said members in the course of the ensuing search inadmissible at the appellant's trial.

The Court certified that it was desirable in the public interest that an appeal should be taken to the Supreme Court on such a point. The appeal was allowed by the Supreme Court in its judgment delivered on 20 March 1990. The headnote of the judgment is reported in Part III of this volume, p. 303, below.

Paul McDermott **for the applicant**
Niall Durnin **for the respondent**

McCarthy J

The applicant was convicted of two offences under the Misuse of Drugs Act 1977/84, the offences being alleged to have taken place on 2 October 1984. On that date, Garda Conway, armed with a search warrant dated 29 September 1984, forced an entry of Flat 1, Ground Floor, 1 Belgrave Place, Rathmines, Dublin, where the applicant resided and he found samples of heroin and various incriminating material. According to the garda, the applicant stated that the flat was his and that he took responsibility for anything that might be found there. Whilst there was other evidence germane to the issue of guilt, it is common case that the admissibility of Garda Conway's evidence concerning what was found and said in the flat turned on the validity of the search warrant.

Section 26, subsection 1 of the Act of 1977, as amended, provides:—

> If a Justice of the District Court or a Peace Commissioner is satisfied by information on oath of a member of the Garda Síochána that there is reasonable ground for suspecting that:—
>
> > (a) a person is in possession in contravention of this Act on any premises or other land of a controlled drug, a forged prescription or a duly issued prescription which has been wrongfully altered and that such drug or prescription is on a particular premises or other land. . . .
>
> Such Justice or Commissioner may issue a search warrant mentioned in subsection (2) of this section

The information sworn by Garda Conway states:—

> I am a member of An Garda Síochána and I suspect, on the basis of information within my possession, that
>
> (a) A person is in possession on the premises or other land Flat 1, Ground Floor, 1 Belgrave Place in contravention of the Misuse of Drugs Act 1977 and 1984 of a controlled drug, namely Diamorphine or Cannabis resin and that
>
> (b) Such drug is on a particular premises or other land Flat 1, Ground Floor, 1 Belgrave Place, Rathmines.
>
> I hereby apply for a warrant to search for and seize the articles named above.

The warrant to search stated:—

Whereas I, the undersigned Peace Commissioner, being satisfied on the information on oath of Garda Matthew Conway of An Garda Síochána that there is reasonable grounds (sic) for suspecting that a controlled drug to which the Misuse of Drugs Act 1977 and 1984, apply namely Diamorphine and Cannabis Resin etc., is in contravention of the said Act or Regulation cited hereunder in the possession or under the control of any person etc.

The trial judge, after evidence from Garda Conway and legal argument, admitted the evidence as to the search, holding that the warrant had been validly issued by the Peace Commissioner. That ruling is the sole issue on this application. The argument for the applicant is that the information sworn by Garda Conway, albeit in an established printed form, does not comply with the requirements of the section in that it does no more than state the suspicion held by Garda Conway on the basis of the information within his possession; it does not state what that information is or its nature, no evidence having been led at the trial as to any further information that Garda Conway may or may not have given to the Peace Commissioner.

A like warrant and information came for consideration by Hamilton P, in *Byrne v Grey* [1988] I.R. 31 in proceedings by way of Judicial Review. There the information on Oath stated at p. 39:—

> I am a member of the Garda Síochána and I have reasonable grounds for suspecting that a plant of the genus cannabis is being cultivated contrary to section 17 of the Misuse of Drugs Act 1977 and 1984, on or in the premises or other land at 50 Whitebrook Park, Tallaght, Dublin 24.

Hamilton P, having cited observations made in *Reg. v I.R.C., Ex P. Rossminster* [1980] A.C. 952 held (at p. 40) that a member of the Garda Síochána seeking the issue of a warrant:—

> must be in a position to and so satisfy either the District Justice or the Peace Commissioner of the relevant facts so that the District Justice or the Peace Commissioner can satisfy himself in accordance with the requirements of the section. He is not entitled to rely on the suspicion of a member of the Garda Síochána applying for the warrant.

As is quite clear from the terms of the warrant, the first respondent in this case relied on the information on oath of the member of the Garda Síochána which merely stated that he, the member of the Garda Síochána, had reasonable grounds for suspicion. I am satisfied that the first respondent acted without jurisdiction in issuing the said warrant because he personally had no information before him that would enable him to be satisfied that there was reasonable grounds for suspicion.

The statutory provision being construed in the *Rossminster* case was the Taxes Management Act 1970, section 20(c), which reads:—

(1) If the appropriate judicial authority is satisfied on information on oath given by an officer of the board that —

(a) there is a reasonable ground for suspecting that an offence involving any form of fraud in connection with or in relation to tax has been committed and that evidence of it is to be found on premises specified in the information; . . . the authority may issue a warrant in writing authorising an officer . . . to enter the premises, if necessary by force, at any time within 14 days from the time of issue of the warrant, and search them. . . .

In his opinion, Lord Wilberforce said at p. 998:—

(2) No warrant to enter can be issued except by a circuit judge, not, as is usually the case, by a magistrate. There has to be laid before him information on oath, and on this he must be satisfied that there is reasonable ground for suspecting the commission of a "tax fraud" and that evidence of it is to be found in the premises sought to be searched. If the judge does his duty (and we must assume that the learned Common Serjeant did in the present case) he must carefully consider for himself the grounds put forward by the revenue officer and judicially satisfy himself, in relation to each of the premises concerned, that these amount to reasonable grounds for suspecting, etc. It would be quite wrong to suppose that he acts simply as a rubber stamp on the revenue's application.

Viscount Dilhorne said at p. 1004:—

It cannot in my view be emphasised too strongly that the section requires that the appropriate judicial authority should himself be satisifed of these matters and that it does not suffice for the person laying the information to say that he is.

Lord Diplock said at p. 1009:—

That subsection makes it a condition precedent to the issue of the warrant that the circuit judge should himself be satisfied by information upon oath that facts exist which constitute reasonable ground for suspecting that an offence involving some form of fraud in connection with or in relation to tax has been committed, and also for suspecting that evidence of the offence is to be found on the premises in respect of which the warrant to search is sought. It is not, in my view, open to your Lordships to approach the instant case on the assumption that the Common Serjeant did not satisfy himself on both these matters, or to imagine circumstances which might have led him to commit so grave a dereliction of his judicial duties. The presumption is that he acted lawfully and properly; and it is only fair to him to say that, in my view, there is nothing in the evidence before your Lordships to suggest the contrary; nor, indeed, have the respondents themselves so contended.

Lord Salmon said at p. 1018:—

The section is, in my view, so drafted that if an officer of the Inland Revenue who had made a long and careful investigation of the respondents' affairs, informed the judge on oath that there was reasonable ground for suspecting that an offence or offences involving fraud in relation to tax had been committed etc., the judge might well make the mistake of misconstruing section 20(c) as meaning that the information given on oath was sufficent to satisfy him that there was reasonable ground for suspicion and to empower him to issue the warrants.

and, later at p. 1019:—

In my view, it provides only one real safegaurd against an abuse of power. That safeguard is not that the Inland Revenue is satisfied that there is reasonable ground for suspecting that an offence involving fraud in relation to tax has been committed, but that the judge who issues the search warrant is so satisfied after he has been told on oath by the Inland Revenue full details of the facts which it has discovered. . . . I am, however, convinced that search warrants like the present are invalid because they recite as the reason for their issue only that an officer of the Inland Revenue has stated on oath that there is reasonable ground to suspecting that an offence involving fraud in relation to tax has been committed. If the judge gives that as his reason for issuing a warrant, it seems to me to follow that his reason for issuing it cannot be that he is so satisfied by the information given to him on oath by an officer of the Inland Revenue of the detailed facts which the officer has ascertained; but that the judge's reason for issuing the warrant was because the officer had stated on oath that there is reasonable ground to suspect, etc.

Lord Scarman said at p. 1022:—

The judge must himself be satisfied. It is not enough that the officer should state on oath that he is satisfied, which is all that the warrants say in the present case. The issue of the warrant is a judicial act, and must be preceded by a judicial inquiry which satisfied the judge that the requirements for its issue have been met. . . . (at p. 1023) It is, therefore, necessary to approach the case upon the basis that the judge did satisfy himself upon the matters which he was required to be satisfied before issuing the warrants.

The majority of the House of Lords held on the evidence that there was no reason to think that the appropriate judicial authority had not considered the relevant facts but, far from disowning the principle upon which Lord Salmon relied, expressly upheld it. It comes back to the simple proposition here that the Peace Commissioner, in deciding to issue a warrant, is acting judicially, must make up his own mind on the facts as presented and must not act merely as a rubber stamp. In the instant case, the learned trial judge stated his reasons for rejecting the applicant's submission as follows:—

It appears to me that the section contemplates that a suspicion is communicated by a Garda Síochána where upon its basis can be enquired into by the District Justice or Peace Commissioner and presumably this would be more likely to be done in certain types of cases than in others. Thereupon it will be, it appears to me, for the District Justice or Peace Commissioner to exercise his jurisdiction in issuing or declining to issue the search warrant sought. It appears to me that it was open to the deceased Peace Commissioner to issue the warrant on foot of the information that was laid before him in the case presently before the court and it appears to me that no such "jump" was made by the Peace Commissioner in compliance with the section as should impugn the warrant actually granted by him. It seems to me that the use of the word "reasonable" necessarily connotes an objective assessment by another person, in this instance the District Justice or Peace Commissioner, and that the absence of an unexplained and undetailed designation such as the word "reasonable" ought not to be fatal to the prosecution case and is not so in this instance.

There was no evidence that the Peace Commissioner inquired into the basis of the garda's suspicion. On the contrary, on the evidence adduced at the trial the only conclusion is that the Peace Commissioner, deceased at the time of trial, acted purely on the "say-so" of Garda Conway as contained in the information. In doing so, he failed to exercise any judicial discretion; he failed to carry out his function under the section and, accordingly, the warrant was invalid.

In these circumstances, the Court is of opinion that the search warrant was invalid and that, accordingly, the evidence as to the search and the statement of the applicant at the time was admitted on an incorrect basis. That does not conclude the matter. Garda Conway believed the warrant to be valid. He had every reason to do so. His good faith was not in question, but having regard to the run of the case the question did not arise as to whether or not the deliberate and conscious act of forcing admission into the applicant's home was a violation of his constitutional rights with the result that the fruits of search consequent on such breach were inadmissible in evidence. The Court requires further argument on this issue and, accordingly, will grant leave to appeal, which appeal will be heard without delay.

30 November 1989

O'Hanlon J

The Court has already ruled in its judgment delivered 15 June 1989, that the learned trial judge erred in law in concluding that the search warrant issued by the Peace Commissioner to Garda Conway was a valid warrant. It follows that the forcible entry by the garda of the flat at Belgrave Place, Rathmines, Dublin, where the appellant resided was unlawful. The Court left over for further consideration the question whether these factors rendered inadmissible the evidence obtained as a result of that unlawful entry, and has had the benefit of further legal argument by counsel on this issue.

The determination of the question involves a consideration of the decision of the Supreme Court in the case of *People (Attorney General) v O'Brien* [1965] I.R. 142, and a number of later decisions of the Supreme Court and the Court of Criminal Appeal.

In *People v O'Brien* the Supreme Court concluded that evidence obtained by means of an invalid search warrant should not be excluded in the circumstances of that particular case. Through inadvertence, a search warrant referring to an incorrect address had been issued and it was not clear whether the garda sergeant noticed the mistake before searching the premises.

The following passages appear in the judgment of Kingsmill Moore J (with whose judgment Lavery and Budd JJ agreed) at p. 161:—

> The mistake was a pure oversight and it has not been shown that the oversight was noticed by anyone before the premises were searched. I can find no evidence of deliberate treachery, imposition, deceit or illegality; no policy to disregard the provisions of the Constitution or to conduct searches without a warrant; nothing except the existence of an unintentional and accidental illegality to set against the public interest of having crime detected and punished.

And at p. 162:—

> Mr Justice Walsh, in the judgment which he is about to deliver, is of opinion that where evidence has been obtained by the State or its agents as a result of a deliberate and conscious violation of the constitutional (as opposed to the common law) rights of an accused

person, it should be excluded save when there are 'extraordinary excusing circumstances', and mentions as such circumstances the need to prevent an imminent destruction of vital evidence or rescue of a person in peril, and the seizure of evidence obtained in the course of and incidental to a lawful arrest even though the premises on which the arrest is made have been entered without a search warrant. I agree that where there has been such a deliberate and conscious violation of constitutional rights by the State or its agents, evidence obtained by such violation should be in general be excluded, and I agree that there may be certain 'extraordinary excusing circumstances' which may warrant its admission. . . . The facts of individual cases vary so widely that any hard and fast rules of a general nature seem to me dangerous and I would again leave the exclusion or non-exclusion to the discretion of the trial judge. . . . This case is not one of deliberate and conscious violation, but of a purely accidental and unintentional infringement of the Constitution. In such cases, as Mr Justice Walsh indicates, the evidence normally should not be excluded.

Since judgment was given in *People v O'Brien* [1965] I.R. 142, the courts have had to consider on a number of occasions what type of conduct may be regarded as deliberate and conscious violation of the constitutional rights of an accused person, and what type of conduct may fairly be regarded as falling outside that category.

It is clear from the decisions in *People v Madden* [1977] I.R. 336, *People v Farrell* [1978] I.R. 13, *People v O'Loughlin* [1979] I.R. 85, *People v Walsh* [1980] I.R. 317, that knowledge of the common law and statute law, and of the constitutional guarantees, must — generally speaking — be imputed to the law enforcement agencies, and that if they are breached in a manner which infringes the constitutional rights of an accused person, it may be regarded as a deliberate and conscious violation without regard to the actual state of knowledge or *bona fides* of the garda officer or other person committing such violation.

The cases referred to were clear-cut. In *People v Madden* [1977] I.R. 336, the Offences Against the State Acts permitted the detention of a person under section 30 of the Act of 1939 for a maximum period of 48 hours, whereas Madden was detained beyond that period while a statement which was being taken from him was being completed. No attempt was made in the course of the trial to justify this course, and the gardaí who gave evidence were aware of the 48-hour time limit. In *People v Farrell* [1978] I.R. 13, no evidence was given at the trial of the giving of the necessary authority to extend the applicant's detension up to 48 hours under the same statutory provisions and therefore the prosecution failed to establish that there had been no deliberate and conscious violation of the applicant's constitutional rights. In *People v Walsh* [1980] I.R. 294 the Supreme Court held that the failure to bring the appellant before a court at the first reasonable opportunity after his arrest (as then required by the express provisions of the Criminal Justice Act 1951, section 15, and as now required by the provisions of the new section substituted for section 15 by the Criminal Justice Act 1984, section 26) resulted in his continued detention being unlawful and in breach of his constitutional rights, but in that case the impugned fingerprint evidence was declared admissible because it had been obtained at a time when his detention had not yet become unlawful. A similar decision was given by the Court of Criminal Appeal in *People v O'Loughlin* [1979] I.R. 85.

These were all cases where the law was clearly established and no justification was put forward in evidence by the prosecution witnesses for their failure to observe the rule of law in their dealings with the accused person.

Different considerations may arise where the law has been generally interpreted and applied in a particular way, without challenge, over a substantial period of time and then, by reason of judicial interpretation, what was formerly regarded as being in accordance with law is found to have been based on an incorrect interpretation of the law and, accordingly, tainted with illegality.

The present case may be taken as an example of that situation. It is common case that the procedure adopted by the garda officer for obtaining a search warrant was in accordance with standard procedure followed in availing of the provisions of section 26 of the Misuse of Drugs Act 1977. The gardaí in applying for search warrants under that section, and District Justices and Peace Commissioners in granting them, had proceeded on the basis that it was a sufficient compliance with the requirements of the section if the application was based on information on oath of a member of the Garda Síochána, deposing that he or she had reasonable ground for suspecting the existence of the matters referred to in the section. Untimately, however, this procedure, and a similar procedure followed in England in relation to analogous legislative provisions in force in that jurisdiction, were challenged in the courts and found to be invalid.

The relevant decision in relation to the English legislation is *Reg. v IRC, Ex p. Rossminister* [1980] A.C. 952, which was followed by the President of the High Court in considering the provisions of the Misuse of Drugs Act 1977, as amended by section 13 of the Misuse of Drugs Act 1984, in the case of *Byrne v Grey* [1988] I.R. 31. These decisions have already been considered and applied by this Court in the judgment already given in the present case in relation to the issue of the legality of the search warrant relied on by Garda Conway in entering the premises of the applicant.

The date of entry was 2 October 1984. Can it be said that Garda Conway was guilty of deliberate and conscious violation of the constitutional rights of the applicant, by reason of his failure to anticipate the decision of the High Court in *Byrne v Grey*, delivered on 9 October 1987, and of this Court delivered on 15 June 1989? And if so, can the Peace Commissioner who issued the search warrant, in common with the other District Justices and Peace Commissioners who have acted on the faith of similar informations on oath since the enactment of the Act of 1977, also be regarded as having been parties to deliberate and conscious violation of the constitutional rights of the persons whose homes were entered in reliance upon warrants which must now be regarded as invalid?

In *People v O'Brien* [1965] I.R. 142 Kingsmill Moore J, in a judgment which had the support of the majority of the Supreme Court, expressed himself as follows in relation to a domiciliary search, unauthorised by a valid search warrant, and which clearly involved an invasion of the constitutional rights of the accused person (at p. 160):—

> It appears to me that in every case a determination has to be made by the trial judge as to whether the public interest is best served by the admission or by the exclusion of the evidence of facts ascertained as a result of, and by means of, illegal actions, and that the answer to the question depends on a consideration of all the circumstances.

> On the one hand, the nature and extent of the illegality have to be taken into account. Was the illegal action intentional or unintentional, and, if intentional, was it the result of an *ad hoc* decision or does it represent a settled or deliberate policy? Was the illegality one of a trivial and technical nature or was it a serious invasion of important

rights, the recurrence of which would involve a real danger to necessary freedoms? . . .

At p. 161:—

> We can do no more than decide the case now before us, and to lay down that in future cases, the presiding judge has a discretion to exclude evidence of facts ascertained by illegal means where it appears to him that public policy, based on a balancing of public interests, requires such exclusion.

> The case is not one of deliberate and conscious violation, but of a purely accidental and unintentional infringement of the Constitution. In such cases, as Mr Justice Walsh indicates, the evidence normally should not be excluded.

The same approach appears to have been adopted in later cases. In *People v O'Loughlin* [1979] I.R. 85, O'Higgins CJ said at p. 91:—

> In this case the Gardaí chose not to charge the applicant when they ought to have done so. Instead, in effect, they held him further for questioning for many hours. This could not have been due to either inadvertence or oversight. It was done by experienced Garda officers who must have had a special knowledge of citizens' rights in such circumstances. It would only have been the result of a deliberate decision by these officers who were aware of the applicant's rights. These rights were disregarded and swept aside because of the concern to continue the investigation into cattle-stealing. This was not such a special circumstance . . . as could excuse the violation of constitutional rights which took place.

> If the mere fact of detention beyond the period allowed by law were sufficient of itself to constitute a deliberate and conscious breach of the constitutional rights of the accused, it would have been unnecessary for the Chief Justice to examine the other circumstances referred to in this part of his judgment.

In *The State (Quinn) v Ryan* [1965] I.R. 70, upon which reliance was placed by the appellant, the Supreme Court found that the long-standing practice of removal of persons from this jurisdiction in reliance on British warrants, backed in Ireland in accordance with the provisions of the Petty

Sessions (Ireland) Act 1851, was invalid as section 29 of that Act was inconsistent with the provisions of the Constitution. However, in considering the question of the culpability of the action of the police officers, and the consequences which flowed from the unlawful removal of the prisoner from the jurisdiction, the judgment of Ó Dálaigh CJ (at pp. 133/4) laid stress on the fact that no instance had been called to the Court's attention where the Act had been operated as it was in the case then before the Court, and that the action of both police groups manifested a determination to avoid any further "Court delays" by presenting the Courts with a *fait accompli*. In other words, the Court embarked upon an investigation as to whether the conduct amounted to deliberate and conscious violation of the constitutional rights of the accused, as had Chief Justice O'Higgins in *People v O'Loughlin* [1979] I.R. 85.

A different approach to the manner in which the phrase "deliberate and conscious breach of constitutional rights" should be construed is evident in judgments of Walsh J in *People v Walsh* [1980] I.R. 294 and in *People v Shaw* [1982] I.R. 1. The report of his judgment in *People v Walsh* contains the following passage at p. 317:—

> The onus is upon the prosecution to establish that there are such extraordinary excusing circumstances where it has been established that there has been a breach of constitutional right. If a man is consciously and deliberately kept in custody in a garda station or anywhere else without a charge being preferred against him and without being brought before a court as soon as reasonably possible, he is in unlawful custody and there has been a deliberate and conscious violation of his constitutional right to be at liberty. That this was the position in the present case is abundantly clear from the evidence given by the police officer at the trial. The fact that the officer or officers concerned may not have been conscious that what they were doing was illegal or that, even if they did know it was illegal, they did not think it was a breach of the Constitution does not affect the matter. They were conscious of the actual circumstances which existed.

The other members of the Supreme Court, O'Higgins CJ and Kenny J, did not, however, express concurrence with that judgment of Walsh J. Again, in *People v Shaw* [1982] I.R. 1 the following passage appears in the judgment of Walsh J, at p. 32 of the report:—

When the act complained of was undertaken or carried out consciously and deliberately, it is immaterial whether the person carrying out the act may or may not have been conscious that what he was doing was illegal, or, even if he knew it was illegal, that it amounted to a breach of the constitutional rights of the accused. It is the doing of the act which is the essential matter, not the actor's appreciation of the legal consequences or incidents of it: *People v Madden* [1977] I.R. 336.

However the other members of the Court concurred in the judgment delivered by Griffin J in the course of which he expressed disagreement with the opinion on this topic which had been expressed by Walsh J in *People v Walsh* [1980] I.R. 294 and again in *People v Shaw* [1982] I.R. 1, the case then before the Supreme Court. He said at pp. 55 and 56 of the report:—

Nor did I find myself able to support the opinion that a person's statement is to be ruled out as evidence obtained in deliberate and conscious violation of his constitutional rights, even though the taker of the statement may not have known that what he was doing was either illegal or unconstitutional. I consider the authorities to be to the contrary effect. For example, in *People (Attorney General) v O'Brien* Kingsmill Moore J (who gave the majority judgment) having held that evidence obtained in deliberate and conscious violation of constitutional rights should be excluded except in "extraordinary excusing circumstances" (which he preferred to leave unspecified), excused as "a purely accidental and unintentional infringement of the Constitution" the violation complained of in that case: see p. 162 of the report. See also *People v Madden* at p. 346 where a "factor such as inadvertence" was recognized as being capable of being one of the "extraordinary excusing circumstances" envisaged in *O'Brien's Case*. In my opinion, it is the violation of the person's constitutional rights, and not the particular act complained of, that has to be deliberate and conscious for the purpose of ruling out a statement.

See also what was said by Henchy J in the course of his judgment in *People v Quilligan* [1986] I.R. 495 as follows:—

The only other ground upon which the statements could be

rejected is if it could be held that they were the fruit of an arrest which was a conscious and deliberate violation of the prisoner's constitutional right to personal liberty. However, that conclusion was not open, for even if it could be said that the arrest was an unconstitutional act, it was not consciously or deliberately so. In arresting the accused under section 30 of the Offences Against the State Act 1939, for a scheduled offence, the arresting gardaí were acting in good faith, because they were merely following a system of arrest which had been followed — and given at least tacit approval in the courts — even since prosecutions were first brought in respect of scheduled offences under that Act. It would follow, therefore, that, regardless of any unconstitutionality in the arrest, the statements were admissible in evidence.

Some confusion appears to have arisen since *People v O'Brien* [1965] I.R. 142 was decided about the application of the concept of "extraordinary excusing circumstances" and it is important to note that the impact of that concept has only to be considered where the Court is of the view that a deliberate and conscious violation of constitutional rights has taken place, but has to go on to consider whether there are, nevertheless, "extraordinary excusing circumstances" which would permit the admission of evidence which could be regarded as tainted by this element of unconstitutionality. Where, however, what has taken place should not be regarded as a deliberate and conscious violation of the constitutional rights of the accused, then the question of the admissibility of the evidence can be considered as a matter for the Court's discretion without having to consider whether "extraordinary excusing circumstances" existed.

Finally, it is of interest to note that a case which provides a close parallel to the present case came before the US Supreme Court in 1984 — *United States v Leon* (1984) 468 U.S. 897. It involved a consideration of the Fourth Amendment of the US Constitution which provides that:—

> the right of the people to be secure in their persons, houses, papers and effects against unreasonable searches and seizures, shall not be violated, and no warrants shall issue, but upon probable cause, supported by oath or affirmation, and particularly describing the place to be searched, and the persons or things to be seized.

The Court held that the Fourth Amendment's exclusionary rule should not be applied so as to bar the use in the prosecution's case in chief of evidence obtained by officers acting in reasonable reliance on a search warrant issued by a detached and neutral magistrate but ultimately found to be invalid.

The rationale lying behind the exclusion of evidence obtained in circumstances involving a breach of these constitutional guarantees was examined by White J, who delivered the Opinion of the Court. He said at p. 906 et seq.:—

> The Fourth Amendment contains no provision expressly precluding the use of evidence obtained in violation of its commands, and an examination of its origin and purposes makes clear that the use of fruits of a past unlawful search or seizure "works no new Fourth Amendment wrong" (*US v Calandra*, 414 U.S. 338/354). . . . The rule thus operates as a "judicially created remedy designed to safeguard Fourth Amendment rights generally through its deterrent effect, rather than a personal constitutional right of the party aggrieved." (*US v Calandra*, supra, at 348).

> Whether the exclusionary sanction is appropriately imposed in a particular case, our decisions make clear, is "an issue separate from the question whether the Fourth Amendment rights of the party seeking to invoke the rule were violated by police conduct" (*Illinois v Gates, supra*, at 223). Only the former question is currently before us, and it must be resolved by weighing the costs and benefits of preventing the use in the prosecution's case in chief of inherently trustworthy tangible evidence obtained in reliance on a search warrant issued by a detached and neutral magistrate that ultimately is found to be defective.

> The substantial social costs exacted by the exclusionary rule for the vindication of Fourth Amendment rights have long been a source of concern. "Our cases have consistently recognized that unbending application of the exclusionary sanction to enforce ideals of governmental rectitude would impede unacceptably the truth-finding functions of judge and jury". *United States v Payner*, 447 U.S. 727, 734. An objectionable collateral consequence of this interference with the criminal justice system's truth-finding function is that some guilty defendants may go free or receive reduced sentences as a result of

favourable plea bargains. Particularly when law enforcement officers have acted in objective good faith or their transgressions have been minor, the magnitude of the benefit conferred on such guilty defendants offends basic concepts of the criminal justice system. *Stone v Powell*, 428 U.S. at 490. Indiscriminate application of the exclusionary rule, therefore, may well "generate disrespect for the law and administration of justice." Id., at 491. Accordingly, "as with any remedial device, the application of the rule has been restricted to those areas where its remedial objectives are thought most efficaciously served."

At p. 916:—

... the exclusionary rule is designed to deter police misconduct rather than to punish the errors of judges and magistrates. Second, there exists no evidence suggesting that judges and magistrates are inclined to subvert the Fourth Amendment or that lawlessness among these actors requires application of the extreme sanction of exclusion. Third, and most important, we discern no basis, and are offered none, for believing that exclusion of evidence seized pursuant to a warrant will have a significant deterrent effect on the issuing judge or magistrate. ...

At p. 922:—

We conclude that the marginal or non-existent benefits produced by suppressing evidence obtained in objectively reasonable reliance on a subsequently invalidated search warrant cannot justify the substantial costs of exclusion.

In many ways it appears to this Court that what was said in *US v Leon* echoes what was said already by Kingsmill Moore J, in *People v O'Brien* as to the manner in which the exclusionary rule should be applied within our own jurisdiction.

In the opinion of the Court, the evidence in the present case, which shows that Garda Conway took all steps believed to be necessary and appropriate for obtaining a valid search warrant, and armed himself with a warrant issued by a Peace Commissioner in purported exercise of his functions under the relevant Act, is a clear indication that there was no deliberate or conscious violation of the constitutional rights of the appellant.

In these circumstances the correct decision for the trial Judge to make in the circumstances of the present case, would have been to admit the evidence obtained as a result of the use made of the search warrant in question. He took this course, but in the mistaken belief that the warrant had been regularly obtained and was a valid warrant. The challenge to the validity of the warrant has been determined in the appellant's favour, but the Court considers that in the circumstances already outlined in this judgment, no miscarriage of justice occurred, and proposes to dismiss the appeal, in exercise of the jurisdiction conferred on it by the provisions of the Courts of Justice Act 1928, section 5, subsection (1)(a).

Solicitor for the appellant: *Padraic Ferry and Co.*   *Eithne Casey*
Solicitor for the respondent: *Chief State Solicitor*   *Barrister*

The People (Director of Public Prosecutions) v Noel Healy*
[C.C.A. No. 20 of 1988]

Court of Criminal Appeal   12 July 1989

Sentence – imprisonment – duration – offences committed while on bail – disparity of sentences between co-defendants – Lesser sentence imposed on co-defendants on ground that it was a consecutive sentence

Totality of sentences – whether consecutive sentence should be adjusted downwards if aggregate of sentence is high – whether duration of sentence to be determined regardless of whether it would be a consecutive sentence

Statute – construction – Criminal Justice Act 1984 (No. 22), section 11

Section 11 of the Criminal Justice Act 1984, provides, *inter alia*, that:—

11.—(1) Any sentence of imprisonment passed on a person for an offence committed . . . while he was on bail shall be consecutive on any sentence passed on him for a previous offence. . . .

The applicant, along with a number of others, was charged in the Limerick Circuit Court with a series of offences arising out of a conspiracy to rob a jewellery premises. The crime involved holding the family of the owner of the premises hostage while the robbery was

*This case is now reported: [1990] 1 I.R. 388.

carried out. After the trial had commenced, the applicant was re-arraigned whereupon he pleaded guilty to two counts, namely, conspiracy to commit false imprisonment and conspiracy to rob. He was sentenced to concurrent terms of 8 years imprisonment on each count. Three of the applicant's co-accused were each sentenced to terms of imprisonment of two, three and four years. As the applicant's co-accused were on bail when these offences were committed, the President of the Circuit Court when sentencing them took into account the total number of years that would be served by them.

Counsel for the applicant stated that he was not arguing that the sentence of eight years imposed on his client was excessive for the crime of robbery, but he stated that different sentencing principles cannot be applied as between all the accused. He submitted that the sentence of eight years was disproportionate to the sentences imposed on the three co-accused, and in particular as the applicant was the youngest, was a petty criminal whereas the other offenders were hardened criminals who were already serving sentences. The applicant, it was stated, was controlled by one of the co-accused and justice required that he should be not be serving a longer sentence.

Counsel for the prosecution submitted that section 11 of the Criminal Justice Act 1984, which did not apply in the applicant's case but did apply to his co-accused, required that a consecutive sentence had to be imposed on them as these offences were committed while they were on bail for other offences and as a result the trial judge adjusted their sentences downwards.

The Court then required counsel for the prosecution to ascertain the attitude of the Director of Public Prosecutions to the trial judge's view that he should look at the total sentencing period where a crime was committed while on bail, and whether or not that was a good ground for reducing significantly the amount of sentence imposed. When the case was resumed counsel stated that the Director of Public Prosecutions' view was that the policy of section 11 of the Act of 1984 was a deterrent one, and that the sentence imposed should be appropriate to the crime regardless of any sentence already being served. Counsel said that the learned President of the Circuit Court looked at the totality of sentences to be served by the co-accused, and in normal circumstances he would have imposed ten or fifteen years on them and the total number of years to be served by the three co- accused were fifteen years, eight years and six years. Counsel submitted that the section required that a judge should disregard the duration of the sentence imposed for the first offence and fix a sentence appropriate to the second crime. He submitted that the Court should not follow the English practice of taking into account the total number of years to be served for all offences.

Held by the Court (McCarthy, Carroll and Barron JJ) in dismissing the application:

(1) That where section 11 of the Act of 1984 applied, the sentencing Court should determine the sentence appropriate to the offence on the indictment without regard to the fact that it must be a consecutive sentence on any sentence for a previous offence. However, in the case of grave offences, the Court should adjust the sentence downwards where not to do so would impose a manifestly unjust punishment on the accused.

(2) In the instant case the sentence imposed was not excessive or founded on any error in principle, and a comparison with the sentences imposed on the other accused which were based on a misconstruction of the Act of 1984, was inappropriate. *People (Attorney General) v Poyning* [1972] I.R. 402 applied.

Case cited in this judgment
People (Attorney General) v Poyning [1972] I.R. 402

The following were cited in argument
S. Edgar, *Craies on Statute Law*, 6th Ed., p. 66
Archbold: *Criminal Pleading Evidence and Practice*, 43rd Ed., para. 5/176 and 5/178

Kevin Haugh SC and Hugh Hartnett **for the applicant**
Thomas O'Connell **for the respondent**

McCarthy J

Noel Healy (the applicant), John Curley, George Royale, Gerard Rodgers and Paul Harte were charged at the Circuit Court in Limerick with a series of offences arising from an elaborate conspiracy to carry out an armed hold-up of Mr Duffy and his family at his home in Limerick, forcing Mr Duffy to open his jewellery premises and thus carry out a large scale robbery. Efficient and comprehensive police action forestalled the plan. After the trial had commenced, the applicant was re-arraigned and pleaded guilty to two counts on the indictment, conspiracy to commit false imprisonment and conspiracy to rob. He was sentenced by the President of the Circuit Court to a term of eight years imprisonment on each count, such sentences to be concurrent.

It is not argued that the sentence itself is disproportionate to the offences nor that there is any intrinsic error in principle. The contention is that the sentence is disproportionate to the sentence imposed on the co-conspirators who have been dealt with in the courts and that this is particularly so since the applicant was the youngest of those involved and the only one to answer to his bail. It is convenient, therefore, to set out in tabular form certain details concerning each conspirator who has been sentenced:—

Accused	Counts	Sentence	Date
Noel Healy	1 and 2	8 years	15-12-1986
Paul Harte	2 and 8	2 years	17-10-1986
George Royale	2	2 years	4-5-1987
Gerard Rodgers	2 and 8	4 years	3-4-1989

The Court has read the transcripts of the sentencing of Messrs. Harte, Royale and Rodgers.

Paul Harte, who was then serving a sentence of 10 years imprisonment for the offence of possession of firearms with intent to endanger life on 3 December 1984, pleaded guilty to an armed robbery in a public house in Wicklow on 4 June 1985, when he was on bail in respect of the December 1984 offences; on 17 October 1986, on his plea of guilty to counts 2 and 8 of the indictment also preferred against the present applicant, he was sentenced to 2 years imprisonment to commence at the expiration of a sentence of 3 years imprisonment imposed in respect of the Wicklow offence. The trial judge stated:—

> I must make it clear that these sentences which may appear very light are being imposed simply because Mr Harte is already serving a sentence of 10 years imposed this year. If it wasn't for that I would have imposed sentences of about 15 years imprisonment for the two offences to which he pleaded guilty today. It amounts to the same thing in the long run.

George Royale was, on 18 February 1987, convicted of an aggravated burglary committed in Wexford, on which charge he was on bail at the time of the commission of the Limerick offence of conspiracy to rob to which he pleaded guilty. In sentencing him on this charge, the trial judge said:—

> Now the question that arises with me is what would have happened if this charge had been mentioned to Judge Buchanan, my colleague, on 28 February, last when you were sentenced to 4 years. If he could have taken it into account, which he couldn't have having regard to the circumstances, what would he have added on? I think he would have added on 2 years which I am going to give you. I am going to impose a 2 year sentence upon you for the present charge again making it quite clear that you are not pleading guilty to the aggravated count, count No. 1, the false imprisonment. I am making it quite clear that I am holding you guilty of a minor part in the conspiracy in imposing 2 years imprisonment only and that it is to be consecutive upon the 4 years already imposed on you.

Gerard Rodgers who pleaded guilty to the conspiracy to rob and the possession of firearms offences was, like Paul Harte and the present applicant, dealt with by the learned President of the Circuit Court. He was not sentenced until 3 April 1989, having absconded after the offences had been committed. Details of the sentences imposed upon the applicant, Paul Harte and George Royale were given to the learned President who said:—

The crimes to which Mr Rodgers has pleaded guilty are very serious. The real sentences imposed by me on Mr Rodgers' co-defendants were 15 years and eight years. Judges, whether they are entitled to is a very doubtful matter, they probably are not but judges when sentences have to be made consecutive have adopted a practice if the sentence to which the new sentence is to be made consecutive is a very long one of imposing very light sentences for the latter offences. Mr Harte was serving 10 years when he came before me. I remember the case well and he came before me and I sentenced him to 3 years consecutive to the 10 years and then 2 years consecutive to the 13 years the effective sentence was 15 years. In Mr Healy's case, there was no question of a consecutive sentence and I sentenced him to 8 years. In Mr Royale's case, which did not come before me, perhaps fortunately for Mr Royale, the effective sentence was 6 years because he was serving 4 years when he came before Judge Buchanan (*recte Judge O'Malley*) and the judge imposed a sentence of 2 years consecutive to the 4 years. So the real sentences were 15 years, 8 years and 6 years.

The facts really speak for themselves, from every aspect of the case. Mr Rodgers has a much better record then Mr Royale, Mr Healy or Mr Harte. They have 18, 14 and 16 previous convictions each, many of them for serious crime. The fair inference from that is that up to the commission of this offence Mr Rodgers was not a hardened criminal nor was he seen on all the occasions on which the gang were seen by the guards in the guards very skilful investigations of the crime. That justifies me in thinking that Mr Rodgers was not as heavily involved as the other four. He may have been but he is entitled to the benefit of the doubt on that point. In other words, I cannot draw a distinction between Mr Rodgers and his 3 co-defendants and hold that he played a more minor role then they did but his role nonetheless was quite major because it involved arming himself with a firearm and laying siege to Mrs Duffy's home for the purpose of robbing her husband to hold her and her family hostage. On that basis I would be justified in sentencing Mr Rodgers to the lowest of all the sentences imposed, although he absconded and attempted to avoid being dealt with. He has, since his arrest, at least had the honesty to plead guilty. He could have put the State to the expense of proving his guilt and with the passage of time some difficulties might have arisen. I will impose a sentence of 4 years imprisonment on the two counts to run concurrently.

John Curley had not been made amenable to justice.

It is clear that the sentences imposed on Messrs. Harte, Royale and Rodgers in respect of those offences in this conspiracy to which they pleaded guilty, were qualified by the effect, as construed by the trial judges, of section 11 of the Criminal Justice Act 1984, which reads:—

11.—(1) Any sentence of imprisonment passed on a person for an offence committed after the commencement of this section while he was on bail shall be consecutive on any sentence passed on him for a previous offence or, if he is sentenced in respect of two or more previous offences, on the sentence last due to expire, so however that, where two or more consecutive sentences as required by this section are passed by the District Court, the aggregate term of imprisonment in respect of those consecutive sentences shall not exceed two years.

(2) Subsection (1) shall not apply where any such sentence is one of imprisonment for life or is a sentence of detention under section 103 of the Children Act 1908.

(3) Subsection (1) shall apply notwithstanding anything contained in section 5 of the Criminal Justice Act, 1951.

This section of the Act came into force on 1 March 1985. At the invitation of the Court, Counsel for the Director has made submissions on the true construction of section 11, suggesting that there are two possible constructions:—

(a) That the sentencing Court should choose the sentence appropriate to the offence regardless of the duration of any existing sentence of imprisonment presently being served.

(b) The sentencing Court should review the aggregate of the sentence being served and the suggested appropriate sentence and, then, consider whether it is just to impose such a sentence — applying a so-called "totality principle".

There is a third possible construction somewhat between the two extremes; that in the graver cases, if the Court considers the aggregate of consecutive sentences to be excessive, then the consecutive sentence or sentences should be lessened accordingly.

This Court is, presently, dealing with an application for leave to appeal against a sentence which is not one within section 11 of the Act of 1984, it is the fact that the argument has depended upon a comparison with sentences that were within section 11 that has led to this examination of those sentences and of section 11 itself. The Court has not heard argument on behalf of an applicant so sentenced; if the section continues to be construed in the manner reflected in the Harte, Rodgers and Royale cases, it is unlikely that the Court will have an application for leave to appeal against sentence in a case where the section has been thus applied. The Court, therefore, takes the opportunity of stating that in the application of section 11 of the Criminal Justice Act 1984, the sentencing Court should determine the sentence appropriate to the offence or offences on the indictment, to which the section applies without regard to the fact that it must be a consecutive sentence under the provisions of section 11, and direct that such a sentence shall be consecutive on any sentence for a previous offence. This is not to say that, in a proper case, the sentencing court, in the case of grave offences, should not adjust the sentence downwards where not to do so would impose a manifestly unjust punishment on the accused.

It follows that a comparison with the sentences imposed upon the other conspirators in the instant case is inappropriate. If they were fortunate in having the section misconstrued in their favour, it does not follow that sentences thus imposed would be a valid basis of comparison. Disparity of sentence is not a ground upon which the Court would, necessarily, intervene. In *People (Attorney General) v Poyning* [1972] I.R. 402 it was stated at p. 408:—

When two prisoners have been jointly indicted and convicted and one of them receives a light sentence, or none at all, it does not follow that a severe sentence on the other must be unjust. If in any particular case one of such joint accused has received too short a sentence, that is not *per se* a ground on which this Court would necessarily interfere with the longer sentence passed on the other. Of course, in any particular case the Court must examine the disparity in sentences where, if all other things were equal, the sentences should be the same; it must examine whether the differentation in treatment is justified. The Court, in considering the principles which should inform a judge's mind when imposing sentence and having regard to the differences in the characters and antecedents of the convicted persons, will seek to discover whether the discrimination was based on those differences.

For all of these reasons, the Court is of opinion that the sentence of 8 years imprisonment was in no way excessive or founded upon any error in principle. The application for leave to appeal is dismissed.

Solicitor for the applicant: *Michael Hanahoe and Co.*
Solicitor for the respondent: *Chief State Solicitor*

Eithne Casey
Barrister

The People (Director of Public Prosecutions) v Patrick O'Brien
[C.C.A. No. 40 of 1988]

Court of Criminal Appeal   21 July 1989

Court of Criminal Appeal – function of Court in review of criminal trial – judge's charge – clear invitation to jury to acquit – verdict of jury – whether perverse – Courts (Supplemental Provisions) Act 1961 (No. 39), section 12

Section 12, subsection (1) of the Courts (Supplemental Provisions) Act 1961, states, *inter alia*, that:—

12.—(1) The Court of Criminal Appeal shall be a superior court of record and shall . . . have full power to determine any questions necessary to be determined for the purpose of doing justice in the case before it.

The applicant was found guilty by a jury on three counts of attempted carnal knowledge contrary to section 1, subection (2) of the Criminal Law (Amendment) Act 1935, and three counts of indecent assault contrary to section 10 of the Criminal Law (Rape) Act 1981. He was sentenced to three terms of five years penal servitude on each of the attempted carnal knowledge charges, and three years imprisonment on each of the indecent assault charges, all sentences to run concurrently. He applied for leave to appeal against conviction. The facts of the case are set out in the judgment and the ground of appeal was that the verdict of the jury was against the weight of the evidence. The offences were committed against three girls who were under the age of fifteen. No complaint was made until about one month after the event.

It was submitted on behalf of the applicant that each girl gave evidence that not only had interference occurred, but also sexual intercourse, however, medical evidence contradicted this, no evidence of penetration having been found. Further it was argued that there were contradictions in the girls' evidence and that not only was there no corroboration but each girl did not corroborate the other. It was also submitted that the trial judge in his charge to the jury invited the jury to acquit. The judge did not withdraw the case from the jury but gave a comprehensive charge on the dangers of convicting in the absence of corroboration, of the different account given by each girl, of the fact that no complaint was made at the time and that there was no evidence of distress. Counsel argued that the verdict was unsafe and referred to the powers of the Court of Criminal Appeal to determine any question necessary for the purpose of doing justice. He referred to the situation in England where the Court of Appeal (Criminal Division) can allow an appeal if it thinks that the verdict of a jury was unreasonable and where that court asks itself the subjective question as to whether it had a "lurking doubt" that injustice may have been done.

Counsel for the prosecution submitted that it was not the case that the verdict was against the evidence, the evidence of the girls amounted to attempted penetration and not penetration, that they were aged under 15 years and consent was no defence, that the girls were not cross-examined as to whether penetration had occurred, that there had been no application at the trial to withdraw the case on the ground that the evidence went to rape and not to attempted carnal knowledge and that the jury was entitled to reach their verdict in the light of the evidence as a whole.

Held by the Court (McCarthy, Barrington and Lardner JJ) in dismissing the application, that the verdict of the jury could not be interfered with. The jury were properly charged by the trial judge and were warned in the most express terms of the danger of acting on the uncorroborated evidence of the complainants. The jury saw the complainants giving evidence, heard them being cross-examined and observed their demeanour throughout and it would be an unwarranted interference with the function of the jury if the Court were not to accept their verdict. *People (DPP) v Kelly (No. 2)* [1983] I.R. 1; *People (DPP) v Madden* [1977] I.R. 336 and *People (DPP) v Mulligan* 2 Frewen 16 applied. *R. v Cooper* [1969] 1 Q.B. 267 not followed.

Semble There may be cases in which the wide powers given to the Court of Criminal Appeal by section 12 of the Act of 1961 may be called in aid to interfere with the verdict of a jury even in a case where technically there was evidence to support the verdict.

Cases cited in this judgment:
People (DPP) v Kelly (No. 2) [1983] I.R. 1; [1983] ILRM 271
People (DPP) v Madden [1977] I.R. 336; 111 I.L.T.R. 117
People (DPP) v Mulligan 2 Frewen 16
R. v Cooper [1969] 1 Q.B. 267; [1968] 3 W.L.R. 1225; [1969] 1 All E.R. 32;
53 Cr. App. R. 82

Additional cases cited in argument:
Attorney General v Lloyd 1 Frewen 32
R. v Stafford [1974] A.C. 878
R. v Turnbull [1977] Q.B. 224; [1976] 3 W.L.R. 445; [1976] 3 All E.R. 549;
63 Cr. App. R. 132

The application for leave to appeal was heard by the Court on 17 July 1989. After the Court delivered its judgment, counsel for the applicant applied for a certificate pursuant to section 29 of the Courts of Justice Act 1924, to enable him to take an appeal to the Supreme Court. The Court refused the application.

Seamus Sorahan SC and Michael Grey **for the applicant**
Miriam Malone **for the respondent**

McCarthy J:

The applicant applies for leave to appeal against conviction on indictment on six counts, three of them attempting to have unlawful carnal knowledge of a girl under the age of 15 years and three of indecent assault. The charges arise upon incidents alleged to have taken place on a date in October 1985, when three girls, two sisters and their cousin, were alleged to have been accosted by the applicant on a street in Kilrush, Co. Clare and invited by him to look for a straying donkey in sheds adjoining a field in the area. Whilst in the second shed the allegation was that the offences were committed. The critical evidence in the case was that of the three girls whose account differed both descriptively and in the alleged sequence of the molesting of each of them. The girls, who made no complaint of what had occurred until about a month after the event, were medically examined and found to be virgins, although each girl specifically alleged that the applicant had had sexual intercourse with her.

The trial took place in February 1988, some 2½ years after the alleged commission of the offences. The case depended upon the evidence of the three girls, there being no corroboration of their evidence and, in a sense, there was medical evidence to contradict their account.

The application is based upon the contention that the verdict of the jury was perverse. Mr Sorahan developed an elaborate argument based upon a comparison of the relevant English Statutes of 1907 and 1968 concerning appeals in criminal cases by contrast with section 12 of the Courts (Supplemental Provisions) Act 1961 with particular reference to the decision in *R. v Cooper* (1969) 53 Cr. App. R. 82, the leading case in England on "lurking doubt" as a ground of appeal, it being a case of visual identification.

The English statute gives jurisdiction to the Court of Appeal to quash a conviction if the Court considers it is unsafe or unsatisfactory. There is no specific power in the Act of 1961 but it is contended that there are wider powers.

That statute has been considered in *People (DPP) v Kelly (No. 2)* [1983] I.R. 1 and in *People (DPP) v Mulligan & Others* 2 Frewen 16.

In *People (DPP) v Madden* [1977] I.R. 336, this Court stated its function in the clearest terms at p. 339. In *People (DPP) v Mulligan* this Court again iterated the reviewing role of this Court.

In the instant case, the learned trial judge gave a clear invitation to the jury to acquit. It is no criticism of his charge to the jury to say that he laid great emphasis on the weakness of the prosecution, in that it depended upon the evidence of three girls, given 2½ years after the alleged event, who themselves had not immediately complained about the alleged incidents. He stressed more than once the dangers of convicting upon the uncorroborated evidence of the three girls and he pointed a number of times to the interior conflicts in their evidence and the conflict produced by the medical evidence. It is to be inferred from his observation that, if trying the case himself, he would have found it difficult to bring in a verdict of guilty. That, however, as the learned trial judge very properly pointed out, was not his function. That, pre-eminently, was the function of the jury. It would, in the opinion of this Court, be an unwarranted interference with and usurpation of the function of the jury if he had done otherwise or if this Court were to do otherwise. This Court does not have the advantage that the jury had — of seeing these girls giving evidence, of hearing them being cross-examined, of observing their demeanour throughout.

There may be cases in which the wide powers given to this Court by section 12 of the Act of 1961 may be called in aid to interfere with the verdict of the jury even in a case where technically there was evidence to support the verdict. This is not such a case. The trial was conducted with exemplary fairness; the jury was warned in the most express terms about the danger of acting on the evidence of these young girls; they were, however, entitled to do so, they did and the verdict must stand.

The application for leave to appeal is dismissed.

Solicitor for the applicant: *Henry Kelly and Co.*
Solicitor for the respondent: *Chief State Solicitor*

Eithne Casey
Barrister

The People (Director of Public Prosecutions) v Paul Murtagh*
[C.C.A. No. 49 of 1987]

Court of Criminal Appeal   27 July 1989

Perjury – subornation of perjury – attempting to pervert the court of justice – charges arising out of false allegations of assault against garda – inciting another to make false statement regarding the alleged assault – suborning another to commit perjury at trial of garda for alleged assault – whether witness for prosecution ranked as an accomplice – failure of trial judge to warn jury on danger of convicting on uncorroborated evidence of accomplice

The appellant was convicted in the Dublin Circuit (Criminal) Court on a charge of subornation of perjury contrary to common law and section 2 of the Perjury Act 1729, and a charge of attempted perversion of the due course of law and justice contrary to common law. Concurrent sentences of two years imprisonment were imposed. Leave to appeal against conviction and sentence was granted by the Court of Criminal Appeal on 4 May 1987, and the appellant was admitted to bail pending the determination of the appeal.

The charges arose out of the arrest of the appellant for an offence of drunken driving. The appellant alleged that after his arrest he had been assaulted by a number of gardaí and as a result of his complaints summonses were issued against a garda. The summons against the garda for assault was heard in the District Court and was dismissed. The appellant was later charged with perjury arising out of the evidence that he gave at the trial of the garda. He was also charged with suborning his friend who was with him at the relevant time to give false evidence at the trial of the garda, and of attempting to pervert the course of justice by inciting the said friend to make a false statement to An Garda Síochána to the effect that she had seen the appellant being assaulted on the night of his arrest for drunk driving.

It was argued on behalf of the appellant that the trial judge in his charge may have conveyed to the jury that they were entitled to draw inferences of guilt when he stated that the accuseds "silence adds weight to the evidence against him, nowhere is the evidence (of the gardaí) contradicted". It was also argued that corroboration was required to prove a charge of attempting to pervert the course of justice by subornation of perjury and that there was no evidence that a lawful oath had been administered to the prosecution witness as she wished to swear on the Koran and none was available. Further the accused believed that he had been assaulted, and he believed that his friend had seen the assault, therefore the *mens rea* required for the offence of subornation of perjury was absent.

The Court of its own motion raised the question as to whether the prosecution witness, the friend of the appellant, ranked as an accomplice and it was on this finding alone that the conviction was quashed.

Held by the Court (Finlay CJ, Costello and Johnson JJ) in allowing the appeal and in ordering a re-trial that, on the charge of subornation of perjury the prosecution witness was an accomplice of the accused and the trial judge failed to warn the jury that, although they might convict on the evidence of an accomplice, it was dangerous to do so unless the evidence was corroborated. Likewise, in a prosecution for the offence of attempting to pervert the course of justice by inciting another to make a false statement to the gardaí, the prosecution

*This case is now reported: [1990] 1 I.R. 339.

witness, by allowing herself to be incited, was an accomplice to the accused's crime and the same warning should have been given.

No cases cited in judgment

Additional cases cited in argument:
Attorney General v Fleming [1934] I.R. 166; 68 I.L.T.R. 223
R. v Bathurst [1968] 2 Q.B. 99; [1968] 2 W.L.R. 1092; [1968] 1 All E.R. 1175;
    52 Cr. App. R. 251
R. v Knill (1822) 5 B & Ald 929
R. v Mutch [1973] 1 All E.R. 178; 57 Cr. App. R. 196
R. v Pratt [1971] Cr. Law Rev. 234
R. v Singh [1958] 1 All E.R. 199
R. v Sparrow [1973] 1 W.L.R. 488; [1973] 2 All E.R. 129; 57 Cr. App. R. 352
R. v Waugh [1950] A.C. 203; [1950] W.N. 173; 66 T.L.R. 554

Other material cited in argument
Archbold, *Criminal Pleading Evidence and Practice* 42nd Ed., 4-431 and 24th Ed.,
    1910, p. 476
Stephen, *History of the Criminal Law of England*, p. 240
O Síocháin, *Criminal Law of Ireland*, 7th Ed., p. 231
O Síocháin, *Criminal Law of Ireland* 6th Ed., p. 236
Perjury Act 1911 (Ch. 6) section 13

Seamus Sorahan SC and Michael Gray **for the appellant**
Erwan Mill-Arden **for the respondent**

Costello J

The appellant was charged in the Dublin Circuit Court with charges of perjury (count 1), subornation of perjury (count 2) and of an attempt to pervert the course of justice (count 3). The jury disagreed on count 1 but found him guilty of the charges contained in counts 2 and 3 and on the 1st of April 1987, he was sentenced to two years' imprisonment in respect of each count, the sentences to run concurrently. Leave to appeal was granted by this Court on the 4th of May 1987, and the appellant was admitted to bail.

The facts which gave rise to the charges against the appellant can be briefly stated as follows. On the evening of the 20th of June the appellant was observed by members of the Garda Síochána coming out of a licensed premises in Swords and getting into his car. Later he was arrested at Seatown Terrace in Swords, brought across the road, put into a police car and brought to Swords garda station. He was charged with drunken driving and subsequently convicted. This Court is not concerned with this conviction but with the circumstances of the arrest and subsequent detention and what happened thereafter. The appellant alleged that he was assaulted whilst being taken across the road at Seatown Terrace and later in the Swords garda station and, as a result of his complaints, summonses were issued by the Director of Public Prosecutions against a number of gardaí, including a Garda O'Sullivan. The summons against Garda O'Sullivan was heard in the Swords District Court on the 17th of July 1984, and dismissed. The charge of perjury arises from the evidence the appellant gave at that trial. The charges of subornation of perjury and attempting to pervert the course of justice arise from the role of a Mrs Sylvia Dunne in the prosecution against Garda O'Sullivan. The charge in count 2 alleged that the accused had between the 15th and 17th of July 1984 (that is, just before Garda O'Sullivan's trial) suborned Mrs Dunne to commit perjury at the trial and the charge on count 3 alleged that on or about the 19th of October 1983, he attempted to pervert the course of justice by inciting Mrs Dunne to make a false statement to the gardaí to the effect that Garda O'Sullivan had assaulted him at Seatown Terrace at the time of his arrest.

The evidence for the prosecution at the appellant's trial consisted of garda witnesses who denied any assault on the accused, medical evidence concerning the appellant's physical condition on the night of his arrest and the day following, and the evidence, crucial to the prosecution case on counts 2 and 3, of Mrs Dunne. She swore that the statement she had made to the gardaí on or about the 19th of October 1983, in which she stated that she had seen the appellant assaulted was false, that the evidence she gave at the trial of Garda O'Sullivan was false, that she had been requested by the appellant to make the statement of the 19th of October, and that he, shortly before the trial, had urged her to give evidence in accordance with it. The appellant gave no evidence at his trial.

The Court granted the appellant leave to amend the grounds of appeal to permit arguments to be advanced relating to the failure of the trial judge to accede to counsel's requisitions at the trial. It also heard submissions on a point which the court itself raised, namely whether Mrs Dunne could properly be regarded as an accomplice of the accused on either count 2 or count 3 and if so, the effect of the failure of the trial judge to give the jury the required warning on the dangers of convicting on the evidence of an accomplice.

As the Court has come to the conclusion that Mrs Dunne was as a matter of law an accomplice in respect of the charge in counts 2 and 3 and that it would be unsafe to allow the conviction on that count to stand, it does not consider it necessary to consider at any length the other points that were canvassed in the course of this appeal.

If, as alleged by the prosecution, the accused had incited Mrs Dunne to commit perjury at the trial of the 17th of July 1984, then by giving perjured evidence she was an accomplice to the crime with which the accused was charged — subornation of perjury contrary to common law — for the perjurer is an accomplice of the suborner. The learned trial judge did not point this out to the jury and did not give them the warning which the law requires a trial judge to give in such circumstances. The Court cannot speculate as to what the jury would have done had the warning been given and its absence renders the conviction unsafe.

With regard to count 3, the prosecution case was that the accused had committed the common law offence of attempting to pervert the course of justice when sometime before the 19th of October 1983, he incited Mrs Dunne to make a false statement to the gardaí to the effect that a member of the gardaí had assaulted him. Such an offence is completed when the words of incitement are uttered, and so the offence is committed even though the incitement fails. In going to the gardaí Mrs Dunne allowed herself to be incited and (assuming the prosecution case to be correct) herself committed the crime of perverting the course of justice by making a false allegation of assault. But in the Court's view she was an accomplice to the accused's alleged offence also when she made the false charge (had she not done so she could not have been implicated in the accused's alleged crime) and a warning on the dangers of convicting the accused on her evidence in respect of count 3 should also have been given. In its absence, the conviction cannot stand.

Both convictions will therefore be quashed and a new trial ordered in respect of the charges on counts 2 and 3.

Solicitor for the appellant: *Henry Kelly and Co.*
Solicitor for the respondent: *Chief State Solicitor*

Eithne Casey
Barrister

The People (Director of Public Prosecutions) v Gerard O'Shea
(C.C.A. No. 111 of 1986)

Court of Criminal Appeal   28 July 1989

Arrest – arrest pursuant to section 30 of the Act of 1939 – suspicion of commission of scheduled offence – detention – extension of period of detention – extension order issued by chief superintendent – suspicion grounding signing of extension order – reliance placed on information furnished by other officers – whether chief superintendent personally formed any suspicion when he directed the extension of the period of detention – continuance of original suspicion – Offences Against the State Act 1939 (No. 13), s. 30(3)

Section 30(3) of the Act of 1939 provides as follows:

> Whenever a person is arrested under this section, he may be removed to and detained in custody in a Garda Síochána station, a prison, or some other convenient place for a period of twenty four hours from the time of his arrest and may, if an officer of An Garda Síochána not below the rank of Chief Superintendent so directs, be so detained for a further period of twenty four hours.

The applicant was convicted of robbery and of having a firearm with intent to commit robbery after a trial before the Special Criminal Court and he was sentenced to eight years imprisonment on each count to run concurrently. He applied for leave to appeal his conviction. The applicant was arrested under s. 30 of the Act of 1939 on suspicion of having committed a scheduled offence under the Firearms Act. He was detained in custody and subsequently an extension order was made pursuant to s. 30(3) of the said Act, and at the trial the Chief Superintendent who made the extension order gave evidence of the making of the said order. Under cross-examination he stated that after some discussions with the officers involved in the investigation it was his opinion that a further period of detention was necessary in the interests of the progress of the investigation and that he was guided by the opinions of the investigating officers. At the conclusion of the prosecution case, counsel on behalf of the applicant applied for a direction on the ground that the continued detention of the accused had been unlawful because there was no evidence that the Chief Superintendent had personally formed a suspicion that the accused had committed a scheduled offence under the Firearms Act at the time he made the extension order.

Held by the Court (Finlay CJ, Barron and Blayney JJ) in refusing the application:

(1) That the Chief Superintendent in deciding whether to make an extension order pursuant to section 30(3) of the Act of 1939 was entitled to rely upon the information and opinions of his subordinate officers with regard to the suspicion they held of the commission of a scheduled offence by the person detained and with regard to the continuance of that same suspicion.

(2) That the evidence of the Chief Superintendent even though it did not include the use of the word 'suspicion' established that he retained at the time he made the extension order a suspicion of the guilt of the applicant of firearms offences for which he had been arrested and that a further period of detention was necessary for the progress of the investigation. *People (DPP) v Byrne* [1987] I.R. 363 followed.

203

(3) That the Court should accept the plain and reasonable meaning of the evidence of the Chief Superintendent in the absence of any challenge raised on behalf of the accused at the trial.

Case cited in this judgment:
People (DPP) v Byrne [1987] I.R. 363; [1989] ILRM 629

Additional cases cited in argument:
People (DPP) v Eccles, 3 Frewen 36
People (DPP) v Farrell [1978] I.R. 13
People (DPP) v Howley [1989] ILRM 629
People (DPP) v Quilligan [1986] I.R. 495; [1987] ILRM 606

Patrick MacEntee SC and Martin Giblin **for the applicant**
Maurice Gaffney SC and Michael McDowell SC **for the respondent**

Finlay CJ

This is an application for leave to appeal against a conviction entered on the 20th of November 1986, after a trial before the Special Criminal Court in respect of the offence of robbery which occurred on the 6th of March 1986, and the offence arising out of the same events of having a firearm with intent to commit robbery. A number of grounds of appeal were entered on behalf of the applicant but two only of those were proceeded with by counsel at the hearing of this application, namely, grounds Nos. 7 and 8 which are in the following terms:

7. The Court erred in law in ruling that no evidence was required from Chief Superintendent Ginty of the suspicion which grounded his signing of the extension order which led to the detention of the applicant for a further period of twenty-four hours.

8. The Court erred in law in refusing the application of the applicant for a dismissal by direction at the close of the prosecution case on the ground that no, or no sufficient, evidence had been produced of the suspicion held or alleged to have been held by Chief Superintendent Ginty which grounded his signing of the extension order.

The facts which are necessary to consider for the purpose of determining these two grounds of appeal are extremely limited, notwithstanding a lengthy trial and a large transcript. Evidence was given by Detective Sergeant Kevin Dillon that at 7.25 a.m. on the morning of the

8th of April 1986, he arrested the applicant under section 30 of the Offences Against the State Act on suspicion of having committed a scheduled offence under the Act, being a scheduled offence under the Firearms Act and he conveyed him to Tralee Garda Station.

Chief Superintendent Sean Ginty who purported to make an extension order pursuant to section 30 of the Act of 1939 gave evidence with regard to the making of that order and the relevant portions of it are as follows:

455. Chief Superintendent, on the 8th of April 1986 pursuant to section 30 of the Offences Against the State Act, did you direct that the accused Mr O'Shea be detained in custody for a further period of twenty-four hours commencing at 7.25 in the forenoon of the 9th of April and expiring at 7.25 in the forenoon of the 10th of April 1986?

That is correct, my lord.

And do you produce that order by you?

Yes, my lord.

And then in cross-examination by counsel on behalf of this applicant the Superintendent was asked as follows:

459. Superintendent, as far as Mr O'Shea is concerned what was your understanding of his position at 11.58 on the evening of the 8th of April 1986? If you could manage without notes I would be obliged.

I had some discussions with the officers involved in the investigation and it was my opinion that it would be necessary to detain him for a further period of twenty-four hours and I directed accordingly.

460. For what purpose?

For the purpose of continuing their interrogation.

461. Had you formed a view as to what his attitude to interrogation was at that point?

Well I knew that the officers concerned in the interrogation felt that a further period of twenty-four hours would be necessary, especially

The People (DPP) v O'Shea
Finlay CJ

having regard to the fact that he would be going to bed at 12 o'clock that night and the interrogation would not resume until the following morning. I was guided by the opinions of the investigating officers and discussed it with them by phone and I was satisfied that a further period of detention was necessary in the interests of the progress of the investigation.

463. Were you told how Mr O'Shea was responding to interrogation up to that point, what attitude he was taking?

I knew in the course of the investigation up to that point that he had taken a defiant attitude in the sense that he was not prepared to give an account of his movements. The gardaí concerned in the investigation were satisfied that he had not given an account of his movements and they were satisfied that he hadn't spoken the truth up to that time.

No other questions of any relevance were then asked on behalf of the applicant and that concluded the evidence of the Chief Superintendent in respect of this applicant.

At the conclusion of the evidence on behalf of the prosecution, counsel on behalf of the applicant at the trial made an application to the Court for a direction or non-suit. The particular ground which is relevant to this application is thus accurately stated in the transcript by the presiding judge in the Court in giving the ruling on that application:

(iii) that even if the arrest and detention of the accused for the original period of twenty-four hours is held to have been lawful, his continued detention pursuant to the extension order made by Chief Superintendent Ginty was unlawful because there was no evidence that the Chief Superintendent personally had formed a suspicion that the accused had committed a scheduled offence under the Firearms Act, and that that was his frame of mind at the time when he made the extension order.

In dealing with that particular submission the Court stated as follows:

The Court is satisfied that Divisional Chief Superintendents are entitled to accept and rely upon information furnished to them by senior officers under their command regarding criminal investigations in which such officers are involved and that they are entitled to make decisions *bona fide* based upon that information. The evidence of Chief Superintendent Ginty makes it clear that before deciding whether or not to authorise the extension of the accused's detention for a further period of twenty-four hours he enquired from the senior officers concerned as to how the investigation was proceeding and why it was thought to be necessary that the interrogation of the accused should be allowed to continue beyond the original period of arrest. In the view of the Court the reasons which he was given fully justified his decision to extend the period of the accused's detention for a further period of twenty four hours as provided for in section 30(3).

The evidence necessary to be given in support of the extension of detention pursuant to section 30 of the Act of 1939 has been considered by the Supreme Court in the case of *People (DPP) v Byrne* [1987] I.R. 363. In that case the Chief Superintendent who had signed the extension order concerned had died prior to the trial of the accused. A specific challenge was raised by counsel on behalf of the accused to the admissibility of any proof of the extension, having regard to the death of the Chief Superintendent. Counsel on behalf of the Director of Public Prosecutions sought to establish the making of the extension order by proving the document itself through the evidence of a member of the Garda Síochána who saw it being signed by the Chief Superintendent to whom the Chief Superintendent handed it. The Supreme Court held that such proof was not sufficient and could not be evidence which was necessary for the hearing of the making of a valid extension order.

In the course of his judgment in that case, Walsh J stated as follows at p. 367:

> If the Chief Superintendent had not died but had been in a position to come and give evidence in the case he would have come to the witness box and given evidence to the fact that he had signed the direction in question, would have identified it and would also have been required to give evidence to the effect that at the time of the signing he entertained the same suspicion as to the commission of the scheduled offence as that upon which the man purported was to have been arrested and of the necessity for the purpose of the investigation of the alleged crime for his further detention.

McCarthy J in a judgment which agreed in its conclusions with Walsh J (both of these judgments forming in effect the majority judgments of the Court) stated as follows at p. 371:

> The real question, in my view, accordingly is whether or not there was evidence upon which a jury would be entitled to hold that Chief Superintendent Joy did, at the time of giving the oral direction on the telephone to Detective Sergeant Murphy or of signing the written direction, suspect the respondent of having committed an offence. True, if the Chief Superintendent were alive at the time of the trial, Detective Sergeant Murphy would not have been permitted to give evidence of the oral direction nor any evidence of the state of the Chief Superintendent's mind. True, if the Chief Superintendent were alive at the time of the trial, he could have been cross-examined as to the genuineness of his alleged suspicion. Is it not, however, a proper inference to draw from the oral direction and the signing of the written direction that the Chief Superintendent had the necessary suspicion? *Omnia praesumuntur rite esste acta* — that an individual who had acted in a public capacity was duly appointed and has properly discharged official duties is common to criminal and civil proceedings. . . . This presumption, however, is limited; there is a wide gap between a presumption in favour of the regularity of acts and against misconduct and bad faith and that degree of proof required not merely in every criminal trial, as such, but, also, in every instance of what is, on its face, a breach of the constitutional right to personal liberty.

This Court is satisfied, firstly, that a Chief Superintendent in approaching the question as to whether or not he will make an extension order pursuant to section 30 of the Act of 1939 is entitled to, and indeed must in common sense, rely upon the information and opinions of his subordinate officers with regard to matters which have given them a suspicion as to the commission of an offence by a person who is being detained and as to the progress of the investigation of the crime in respect of which that suspicion exists and of the continuance of that suspicion, having regard to the investigation that has so far taken place.

All of these matters are, in the opinion of the Court, clearly contained, though in an abbreviated form, in the answers given by the Chief

Superintendent upon being questioned as to his reasons for making the extension order. It is quite unreal and quite artificial in the view of the Court, to suggest that the answers which are shortly quoted in this judgment of the Chief Superintendent on examination and more particularly on cross- examination, merely because they do not include the word 'suspicion', could be construed otherwise than as indicating that he retained at the time he made this extension order a very definite suspicion of the guilt of the applicant of the crime of use of firearms in respect of which he had been arrested and that he was satisfied, having regard to the information obtained by him from his subordinates of the progress of their investigation, that a further period of detention was necessary.

Notwithstanding the quite unqualified onus of proof which rests upon the prosecution in any case to establish its case beyond reasonable doubt, and notwithstanding the fact that there can never be any onus on the defendant to establish any particular matter it is clear that if an answer such as the answers that are found in the transcript in this case are given by a witness which have a plain, reasonable meaning attached to them, that if counsel on behalf of the accused wished to challenge that meaning or to put to it some particular qualification or exception that challenge must be raised or the proper meaning should be accepted by the Court. The Court is, therefore, satisfied that this application must be refused.

Solicitor for the applicant: *Edward O'Sullivan & Co.*
Solicitor for the respondent: *Chief State Solicitor*

Eithne Casey
Barrister

The People (Director of Public Prosecutions) v Nicholas Buckley*
[C.C.A. No. 78 of 1987]

Court of Criminal Appeal   31 July 1989

Evidence – admissibility – incriminating statements made by accused – previous incriminating statements ruled inadmissible by trial judge – subsequent statements admitted in evidence – whether subsequent statements voluntary

The applicant was convicted of the offence of robbery by the Special Criminal Court. He had been arrested pursuant to section 30 of the Offences Against the State Act 1939, on suspicion of having committed a scheduled offence under the Firearms Acts, and during his interrogation he made a number of verbal statements of an incriminating nature. The Court of trial in the exercise of its discretion ruled out of evidence the first and second statements the grounds being that the first statement was obtained in breach of Rule 8 of the Judges' Rules in that the applicant was given the statement of his co-accused and a member of the Garda Síochána read it to him at his request, and having done so the applicant was then asked to tell the truth. His reply was ruled inadmissible on the ground that the request to tell the truth constituted an invitation to make a reply and accordingly was in breach of the Judges' Rules.

The second statement was ruled inadmissible on the grounds that the circumstances were such that a new caution should have been administered to the accused. A further interview took place and after caution, the accused made incriminating verbal statements which were admitted in evidence at the trial. It was argued that these statements should also have been excluded on the ground that as the applicant had already made incriminatory statements in circumstances ruled inadmissible by the trial Court, that this must be taken to have coloured the making of the subsequent statements such that he must no longer be considered to have had a free will.

Held by the Court (Finlay CJ, Carroll and Johnson JJ) in refusing the application:

(1) That where an accused person made an incriminatory statement and had previously been induced to make a statement either by promise, threat or oppression which was thereby rendered inadmissible, then the Court must have regard to the possibility that the threat or inducement remained so as to affect the voluntariness of the later statement, even though no immediate threat, inducement or oppression surrounded it.

(2) That, in the instant case, the earlier statements had been ruled inadmissible by virtue of the exercise by the Court of a discretion concerning a breach of the Judges' Rules and not by virtue of any oppressive circumstances, inducement or threat and having regard to the lapse of time and the fact that the accused was duly cautioned, the statements were properly admitted.

Cases cited in this judgment:
People (DPP) v Lynch [1982] I.R. 64; [1981] ILRM 389
People (Attorney General) v Galvin [1964] I.R. 325
Rex v Maynell (1834) 2 Lew C. C. 122
Reg. v Rosa Rue (1876) 13 Cox. C. C. 209
Reg. v Smith [1959] 2 Q.B. 35; [1959] 2 W.L.R. 623; [1959] 2 All E.R. 193

*This case is now reported: [1990] 1 I.R. 14.

Martin Kennedy SC and Anne Watkin **for the applicant**
Kevin Haugh SC and Denis Vaughan Buckley **for the respondent**

Finlay CJ

This is an application for leave to appeal against a conviction entered after trial in the Special Criminal Court on the 24th of June 1987, against the applicant in respect of the offence of robbery.

Four grounds of appeal were submitted on behalf of the applicant but the issue arising in the case was in effect argued on ground No. 1 of those grounds, which was in the following terms:

> 1. That the Special Criminal Court erred in law in holding that the alleged verbal admissions made by the accused to Detective Garda Mahony and Detective Sergeant Kevin Dillon were admissible in evidence.

The applicant was arrested pursuant to section 30 of the Offences Against the State Act 1939, on suspicion of having committed a scheduled offence under the Firearms Act, being the use of firearms in connection with the robbery. He was then brought to Tralee Garda Station and was interviewed by a number of members of the Garda Síochána.

Relevant to the issues arising in this case are three interviews. The first of those was an interview with Gardaí Hanley and Walsh, at which there was supplied to the applicant a statement alleged to have been made by one of his co-accused, Mr Galvin. Upon being given that statement the applicant on the evidence asked the gardaí to read it to him and they did so. After the conclusion of the reading the applicant asked the gardaí certain questions concerning the statement and after that he was asked by the members of the gardaí present to tell the truth. Having been so asked, he made the remark: 'Haven't ye got the story there?'

This verbal admission was ruled as inadmissible by the Special Criminal Court on the grounds that the request by the gardaí to the applicant after the reading of the statement of his fellow accused constituted an invitation to make a reply to that statement and that accordingly it was in breach of Rule 8 of the Judges' Rules and they exercised their discretion to exclude it in evidence.

Shortly after that had occurred, two other members of the Garda Síochána entered the room in which the applicant was with the co-accused, Mr Galvin. A conversation then took place between Mr Galvin and the applicant, and this conversation was tendered in evidence. The Special Criminal Court held that the entry of Mr Galvin into the room was a *novus actus interveniens* and that a new caution should have been given to the applicant, though he had been previously cautioned, and that in those circumstances certain statements made by the applicant which were incriminatory in nature should be ruled out of evidence as inadmissible.

This interview had concluded at approximately 5 p.m. to 5.15 p.m.

A further interview then commenced at approximately 6.45 p.m. between the applicant and Detective Sergeant Dillon and Detective Garda Mahony. On the evidence as accepted by the trial Court, the applicant was then cautioned and was asked to tell the truth about Sunday night. In reply to that the following conversation took place. The applicant said: 'Ye know all about that', and on being asked what he meant: 'Sure Galvin told you who loaded the lorry. I'll give you no names anyhow'. He was then asked to tell his own part in the affair and his reply was: 'You know I was on the job and I told the other two lads. It was hard luck that I was stopped so near that farm place'. He was then asked about the robbery and he stated: 'I was there. Ye know that. I am saying nothing more about that'.

It is in respect of these last verbal statements at the interview commencing at approximately 6.45 p.m. which were admitted in evidence by the trial Court that the whole issue on this appeal arises.

It is submitted on behalf of the applicant that by reason of the fact that the applicant had already, on two separate occasions, made incriminatory statements to other members of the Garda Síochána, in circumstances which have been ruled inadmissible by the trial Court, that this must be taken to have coloured the making of the subsequent statements, notwithstanding the intervening caution, and in particular, that he must no longer be considered to have had a free will in relation to whether or not he would admit guilt at the time of the making of these statements.

Reliance was placed on the cases of *People (DPP) v Lynch* [1982] I.R. 64; *Rex v Meynell* (1834) 2 Lew C.C. 122; *Reg. v Rosa Rue* (1876) 13 Cox C.C. 209; and *Reg. v Smith* [1959] 2 QB 35. Reference was also made on behalf of the respondent to the decision in the case of *People (Attorney General) v Galvin* [1964] I.R. 325.

This Court is satisfied that the cases to which reference has been made would appear to establish a principle that where an accused person makes a statement which is incriminatory in nature and has previously been induced to make a statement either by promise, threat or oppression, also incriminatory in nature, which is by that fact rendered inadmissible, that the Court must in respect of the later statement, even though no immediate circumstances of oppression, threat or inducement surround it, have regard to the possibility that the threat or inducement remains so as to effect the free will of the party concerned and, therefore, the voluntary nature of the statement.

The Court is, however, satisfied that very different considerations apply and arise in a case where a previous admission of guilt has been made which is rendered inadmissible, not by virtue of any oppressive circumstances, nor by the holding out of any inducement or threat, but rather by the exercise by the Court of a discretion concerning a breach of the Judges' Rules.

In this case the Court is satisfied that having regard to the lapse of time and having regard to the uncontested evidence that at the interview which commenced at 6.45 on the evening of the 2nd of September, that the applicant was duly and properly cautioned and that in a very short time after that he made these incriminating statements, that the Special Criminal Court was correct in having reached a conclusion that since they were not tainted by the continuance of any oppression, inducement or threat, and since the earlier statements had been ruled out on a different ground from that of inducement or threat that they were properly admissible in evidence. The Court is satisfied that once that ruling was correct that there was sufficient evidence to support a conviction in this case and the application for leave to appeal must be refused.

Solicitors for the applicant: *Pierse O'Sullivan & Co.*
Solicitor for the respondent: *Chief State Solicitor*

Eithne Casey
Barrister

The People (Director of Public Prosecutions) v John McGrail
[C.C.A. No. 142 of 1988]

Court of Criminal Appeal   18 December 1989

Criminal law – evidence – imputation on character of prosecution witnesses – whether character of accused put in issue – fair procedures – discretion of Court – whether Court should give prosecution leave to cross-examine accused as to previous convictions

Statute – construction – Criminal Justice (Evidence) Act 1924 (No. 37), section 1(f)(ii)

Section 1 of the Criminal Justice (Evidence) Act 1924 states *inter alia* as follows:—

(f) A person charged and called as a witness in pursuance of this Act shall not be asked, and if asked shall not be required to answer, any question tending to show that he has committed or been convicted of or been charged with any offence other than that wherewith he is then charged, or is of bad character, unless —

(ii) He has personally or by his advocate asked questions of the witnesses for the prosecution with a view to establish his own good character, or has given evidence of his good character, or the nature or conduct of the defence is such as to involve imputations on the character of the prosecutor or the witnesses for the prosecution. ...

The applicant was convicted in the Dublin Circuit (Criminal) Court on three counts involving firearms, including possession of firearms with intent to endanger life, and he received sentences of imprisonment totalling twelve years. The facts of the case were that a number of detectives gained entry to the ground floor flat of a house on foot of a search warrant which had been issued pursuant to section 29 of the Offences Against the State Act 1939. Shortly thereafter the applicant was arrested pursuant to section 30 of the Act of 1939, on suspicion of having committed a scheduled offence under Part V of the Act, namely unlawful possession of firearms. The case for the prosecution was that the accused dropped the keys to the flat and attempted to leave through a window when the detectives gained entry. He was apprehended and it was alleged that while lying on the floor he was asked by one of the detectives 'are there guns here' and he replied 'up there'. A gun was found in the place pointed to by the applicant and he was asked 'what was this', and it was alleged that his reply was 'you know fucking well what it is'. In all, three firearms, ammunition, false moustaches, masks and a balaclava were found. The fingerprints of the accused were found on a black plastic bag which contained one of the guns. It was alleged by the prosecution that the accused made a number of other verbal statements after caution which were taken down in writing but he refused to sign them.

The case for the defence was that the accused did not make any verbal admissions to the detectives, that he did not point out any hiding place for the guns, or anything else of an incriminating nature, and that the members of the gardaí were trying to convict him by inventing verbal statements.

Counsel for the prosecution at the trial applied for leave to cross-examine the accused as to his own character on the grounds that the nature of the defence case, whereby it was put to one of the garda witnesses that he had invented the verbal statements, involved

214

imputations on the character and credibility of the garda witness. The trial judge indicated that he would grant such leave and the applicant, in his direct evidence, stated that he had previous convictions which related to motor vehicles. He denied making any incriminating statements to the gardaí and said that his purpose in going to the flat was to pay the rent to oblige a friend.

Counsel for the applicant submitted that fairness required that the accused be able to deny that he made any incriminating statements without exposing his character to cross-examination.

Held by the Court (Hederman, Egan and Barr JJ), in allowing the application and in ordering a re-trial:

(1) That the trial judge erred in principle in ruling that the case made by the defence put the character of the prosecution witnesses in question. Fair procedures required that an accused must not be put at risk of having his character put in evidence if he alleges that the witnesses for the prosecution had fabricated evidence of verbal admissions. *R. v Tanner* (1977) 66 Cr. App. R. 56 and *R. v Britzman and R. v Hall* [1983] 1 W.L.R. 350 not followed.

(2) In challenging the veracity of the evidence of prosecution witnesses an accused was not required to confine himself to suggesting a mistake or other innocent explanation in order to avoid the risk of having his own character put in issue.

(3) The provisions of the Act of 1924 applied only to imputations of bad character of the prosecutor or his witnesses which related to matters unconnected with or independent of the proofs of the instant case, and in such a case, the trial judge had a discretion, because of the dangers of unfairness to an accused who had previous convictions, to refuse leave to cross-examine. The trial judge had, however, no discretion to permit cross-examination of an accused when the matters related directly to the evidence of the case at hearing. *Attorney General v Campbell*, 1 Frewen 1, distinguished.

Cases cited in this judgment:
Attorney General v Campbell 1 Frewen 1
R. v Britzman and R. v Hall [1983] 1 W.L.R. 350; [1983] 1 All E.R. 369; (1983) 76 Cr. App. R. 134
R. v Tanner (1977) 66 Cr. App. R. 56

Cases cited in argument:
R. v Flynn [1963] 1 Q.B. 729; [1961] 3 W.L.R. 907; [1961] 3 All E.R. 58
Selvey v DPP [1970] A.C. 304; [1968] 2 W.L.R. 1494; [1968] 2 All E.R. 497; (1968) 52 Cr. App. R. 443

Denis Vaughan Buckley SC and Anthony Salmon **for the applicant**
Thomas O'Connell **for the respondent**

Hederman J

The accused was convicted in the Circuit (Criminal) Court on three counts contrary to the Firearms Act 1925, as amended. The counts on which he was convicted were possession of firearms without a licence, possession in such circumstances as to give rise to a reasonable inference that he had not got them in his possession for a lawful purpose, and possession of firearms with intent to endanger life. The prosecution alleged that all the offences occurred on the 23rd of March 1988. After conviction and sentence the accused sought leave to appeal on a number of grounds but the Court indicated to counsel for the prosecution that they required to hear submissions from him in reply to the submissions made by counsel on behalf of the applicant on two grounds of appeal only. They were grounds No. 10 that the learned trial judge erred in law and on the facts in permitting evidence to be given of the applicant's previous convictions and ground No. 11 that the trial was in all the circumstances most unsatisfactory.

Summary of the evidence for the prosecution

John Meers, a son of the owner of the premises 146 Tritonville Road, on the 20th of January 1988, let a downstairs front bed-sitting room to two young men of whom he asked no questions. He did not know their names or anything about them nor did he give them a rent book. The rent was agreed at £35 per week and was to be left in the flat every Wednesday. He took a deposit of £70 but did not give a receipt. Mr Meers said he did not see the tenants very often and the flat looked as if it had not been lived in. Before the flat was let to these two young men it had been cleaned on that morning by a Mrs Channing, who had earlier on the same day shown the flat to these men.

Miss Kim Woods gave evidence that in the month of March 1988, she was the owner of a motor-car registration no. LZW 288. She was a hairdresser. The accused from time to time got his hair done in the hairdressing salon in which she then worked. From time to time he got a loan of her car to help her get various repairs done to the car. On the 23rd of March 1988, at about 12 noon the accused collected her car at the hairdressing salon to get a puncture repaired. When the car had not been returned by 5.30 p.m. she went home and phoned the accused's mother to enquire about her car. On the 18th of April, she identified her car and the keys of her car to Detective Sergeant Donnellan.

Detective Garda Noel Clarke was on duty with Detective Garda Loughlin in Serpentine Avenue, Sandymount. He saw a red Toyota Corolla car registration No. LZW 288 crossing the railway tracks travelling along Serpentine Avenue from the Merrion Road direction. There were three people in the car. He later saw the driver of the car whom he identified as the accused walk into the front garden of 146 Tritonville Road. He passed a message to Detective Garda Mitchell by way of a walkie-talkie sometime after 2.30 p.m. Detective Garda Mitchell was on duty on that day in the vicinity of Tritonville Road at about 2.50 p.m., with him were Detective Sergeant Ryan, Detective Garda O'Driscoll and Detective Garda Burke. They went to the front door of 146 Tritonville Road. Detective Garda Ryan had a search warrant under section 29 of the Offences Against the State Act 1939 to search the ground floor flat of 146 Tritonville Road. The door was slightly open. The door into the right hand garden flat was opened from within by the accused. When the accused saw the gardaí he went to run back into the flat, he went to the rear of the flat and he tried to open the window. He did not make it as far as the window. He was attempting to climb by a table to get at the window when the witness assisted by Detective Gardaí O'Driscoll and Burke prevented him from getting any further. As he ran to the window he dropped a set of keys, later identified as the keys to the flat. Before going into the flat Detective Sergeant Ryan announced to the accused that they were gardaí and that he, Detective Garda Ryan, had a search warrant to search the flat. The accused, when arrested was lying on the ground in the flat. The witness Detective Sergeant Garda Mitchell searched the accused and took possession of the keys of the Toyota Corolla motor-car. Immediately afer the arrest and while the accused was still on the ground Detective Sergeant Ryan asked the accused 'What is your name?' and he replied 'John McGrail'. Detective Sergeant Ryan then asked 'Are you armed?' and the accused replied 'No'. Detective Sergeant Ryan further asked 'Are there guns here?' and the accused replied 'Up there', pointing up over the window. At that stage the witness climbed up with the assistance of a table and chair to the top of the window and removed the plastic bag with what appeared to be a gun concealed inside. Detective Sergeant Ryan cautioned the accused. The witness pulled back the top of the plastic bag and there appeared to be a stock of a gun protruding from the black plastic bag referred to. The witness showed it to the accused and asked him 'What this was?' and he replied 'You know fucking well what it is'.

The witness then opened a second black refuse bag and there appeared to be a gun wrapped up in what appeared to be a balaclava. The witness asked the accused 'What is this?' and the accused replied 'I think that is the magnum'. There was a third gun in the bottom of the bag. Later the witness heard Detective Garda O'Driscoll ask the accused 'What else was in the place?' and the accused replied 'There is some more stuff up there', he pointed over the window immediately inside the door of the flat. Detective Garda Burke climbed up to search the top of the window, he pulled down a sock and a balaclava. As he was handing the sock down a bullet fell from it (counsel for the applicant at this stage objected to evidence of any further statements allegedly made by the accused as being immaterial to the charge, but the learned trial judge refused his application).

The witness then heard Detective Garda O'Driscoll ask the accused 'Anything else' and the accused replied 'There is gear in the press for plating motors' motioning over to the press on the right-hand side of the fireplace. The witness then asked the accused 'What do you use this place for?' and he replied 'For strokes'. The witness then asked 'Is that what the clothes are for?' and he replied 'Yea'. At this stage Sergeant Ryan read over to the accused some notes which he had made after again cautioning him and the accused replied 'I was only paying the rent'. Detective Sergeant Ryan asked 'Whose flat is it?' and the accused replied 'It is my flat'. When asked to sign the notes by Detective Sergeant Ryan, he refused to do so. The witness then asked the accused 'What were the keys you dropped?' and the accused replied 'They are mine for the gaff'. At this stage witness arrested the accused under section 30 of the Offences Against the State Act 1939, on suspicion of having committed a scheduled offence under Part V of the Act, that is unlawful possession of firearms at 146 Tritonville Road.

At 8.40 p.m. witness in the presence of Detective Garda O'Driscoll at Kevin Street Garda Station read over his notes of the conversations he had with the accused at the time of the arrest. He cautioned the accused and advised him to sign the notes, the accused did not reply nor did he sign the notes. Detective Garda O'Driscoll and witness then signed the notes. Garda Mitchell was then cross-examined by counsel for the applicant and during the course of his cross-examination he was asked a number of specific questions.

Question: 'Weren't you one of the guards, who held the accused on the ground?'

Answer: 'Yes".

Question: 'I put it to you whilst you did that on a number of occasions you hit him on the back with some object, he does not know what?'

Answer: 'That is not correct'.

Question: 'I put it to you you did?'

There was no answer to that question.

Later during his cross-examination counsel said to the witness:

Question: 'I have to put it to you did Sergeant Ryan say to the accused are there guns here?'

Answer: 'He never said anything of the kind.'

Answer: 'That is not correct.'

Question: 'I have to put it to you again, as soon as you got the accused on the floor in the flat, members of the gardaí jumped up on the table to pull down items from above the window without them even being pointed out to by the accused'.

Answer: 'That is not correct'.

Question: 'I put it to you the accused never pointed out any items in that flat to any member of the gardaí'.

Answer: 'That is not correct'.

Question: 'In particular he did not point out a point on the top of the window'.

Answer: 'That is not correct'.

Question: 'I further put it to you you did not at any stage show the stock of the gun to the accused while you were in the flat'.

Answer: 'That is not correct'.

Question: 'And at no stage did the accused say to you or any other member "you know fucking well what it is".'

Answer: 'That is not correct'.

Question: 'I further put it to you at no stage did you produce to the accused what appeared to be a gun wrapped in a bag'?

Answer: 'That is not correct'.

Question: 'I put it to you at no stage did the accused say "I think that is a Magnum".'

Answer: 'That is not correct'.

Question: 'I put it to you you did not produce the third gun to the accused either'.

Answer: 'That is not correct'.

Question: 'I further put it to you the accused did not say "there is more stuff up there" pointing up'.

Answer: 'That is not correct'.

Question: 'I put it to you the accused never said there is gear in the press for plating motors'.

Answer: 'That is not correct'.

Question: 'I put it to you he never said to you the place was used for strokes'.

Answer: 'That is not correct'.

Later during the continued cross-examination of the witness counsel for the accused put to him the following question.

'I have to put it to you at no stage did the accused make any verbal admissions of any kind to you or any member of the gardaí, and that what you are trying to do is to convict him by inventing a verbal statement.'

Answer: 'That is not correct'.

Detective Sergeant William Ryan corroborated in his direct evidence the evidence already given by Detective Garda Mitchell. He further gave evidence that at 10.45 a.m. on 24 March 1988, at Kevin Street Garda Station accompanied by Detective Inspector Butler, he saw the accused in an interview room and read over questions and answers made to the witness and noted by him at the time of the arrest. The accused replied 'I cannot remember or I do not remember that' and then declined to sign the notes. In cross-examination counsel for the accused put to Sergeant Ryan the following:—

Question: 'I put it to you he at no time told you that the flat was his'.

Answer: 'That is not correct'.

Question: 'I put it to you at no time did he point out any place in the flat to yourself or to your colleagues'.

Answer: 'That is not correct, he did.'

Question: 'I further put it to you at no stage did he attempt to make his escape from the flat'.

Answer: 'He ran back towards the window from the door'.

Question: 'I put it to you you stated "are there any guns?" and you said his reply was "up there". I put it to you that did not happen'.

Answer: 'It did, yes'.

Later during cross-examination counsel for the accused asked the witness:—

Question: 'I put it to you at no stage did the accused point out anything to Garda O'Driscoll and that he never acknowledged in your presence that he pointed out anything to Detective Sergeant Driscoll'.

Detective Garda O'Driscoll was the next prosecution witness. He corroborated the evidence given by Detective Garda Mitchell and the admissions made by the accused while in the flat. In cross-examination counsel for the accused put to this witness that the accused made no admissions of any nature to the gardaí at 146 Tritonville Road and did not point out any hiding place for guns or anything incriminating.

Detective Garda Burke who was also present at 2.50 p.m. on the 23rd of March 1988 at 146 Tritonville Road corroborated the evidence of Detective Sergeant Ryan, Detective Garda Mitchell and Detective Garda O'Driscoll. In cross-examination it was put to him by counsel for the accused:—

Question: 'I further put it to you at no time did the accused make any of the verbal admissions you referred to in your evidence'.

Answer: 'No, all the verbals are true and accurate'.

Other witnesses called by the State proved that false moustaches, masks, and the balaclava with the appropriate holes were found in the flat as well as fingerprints of the accused on the black plastic bag and evidence of other items which might associate the accused with the firearms was also given.

Further evidence was given of the firearms found hidden in the vicinity of the window, they were an SLR self-loading rifle semi- automatic, it is a military rifle, it was complete with a magazine which contained 20 rounds of 7.62 by 51 millimetre ammunition. The rifle and magazine were ready for use, also found was a revolver point 357 Magnum, sturmroger, it is called a black hawk revolver. This revolver contained four rounds of ammunition, it also had a shoulder strap for it. A third weapon was found on the premises according to the evidence of the prosecution, that was a Webley mark 4 point 455 calibre revolver fully loaded with six rounds, a sock containing three rounds of 7.62 millimetre by 51 ammunition. A ballistic expert gave evidence that all the weapons and bullets were in good condition.

Application by defence and evidence of accused

At the end of the State case on the second day of the trial counsel for the accused applied for a direction. The learned trial judge refused this application. Having dealt with the application Mr Vaughan Buckley SC, counsel for the accused said to the learned trial judge:

> One other matter My Lord, Mr O'Connell has indicated that if the accused was to give evidence in this case there would be an application made to permit him to cross-examine the accused as to his character.

He is alleging apparently by my cross-examination of the gardaí, relating to the alleged verbal statements I put to the accused. In particular I think he will be alleging by putting it to one of the gardaí that he invented the verbal statements I put the accused's character in issue. I would submit that that issue as to the question of whether the accused made verbal statements or not in this case is the central issue in the trial and to put it to a garda, who was giving evidence concerning those alleged verbal admissions that he invented them, which could only be the proper inference if the accused's instructions are correct, that I would submit is a central issue in this case and I would submit that by doing that I certainly did not put my client's character in issue.

Mr O'Connell for the prosecution submitted to the trial judge:

> ... that the nature and conduct of the defence in this case involved implications on the character and credibility of the garda witnesses. Mr Buckley specifically put it to Detective Garda Mitchell bluntly that he was inventing verbal statements against his client. There is a lot of recent authority on it, I do not think on this particular aspect there is any Irish case.

At this stage the learned trial judge intervened and said to counsel for the prosecution:

> I think the practice up to now has been to allow the accused's character in issue following what I might call general accusations of either malpractice or indeed improper practice.

Mr O'Connell for the prosecution:

> I think the proper legal position is even if Your Lordship were to hold that the conduct of the defence involved imputations against the character of prosecution witnesses Your Lordship still has a discretion in the matter whether or not to permit cross-examination of the accused in relation to previous convictions, in the interest of overall fairness of the trial, but certainly there are a number of recent authorities from the English Courts arising out of very similar circumstances to what occurred in this particular case.

Counsel for the prosecutor then went on to cite from the case of *R. v*

Hall [1983] 1 All E.R. 369. He also referred to the most recent edition of *Archbold* at para. 4 of p. 360. Mr Buckley then for the defence submitted to the learned trial judge that his client's previous convictions were for motoring offences and he said:

> just to let Your Lordship know in relation to that but in relation to the situation generally I could not have defended Mr McGrail in this case without making the accusations I made. We are alleging he was verballed by the gardaí, how could he be defended except he had to put this to the gardaí.

Counsel for the defence further submitted to the learned judge that he had never heard of a court in this land to go so far as to grant leave to the prosecution under those circumstances.

The learned trial judge stated:

> what I am primarily concerned with is the guilt or innocence of the accused man on the chages before this Court, and this is of course what I will tell the jury, nevertheless it does appear to me that on the authority of the *Attorney General v Thomas Campbell* 1 Frewen 1 that as a grave imputation has been made against the character of the prosecuting witnesses the character of the accused man has been put in issue and I am supported also by the cases of *R. v Tanner* (1977) 6 Cr. App. R. 56 and *R. v Hall* [1983] 1 All E.R. 369. So there is leave to cross-examine the accused as to his character if required.

The defence then went into evidence and the first witness called was Mr Henry Kelly, who was the solicitor acting for the accused and who visited him at Kevin Street Garda Station on Wednesday, 24th of March 1988, around mid-day. He gave evidence that the accused gave a statement to him which was an exculpatory statement and that he informed the gardaí of this statement, and he believed they had taken a copy of it. The accused was then called and counsel for the defence almost immediately put the following questions to his client.

Question: 'So the jury won't be left under any illusion Mr McGrail, I think you are not as far as the criminal law is concerned snow white, isn't that correct?'

Answer: 'That is correct, yes'.

Question: 'Do you have some previous convictions?'

Answer: 'I do, yes'.

Question: 'I think in fact you have a large number of previous convictions for mainly road traffic offences, in fact I think nearly all are for road traffic offences'.

Answer: 'That is right, yes'.

Question: 'I think you have also a conviction for house-breaking implements, but the vast majority of your convictions are in fact for interfering with motor-cars'.

Answer: 'That is right, yes'.

Question: 'Have you ever been convicted or been involved in an armed robbery or anything of that kind?'

Answer: 'Never'.

Question: 'Have you ever been convicted or charged with any offence in relation to firearms?'

Answer: 'Never'.

Question: 'Would you have anything whatsoever to do with armed robberies or firearms?'

Answer: 'No'.

Counsel then went on to examine his client on the events of 23 March 1988. The accused then went on to say he denied knowledge of any of the ammunition, the balaclava, false moustaches or any of those items that were in the flat. While still giving evidence counsel for the defence addressing the accused said:

> Sorry my junior colleague has just corrected me in relation to the housebreaking implements case, I think in fact you were not convicted of that, I was wrong in suggesting you were, that on appeal that conviction was set aside, you were acquitted of that offence. It would appear that your only previous convictions appear to be for motoring offences as far as I can see. You have a long number of convictions for interfering with cars?

Answer: 'I have, yes'.

Question: 'Why do you interfere with cars, the jury might like to know'.

Answer: 'I do not know'.

Question: 'It is a stupid thing to do at any rate'.

Answer: 'It is a stupid thing, I am immune to cars'.

The witness then went on to deny that he had made any admissions to the gardaí and he indicated that he went to pay the rent for a named friend of his and that he had no connection with the flat other than to oblige his friend by leaving him the rent when so requested.

The accused was then cross-examined by counsel for the prosecution. Early during his cross-examination counsel put this question:

Question: 'Let's examine your reputation for honesty? Is it true to say you simply had convictions for interfering with motor-cars, in fact you have seven convictions for the unlawful taking or in colloquial language stealing of motor-cars. Isn't that right?' Seven convictions for pinching people's motor-cars, true or false, Mr McGrail?'

Answer: 'That is right, yes'.

Question: 'You also have another conviction for dishonesty, of larceny from a motor-car, do you remember that Mr McGrail?'

Answer: 'No, I don't remember that, no'.

Question: 'You don't remember that, no'. 'It is on your record'.

During cross-examination of the accused he persisted in denying having made any of the statements or of knowing of the contents of the flat or of having anything to do with the contents of the flat. When asked 'when the gardaí came into the flat and you were coming out the door didn't Detective Sergeant Ryan tell you that they were members of the gardaí and that they had a warrant to search the premises?'

Answer: 'He did not tell me anything, when I was coming out the door I just seen about five or six gardaí running in.

Well there were not five or six, we know there were four policemen running charging into the place.

Question: 'You ran, Mr McGrail?'

Answer: 'I did not run'.

Question: 'To try and get out the window because you knew the firearms were in the flat, isn't that right?'

Answer: 'No, that is not right'.

Question: 'Why did you drop the keys?'

Answer: 'I got a fright when I opened the door and I seen these men running in with guns in their hands, the keys just fell on the ground.'

The accused denied he was throwing away the keys. He again denied pointing out anything to the gardaí and he denied persistently all the verbal admissions that the gardaí had sworn he had made.

He was asked by the judge what would you understand by plating a car, does that mean changing the number plates and he answered 'it does, yes'. And what does strokes mean? Answer: 'I do not know what it means'.

You do not know what it means? No.

Question: 'Isn't a stroke, Mr McGrail, the slang for robbery'.

Answer: 'I do not know'.

Question: 'You have never heard it being used, the word stroke?'

Answer: 'No'.

Question: 'And that you said when asked what do you use the place for, you said for strokes?'

Answer: 'I never said that'.

He was then asked about the guns, balaclava, wigs, beards and so on. He said: 'I do not know what it was used for'.

When making his submissions to this Court on the ruling of the learned trial judge to allow the accused to be cross-examined as to his convictions counsel for the accused said 'the ruling having been made, I then decided it was in the accused's interest, doing the best I could, for me to elicit his previous convictions rather than to present him as a person who had no convictions and then to have the information elicited in cross-examination.'

The law

In the view of the Court the trial judge erred in principle in ruling that the case made by the defence put the character of the prosecution witnesses in question.

Every criminal trial involves an imputation as to the character of somebody. The mere fact that the accused is accused of a criminal offence and evidence is offered to support that view is in effect an imputation against the character of the accused. If the accused either by giving evidence or through his counsel's cross-examination of the witnesses for the prosecution suggests to them that they are not to be believed, that is also an imputation as to their character in as much as it is suggested they are telling an untruth, if that is the way the matter is put to them. The defence may even require, in its efforts to rebut the prosecution case, to suggest to the witness and to the Court, that in fact the real author of the crime, if it has been proved to have been committed, is not the accused but one or other, perhaps, of the witnesses for the prosecution. Such a course of conduct is inevitable if an accused person is not to be seriously hampered in the conduct of his defence. Any ruling otherwise would have the effect of inhibiting the conduct of the defence in that an accused person, who may have a criminal record, may be intimidated into abandoning an effort to put in issue the truth of the evidence of a prosecution witness lest his own character outside the facts of the trial be put in issue. For example, in a prosecution for rape, if the accused's case is that the alleged sexual intercourse was by consent, to put that case to the complainant, in effect is to say that she was guilty of immoral and not unlawful conduct. Such suggestion or inference is not based on any matter independent of the evidence given by the complainant. It would be a totally different matter if it was put to the complainant that she behaved in a similar immoral fashion on occasions or in situations quite independent of the facts of the case in issue. Even such an attack on the character of the complainant is now restricted by section 3 of the Criminal Law (Rape) Act 1981. Thus to suggest to her that she was a common prostitute or had had sexual relations by consent with other persons independently of the accused would be to put her character in issue for the purpose of discrediting her testimony.

Similarly when the case against an accused person is based on confessions alleged to have been made by him and he denies that he made any such statements to the police, the inescapable inference is of course that the police are not telling the truth. But that again is a matter which is not independent of the facts of the case. It would be different if it had been suggested to the police that this was their usual practice in respect of any persons they prosecuted, for the purpose of discrediting their testimony in the case at hearing. It would be quite an intolerable situation if an accused person in the conduct of the defence in cross-examining prosecution witnesses, the veracity of whose evidence he was challenging, should be required to confine himself to suggesting a mistake or other innocent explanation to avoid the risk of having his own character put in issue.

The provisions of the Criminal Justice (Evidence) Act 1924, prohibit putting in evidence the bad character of the accused unless 'the nature or conduct of the defence is such as to involve imputations on the character of the prosecutor or the witnesses for the prosecution'. The question is what construction is to be put on the words '*imputations on the character of the prosecutor or the witnesses for the prosecution*'. In the view of the

Court this must be construed as applying only to imputations made on the character of the prosecutor or his witnesses independent of the facts of the particular case, as, for example, when it was suggested that the witnesses are of such general ill-repute that they are persons who are not to be believed. To put to a prosecution witness that he fabricated the evidence he is giving or that he and other witnesses for the prosecution combined together to fabricate evidence for the particular trial in question may be necessary to enable the accused to establish his defence, if in fact, his defence is that he made no such statement to one or more of the prosecution witnesses. It seems immaterial whether the allegation of untruthfulness is made directly to the witness or witnesses or is a necessary inference on the questions put. If the accused gives evidence and if, for example, he denies the facts of the offence alleged against him and it is put to him that he is not telling the truth, is that to be taken as an attack by the prosecution on his character? The Court thinks not. A distinction must be drawn between questions and suggestions which are reasonably necessary to establish either the prosecution case or the defence case, even if it does involve suggesting a falsehood on the part of the witness of one or the other side. It is otherwise when an imputation of bad character is introduced by either side relating to matters unconnected with the proofs of the instant case.

Even in such an event as the latter one, the danger of unfairness to an accused person who has had previous convictions cannot be overlooked and in such an event, the trial judge has a discretion when he thinks proper, to refuse leave to cross-examine an accused person about his previous convictions or his alleged bad character. In the view of the Court he has no discretion to permit cross-examination of the accused when the matters complained of related directly to the evidence given in the case at hearing either by way of suggesting the untruthfulness of witnesses or an agreement between the prosecution witnesses to concoct a case against the accused. There can be many instances where it could be shown that witnesses for the prosecution have a financial interest in the conviction of an accused person. If they were asked if their evidence was coloured by that fact it could scarcely be objected to.

In the present case the learned trial judge relied upon the decision of the former Court of Criminal Appeal in *Attorney General v Thomas Campbell* 1 Frewen 1. In that case the allegation made was that a Detective Sergeant had coerced the witness into giving false evidence and that the

Detective Sergeant in question had conspired with business competitors of the accused person to keep him out of business and that for this extraneous purpose they were ready to concoct evidence. This was held to amount to a direct imputation on the character of the persons who gave evidence, namely, the merchants in question and the Detective Sergeant. It involved a general conspiracy to ruin anybody who might come into commercial competition with the dealers in question.

This decision, which was the very first ever given under the terms of the 1924 statute in relation to this matter appears to the Court to have been an over literal interpretation of the statute, in so far as the case dealt with the suggestions made to the Detective Sergeant that his evidence was untrue. In so far as the defence case imputed the existence of a general conspiracy to ruin anybody in competition with the other dealers concerned, thereby putting in issue a different matter, it probably did fall within the terms of the statute. The Court is of opinion that this decision should not be followed in so far as it dealt with imputations or suggestions of untruthfulness in the evidence of the Detective Sergeant, but in so far as it was suggested that he was a party to a general conspiracy to ruin competitors that was a different matter. In our view the decisions in *R. v Tanner* (1977) 66 Cr. App. R. 56, *R. v Britzman* and *R. v Hall* [1983] 1 All E.R. 369 should not be followed in so far as they hold that the challenge to the veracity of the evidence of the prosecution was sufficient to open the way to a cross-examination of the accused as to his character or to put in evidence, evidence of his previous character. This Court is of the view that the principles of fair procedures must apply. A procedure which inhibits the accused from challenging the veracity of the evidence against him at the risk of having his own previous character put in evidence is not a fair procedure. The gratuitous introduction of material by way of cross-examination or otherwise to show the witness for the prosecution has a general bad character divorced from the facts of the case at hearing is a different matter.

In the opinion of the Court the learned trial judge misdirected himself in indicating that he would permit the accused's character to be put in issue and the course taken subsequent to the case was brought about by that decision. In the view of the Court this application for leave to appeal should be allowed, the application should be treated as the hearing of the appeal and the conviction should be quashed and a new trial ordered.

Solicitors for the applicant: *Michael J. Staines & Co.*
Solicitor for the respondent: *Chief State Solicitor*

Eithne Casey
Barrister

Procedural Direction

9 November 1987

Hederman J

Where counsel on behalf of an accused applies for leave to appeal to a trial judge after conviction by a jury, he or she should at the same time apply for a legal aid certificate. Legal aid should then be granted by the trial judge if the accused's circumstances warrant it. This would expedite the proper appeals procedure in accordance with the rules of court and ensure that proper grounds of appeal were lodged by the legal representative of an accused within time and avoid unnecessary administrative or unwarranted delay.

Part II

EX TEMPORE RECORDED JUDGMENTS

and

EX TEMPORE JUDGMENTS

The People (Director of Public Prosecutions) v Denis McGinley
[C.C.A. No. 47 of 1987]

Court of Criminal Appeal   18 June 1987

Ex tempore judgment

Arrest – detention – subsequent arrest – admissibility of statements – applicant held for one hour on roadway in motor vehicle – stated purpose to make enquiries regarding driving licence – enquiries not pursued – subsequently arrested pursuant to section 30 of the Act of 1939 by a different garda – whether detention prior to arrest unlawful – whether detention invalidated the arrest – whether connection between applicant's detention and subsequent arrest – Offences Against the State Act 1939 (No. 13), section 30

The applicant was convicted in the Dublin Circuit Court of robbery, burlary, aggravated burglary, malicious damage and two counts of assault. He received sentences of fourteen years, ten years, ten years and one year imprisonment and a sentence of five years penal servitude respectively. The applicant applied for leave to appeal against both conviction and sentence.

The relevant facts were that the applicant, along with a co-accused, was stopped at a checkpoint, his driving licence was taken to be checked, and he was asked to wait. He was detained at the side of the road for one hour in the presence of two gardaí and a soldier. Subsequently, another garda arrived and arrested the applicant pursuant to section 30 of the Act of 1939. The principal ground of appeal related to the circumstances of the applicant's detention prior to being arrested. The convictions rested substantially on evidence of admissions made while in custody pursuant to section 30 of the Act of 1939.

Counsel for the applicant submitted that the stated reason for holding the applicant was merely a colourable device used in order to hold him until some persons would arrive and arrest him under section 30 of the Act of 1939. Counsel conceded that the gardaí have powers under the Road Traffic Acts to stop and inspect a driving licence but if it trips into another area and another act is done, then the person must be told that he is free to go. Counsel submitted that there was no lawful reason for holding the applicant, and that the trial judge erred when he concluded that the applicant was not in custody prior to his arrest. Counsel stated that there was no half way house between liberty and arrest, and that the arrest was invalid.

Counsel for the prosecution stated that under the Road Traffic Acts a garda is entitled to stop and ask certain questions and he has a right to make reasonable enquiries as to the truth of the answers. Counsel did not accept that the applicant's detention amounted to arrest and he submitted that even if he was stopped unlawfully, all that the State had to establish was that the subsequent arrest under section 30 was totally independent of that prior detention. Counsel submitted that the applicant's legal status at the time when he was held was irrelevant, and even if he had been delayed unconsciously long, a lawful arrest pursuant to section 30 of the Act of 1939 had been made and that the gardaí do not have to undergo a charade whereby a person must be released before a section 30 arrest could be made. Counsel argued that the tort of false imprisonment, even if established, could not prevent another garda performing a lawful arrest unless that arrest was the fruit of a deliberate and conscious violation of the accused's constitutional rights or in other words if it was part of

233

The People (DPP) v McGinley
Hederman J

a conspiracy to hold the accused. It was submitted that all the evidence showed that there was no plan to keep the accused where he was, and that there was no connection between the holding of the applicant and his subsequent arrest under section 30 of the Act of 1939. Counsel submitted that whatever the applicant's status was prior to the section 30 arrest that status terminated once a valid section 30 arrest was made and that his prior status then became irrelevant.

In reply counsel for the applicant stated that the trial judge never considered the question of whether or not there was a causal connection between the detention and the subsequent arrest under section 30 of the Act of 1939. The trial judge simply stated, he said, that he was not satisfied that the accused was detained prior to the arrest.

Held by the Court (Hederman, Gannon and Barrington JJ) in quashing the conviction and in ordering a retrial:

(1) That having regard to the circumstances of the case — the stopping of the applicant at the checkpoint, the taking of his driving licence, the fact that he was held for one hour, the fact that the checks made had nothing to do with the Road Traffic Acts and the presence of garda and army personnel — the applicant's detention amounted to arrest.

(2) That the fact that the applicant was arrested would not necessarily invalidate a subsequent *bona fide* arrest pursuant to section 30 of the Act of 1939, but would place a heavy onus on the State to prove that there was no connection between his detention at the checkpoint and his subsequent arrest under section 30 of the Act of 1939.

(3) That in the instant case, the trial judge did not make clear beyond reasonable doubt that there was no connection between the detention at the checkpoint of the applicant and his subsequent arrest.

The court quashed the conviction and ordered a retrial, however subsequently a *nolle prosequi* was entered by the Director of Public Prosecutions.

Case cited in this judgment:
  The State (Trimbole) v The Governor of Mountjoy Prison [1985] I.R. 550; [1985] ILRM 465

Additional cases cited in legal argument:
  The People (DPP) v Gilbert [1973] I.R. 383; 107 I.L.T.R 89
  The People (DPP) v Coffey [1987] ILRM 727
  The People (DPP) v Lynch [1982] I.R. 64; [1981] ILRM 389
  The People (DPP) v O'Loughlin [1979] I.R. 85; 113 I.L.T.R. 109
  Dunne v Clinton [1930] I.R. 336; 64 I.L.T.R. 136
  The People (DPP) v Kehoe [1985] I.R. 444; [1986] ILRM 690

Adrian Hardiman SC and Hugh Mohan **for the applicant**
Michael McDowell SC and Erwan Mill-Arden **for the respondent**

Hederman J

On reading the submissions the central issue in the application for leave to appeal herein is whether the trial judge erred in law in holding that the applicant was not detained at the checkpoint at Blacklion, at 11 a.m. on 29 April 1985. After hearing a lengthy argument the trial judge ruled:

> Garda Kilgallon stopped a car driven by the accused, McGinley, at Blacklion permanent checkpoint at 11 a.m. on 29 April 1985. The accused man, McGinley, produced a Northern Ireland driving licence in the name of Denis McGinley. Garda Kilgallon stated that he was not satisfied with the address on the driving licence as he had previously been supplied with two other addresses within the State by the said Denis McGinley. Garda Kilgallon decided to check the identity of Denis McGinley and, incidentally, that of his passenger, Michael Maughan, insofar as it related to McGinley. For this purpose Garda Kilgallon went into to Blacklion Garda Station and was there instructed by Sergeant Murphy to return to duty whilst Garda Gallagher was detailed to check out the particulars.

> Before the checking was completed Garda Hennelly arrived from Manorhamilton at or about midday. Garda Hennelly knew that a Denis McGinley and a Michael Maughan were wanted for questioning. He also knew, from information he had received at Manorhamilton, that a Denis McGinley and a Michael Maughan had been stopped at Blacklion at the permanent garda checkpoint. When Garda Hennelly saw these two men in Blacklion he recognised them from photographs already seen by him as the men wanted for questioning and, accordingly, he arrested them under section 30.

> Garda Kilgallon had a right to stop and demand the driving licence of McGinley and to check it out. The checking took a protracted time. The reason given for this was because there was another person named Denis McGinley who was, in fact, wanted in the immediate area of the garda station.

> I am satisfied from the evidence that McGinley did not object to the checking. In fact, he co-operated fully with the gardaí.

> Michael Maughan gave evidence that he was afraid of the guards and the army, and that he felt himself detained. In fact, it would appear that the checking done was in relation to the identity of McGinley and the car, and not Michael Maughan, who was well known to a member of the station party.

In this matter I am primarily concerned with the length of time that the checking took and also the purpose for which the car was held at Blacklion. If the length of time taken was of such a time as to amount to harrassment, then clearly there would be a detention which would be unlawful. Also, if the purpose of the stopping of the vehicle altered from a road traffic check to that of a holding operation, there would, likewise, be an unlawful detention. I have considered the case of *State (Trimbole) v The Governor of Mountjoy Prison* [1985] I.R. 550, in which there was an arrest under section 30 of the Act of 1939, for the purpose of detaining Trimbole until extradition proceedings could be brought.

The facts of this case are different as Garda Kilgallon had the right to examine and check the driving licence and to stop the vehicle whilst the same was being done. On the evidence I am not satisfied that either accused man was, in fact, detained.

Accordingly, I hold that there was no illegal detention in the circumstances of this case, and I further hold that the arrest under section 30 was lawful.

The trial judge went on to say that he was satisfied that the applicant had not been detained. In the opinion of the Court and having regard to the circumstances in the particular case, that is the stopping of the applicant at the checkpoint, the taking of the licence, the checking of security files and other checks carried out by the gardaí which had nothing to do with the Road Traffic Acts — in fact there was no check made on the garda computer in relation to the licence — but the applicant was held for over one hour in circumstances where there were many gardaí present in the area as well as army personnel, on these facts the Court is satisfied that the applicant's unnecessary detention at the checkpoint was tantamount to an arrest.

The Court therefore is not satisfied that the trial judge could have been satisfied beyond reasonable doubt that the applicant was not detained while in the car. But even if he was arrested, this would not necessarily to invalidate his subsequent arrest under section 30 of the Act of 1939, but it would place a heavy onus on the State to prove that there was no connection between the holding of the applicant at the checkpoint and his subsequent arrest under section 30.

Unfortunately the trial judge does not make clear that there was no connection between the detention at the checkpoint and the subsequent arrest under section 30. The conviction must therefore be quashed and a retrial ordered.

Solicitors for the applicant: *Claffey Gannon & Co.*
Solicitor for the respondent: *Chief State Solicitor*

Eithne Casey
Barrister

The People (Director of Public Prosecutions) v Patrick Ryan
[C.C.A. No. 14 of 1987]

Court of Criminal Appeal   16 February 1989

Ex tempore judgment, recorded

Trial – delay – falsification of accounts – delay in investigating offence – whether delay excessive – whether accused's right to a fair trial prejudiced

The applicant was convicted in the Galway Circuit Court on two counts of falsification of the accounts of the National Manpower Service contrary to section 2 of the Falsification of Accounts Act 1875. He was sentenced to two years imprisonment on each count, which was suspended, and he was fined £500 on each count. The offences related to the making of false entries on application forms for reimbursement of allowances paid to participants in the Work Experience Programme.

It was stated on behalf of the applicant, *inter alia*, that the charges related to dates unknown between the 1st of November 1981, and the 6th of April 1982. A complaint was made in September 1982 and all the relevant files and documents were given to the gardaí, and it was not until December 1985 that the applicant was arrested and charged, and the trial took place in January 1987. Counsel submitted that in the trial which took place and the infirmities that were anticipated occurred in that the witnesses' recollection of events was unclear and the quality of the evidence that was given rendered the verdict unsafe because of the lapse of time. Counsel stated that the trial judge failed to vindicate the right of the accused to a speedy and fair trial in view of the delay between the events complained of and the arrest of the accused.

Held by the Court (Walsh, Barr and Blayney JJ):
(1) That where at the trial of a person charged with a criminal offence, there has been an excessive delay in investigating the offence, the nature of the delay having regard to the circumstances of the case must be examined and the Court must determine whether the defendant had suffered prejudice such that his right to a fair trial was jeopardised. *The State (O'Connell) v Judge Fawsitt* [1986] I.R. 362 distinguished.

(2) The delay in investigating the offence occurred because of the complicated nature of the case. The trial took place and from the record of what did happen at the trial there was nothing to support the claim that the delay prejudiced the accused's right to a fair trial.

Case cited in this judgment:
The State (O'Connell) v Judge Fawsitt [1986] I.R. 362; [1986] ILRM 639

Additional cases cited in argument:
Bell v Director of Public Prosecutions [1985] A.C. 937; [1985] 3 W.L.R. 73; [1985] 2 All E.R. 585
The State (Healy) v Donoghue [1976] I.R. 325; 110 I.L.T.R. 9; 112 I.L.T.R.

Conor Maguire SC and Padraic O'Higgins **for the applicant**
Feargus Flood SC and Erwan Mill-Arden **for the respondent**

Walsh J

The Court has carefully considered this application for leave to appeal and has come to the conclusion that the application should be refused. The most substantial ground offered was really connected with the delay in bringing the proceedings. The events in question started way back in about 1977. The actual trial took place ten years later, in 1987. So far as the Court proceedings are concerned they cannot be faulted because of the lapse of time. The warrants were issued in 1985 and the return for trial was in 1986 and the trial took place in January 1987. All things considered it was quite a speedy procedure having regard to the nature of the case. But undoubtedly there was a long delay in the investigation of the case.

Anybody reading the transcript could not fail to be struck by the fact that it was a most complicated case. The actual amount of money involved was comparatively little but it was a very complicated matter to track it through the evidence and one must pay tribute to the late Judge Esmonde for the skill with which he did marshall the facts of this very complicated case in his charge to the jury. I am afraid not every judge could have done it quite so skilfully or so clearly from the jury's point of view.

Mr Maguire has made very able submissions to this Court. He laid great emphasis on the prejudicial effect of the long pre-Court delay. There is no doubt whatever that everybody is entitled to fair procedures as part of his constitutional rights. The applicant has invoked this right here. One must examine this in the circumstances of the case. Some of the cases cited particularly *The State (O'Connell) v Judge Fawsitt* [1986] I.R. 362 referred to the length of the Court procedure itself. What is in issue here is the effect upon the Court procedure of the delay incurred before the Court procedures started. Having regard to the complicated nature of the matter and the number of documents which had to be examined in this case the delay which at first sight appears to be long it is not completely inexplicable. But the most important thing is that there is really no evidence to show that it has prejudiced the fairness of the trial in any way. If anybody can have been prejudiced it must be the prosecution because some of their witnesses could, by the skilful way Mr Maguire conducted the defence, have been pushed into uncertainties of memory which, perhaps, they had not felt when they went into the witness-box. That would be a weakness in the prosecution case. But nonetheless their evidence is there, so what we are examining is a trial which did take place, not one which has not taken place and which somebody fears might be prejudicial if it did take place. Looking at the record of what did happen the Court cannot see any point to support the claim that this delay in anyway damaged the defence's right to a fair trial. The other specific issue which arose in the course of Mr Maguire's submissions to this Court is the question of the letters which were written by the solicitors for the companies. Possibly it could have had some prejudicial effect if the jury was left under the impression that these amounted to acknowledgments or admissions on behalf of the accused to the effect that he was in some way guilty. But they do not and no such impression was left to the jury. On the other hand it is quite clear from the evidence that Mr Ryan was associated with these companies and there was evidence of the fact that monies did reach those particular companies. Furthermore on the question of the handwriting, on which Mr Maguire placed great emphasis, the Bank Manager although initially saying he remembered quite well Mr Ryan signing this, eventually reached the point where he could not exactly remember completely because of the lapse of time, but he reinforced himself by saying that he would never have agreed to such a document being completed unless he were satisfied as to the person who was signing it. This was a matter which of course could have been the subject of considerable comment and no doubt it was the subject of a comment by Mr Maguire in his address to the jury as disclosing perhaps some uncertainty in the evidence of authentication of the signature. As against that a handwriting expert was called. There was criticism of the judge in pulling him up at the point at which he did, that is where the witness should not state as a fact that it was not Mr Ryan's handwriting, particularly as he had not yet reached the point of giving his comparisons and disparities etc. The judge was quite correct in that and eventually having given all his evidence he was allowed, and without any interruption or qualification, to state in his opinion the handwriting was not that of Mr Ryan's when compared with the signature of Mr Ryan in his statements to the police. That of course is not the end of the matter. The jurors under our system are themselves the judges of the writing and they had to compare the handwriting together with the advice or any expert material which may be put before them as to the differences or otherwise. They are the final judges on whether the two were written by the same hand or not, and it is quite clear they decided they were. That is evident from the verdict.

The suggestion that the learned trial judge should have commented on the fact that the State did not call a handwriting expert is really a matter of advocacy. It is not the judge's function to make points like that. That is a defence point which no doubt was made. Any counsel, I am sure, particularly one of Mr Maguire's experience would have made the point that here is a bank manager, who appears to have had some uncertainties. There was no handwriting expert called by the State and the defence called one. Nonetheless the jury was quite within its rights in finding as it did, and the fact that the judge did not endeavour to throw more doubt on it by referring to the absence of a hypothetical witness is not a matter the judge should be expected to do in the circumstances of that case. There may be other cases where somebody has been mentioned throughout the case as having a connection with the case and then eventually is not called, which could well be a legitimate subject for comment.

I do not think the submissions made in respect of the judge's failure to refer to the fact that the State did not call a handwriting expert are good grounds for upsetting this particular verdict. There is no doubt whatever that the evidence in the case was more than sufficient to warrant the convictions. Therefore in effect the application for leave to appeal is directed at matters from which it might be deduced that the trial, though procedurally sufficient, must, because of the delays complained of, necessarily be regarded as unfair. The Court cannot reach that conclusion in all the circumstances of this case. The Court has read the very voluminous transcript in this case and has noted that it was a complicated case which was skilfully handled by everybody who had to deal with it. It cannot be said that either the verdict was unsupported by the evidence or was flawed by any procedural defects.

In the result the Court refuses the application for leave to appeal.

Solicitor for the applicant: *Leonard Silke and Co.*
Solicitor for the respondent: *Chief State Solicitor*

Eithne Casey
Barrister

The People (Director of Public Prosecutions) v O'Byrne
[C.C.A. No. 105 of 1987]

Court of Criminal Appeal   24 April 1989

Ex tempore judgment

Road Traffic – disqualification from driving – restoration of driving licence – whether imposition of a disqualification on driving a primary punishment – matters to be considered by the Court as to whether or not to restore driving licence

The applicant was convicted in 1982 in the District Court of driving a car without the consent of the owner and was sentenced to six months imprisonment and disqualified from driving for twelve months. He appealed to the Circuit Court and the learned trial judge dismissed the appeal and varied the sentence to one of twelve months imprisonment and disqualified the applicant from driving for a period of ten years. The applicant served the prison sentence and subsequently brought an application for the removal of the disqualification order imposed on him. That application was heard by the same Circuit Court judge who had heard the appeal, and he refused to restore the driving licence. The applicant appealed to the Court of Criminal Appeal pursuant to section 29(6)(ii) of the Road Traffic Act, 1961. The Court heard the evidence of the investigating garda as to the subsequent conduct of the applicant and he stated that he had no objection to the restoration of the driving licence and the Court heard evidence from the applicant himself.

Held by the Court (Finlay CJ, Barron and Johnson JJ) in allowing the application and restoring the driving licence, that disqualification from driving was not a primary punishment but an adjudication on an accused's fitness to drive. In the instant case the wrong principles were applied by the trial judge to the disqualification and its removal. Matters which the Court must consider in deciding whether or not to restore a driving licence include the applicant's fitness to drive, the nature of the offence, and his conduct since the original conviction.

Case cited in this judgment:
Conroy v The Attorney General [1965] I.R. 411

Fergal Foley **for the applicant**
John Whelan **for the respondent**

Finlay CJ

This application was brought pursuant to section 29(6) of the Road Traffic Act, 1961, on appeal from the decision of His Honour Judge Martin concerning an application to that Court for the removal of a disqualification imposed on driving.

In 1982 when aged 17 years the applicant was convicted in the District Court of driving a car without the consent of the owner, and was sentenced to six months' imprisonment and disqualified from driving for twelve months. The applicant paid £700 compensation to the owner of the car, and he appealed his sentence to the Circuit Court, whereupon Judge Martin doubled his sentence and ordered that he be disqualified for a period of ten years. The applicant served his prison sentence and subsequently applied to have the driving disqualification removed in 1987, and having heard the outline of the case the learned Circuit Court judge said that he remembered the case and that there was evidence that the keys of the car had been removed from the owner in a robbery, and he refused to grant the application.

The Supreme Court stated in the case of *Conroy v The Attorney General* [1965] I.R. 411 that a disqualification from driving not a primary punishment but an adjudication on the applicant's fitness to drive. This view is borne out by section 29 of the Act of 1961 which provides for the removal of disqualification orders, which states that the character of the applicant, his conduct since his conviction, the nature of the offence, and any other relevant matters must be considered in deciding whether or not to grant the application. These matters are relevant to the disqualification, but the disqualification itself was not a statutory punishment.

The Court was quite satisfied that the Circuit Court judge was wholly wrong in his attitude to the disqualification and its removal. The applicant has been in no trouble since the original offence, and he helps his father in his business, and the Court is satisfied that the order of the Circuit Court should be reversed and the disqualification removed.

Solicitors for the applicant: *Devaney & Ryan*
Solicitor for the respondent: *Chief State Solicitor*

Eithne Casey
Barrister

The People (Director of Public Prosecutions) v Richard Kavanagh
[C.C.A. No. 63 of 1988]

Court of Criminal Appeal   13 November 1989

Ex tempore judgment, recorded

Trial – composition of jury – brother of garda on jury – garda stationed in garda station where investigation of crime took place – accused given option of new trial before a differently constituted jury – accused requested trial to continue – whether right to fair trial prejudiced

Evidence – only evidence implicating applicant in crime was incriminating verbal statements – whether such statements require corroboration

The applicant was tried before a jury for *inter alia* the offence of robbery. On the last morning of the trial, the defence was informed by the prosecution that a member of the jury was a brother of a garda who was stationed in the garda station in which the investigation of the crime had taken place, and who was in charge of some of the exhibits during the course of the case. The applicant was given the option of a new trial before a differently constituted jury. After consulting with his client counsel for the applicant stated to the trial judge that his client did not wish to have the jury discharged, and the trial continued whereupon the applicant was convicted. Counsel submitted to the Court, that in spite of the instructions he received, the matter was prejudicial to this client.

Counsel also submitted that there was no evidence against the applicant other than oral statements allegedly made by him in the course of a serious of interrogations, which statements he never signed, and which he denied making. Counsel submitted that an accused should not be convicted solely on such statements without corroboration.

Held by the Court (Finlay CJ, Barron and Johnson JJ) in dismissing the application:

(1) That the applicant was given the option of whether he wished his trial to continue or have the jury discharged. He had the benefit of legal advice and it was his decision to continue with the trial, and the highest standards of fair procedures were applied.

(2) The concept of corroboration does not apply to incriminatory oral statements made by an accused whilst in custody. Such statements are subject to the Judges Rules and they are not admitted into evidence if their admission would be unsafe or unfair. No breach of the Judges Rules was raised at the trial or before the Court and the Court is satisfied that all the issues were put before the jury and that their findings cannot be disturbed.

Rex Mackey SC and Gregory Murphy **for the applicant**
Vincent Landy SC and Michael Durack **for the respondent**

Finlay CJ

The Court has considered the first ground of appeal of the three grounds of appeal put forward in this case and as both counsel were agreed, it takes the form of a preliminary ground and should be dealt with as that.

The ground of appeal is that at the conclusion, or towards the conclusion, of the trial of the accused by a judge sitting with a jury in the Dublin Circuit Court the State became aware that a member of the jury was the brother of a member of the Garda Síochána who was stationed in the garda station in which the investigation of the crime had taken place and was in fact involved to the extent of being in charge of some exhibits during the course of the case. These facts were immediately made aware to the counsel and solicitor acting on behalf of the accused by the judge, apparently in the ordinary channel of discussion with both counsel present at the same time in his room, that is to say, the counsel for the prosecution and the counsel for the accused.

After consideration, as appears from the transcript, senior counsel acting on behalf of the accused said that he had explained the circumstances fully to his client and that his specific instructions were that his client does not wish the jury to be discharged. This Court has carefully considered the suggestion made by counsel on behalf of the applicant that although that decision was arrived at, as it says, *bona fide* it was in disregard to the principle that justice must not only be done and must appear to be done, and that the applicant's right to a fair trial was prejudiced. The Court is satisfied it must reject this contention. What was done on this occasion is in accordance with the highest standards of fair procedure; the accused was informed of the relationship between one of the jurors and a person who might be considered to have an interest in the case; and was given the complete option of whether he wished the trial which was coming to its close to continue or to have the jury discharged and a further trial to take place before a differently constituted jury. He had the benefit of legal advice from an experienced counsel on that and his decision was a decision to continue on with the trial. The Court is quite satisfied that on that evidence and on the information that is available to it on the transcript and the agreed statement of what occurred prior to the matter in the transcript that there is no chance that this fact caused a want of fair trial or indeed that there was any appearance of a want of justice or fair trial in that. One can well conceive the member of the public entitled to attend at a case of this description who if subsequently told that the accused having asked specifically with the assistance of his counsel and presumably having taken the advice of his counsel, having asked specifically for the trial to continue, that if a court subsequently were to set aside the verdict of that trial, that is the situation which might appear to a member of the public to lack justice. In those circumstances, this ground of appeal must be refused.

The two remaining grounds of appeal in this case have on the submissions that were made been taken together and dealt with as an interrelated and in a sense a single ground. Those grounds are that the conviction was unsatisfactory and should be set aside on the ground that the only evidence against the applicant is alleged uncorroborated, oral and unsigned incriminatory statements obtained under interrogation while the accused was in police custody and, secondly, the alibi evidence led on behalf of the applicant was unshaken and uncontradicted.

The oral incriminating statements which are referred to in these grounds were admitted in evidence during the course of the trial by the learned trial judge after a trial within a trial on which he ruled on their admission in evidence in accordance with the rules of evidence. No ground of appeal against the correctness in law and on the facts that were available of that ruling has been submitted to this Court. No application has been made to this Court to add such a ground to the existing grounds of appeal and no submissions were made to this Court on the incorrectness or any alleged incorrectness or suggested incorrectness in that ruling. The Court, therefore, having considered the issues which were before the learned trial judge and the discretion which the law vests in him, is satisfied that the admission of the alleged incriminating statements must be considered as to have been properly allowed, having regard to the rules of evidence.

There was no application at the conclusion of the evidence for the State before the jury, which of course included the evidence of the making of these statements, for a direction. That does not mean that the question of the sufficiency of the evidence then tendered by the State may not, in exceptional circumstances, be considered by this Court in the interests of justice, but it is taken, even in a criminal case, as something indicating the course of the trial as it appeared to counsel engaged in it at that time, and is of some relevance in considering the evidence.

It is correct to say that the oral statements of which the members of the Garda Síochána gave evidence were made by the accused and which are incriminating him in the crime and asserting a participation in the crime or admitting in a participation in the crime were not acknowledged by him by any signature. The correct procedure, having regard to the Judges' Rules, was, it would appear from the transcript, followed by the members of the Garda Síochána in every case, that is to say, that one of the members of the Garda Síochána taking part in the interviews made notes of these statements and read out those notes to the accused at the conclusion of the interview, tendered them for signature by him and when he refused to sign them, as happened in each instance, that garda himself and the other members of the Garda Síochána present — there were two on all occasions — signed the statement in the notebook so as to identify what had been read out to the accused. Some criticism was made of that, not so much as being improper or anything like that, but merely saying it does not corroborate the making of the statements, and that is perfectly true but there can be no question that the Court is satisfied that it is in any way incorrect and, in fact, it is a desirable practice to try and ensure as far as possible that the Court has some satisfactory method of knowing what was read out on the occasion or whether the notes were in fact contemporaneous.

The real issue on the trial of this case was whether these statements were in fact made by the accused whilst in the custody of the Garda Síochána or whether they were invented or created by members of the Garda Síochána. That was identified very clearly by the learned trial judge in the course of his charge to the jury as being the real and dominant issue in the case and it was confirmed by counsel here in the course of his submissions on behalf of the applicant that that was the real issue that arose in the case, and it is the reason why, and a very good reason why, there was no application for a direction at the hearing of the case.

The law either created by judges or by statute requires in a limited number of criminal cases corroboration of particular types of evidence in order to support a conviction, and a conviction may not be entered without such corroboration. In a much greater number of cases, and more frequently, the law created again by judicial interpretation and to a limited extent by statute, has deemed it necessary and desirable that a jury dealing with particular types of evidence or evidence from particular types of persons would be warned against acting upon it unless they find it satisfactorily and independently corroborated, but such warnings of the necessity for corroboration in such cases have got the saver attached to them of which the jury must also be told, that if having regard to that warning they are satisfied to act on the evidence, they are entitled to do so.

Neither of these two categories or involvement of the concept of corroboration with regard to the conviction in criminal cases applies to oral statements of admission or incriminating oral statements made by an accused person whilst in the custody of the police. Such statements are, however, subject to certain judicial rules which have been applied to them and they are of very great importance. They are known to lawyers as the Judges' Rules, and they are so framed as to try and ensure that the making of such statements, oral or otherwise, but certainly of oral statements in police custody as a result of interrogation, are not admitted into evidence when their admission would be unsafe or when it would be unfair. No breach of the Judges' Rules has been established in this case, nor was any issue raised by the applicant before this Court of any breach of those Rules. Quite apart from that it is quite clearly, in the view of the Court, possible to conceive of cases in which if the only evidence being alleged against an accused is oral statements made by him, for example, as occurred in this case there are grounds for saying that those oral statements themselves may be inconsistent one with the other and that a judge should point out in a very definite way to the jury precisely what the state of the evidence with regard to a conviction is. Having carefully considered the learned trial judge's charge, and again this Court is going beyond the grounds of appeal put before it in the interests of justice, because no query or challenge to the charge of the learned trial judge was made in this Court, but this Court having considered the terms of that are quite satisfied that the learned trial judge has brought clearly to the notice of the jury, which was the essential thing, not only the defence being made by the defendants, but that the evidence of these statements made by the accused in the custody of the Garda Síochána was the only evidence associating him with the commission of the crime, and that having been put before the jury and the jury having reached the conclusion they did, this Court is satisfied that their finding and conviction cannot be disturbed and the appeal must be refused.

The Court has considered the application made on behalf of the applicant for a certificate pursuant to section 29 of the Courts of Justice Act 1924, on the basis that a question of law, as to whether in the case of evidence of oral admissions made by a person in the custody of the members of the Garda Síochána going to a jury, the jury should be warned in terms similar to that of visual identification with regard to the necessity or desirability of other corroborating evidence, should be stated for the consideration of the Supreme Court. The Court is quite satisfied that that issue was never raised at the hearing of this trial, was never raised on the grounds of appeal nor on the submissions of appeal made in this trial, that it would be a moot point and that therefore it is outside the terms of the section and the court must refuse a certificate.

Solicitors for the applicant: *Ferrys*
Solicitor for the respondent: *Chief State Solicitor*

Eithne Casey
Barrister

The People (Director of Public Prosecutions) v Michael Walsh
[C.C.A. No. 9 of 1989]

Court of Criminal Appeal   20 November 1989

Ex tempore judgment, recorded

Sentence – severity – application for adjournment to bring motion to adduce further evidence – opinion of investigating member of the Garda Síochána – whether opinion of person other than an expert can be accepted by a court

Sentence – function of Court in reviewing sentences – function of executive

The applicant was convicted on a plea of guilty of being an accessory before the fact of an armed robbery of a bank. He was sentenced to eight years imprisonment and applied to the Court for leave to appeal the severity of sentence.

At the hearing counsel for the applicant applied for an adjournment on the ground that he wished to bring a motion for leave to adduce further evidence. Counsel submitted that justice required that the Court should hear evidence from the two detectives who investigated the crime. Counsel stated that the trial judge should not have admitted evidence of an opinion of one of the detectives who stated at the trial that the applicant took part in the planning of the robbery. Counsel submitted that opinion evidence cannot be admitted except expert evidence and that both detectives could clarify matters with further evidence.

On being refused an adjournment, counsel, *inter alia*, asked for leniency and mercy for the applicant in the all the circumstances that had happened since his imprisonment. He stated that the applicant was a model prisoner and was very anxious to reform.

Held by the Court (Finlay CJ, MacKenzie and Lavan JJ), in refusing the application and affirming the sentence:

(1) That the application to adduce further evidence on the hearing of an appeal did not fall into any of the principles or procedures for the availability of further evidence in the interests of justice and it was undesirable that members of the Garda Síochána should be called and asked to review or alter an expression of opinion they made at a trial.

(2) That the trial judge was entitled to accept an opinion of the investigating detective

based on the evidence he gave, that the applicant had a significant part in the crime.

(3) That there was a clear division between the function of the Court in reviewing sentence, which was to see if an error had occurred, and the function of the Executive. The matters brought to the Court's attention were matters appropriate to a petition to the Minister and were not part of the function of the Court.

Seamus Sorahan SC **for the applicant**
Martin Kennedy SC and Maureen Clark **for the respondent**

Finlay CJ

This is an application for leave to appeal against severity of sentence the applicant having pleaded guilty to the offence of being an accessory before the fact of an armed robbery of a bank carried out in the middle of the day in Waterford. The armed robbery consisted of one person armed with a sawn-off shotgun, another person with a knife and the applicant's part in the matter was, it was established, that he was the driver of the "getaway" car, as it is ordinarily called.

The application (though no previous motion was served) eventually was made by Mr Sorahan on the basis that the interests of justice required that there should be an adjournment of the case in order to permit him, Mr Sorahan, to call evidence which he says he could get and which might affect the view of the Court with regard to sentence from a Detective Sergeant Burke. Detective Sergeant Burke was one of the witnesses involved in the investigation of the crime and was one of the witnesses who gave evidence concerning the crime at the hearing regarding sentence, after the plea of guilty by the applicant. He was not asked any questions with regard to what might be described as the relativity of responsibility between the applicant and the other two persons who were clearly involved in the crime. Detective Sergeant McDermott was asked these questions and expressed the view based on certain observations that he had made prior to the commission of the crime, that whereas Mr Walsh had made a written statement at the time of his arrest, he being arrested, one might say, very shortly after the crime, that whereas he had made a written statement indicating that he had a very minimal part, that he knew something unlawful was going on but did not even know what it was, the view of Detective Sergeant McDermott was that he had taken part in the planning, and whilst he put him as being a less important instigator of the crime than one of the other two accused, he put him as more important than the third. The suggestion made by Mr Sorahan is that there should be an adjournment and that both Detective Sergeant McDermott as a matter of justice should be adduced in evidence to give further evidence to this Court and so should Detective Sergeant Burke. The Court has carefully considered this application and is quite satisfied that it must be refused.

It does not fall within any of the principles or procedures laid down by this Court for the availability of further evidence in the interests of justice on the hearing of an appeal against either conviction or sentence. It is suggested that it is based on some informal conversations between members of the gardaí and solicitors acting for the accused. The idea that at a late stage when the matter comes on on appeal before this Court members of the Garda Síochána should be called and asked to review or alter or to contemplate altering the expression of opinion they made, seems to this Court to be very undesirable and not to be required in the interests of justice in this case.

The Court has, however, considered the application for leave to appeal. The crime that was committed was as the learned trial judge pointed out, a bold and flagrant breach of the law, conducted in the middle of the day in a busy bank with a great number of ordinary customers in it, and was done with roughness and risk and danger to the people concerned. The fact that the money was recovered is irrelevant; it was only good police work that achieved that, and the Court must accept what the learned trial judge accepted, and he was entitled to accept, namely, an opinion of Sergeant McDermott based on the evidence that Sergeant McDermott gave as the reason for his opinion, that this applicant had a significant part in the crime.

In those circumstances it is not possible in the view of the Court to say that a sentence of eight years' imprisonment which was imposed by the learned trial judge is incorrect or is a sentence which has in some way been reached as a result of some error in principle. Neither can it be said to be out of alignment with the other sentences imposed in the case, one of them by another judge, at least, on the other person who had been convicted at the time of the sentencing of this applicant.

There are matters set out in a statement from the applicant and repeated and pointed out by Mr Sorahan here in his submission on behalf of the applicant which would call for or raise the question of leniency and mercy towards this man in all the circumstances that have happened. There is a very clear division between the function of this Court which is to review sentences imposed on the basis on which they were imposed and to see if an error has occurred and the function of the Executive which is to deal with questions of leniency and mercy. In particular, this is highlighted by the fact that one of the matters which Mr Sorahan has stated, which I am sure is correct is that this man has been an ideal or model prisoner and has not given any trouble in prison and is very anxious to reform. We have had a letter indicating that kind of approach from a human point of view. All these cases are sad and the Court must view that, but would point out that that would be a matter properly to be included if a petition were brought to the Minister and it might well be that the Minister would see fit to alleviate the sentence that has been imposed but it is not part of the function of this Court nor should it do it, in the view of the Court. Therefore, the application for leave to appeal will be refused.

Solicitor for the applicant: *Kieran Cleary & Co.*
Solicitor for the respondent: *Chief State Solicitor*

Eithne Casey
Barrister

The People (Director of Public Prosecutions) v John McGinley
[C.C.A. Nos. 96 and 99 of 1988]

Court of Criminal Appeal   27 November 1989

Ex tempore judgment

Sentence – appeal against severity – probation officer seen by trial judge in chambers in absence of accused – whether justice administered in open court

The applicant pleaded guilty to a series of offences consisting of *inter alia* unauthorised taking of a mechanically propelled vehicle, burglary, malicious damage and receiving stolen goods. He was sentenced to concurrent terms of detention, the longest being five years. He came from a disadvantaged background, suffered from depression and was addicted to sniffing glue.

The Court ordered the applicant to be psychiatrically examined and a report on such examination be prepared for the use of the Court.

At the trial, prior to sentencing the applicant, the trial judge saw a probation officer in his chambers in the absence of the applicant and his legal representatives. While that was not a ground of appeal the Court stated the legal position regarding such an occurrence.

Held by the Court (Hederman, Lynch and Blayney JJ) in allowing the application and reducing the sentence to three years detention, that justice must be administered in open

Court and no part of a criminal trial shall be held in a judge's chamber in the absence of the accused.

Peter McMorrow **for the applicant**
Una McGurk **for the respondent**

Hederman J

In this case the trial judge saw a probation officer on her own in his chambers before hearing the open Court evidence regarding sentence. Because this has happened on one or two previous occasions the Court wants to state certain principles which govern all criminal trials. By virtue of the obligation under the Constitution, and in order to ensure that justice is done, a criminal trial must be held in public and the accused should always be present during all of a criminal trial on indictment which includes sentencing. It is not in accordance with law that any part of a criminal trial should be held in a judge's chamber and in the absence of the accused. Nor would it be proper, though it did not occur in this instance, for any report to be made available to the judge which was not also available to the parties, and in particular to the defence. Justice must be administered in open court and everything pertaining to a criminal trial and to the sentencing of a person who has been convicted must be in open court. Because this has happened on two or three occasions the Court is anxious to affirm that that is the law in this jurisdiction.

In regard to this particular appeal the Court has had with the assistance of the State and the cooperation of the defence an up to date report on Mr McGinley. Mr McGinley cannot be released now because of the nature of the offences and the gravity of them and the persistence of them. But what the Court proposes to do is to reduce on Bill No. 9 the five years imprisonment to three years so that the maximum term that Mr McGinley will serve from the date of the second sentence will be three years from that date.

Solicitor for the applicant: *John B. Doherty & Co.*
Solicitor for the respondent: *Chief State Solicitor*

Eithne Casey
Barrister

The People (Director of Public Prosecutions) v Thomas Dennigan
[C.C.A. No. 89 of 1989]

Court of Criminal Appeal   27 November 1989

Ex tempore judgment, recorded

Sentence – severity – extenuating circumstances – home environment – applicant's efforts to rehabilitate himself while awaiting trial – whether sentences totalling four years excessive for offences relating to burglary, unauthorised taking and malicious damage – a further series of offences committed while on bail – consecutive sentence not imposed

Statute – interpretation – whether court has power to suspend consecutive sentence where the Act of 1984 applies – Criminal Justice Act, 1984 (No. 22), section 11

The applicant came before the Midland Circuit Court, and pleaded guilty to a series of offences contained on two bills of indictment. The second series of offences were committed while on bail in respect of the first. The first bill of indictment contained eight counts and included counts of possession of housebreaking implements, unauthorised taking of a mechanically propelled vehicle, breaking into a school, malicious damage and larceny. He was sentenced to concurrent terms of imprisonment, the longest being four years.

The second bill of indictment included a count of breaking into a garda station and stealing two walkie-talkies, two garda caps, handcuffs and a baton. The trial judge imposed a sentence of five years to run concurrently with the other sentences imposed.

The arguments before the Court were in relation to two issues:

(1) The personal circumstances of the accused.

(2) While it was agreed that a consecutive sentence should have been imposed pursuant to section 11 of the Act of 1984, as to whether the Court had power to suspend the said consecutive sentence.

Counsel for the applicant asked for clemency on the grounds that his client was aged 17 years, was unemployed, came from a family of 16 children, and that he was out of parental control when the offences were committed. It was submitted that the most serious crime was theft from the garda station, but it was stated that the items taken were used for mindless petty crimes and did not form part of any grand plan. Counsel stated that the applicant had attended a training centre since these charges arose and for the first time he was coming to grips with the maturing process. In addition, his mother gave evidence on his behalf at the trial, and she was now taking an interest in him. Counsel for the applicant submitted that with regard to section 11 of the Act of 1984, the Court had power to suspend either or both of the sentences and if the Oireachtas intended that the Court should not have such power then it would have been clearly stated.

Held by the Court (Hederman, Egan and Barr JJ) in allowing the application:

(1) That there were extenuating circumstances which had not been taken into account by the learned trial judge, namely, the fact that the applicant was one of a family of 16, and came from a very difficult home environment, that he committed the offences with people older than himself, that sufficient weight was not given to the mother's evidence in support

of her son, and that genuine efforts were made by the applicant subsequent to the commission of the offences to rehabilitate himself.

(2) That the Court had power under section 11 of the Act of 1984 when imposing a consecutive sentence to suspend that sentence in appropriate circumstances.

(3) The circumstances of the instant case were too serious to warrant suspending any of the sentences. However, the Court would substitute a sentence of one year in respect of the offences on the first bill of indictment and would substitute a consecutive sentence of three years for the offences on the second bill.

Per curiam: The provisions of the Criminal Justice Act, 1984, section 11 were not drawn to the attention of the court of trial and the Court reiterated that, as was stated in *People (DPP) v Stafford* 2 Frewen 119, it was the duty of counsel whether for the prosecution or the defence to give all assistance to the trial judge.

Case cited in this judgment:
People (DPP) v Stafford 2 Frewen 119

Henry Abbott **for the applicant**
Edward Walsh **for the respondent**

Hederman J

This is an application for leave to appeal against the severity of a sentence. Mr Dennigan was sentenced before the Circuit Court judge on the 12th of July 1989. Prior to sentence being imposed evidence was given of previous convictions. Mr Dennigan had a previous conviction of a road traffic offence. At Mullingar Circuit Court on the 16th of February 1988 he had 18 charges taken into account, when he was sentenced to 18 months detention in St. Patrick's Institution. That sentence had expired prior to his coming for sentence before the Circuit Court on the 12th of July. On that date there were two bills of indictment. The first bill contained eight counts which included possession of house-breaking implements, pliers, cutters and gloves, the use of a vehicle without the owner's consent, breaking into a school and taking £26, damage to the extent of £45 to windows and malicious damage in the sum of £40, and there were other summary type offences.

This Court must accept that the offences were committed during the night-time and therefore they are burglary counts. The learned trial judge sentenced him on some of the charges to four years and the others two years. In respect of the motor-car offences he was sentenced to one year and six months.

Submissions were made to this Court about the severity of that sentence. In normal circumstances where a person, even a young person of the age of the applicant, commits those offences, the Court might not regard four years as excessive. But there are a number of extenuating circumstances which the Court is satisfied the learned trial judge did not take into account. One was the fact that the applicant is one of a family of 16 and that part of the social problem in which he found himself involved, committing these crimes with two people, both of whom were older than himself, emanated from the home environment. Mrs Dennigan gave evidence in support of her son. The Court feels that the learned trial judge did not give sufficient weight to the evidence that Mrs Dennigan, the mother of the applicant and 15 other children, gave to the learned Circuit Court judge.

The Court must also taken into account the genuine efforts that were made by the applicant subsequent to the commission of these offences, his endeavour to rehabilitate himself despite the problems which he faced. This Court feels that in all the circumstances the sentences were excessive. The fact that he was the youngest of three perpetrators in no way diminishes the seriousness of the type of crimes, and in no way diminishes the fact that burglary of itself is a serious crime. But having regard to his youth, to his family circumstances, to his mother's evidence on his behalf, and his own efforts to rehabilitate himself, what the Court proposes to do is on all the counts that had six months or twelve months imposed, they would stand, and the sentences of two years and four years respectively will be reduced to one year. For all these offences he will serve one years imprisonment for the reasons for which the Court has indicated.

Now with regard to the other sets of offences which were subsequently committed on the 11th and 12th of March, they were as follows — the burglary in the fashion house and the stealing of £60, the same night the burning in a house and the stealing of £100 from there. On the 8th of May that is some months later in Makins the larceny of £2.39, from James Murnaghan I think it was £2, from Noonan and Dowdalls £30, malicious damage £20, Streamstown Post Office £19.30, that was on the 12th of May. The very serious offences was the breaking-in to the garda station and the stealing of two walkie-talkies, two garda caps, garda handcuffs and one baton — value £2,370, all of which property was recovered. Then also on the 12th of May the malicious damage in the sum of £100 to the property of the Department of Justice and the last two offences were the taking of a vehicle without the consent of the owner and the use of it without any insurance.

All these offences were offences which were committed while the accused was on bail. Under section 11 of the 1984 Criminal Justice Act sentences must be consecutive and not concurrent. The learned trial judge imposed a concurrent sentence of five years for these offences which he was not entitled to do. The Court while it will not suspend that sentence and proposes to impose a custodial sentence, is of the view that the proper interpretation of section 11 of the 1984 Act is that a court may in appropriate circumstances suspend a consecutive sentence, which must be imposed pursuant to section 11 of the 1984 Act. But the Court in the circumstances of this case cannot even contemplate such a course of action. The offences were committed by somebody who had a number of previous offences, the most serious one being the offence of taking the garda property, but all the offences are serious. In respect of all those offences the learned trial judge imposed a sentence of five years, but again this Court is satisfied that in imposing that sentence the learned trial judge did not give sufficient weight to the circumstances of the accused and his family, and did not give sufficient weight to his own genuine endeavours to try and rehabilitate himself. The Court proposes to impose a sentence of three years consecutive on the twelve months for the offence committed in the first bill of indictment.

The provisions of the Criminal Justice Act 1984, section 11, were not drawn to the attention of the court of trial and the Court reiterates that, as was stated in *People (DPP) v Stafford* 2 Frewen 119, it was the duty of counsel whether for the prosecution or defence to give all assistance to the trial judge.

Solicitor for the applicant: *John J. Quinn and Co.*
Solicitor for the respondent: *Chief State Solicitor*

Eithne Casey
Barrister

The People (Director of Public Prosecutions) v Michael Farrell
[C.C.A. No. 84 of 1989]

Court of Criminal Appeal   27 November 1989

Ex tempore judgment, recorded

Sentence – offences committed while on bail – concurrent sentences imposed – appeal against severity – application for leave to abandon appeal refused – whether Court has obligation to ensure that correct sentence imposed – sentence varied – consecutive sentences imposed – Criminal Justice Act, 1984 (No. 22), section 11

The Criminal Justice Act, 1984, section 11, states as follows:

> 11.—(1) Any sentence of imprisonment passed on a person for an offence committed ... while he was on bail shall be consecutive on any sentence passed on him for a previous offence or, if he is sentenced in respect of two or more previous offences, on the sentence last due to expire. ...

The applicant was sentenced to two terms of two years detention to run concurrently on various charges relating to larceny and burglary to which he had pleaded guilty. One of the sentences related to an offence committed while on bail. Originally when the case appeared before the learned trial judge, he imposed consecutive sentences and he suspended the issue of the warrant for a year to enable the applicant to undergo a period of probation and he indicated that he would suspend the sentences if the applicant kept out of trouble. However, when the matter came before the Circuit Court again, evidence was given that the accused had not kept out of trouble, and had committed further offences for which he had been sentenced to six months in the District Court. The learned trial judge then imposed concurrent sentences of two years detention in respect of the original offences and these sentences were to run concurrently to the sentence of six months imposed by the District Court.

The applicant applied for leave to appeal the severity of sentence. However, at the hearing of the application, the applicant then applied for leave to abandon the application. Leave to abandon was refused.

Held by the Court (Hederman, Egan and Barr JJ) in refusing the application and in varying the sentence:

(1) That the Court had a duty to see that the sentence imposed was a lawful and proper sentence and by virtue of section 11 of the Act of 1984 it was mandatory on the Court to pass a consecutive sentence in respect of any sentence committed while on bail.

(2) That the Court would suspend the first sentence of two years in respect of the offence which was not committed while on bail and the applicant would serve the second sentence of two years detention for the offence committed while on bail, at the termination of the last of the sentences imposed by the District Court.

John O'Kelly for the applicant
Fergal Foley for the respondent

The People (DPP) v Farrell
Hederman J

Hederman J

This is an application for leave to appeal against the sentence imposed on the applicant by Judge Sheridan on the 26th of November 1987 on the number of charges for which he had pleaded guilty. On that occasion the learned trial judge did not impose any sentence as he was endeavouring to give Mr Farrell an opportunity and he adjourned the case until the Summer session. The matter then came before Judge Sheridan on the 13th of July 1988 and Garda Sullivan gave evidence that on the 28th of December Mr Farrell with others had drinks taken which they had stolen from the Greenery Restaurant. He was charged with that offence in the District Court on the 3rd of February and he pleaded guilty to a charge of receiving that drink. The District Justice adjourned it to the 20th of July on hearing that the defendant would be appearing in the Circuit Court. He had, on the first occasion, given an undertaking that he would go to a hostel but he had in the intervening period left the hostel and on the second occasion he was living at home with his parents. The judge, on that occasion, stated that it was a proper course for the Court to adopt having regard to the December incident to take into consideration and to impose a sentence but postpone the issue of the warrant for a year while he was on probation, and whilst he attended the aftercare regime with the hostel, which apparently he said he was prepared to do. The judge said:

"I think the proper course, taking the worst ones into account and the one in relation to Catherine Lydon which was close to the value of £760, the larceny of a camera. One was committed while on bail but what I propose to do in relation to Mr Farrell, I am going to sentence him to two years detention in St. Patrick's Institution on the burglary charge and two years detention in Miss Lydon's case, and make these consecutive.

I am taking all the other counts including the count before the District Justice into account and I will suspend the issue of a warrant for a yeare to enable him to undergo the regime of the Probation Officer and also to attend the aftercare service provided if he keeps out of trouble for a year and does not offend again, I will most likely suspend the sentence. But if there is more trouble from this young man he must be brought before me anywhere I may be sitting and I will remove the stay on the warrant".

On the 19th of July 1989, one year later, the matter again came before the learned trial judge, and the officer who was giving evidence, Garda Sullivan said "that the accused appeared before the Wexford District Court on the 15th of February 1989 on a charge of burglary and malicious damage. He pleaded guilty and he was convicted and sentenced to six months detention in the District Court and then later he was brought to the District Court again in custody and there were further offences which took place, namely burglary on the 26th of January, another burglary on the 26th of January and a third one during the same night. There had been an earlier burglary on the 18th of January 1989. He pleaded guilty to all of these. All of these crimes were committed in January 1989".

The learned trial judge then having heard the evidence of Miss Barry, the social worker, and of Mr Farrell himself imposed two sentences concurrent and concurrent with the sentence he is already serving, that is with the District Court sentence. Now the Court has refused leave to withdraw the appeal because the Court is satisfied that its duty is to see that the sentence which was imposed was a lawful and proper sentence. The 1984 Criminal Justice Act, section 11, makes it mandatory on a court to pass a consecutive sentence on any person who while on bail commits an offence and that is the obligation that the courts have to discharge in accordance with section 11 of the 1984 Act. What the Court proposes to do is to suspend the original sentence of two years imposed on Mr Farrell prior to committing any offence whilst on bail. Mr Farrell will have to serve the sentence that were imposed by the District Justice under section 11 of the 1984 Act because they were imposed on a person who was on bail in respect of other crimes to which he had pleaded guilty. The sentence of the Court will be under section 11 for the offences which were committed while the accused was on bail, that is two years from the termination of the last of the District Court sentences.

Solicitors for the applicant: *Huggard Brennan & Murphy*
Solicitor the the respondent: *Chief State Solicitor*

Eithne Casey
Barrister

The People (Director of Public Prosecutions) v Patrick Anthony Walsh
[C.C.A. No. 46 of 1989]

Court of Criminal Appeal   11 December 1989

Ex tempore judgment, recorded

Arrest – detention – arrest pursuant to Offences Against the State Act 1939 on suspicion of having committed scheduled offence of malicious damage to clothing of victim – clothing pierced by weapon – questioning in respect of non-scheduled offence – whether arrest lawful – Offences Against the State Act 1939 (No. 13), section 30

The applicant applied for leave to appeal conviction and sentence on charges arising out of the stabbing of two ladies. The principal ground relied on was that the arrest of the applicant pursuant to section 30 of the Offences Against the State Act, 1939, on suspicion of having committed a scheduled offence, namely malicious damage, was unlawful and that the statements obtained during the ensuing detention were inadmissible. The malicious damage concerned damage to clothing worn by the victims which was pierced in the course of the stabbing. It was argued on behalf of the applicant that the powers conferred by section 30 of the Act of 1939 did not lie in such circumstances and that the arrest for malicious damage was merely a "colourable device" to do something that the gardaí could not otherwise do.

Held by the Court (Walsh, Barr and Johnson JJ), in treating the application for leave to appeal as the appeal and in allowing the appeal:

(1) That section 30 of the Act of 1939 cannot be used as either a pretext or a colourable device for arrest.

(2) That in the instant case the gardaí were not justified in availing of the powers of section 30 of the Act of 1939 to arrest the applicant because the arrest and subsequent interrogation was not directed towards the investigation of an offence of malicious damage to clothing. There must be a genuine investigation of a genuine offence of malicious damage which was worthy of investigation in itself. It was not, however, a case of deceit or trickery on the part of the gardaí but arose out of a mistaken belief that once a matter was within the terms of the Offences Against the State Act, 1939, by reason of it being a scheduled offence, that the section automatically applied. *People (DPP) v Quilligan* [1986] I.R. 495 and *People (DPP) v Howley* [1989] ILRM 629 distinguished.

Cases mentioned in this judgment:
People (DPP) v Howley [1989] ILRM 629
People (DPP) v Quilligan [1986] I.R. 495; [1987] ILRM 606

Additional cases cited in argument:
People (DPP) v Walsh [1986] I.R. 722; [1988] ILRM 137
The State (Bowes) v Fitzpatrick [1978] ILRM 195

Blaise O'Carroll SC and Sean O'Donovan **for the applicant**
Fergal Foley **for the respondent**

Walsh J

In this case the Court is of opinion that this application for leave to appeal should be allowed.

There were three main issues brought in the appeal. The first arises in respect of the query by the foreman of the jury after the lunch interval on the first day of the hearing. The facts of that are simply that some member or members of the jury observed the accused being led out to his lunch still handcuffed. The background to this is that an application to keep him in custody during lunch was made and acceded to by the judge. The accused had been on bail. When he surrendered his bail he was then in the custody of the Court and it was a matter for the Court then to decide to what extent he should be released during the trial. In my view this is not a sustainable ground. First of all there is no indication from what the jury man said that the jury had formed any view. It seemed that the nature of the query could be interpreted as an expression of disapproval of the handcuffing or that the jury thought that perhaps it was prejudicial or could be prejudicial. They did not expressly state that any prejudice had been caused by the fact that he was in handcuffs. From then on the judge took care to see that that situation was not repeated. It is desirable of course that nothing should be done that might be interpreted by juries as an indication that guilt had been established or was to be inferred from the treatment of the prisoner during the hearing. On the other hand there are many cases in which some form of restraint has to be exercised even in the presence of the jury. I am not saying that this is necessarily one of them. But as a ground of appeal amounting to a claim that this was prejudicial to a fair trial by a jury, I think it must fail. Nothing was indicated by the jury to show they were so influenced. It was simply at the very beginning of the trial and the mere fact that the accused was in Court at all and was identified as the person being accused would itself, I thought, be as prejudicial as being in handcuffs.

The second ground of appeal refers to what I might call the general condition of the accused at the time he made the statements which are referred to in this case. The accused had been taken into custody fairly early in the morning and shortly after being taken into custody he was attended by his legal adviser and by members of his family. Some time later in the day before any statements were taken he took what I can only call an overdose of water, but anyway whether it went down into his lung or where it went it is not clear. The gardaí acted with commendable promptitude and did everything they could to relieve him of the effects of what had happened and applied what the doctor described as the correct technique.

The technique involved a sudden application of force to the abdomen I think, as well as other efforts they made. This did relieve him and very likely saved him from serious injury or even death. The gardaí can scarcely be faulted for that. They would certainly be faulted if they had done nothing about it. It was suggested that this in some way would make the accused so grateful to the garda for what they had done that he would then make a statement which was untrue, as a token of his appreciation and gratitude for their assistance. The Court is satisfied there is no evidence whatsoever to support that view.

Mr O'Carroll has also dealt in some detail, and at great length, with other aspects closely related to that which might or might not arise in some other case, but they certainly, in the view of the Court, do not arise in this case, and concerned various excursions into the psychology of accused persons and so on.

We are aware that there was some reason to believe that this particular accused had certain medical disorders but no point was raised about those at the trial nor was any effort made to take advantage of them by the accused or to seek to rely upon them, which itself is a problem. But on the evidence given in the case the judge's ruling on that aspect of the case cannot be faulted.

The third and the most important issue in this case is the actual arrest. The charge for which this man was tried was for the stabbing of two ladies. The two ladies wore clothes at the time. Obviously when they were penetrated by a sharp instrument causing the stabbing the clothes would have been penetrated, so there was malicious damage to the clothes in the strict sense. Section 30 of the Offences Against the State Act, 1939, is itself an extraordinary limitation on the rights of persons, who are about to be charged or may be charged in that they may be arrested and held for up to 48 hours without being charged or being brought before a court.

In this particular case the prosecution relies here in this Court upon the decisions in *The People (DPP) v Quilligan* [1986] I.R. 495 and *The People (DPP) v Howley* [1989] ILRM 629. A close reading of these judgments would indicate that what the Court was dealing with in each case were matters which were quite serious in themselves and unconnected in time and place, to a greater or lesser extent, with the crime which was being charged. Each of those crimes was a substantial crime in the sense that it was worthy of being prosecuted on its own account and the garda in each case were generally pursuing the investigation and perhaps the ultimate solution of those offences.

In the present case the matter is quite different. Here is a stabbing offence against a person and if the part of the body which was stabbed was clothed, there is nothing in the evidence here that would suggest that there was any genuine or serious investigation by the garda or that they were the least bit concerned about pursuing a case of malicious damage to clothing. What they were concerned with was pursuing a very serious case of the wounding of a very innocent person. This is not a case of the garda being deceitful or being engaged in trickery of any description. They have shown in the case itself and during the investigation of the case that they were very concerned. I think it is a case where they were mistaken as to the law. It is not correct that simply because something is within the Offences Against the State Act, 1939, by reason of it being a scheduled offence, that such an act automatically brings into play section 30 of the Act of 1939. In this case it did not. Both *The People (DPP) v Quilligan* and *The People (DPP) v Howley* make it quite clear that the use of section 30 must not be either a pretext or a colourable device for arrest. That means that in effect it must be a genuine investigation of a genuine offence of malicious damage which had been treated genuinely as something which was worthy of an investigation in itself. No such evidence was forthcoming in this case. The fact that the accused was arrested under section 30 of the Act of 1939 was not in doubt. While Detective Garda O'Leary did not actually in the course of his evidence, mention that he said section 30 was what he was operating under, the accused, in his evidence supplied that omisson by saying "yes", that section 30 had been mentioned, but he denied the other details.

The Court is quite satisfied that the garda in question did say that the arrest was being effected under section 30 and then went on, as he must do, to specify in respect of what particular offence he had the suspicion that warranted the arrest. As it happened at the end of his detention under section 30 the accused was in fact released, so there is no question of his being pursued for the so-called malicious damage case. With regard to the mistake in law on the part of the gardaí it is well established, even as recently as last week by the Supreme Court, that that is sufficient to set aside the whole arrest as being illegal.

We are not questioning the good faith of the garda or holding that there was any malicious act or deliberate act of trickery on the part of the garda. It was simply a mistaken view of what the law permits. One must look at it in context. If the proposition which the prosecution seeks to establish were correct it would mean that every charge of ordinary common assault which, if somebody's shirt button was torn off or some minor damage to his shirt or clothing occurred it would bring into effect section 30 of the Act of 1939. Such is not the case and in the present instance the ultimate trouble was that the learned trial judge appears to have taken the view that once it is established that the arresting garda did effect the arrest in the terms of section 30 and set out the scheduled offence or the offences concerned, that that was sufficient. It is not sufficient. It is a correct formality but that observance of bare formality does not make the arrest legal.

The learned trial judge was perhaps so preoccupied with the other arguments in the case about the voluntariness of the statement and the rather complex argument put forward dealing with it that he did not give the question the attention which he ought to have given it.

In the result the Court is of opinion that these statements were inadmissible because of the illegality of the arrest and detention during which they were taken. There was other evidence in the case which could possibly persuade the jury that the accused was the guilty person. There was the question of identification by the victims and that in itself would have been sufficient evidence, if accompanied by the warnings by the judge of the dangers of such evidence. Normally what the Court would do is to quash this trial and verdict and order a new trial. But the Court must have regard also to the general justice of the case. This would be a fourth trial if it were ordered. The accused person has already served over a year in custody which, if a sentence of three years were to stand, would be more than 50 per cent of what he would actually serve.

In those circumstances the Court is of opinion that the proper course to follow in this case is to quash the conviction entirely and not order any new trial. But I would like to add that I think it would be in the interest of everybody and of the accused if the proper medical treatment were applied under the provisions of the non-penal legislation because what we have been dealing with so far is a case which appears, on the evidence, to be one where the solution really lies in the medical condition of the accused person. But that point was not raised as such in the trial.

On the grounds given the Court will make the orders already mentioned for the accused to be released.

Solicitors for the applicant: *Deane & Co., Cork*
Solicitor for the respondent: *Chief State Solicitor*

Eithne Casey
Barrister

The People (Director of Public Prosecutions) v Simon Maguire and Patrick McDonagh
[C.C.A. Nos. 44 and 39 of 1989]

Court of Criminal Appeal   11 December 1989

Ex tempore judgment, recorded

Sentence – review – rape – plea of guilty – circumstances and youth of accused – whether sentence of 14 years excessive

The applicants were arraigned on counts of rape, buggery, indecent assault and burglary before the Dundalk Circuit Court.

On the day of the trial they pleaded guilty to the count of rape, and a *nolle prosequi* was entered on the other charges. A sentence of 14 years' imprisonment was imposed on both applicants.

The facts were that the victim, a married woman in her forties with five children, was alone in her father's licensed premises while her father was in hospital. After closing time three men broke into the premises and demanded money and threatened 'to blow her brains out'. She was taken upstairs where she was raped and buggered by all three men.

Counsel for the first applicant stated that the circumstances of the crime were such that there was nothing that could be said that mitigated it, however, he submitted that when passing sentence the trial judge did not give adequate consideration to the applicant's circumstances, his youth, the fact that he had only one previous conviction, and his plea of guilty. Counsel submitted that the trial judge sentenced both accused together rather than as particular individuals and that the sentence was excessive.

Counsel for the second applicant submitted that on any view, the sentence of 14 years was in the top range, in particular as his client would serve his twenties in prison. Counsel referred to *The People (DPP) v Tiernan* [1988] I.R. 250, and stated that while he was not saying that a tariff should be laid down, in that case the applicant had an appalling record of previous convictions involving violence. Counsel stated that the trial judge believed that there was a range of sentences within which the present sentence should be accommodated and that he did not have sufficient regard for the youth of the applicant. Counsel stated that his client pleaded guilty although not at an early stage, and, with regard to his previous convictions, only one involved violence.

Held by the Court (Walsh, Barr and Blayney JJ), in refusing the application, that the circumstances of the instant case were such that the sentence of 14 years was not excessive.

Per Curiam: If the applicants had been found guilty by a jury after a plea of not guilty a sentence of 20 years would not have been unduly severe.

Editor's note: The court ordered that the sentence of 14 years imprisonment imposed in respect of the conviction be corrected by substituting a sentence of 14 years penal servitude as provided for by section 48 of the Offences Against the Person Act 1861.

Cases cited in this judgment:
The People (DPP) v Tiernan [1988] I.R. 250
The People (Attorney General) v Poyning [1972] I.R. 402

Turlough O'Donnell **for the first applicant**
Patrick Gageby **for the second applicant**
Thomas O'Connell **for the responent**

Walsh J

The Court sees no reason to interfere with the sentence. Mr Maguire put the victim in fear for her life and threatened to 'blow out her brains'. What is of importance is the serious views of this Court and of the Supreme Court concerning these type of offences which were expressed before the commission of these offences. Lack of knowledge of what is likely to happen is not to be taken into account but none the less great publicity has been given to the views which this Court and the Supreme Court have expressed and many trial judges have taken these into account when dealing with these particular offences.

The offence of rape is bad enough and in this case it could scarcely have been worse. But to be combined with the other offence to which the unfortunate victim was subjected, in what I can only describe as a gang rape, with the threat of death from firearms raises the matter to a new level of depravity. Next to murder it is probably the most serious offence one could contemplate. Nevertheless it was carried out by people of sound mind and full age. The Court bears in mind all the observations made in the Supreme Court in *The People v Tiernan* [1988] I.R. 250 and indeed, in other cases. As was pointed out in *The People v Poyning* [1972] I.R. 402 which, of course, is not in any way comparable to this case what the Court is concerned with here is what is adequate punishment for these offences.

If these people had been found guilty by a jury of these offences after a plea of not guilty, a sentence of 20 years would not have been regarded by this Court as being unduly severe. The fact that they had either good advice or the good sense to plead guilty in these cases, probably saved them six to seven years imprisonment.

In the circumstances of this case which can only be described as really atrocious and abominable I think that no court could hold that 14 years was in any sense an excessive sentence. The application for appeal against sentence should be dismissed and the sentence confirmed.

Solicitors for the first applicant: *Branigan, Berkery and Co.*
Solicitors for the second applicant: *Ahern and McDonnell*
Solicitor for the respondent: *Chief State Solicitor*

Eithne Casey
Barrister

The People (Director of Public Prosecutions) v Jack Maloney
[C.C.A. No. 66 of 1989]

Court of Criminal Appeal   12 December 1989

Ex tempore judgment, recorded

Sentence – severity – burglary – property recovered – plea of guilty – refusal to name other parties involved – whether such refusal is a valid reason for imposing a more severe sentence

The applicant was sentenced to five years imprisonment for burglary. It was submitted on his behalf that the sentence was excessive in view of the fact that the applicant had pleaded guilty, was only 18 years old, and all the property was recovered. It was further submitted that the trial judge before sentencing the applicant asked him to name a 'fence' and when the applicant refused the trial judge then asked what the maximum sentence was, and proceeded to impose a sentence of five years imprisonment. Counsel stated that the trial Judge over-reacted when he stated that the applicant was unrepentant and uncooperative.

Held by the Court (Finlay CJ, Costello and Blayney JJ) in allowing the application:
(1) That the applicant was apprehended in circumstances that did not give him much option but to plead guilty and his plea was a hard-headed approach to the case and did not amount to a special ground for leniency. *The People (DPP) v Tiernan* [1988] I.R. 250 applied.
(2) That the trial judge may have over-reacted to the attitude of the applicant and whereas co-operation by an accused with the gardaí in finding out persons involved in a crime may be a ground for imposing a more lenient sentence than otherwise, it was not a principle of sentencing that failure to give information should lead to an increased sentence. Accordingly, in the circumstances the Court directed that that the sentence be varied by substituting a sentence of three years imprisonment.

The People (DPP) v Maloney
Finlay CJ

Case cited in this judgment:
The People (DPP) v Tiernan [1988] I.R. 250; [1989] ILRM 149

James O'Mahony **for the applicant**
Thomas O'Connell **for the respondent**

Finlay CJ

This is an application for leave to appeal against a sentence imposed on the applicant Mr Maloney on the 5th day of May 1989 before His Honour Judge Murphy in Cork. The applicant was then 18 years of age, approximately, and pleaded guilty to what was a very serious burglary at night in a household. The seriousness of it was the quantity of goods that were stolen and the fact that on the scene of it were found instruments which indicated that those taking part were prepared to use or threaten to use considerable violence, namely a hammer and another offensive weapon. The property was all recovered but that was not due to anything done by any of the persons involved in the crime of whom there were three, but rather to good police work.

The matter is put by Mr O'Mahony to this Court very economically and none the worse for being economically put, on two bases, or three bases, really. He suggests that the learned trial judge as indicated by the transcript, did not give any credit or take into account the fact that this applicant pleaded guilty to the crime. He suggests that the learned trial judge, as appears from the transcript, in his submission, over-reacted to the attitude of the applicant when called before him, and he suggests that there was something incorrect in principle in the attitude of the judge which appeared to be that he was imposing a sentence of a severity associated with the fact that the applicant when asked to give the name of the 'fence' said he could not do so.

The Court has considered all these submissions. With regard to the first one, namely, the failure to give or state that any credit was being given for the plea of guilty, it would appear that the applicant was well and truly apprehended under circumstances which did not give him much option and that the plea of guilty as was stated by the Supreme Court in the case of *The People v Tiernan* [1988] I.R. 250 in those sort of circumstances may be no more than a hard-headed approach to the case and may not be a special ground for leniency of sentence.

With regard to the over-reaction, the Court is satisfied that the transcript and the terms in which the sentence was imposed and the absence of any measured consideration of the grounds on which such a sentence was being imposed, do lend support to a suggestion that the learned trial judge over-reacted on this occasion and may have been led by that to impose too harsh a sentence.

Thirdly, whereas co-operation by an accused or convicted person with the police authorities in finding other persons who are involved in the crime may be a ground and often is a ground for imposing a more lenient sentence than otherwise would be appropriate, it is not part, in the view of the Court, of a proper principle of sentencing that there should be an actual increased severity of sentence by reason of the failure of a person to give information when called upon in Court to do so.

In all those circumstances the Court is satisfied that this application should succeed and will treat it as the hearing of an appeal and will reduce the sentence, but having regard to the unfortunately bad record of the applicant in previous years, together with the seriousness of this crime and the type of crime it was, the Court can only reduce it to a sentence of three years to date from the date on which the original sentence was imposed.

Solicitor for the applicant: Not available
Solicitor for the respondent: *Chief State Solicitor*

Eithne Casey
Barrister

The People (Director of Public Prosecutions) v Luke Egan
[C.C.A. No. 34 of 1989]

Court of Criminal Appeal   13 December 1989

Ex tempore judgment, recorded

Trial – rape – evidence – findings of fact – verdict of jury – jury correctly charged by trial judge – function of Court of Criminal Appeal – principles to be applied when considering verdict of jury – whether Court has jurisdiction to substitute its own verdict contrary to that of jury based on its own subjective view of case – whether concept of 'lurking doubt' inherent in jurisdiction of Court – Courts (Supplemental Provisions) Act 1961 (No. 39), s. 12

The applicant was convicted of rape and was sentenced to ten years penal servitude. He applied for leave to appeal both conviction and sentence and the grounds are set out in the judgment *post*. The defence case was that sexual intercourse took place with the consent of the complainant.

Counsel on behalf of the applicant submitted that, notwithstanding the learned trial judge's full and detailed charge to the jury, and the warning that he gave of the dangers of acting on the evidence of the complainant alone, and the fact that it was his, the trial judge's opinion, that there was no corroboration, the Court could and should substitute its own verdict for that of the jury. Counsel stated that every single circumstance of the prosecution's case was consistent with the innocence of the applicant and that where the Court had a 'lurking doubt' on any material leading to the conviction of an accused the Court should substitute its own verdict if it felt that the jury acted on insufficient evidence. Counsel submitted that by virtue of the Courts (Supplemental Provisions) Act 1961, s. 12, the Court had full powers to determine any question necessary for the purpose of doing justice and that this was not confined to questions of law.

The case for the prosecution was that the complainant, having left a public house to catch the last bus to her sister's home, and having missed it, decided to walk. She became aware of the applicant whom she saw running into a public park. She ran past the entrance of the park and as she did so the applicant dragged her into the park and raped her and in the course of the rape he struck her face and threatened that if she did not stop screaming he would 'rearrange her face'. In the course of the struggle one of her shoes fell off and ended up outside the park railings. Following upon the rape the complainant allowed the applicant to walk her home at his request because she said she was terrified to refuse. During the journey home the applicant disclosed many details about himself. They passed other people, as well as a garda station, and the complainant made no attempt to get away. During the course of the trial the evidence relied on by the prosecution by way of corroboration was the fact that the complainant's shoe was outside the railings of the park, her facial injuries, dirt on her clothing, her distress when she complained of the rape as soon as she arrived at the home of her sister, and details of the applicant's statement to the gardaí which were false. Counsel for the prosecution submitted that the concept of a "lurking doubt" was not part of the jurisdiction of the Court and was inconsistent with decided cases.

Held by the Court (Hederman, Gannon and Johnson JJ) in dismissing the application, that the superior Courts in exercising the jurisdiction conferred by the Constitution cannot interfere with findings of primary fact by juries and that the concept of a lurking doubt or a subjective test on the part of an appellate court was not part of the jurisdiction. The jury saw and heard the witnesses and their verdict was consistent with the instructions they received from the learned trial judge. *People (DPP) v Madden* [1977] I.R. 336 applied. *R. v Cooper* [1969] 1 Q.B. 267 not followed.

Cases cited in this judgment:

Banco Ambrosiano S.P.A. (in liquidation) v Ansbacher and Co. Ltd [1987] ILRM 669
Hanrahan v Merck Sharp and Dohme (Ireland) Ltd [1988] ILRM 629
People (DPP) v Madden [1977] I.R. 336; 111 I.L.T.R. 117
People (DPP) v Kelly (No. 2) [1983] I.R. 1; [1983] ILRM 271
Northern Bank Finance Corporation Ltd v Charlton [1979] I.R. 149
R. v Cooper [1969] 1 Q.B. 267; [1968] 3 W.L.R. 1225; [1969] 1 All E.R. 32; 53 Cr. App. R. 82

The application for leave to appeal was heard by the Court on 13 December 1989. The Court delivered an *ex tempore* judgment which was recorded and at the conclusion thereof counsel for the applicant applied to the Court pursuant to the Courts of Justice Act 1924, section 29, to certify that its decision involved a point of law of exceptional public importance, and that it was desirable in the public interest that an appeal should be taken to the Supreme Court. The application was allowed and the point of law certified was as follows:—

> Was the Court of Criminal Appeal correct in holding that it had no jurisdiction to substitute its own subjective view for the verdict of the jury in this case?

The Supreme Court delivered its judgment on the question certified on 30 May 1990, and the decision of the Court of Criminal Appeal was upheld [1990] ILRM 780.

Rex Mackey SC and Adrian Mannering **for the applicant**
Thomas O'Connell **for the respondent**

Hederman J

On 26 January 1988, after a three day trial, the applicant, Luke Egan, was convicted of rape contrary to section 2 of the Criminal Law Rape Act 1981, and section 48 of the Offences against the Person Act 1861, and he was sentenced to ten years imprisonment.

From that verdict the applicant has appealed to this Court on three grounds. The grounds of appeal are:

1. That the verdict of the jury was unsupported by the evidence which was inconsistent with the lack of consent by the prosecutrix.

2. The said verdict lacking as it did any sufficient corroboration of the evidence of the prosecutrix is dangerous to sustain.

3. The circumstances suggested to be corroborative of the evidence of the prosecutrix are consistent with the innocence of the applicant.

At the end of the prosecution case no application was made for a direction nor at the end of the evidence given by the defendant was any application made to have the case withdrawn from the jury. Counsel for the accused laid emphasis on the fact that the instructions to the jury by the learned trial Judge could not be challenged and that that instruction was in accordance with all the requirements of the law. There was, the Court is satisfied, evidence from the complainant of absence of consent and this was an essential element in the case for the prosecution. The inconsistencies in the complainant's evidence were pointed out on a number of occasions during a lengthy and careful charge by the learned trial judge to the jury. The danger of convicting without corroboration and relying solely on the evidence of the complainant was explained on at least two occasions by the learned trial judge to the jury. The importance of looking for corroboration was explained to the jury. The weakness of the evidence referred to as purporting to be corroboration was carefully pointed out to the jury by the trial judge during his charge to the jury. The jury was correctly instructed that they were entitled to reach a verdict of guilty if they were convinced of the truth of what the girl said of lack of consent and if they felt that there was no corroboration they were still entitled to convict.

In all these respects the jury was correctly instructed in accordance with the law and counsel for the accused finds no fault in the directions that were given by the trial judge to the jury. The judge said as I have indicated at the end of his lengthy charge to the jury that, in his opinion, there was no corroboration of the evidence of the prosecutrix and they would rely solely on her evidence. Nevertheless counsel relies on the extract from the judgment of the Court of Appeal in *R. v Cooper* (1969) 53 Cr. App. R. 82 and it is a portion of the judgment of Widgery L.J. which is to be found at p. 85 and I quote:

> The important thing about this case is that all the material to which I have referred was put before the jury. No one criticises the summing-up, and, indeed, Mr Frisby for the appellant has gone to some lengths to indicate that the summing-up was entirely fair and that everything which could possibly have been said in order to alert the jury to the difficulties of the case was clearly said by the presiding judge. It is, therefore, a case in which every issue was before the jury and in which the jury was properly instructed, and, accordingly, a case in which this Court will be very reluctant indeed to intervene. It has been said over and over again throughout the years that this Court must recognise the advantage which a jury has in seeing and hearing the witnesses, and if all the material was before the jury and the summing-up was impeccable, this Court should not lightly interfere. Indeed, until the passing of the Criminal Appeal Act 1966 — provisions which are now to be found in section 2 of the Criminal Appeal Act 1968 — it was almost unheard of for this Court to interfere in such a case.
>
> However, now our powers are somewhat different, and we are indeed charged to allow an appeal against conviction if we think that the verdict of the jury should be set aside on the ground that under all

the circumstances of the case it is unsafe or unsatisfactory. That means that in cases of this kind the Court must in the end ask itself a subjective question, whether we are content to let the matter stand as it is, or whether there is not some lurking doubt in our minds, which makes us wonder whether an injustice has been done. This is a reaction which may not be based strictly on the evidence as such; it is a reaction which can be produced by the general feel of the case as the Court experiences it.

This element of the lurking doubt is not part of our law and it is inconsistent with the decisions in this Court as presented to us by Mr O'Connell for the State in *The People (DPP) v Madden* [1977] I.R. 336 when he referred to a part of the judgment of the then Chief Justice O'Higgins at p. 339 and I quote:

Function of the Court of Criminal Appeal

A person convicted by the Special Criminal Court has a right of appeal to the Court of Criminal Appeal from conviction and sentence (or from conviction or sentence) upon obtaining from the Special Criminal Court, or from the Court of Criminal Appeal, leave to appeal. This right of appeal is provided by section 44 of the Offences Against the State Act, 1939, which also applies sections 28-30 and sections 32-35 of the Courts of Justice Act 1924, and sections 5-7 of the Courts of Justice Act 1928, to appeals from the Special Court in the like manner as they apply to appeals under section 31 of the Act of 1924. Section 12 of the Courts (Supplementary Provisions) Act 1961, replaces section 30 of the Act of 1924 and provides that the Court of Criminal Appeal shall be a superior court of record and shall have power to determine any questions necessary to be determined for the purpose of doing justice in the case before it, and vests in the Court of Criminal Appeal all jurisdiction which, by virtue of any enactment applied by section 48 of the Act of 1961, was vested in the former Court of Criminal Appeal immediately before the operative date. Unlike the appeals in civil matters from courts of first instance, the appeal to the Court of Criminal Appeal is not described as a re-hearing. Therefore, it would seem that the Court of Criminal Appeal, in exercising its functions as an appellate court from decisions of the Special Criminal Court, should apply the following statements of principle which are taken from the judgment of Holmes L.J. delivered in the Court of Appeal in *Aberdeen Glen Line Steamship Co. v Macken: The SS. "Gairloch"* [1899] 2 I.R. 1 at p. 18:—

When a Judge after trying a case upon *viva voce* evidence comes to a conclusion regarding a specific and definite matter of fact, his finding ought not to be reversed by a Court that has not the same opportunity of seeing and hearing the witnesses unless it is so clearly against the weight of the testimony as to amount to a manifest defeat of justice. The same rule does not apply, at least in the same degree where the conclusion is an inference of fact. It often happens, as in the present instance, that the decisive finding is a deduction from facts hardly disputed or easily ascertained. In such a case the appellate tribunal is in as good a position for arriving at a correct conclusion as the Judge appealed from, and it would be an undue restriction of the functions of the former if it were to hold itself bound by what has been found by the latter. Of course the view of the Judge who tried the case is of the greatest weight, and for my own part I would only depart from it with much hesitation when, as here, we have not been furnished with a report or note of the judgment appealed from.

In the appeals now before this Court, we have transcripts of the rulings of the Special Criminal Court made in the course, and at the end, of the trial on questions of law and findings of facts in relation to the admissibility of evidence, the sufficiency or cogency of the evidence, and the reasons for the rulings and verdicts given. Therefore, subject to the grounds of appeal, it would seem to be the function of this Court to consider the conduct of the trial as disclosed in the stenographer's report to determine whether or not the trial was satisfactory in the sense of being conducted in a constitutional manner with fairness, to review so far as may be required any rulings on matters of law, to review so far as may be necessary the application of the rules of evidence as applied in the trial, and to consider whether any inferences of fact drawn by the court of trial can properly be supported by the evidence; but otherwise to adopt all findings of fact, subject to the admonitions in the passages cited above.

The judgment in *People v Madden* [1977] I.R. 336 was subsequently approved in the decision of the Supreme Court in *People v Kelly* [1983] I.R. 1.

In our view there is no difference in the principles to be applied in considering the verdict of the jury, be it a criminal or a civil case. Our attention has been drawn also by Mr O'Connell for the prosecution to *Northern Bank Finance Corporation Ltd v Charlton* [1979] I.R. 149, *Banco Ambrosiano S.P.A. (in liquidation) v Ansbacher & Co. Ltd* [1987] ILRM 669 and *Hanrahan v Merck Sharp and Dohme Ltd* [1988] ILRM 629, although he did not cite from any of the cases.

We are of opinion that the Superior Courts in this country in exercising the jurisdiction conferred by our Constitution have consistently refused to interfere with findings of primary fact by juries and that the concept of a lurking doubt or a subjective test by an appellate Court is not part of the jurisdiction, having regard to the cases cited to us by counsel for the prosecution. We are not prepared to follow the decision in *R. v Cooper* 53 Cr. App. R. 82 as an authority which would allow us on a subjective test to substitute a verdict contrary to that returned by the jury. They saw and heard the witnesses and their verdict is consistent with the instructions they received from the learned trial judge in his charge.

For these reasons the Court will treat the hearing of the application for leave to appeal as the hearing of the appeal and will disallow the same.

Solicitor for the applicant: *Michael E. Hanahoe & Co.*
Solicitor for the respondent: *Chief State Solicitor*

Eithne Casey
Barrister

The People (Director of Public Prosecutions) v Thomas Johnston
[C.C.A. No. 90 of 1988]

Court of Criminal Appeal   18 December 1989

Ex tempore judgment, recorded

Manslaughter – charge of murder – trial – verdict of manslaughter returned – sentence of penal servitude for life imposed – whether life sentence should be reserved for worst type of manslaughter that could be committed – whether indeterminate sentence destroyed hope of rehabilitation – disparity of sentences between co-accused – whether admissions amounted to a mitigating factor – whether error in principle

The applicant, along with two co-accused, was convicted of various charges arising out of an armed robbery on the premises of a Credit Union. A member of staff died of gunshot wounds during the ensuing pursuit of the raiders.

The applicant initially denied any complicity in the crime, but during his second interrogation by the gardaí, after having been informed that one of his co-accused had implicated him, he made a statement admitting involvement in the crime, however, he stated that he believed at the time that the gun which he carried did not contain live ammunition. The applicant was charged with, *inter alia*, murder and possession of a firearm with intent to endanger life. He pleaded not guilty to both these charges, but at all times offered a plea of guilty to manslaughter.

The jury acquitted him of murder, convicted him of manslaughter, and the firearms charge. The applicant was sentenced to penal servitude for life in respect of the former, and ten years imprisonment for the firearms offence. His two co-accused were convicted of robbery and sentenced to ten years and four and a half years respectively.

It was argued on behalf of the applicant that the trial judge erred in imposing the maximum sentence of penal servitude for life in respect of manslaughter in that it was inappropriate having regard to the sentences imposed on the co-accused who were involved in the same enterprise; that the applicant made a statement admitting the broad facts of the crime; that before imposing the maximum sentence, the trial judge should be satisfied that it was the worst type of case conceivable and that there should be some light at the end of the tunnel and hope of eventual rehabilitation into society. Counsel stated that at all times the applicant had been prepared to plead guilty to manslaughter and while there should not be an enormous discount for a plea, there should be a substantial reduction.

Held by the Court (Finlay CJ, Carroll and Murphy JJ) in allowing the application and in varying the sentence:

(1) That the crime committed was not the worst type of manslaughter that could be committed and that in broad terms the maximum sentence should be confined to that, and that there was insufficient hope of rehabilitation where an indeterminate sentence was imposed as distinct from a lengthy finite term, the Court was satisfied therefore that there was an error in principle in the imposition of the maximum sentence and that the appropriate sentence was one of 17 years penal servitude.

(2) That there was no error in the disparity of sentences imposed as between all the accused.

(3) That the admissions made by the applicant in his statement at the time and in the

276

circumstances in which it was made was not a factor of any significance in mitigating the sentence as it was a hard-headed assessment of the situation made by the applicant in the knowledge that he had been implicated by his co-accused. *The People (Director of Public Prosecutions) v Tiernan* [1988] I.R. 250 and *The People (Director of Public Prosecutions v Conroy (No. 2)* [1989] I.R. 160 followed.

Cases cited in this judgment:
  The People (Director of Public Prosecutions) v Tiernan [1988] I.R. 250;
    [1989] ILRM 149
  The People (Director of Public Prosecutions) v Conroy (No. 2) [1989] I.R. 160;
    [1989] ILRM 139.

The application was heard on the 18th of December 1989, and the Court substituted a term of fifteen and a half years penal servitude which took account of the period of sentence already served.

Patrick MacEntee SC and Anthony Sammon **for the applicant**
Martin Kennedy SC and Patrick Marrinan **for the respondent**

Finlay CJ

This is an application by way of appeal against the refusal of a certificate for leave to appeal in respect of the sentence imposed on the applicant arising out of a conviction in respect of a frustrated armed robbery. The particular sentence with which the Court is concerned is the sentence imposed on the applicant on the first count on which he was found guilty, that is to say, a charge of murder on which the jury found him guilty of manslaughter and not guilty of the murder. The sentence which was imposed was the maximum sentence of penal servitude for life.

The matter is put by Mr MacEntee under, in effect, four separate headings — three and an extended one — the first being that the maximum sentence was inappropriate having regard to the sentences imposed on two of the applicant's co-accused. The two co-accused who were involved in the same enterprise were sentenced respectively to ten years and four and a half years on a count of robbery, but neither of these two co-accused was found guilty of manslaughter, and in those circumstances the Court is not satisfied that there can be said to be a disparity of an unexplained or unsatisfactory kind between the sentence imposed on those two accused and the sentence imposed on this accused. Taking the actual charge in respect of which they were convicted, one of those two co-accused was sentenced to ten years for the robbery, that is the precise sentence that was imposed on the accused in this case.

The next matter is a reliance on the fact that the applicant made a statement, though not on the first opportunity. When he was first interrogated he denied any form of complicity but on the second opportunity and having been informed that one of his co-accused had named and identified him (the applicant) as having been involved in the crime, he made a statement in which the broad facts of the crime were admitted by him, but he stated in the course of that statement and subsequently stated on sworn evidence at the hearing of the trial that he believed that the gun which contained a cartridge contained only a blank cartridge and not a live round, or a loaded round. That assertion in his evidence was clearly interpreted by the learned trial judge, and correctly interpreted by the learned trial judge, as having been rejected by the conviction of the applicant in respect of a count of possession of a firearm with intent to endanger life to which he had pleaded not guilty. With regard to that aspect, the position concerning admissions of guilt and pleas of guilty has been set out by the Supreme Court, both in the case of the *The People v Tiernan* [1988] I.R. 250 and in the case of *The People v Conroy* [1989] I.R. 160 to which we have been referred. Following and accepting those principles as this Court is bound to do, the Court is not satisfied that on the facts of this particular case the admission in the form in which it was made and at the time at which it was made and in the circumstances in which it was made is a factor of any real significance in mitigating the sentence which would be appropriate to impose for the commission of this crime. It appears to be a business-like and hard-headed assessment of the situation in which the applicant was and, as such, has not got any of the mitigating factors which are considered in the two cases to which the Court has referred.

The next matter, really in a sense two matters taken together or two taken separately whichever way it is, and the first is that this particular crime of manslaughter, on the facts established before the learned trial judge, should not or could not be described as the worst possible type of manslaughter and that the maximum sentence, in broad terms, should be confined to that, and the second one associated with that is that having regard to the nature of the crime committed and coming back to the sense of it not being the most appalling of the crimes of manslaughter that can be committed, that having regard to the nature of that there is insufficient hope of rehabilitation to be found in an indeterminate sentence as distinct from even a lengthy finite sentence. The Court accepts these two combined pleas in regard to the sentence in this case. This was an extremely savage crime, and in the sense that it was a premeditated crime involving the use of a firearm and the whole history of recent crime would indicate that any person setting out on such an enterprise must be aware that there is likely to be the loss of innocent life, and that is exactly what occurred in this case, but it does not have the savage brutality of certain other types of case which have come before the courts as manslaughter cases and this Court having regard to that fact and having regard to the necessity at all costs to try and give to the applicant some hope of rehabilitation and some light at the end of the tunnel that would permit him to try and bring himself back into a frame of mind that would restore him as a reasonable member of society on his release whenever it should take place, is satisfied that there was an error in principle in the imposition of the maximum sentence in this case. The sentence which, in the view of this Court, would have been appropriate to be imposed at that time short of the maximum, would be a sentence of 17 years. The Court has inquired of Mr MacEntee and Mr Kennedy if it is correct to say that the sentence is a sentence of penal servitude for life, not imprisonment. Both phrases are used by the learned trial judge in the course of his summing up.

The appropriate sentence is penal servitude. In those circumstances, obviously, the sentence must be imposed only from today and, therefore, the sentence to be imposed to effectuate the view of the Court as to what should have been the sentence last July would be 15 and a half years' penal servitude imposed as from today.

Solicitor for the applicant: *Michael J. Staines & Co.*
Solicitor for the respondent: *Chief State Solicitor*

Eithne Casey
Barrister

Part III

REPORTED JUDGMENTS 1984-1989

This brief section contains the headnotes of judgments delivered by the Court of Criminal Appeal during the period 1984-1989, all of which judgments are reported in full in the Irish Reports and Irish Law Reports Monthly.

The People (Director of Public Prosecutions) v David Douglas and George Raymond Hayes
[C.C.A. Nos. 19 and 20 of 1983]

Court of Criminal Appeal   21 May 1984

Criminal law – mens rea – shooting with intent to commit murder – whether necessary to establish intention to commit murder – whether reckless disregard of risk of killing as a likely outcome sufficient to constitute required intent – Offences Against the Person Act 1861 (24 and 25 Vict. c.100), section 14

The applicants were convicted of shooting with intent to commit murder contrary to section 14 of the Offences Against the Person Act 1861. The court of trial held that it was sufficient to constitute the offence where the natural consequence of shooting would be to kill or seriously injure and that the shots were fired with reckless disregard of the risk of killing, in the sense that it would be the likely, but not necessarily the desired, outcome of shooting. Section 14 of the 1861 Act provides that whosoever 'shall shoot at any person . . . with intent . . . to commit murder, shall, whether any bodily injury be affected or not, be guilty of a felony'. The applicants sought leave to appeal on the ground that the necessary intent to constitute the offence had not been established.

Held by the Court of Criminal Appeal (O'Higgins CJ, McWilliam and Barron JJ) in granting leave to appeal and quashing the convictions:

(i) While it was anomalous that where a person shoots at another intending to cause serious injury and that person dies, the offence of murder has been committed, while if he does not die the offence of shooting with intent to murder has not been committed, section 14 of the 1861 Act specifically required proof of an intent to kill and it was irrelevant that the court of trial was satisfied that those who fired the shots would have been guilty of murder had any person been killed. *Cawthorne v H.M. Advocate* 1968 JC 32 considered.

(ii) In order to determine whether an intent to kill existed, a court may take into account that a reasonable man would have foreseen that the natural and probable consequence of the acts was to cause death and that the accused acted in reckless disregard of that likely outcome of the acts, but such factors of themselves would not constitute proof of such intent. *Dicta* of Wien J in *Reg. v Belfon* [1976] 1 W.L.R. 741 applied. *Reg. v Smith* [1961] A.C. 290 and *Reg. v Hyam* [1975] A.C. 55 considered.

Cases cited in this judgment:
Cawthorne v H.M. Advocate 1968 JC 32; 1968 SLT 330
Cunliffe v Goodman [1950] 2 K.B. 237
Reg. v Belfon [1976] 1 W.L.R. 741
Reg. v Hyam [1975] A.C. 55
Reg. v Mohan [1976] Q.B. 1
Reg. v Smith [1961] A.C. 290
Reg. v Whybrow (1951) 35 Cr. App. R. 141

[1985] ILRM 25

The People (Directory of Public Prosecutions) v Brendan McCaffrey

Court of Criminal Appeal   30 July 1984

Criminal law – arrest – suspicion – offences against the state – whether suspicion of arresting officer required – whether suspicion of other person, communicated to arresting officer, sufficient – Offences Against the State Act 1939 (No. 13), section 30

The applicant was arrested pursuant to section 30 of the Offences against the State Act, 1939. During his trial it was argued that his arrest was invalid, on the ground that the arresting officer in evidence stated that he had formed a personal suspicion that the applicant had committed a scheduled offence under the Act. He stated that the basis for the suspicion had been communicated to him by a superior officer. The applicant was convicted of a number of offences. On appeal by the applicant:

Held by the Court of Criminal Appeal (Henchy, Gannon and Egan JJ) in dismissing the application:

(1) The arresting officer, in stating in evidence that his arrest under section 30 of the 1939 Act was on suspicion that a scheduled offence had been committed, had sufficiently complied with the requirements of section 30, and it was irrelevant that the suspicion derived from the mental processes of a superior officer rather than from the arresting officer's.

(2) To construe section 30 as requiring communication of the superior officer's information to the arresting officer would be inconsistent with the declared objective of the Offences Against the State Act 1939.

No cases cited in judgment

[1986] ILRM 687

The People (Director of Public Prosecutions) v Nicholas Kehoe

Court of Criminal Appeal   17 December 1984

Criminal law – arrest – restraint – whether constitutes arrest – whether subsequent arrest pursuant to statute required release of arrested person to be valid – Offences Against the State Act 1939 (No. 13), section 30

Criminal law – arrest – detention – extension – statutory power – extension of period of detention under statute – whether required to be in writing – format of document extending period of detention – Offences Against the State Act 1939 (No. 13), section 30(3)

Criminal law – trial – whether defendant lawfully before court – whether defendant in unlawful custody at time of being charged in court – whether relevant to jurisdiction of court to try case – Offences Against the State Act 1939 (No. 13), section 43

The applicant was charged before the Special Criminal Court on various charges. It was argued that at the time the applicant was in unlawful custody and that therefore the court did not have jurisdiction to try him pursuant to section 43 of the Offences Against the State Act 1939. The applicant was convicted on a number of charges. On appeal:

Held by the Court of Criminal Appeal (McCarthy, O'Hanlon and Barron JJ) in dismissing the application:

(1) The Special Criminal Court has jurisdiction under section 43 of the Offences Against the State Act 1939 to try a scheduled offence where the Director of Public Prosecutions directs trial before that court, and that jurisdiction does not depend upon the technical validity of the manner in which an individual may be physically present before that court.

(2) Without expressing a concluded view, the physical restraint placed on the applicant, before his arrest pursuant to section 30 of the 1939 Act, did not in itself amount to an arrest, and was part of the sequence of events at the scene of a crime during which a great number of shots were fired; but even had there been a common law arrest, this did not mean that a lawful arrest could not have been effected under section 30 without going through the colourable manoeuvre of an apparent release from custody. *Dicta* of Henchy J in *The State (Walsh) v Maguire* [1979] I.R. 372 discussed.

(2) While there is no formal requirement that the direction of an extension of the period of detention under section 30(3) of the 1939 Act be in writing, such a practice is desirable; but it is unnecessary and undesirable, having regard to the possibility of *bona fide* errors, that the exact time of commencement and termination of the further period be stated, and it would be preferable that the direction merely state that the person arrested is to be detained for a further period of 24 hours commencing upon the expiry of the period of 24 hours from the time of his arrest.

Cases cited in this judgment:
Attorney General v Burke [1955] I.R. 30
In re Ó Laighléis [1960] I.R. 93
R. v Hughes (1879) 4 Q.B.D. 614
The State (Attorney General) v Fawsitt [1955] I.R. 39
The State (Attorney General) v Roe [1951] I.R. 172
The State (Walsh) v Maguire [1979] I.R. 372

[1985] I.R. 444; [1986] ILRM 690

The People (Director of Public Prosecutions) v Eugene Prunty
[C.C.A. No. 16 of 1985]

Court of Criminal Appeal   15 May 1986

Criminal law – appeal – defect in trial – proviso – whether miscarriage of justice actually occurred – whether shown that trial court disregarded inadmissible evidence

Criminal law – trial – evidence – hearsay – telephone calls – tracing of calls – whether evidence as to voice on telephone established by hearsay – whether admissible – whether retrial should be ordered – proviso

Criminal law – trial – evidence – tape recordings – telephone calls – whether admissible – whether defect in quality affects admissibility – factors affecting weight to be given to evidence – whether recording of telephone call made to person not then on trial admissible if part of transaction as a whole

The applicant was charged with various offences, based partly on evidence of telephone calls relating to the payment of a ransom. His voice was identified at the trial from recordings made; and the process of tracing these calls was also put in evidence. Objection was taken to the method of proof of these tracings, on the ground that part of the proof of such tracings was established by hearsay evidence. The trial judge ruled the evidence was admissible. The applicant subsequently gave evidence accounting for his movements, but was convicted. On appeal:

Held by the Court of Criminal Appeal (McCarthy, D'Arcy and Egan JJ) in allowing the appeal and ordering a re-trial:

(1) The evidence as to tracing involved an element of hearsay in the chain of proof, and as there was no question of an essential witness being unavailable it was not admissible. *Myers v Director of Public Prosecutions* [1965] AC 1001 distinguished.

(2) There was ample and clear independent proof to support the conviction made, and the supportive evidence of tracing was not vital, but the court could not be satisfied that the trial jury had not taken account of inadmissible evidence, and the defence had been required to go into evidence, so that the court could not apply the provision in section 5(1) of the Courts of Justice Act 1928 but would order a re-trial. *The People v Ruttledge* (1946) 1 Frewen 75 applied.

(3) In a trial where a significant part of the evidence consists of a tape recording, and the tape is shown to be authentic, defects in sound quality, disputes as to the identity of the speakers or the fact that there were available more persons to give evidence as to the identity of the speakers are no grounds for excluding it from evidence; but the trial judge should always direct the jury as to sound quality if evidence on this point has been given by the defence.

(4) Where an offence is alleged to have been committed by two or more persons, there is no rule of evidence excluding personal accounts of recipients of telephone calls or mechanical recordings of them on the ground merely that they were not made by the person then on trial, if it is shown that they were made as part of the transaction as a whole.

Cases cited in this judgment:
Attorney General v Hurley (1937) 71 I.L.T.R. 31
Myers v Director of Public Prosecutions [1965] A.C. 1001; [1964] 2 All E.R. 881
R. v Robertson (1936) 25 Cr. App. R. 208
R. v Thompson [1914] 2 K.B. 105
The People v Campbell (1983) 2 Frewen 131
The People v Ruttledge (1946) 1 Frewen 75

[1986] ILRM 716

The People (Director of Public Prosecutions) v Patrick (Pa Ned) Walsh
[C.C.A. No. 86 of 1984]
[S.C. No. 14 of 1986]

Court of Criminal Appeal   20 December 1985

Supreme Court   25 July 1986

Criminal law – arrest – statutory power – offences against the state – motive – arrest in respect of scheduled offence – questioning in relation to non-scheduled offence – non-scheduled offence more serious – whether arrest lawful – whether arrest merely colourable device – purpose of statute – whether applicable to subversive and non-subversive crime – Offences against the State Act 1939 (No. 13), sections 30, 45

The appellant had been charged with murder and malicious damage, and later tried for murder only. The murder related to the death of a person whose shop premises and house had been broken into and which involved malicious damage to the premises. The appellant was arrested pursuant to section 30 of the Offences against the State Act 1939 in respect of the malicious damage offences, which was a scheduled offence under the Act. In the course of his detention under section 30, he was questioned in relation to the murder which the Gardaí were investigating. At his trial, evidence was given that the Gardaí were investigating the death involved in the entering the premises, and that both events were regarded as 'part and parcel of the one act'. Counsel objected to the admissibility of evidence obtained from the appellant on the ground that the arrest under section 30 had been used purely as a device to question him in relation to the murder.

Held by the trial judge (O'Hanlon J) in ruling the evidence admissible:
while the Gardaí were more concerned with the murder investigation in their questioning of the accused when he was in custody under section 30 of the Offences against the State Act 1939, and while the malicious damage was not likely to have caused damage in excess of £50, nonetheless it was not obviously spurious to have arrested the accused in respect of malicious damage having regard to the possibility that only one person might be

charged with murder and that the seriousness of the malicious damage had yet to be ascertained, as well as the circumstances in which the malicious damage was committed for the purpose of gaining forcible entry with the intent of robbery which would constitute a serious criminal matter regardless of the amount of damage done. *The People v Towson* [1978] ILRM 122 and *The State (Bowes) v Fitzpatrick* [1978] ILRM 195 applied.

The appellant was convicted of murder. On appeal pursuant to the trial judge's certificate of leave to appeal.

Held by the Court of Criminal Appeal (Finlay CJ, Egan and Barr JJ) in dismissing the appeal:

(1) The provisions of section 30 of the 1939 Act were clear and unambiguous in their terms and the Government, in making an order providing that offences under the Malicious Damage Act 1861 be scheduled offences for the purposes of section 30, provided that all offences under the 1861 Act came within the power of arrest under section 30, whether the malicious damage in question was or was not caused for subversive reasons, and the power in section 45 of the 1939 Act vested in the Director of Public Prosecutions to direct a trial in the ordinary courts in respect of a scheduled offence was presumably granted for the purpose of taking account of the distinction between subversive and non-subversive malicious damage.

(2) The trial judge was correct in taking account not only of the amount of damage caused but also the place and circumstances and time at which it is alleged to have taken place, and that in the circumstances of this case the malicious damage was a real offence and was necessarily involved as part of the same incident or transaction as the murder and that the arrest was therefore justified. *The People v Towson* [1978] ILRM 122 and *The State (Bowes) v Fitzpatrick* [1978] ILRM 195 followed.

(3) Since the malicious damage and the murder formed part of the same transaction or series of transactions there was no basis for restricting the ability of the Gardaí to question the appellant in respect of the malicious damage only. On appeal pursuant to certificate granted by the Court of Criminal Appeal.

Held by the Supreme Court (Walsh, Henchy, Griffin, Hederman and McCarthy JJ) in dismissing the appeal:

(1) The fact that there was a great disproportion between the nature of the offences in question, and that a greater concentration of police effort was on the investigation of the murder, was not of itself sufficient to establish as a reasonable probability that the arrest in respect of the malicious damage charge was simply a colourable device to hold the accused in custody for an ulterior purpose on an alleged offence in which the Gardaí had no real interest, and in view of the connection between the two offences and the genuine interest of the Gardaí in pursuing the malicious damage claim the arrest was a valid one.

(2) The provisions of the 1939 Act were not merely applicable to 'subversive' offences, and so they were applicable to the circumstances of this arrest. *The People v Quilligan* [1987] ILRM 606 applied.

Cases cited in the Central Criminal Court ruling
The People v Towson [1978] ILRM 122
The State (Bowes) v Fitzpatrick [1978] ILRM 195

Cases cited in the judgment of the Court of Criminal Appeal
  The People v Towson [1978] ILRM 122
  The State (Bowes) v Fitzpatrick [1978] ILRM 195

Case cited in Supreme Court judgment
  The People (DPP) v Quilligan [1986] I.R. 495; [1987] ILRM 606

[1986] I.R. 722; [1988] ILRM 137

The People (Director of Public Prosecutions) v Charles Conroy
[C.C.A. No. 5 of 1984]
[S.C. No. 24 of 1986]

Court of Criminal Appeal   6 June 1985

Supreme Court   31 July 1986

Criminal law – evidence – admissibility – garda custody – access to solicitor – whether arises as a constitutional right – Constitution of Ireland 1937, Article 40.3 – Criminal Justice Act 1984 (No. 22), section 4

Criminal law – trial – voir dire – evidence – admissibility – effect on subsequent trial – accused alleging detention in garda custody unlawful – onus of proof – whether issue to be tried by judge on voir dire or by jury – whether jury likely to be prejudiced by determining issue of lawfulness of detention or admissibility of evidence – Constitution of Ireland 1937, Articles 38.1, 38.5 – Criminal Justice Act 1984 (No. 22), section 25

The appellant had been charged with murder. In the course of his trial before a judge and jury in the Central Criminal Court, his counsel challenged the admissibility of inculpatory statements made by him while in garda custody. Counsel stated that the appellant would allege in evidence that he requested access to a solicitor and that this was denied him, and that he was not told he was free to leave the garda station even though at the time he had not been charged with any offence. Counsel requested that these issues be determined by the jury in accordance with the decision of the Supreme Court in *The People v Lynch* [1982] I.R. 64; [1981] ILRM 389. The trial judge determined the issues on his own, and determined that all statements made by the accused were admissible in evidence; and that in relation to the issue of whether the appellant was in unlawful detention at the time he made the statements that he had failed to make out a *prima facie* case of unlawful detention. The appellant applied for leave to appeal to the Court of Criminal Appeal on the basis that the trial judge had failed to follow the procedure set out in *The People v Lynch*.

Held by the Court of Criminal Appeal (McCarthy, Costello and Murphy JJ) in dismissing the application:
  the trial judge was entitled to make a determination on his own in relation to the issue

raised as to the admissibility of the evidence in question, and there was no requirement that all issues as to the admissibility of evidence be tried by a jury, particularly where the trial judge determined that there was no real conflict of fact as to what occurred in garda custody. *The People v Lynch* [1982] I.R. 64; [1981] ILRM 389 explained.

On appeal to the Supreme Court pursuant to certificate of leave to appeal

Held by the Supreme Court (Finlay CJ, Walsh, Henchy, Griffin and Hederman JJ) in ordering a re-trial:

(1) (Walsh J dissenting) the practice which had operated since the foundation of the State of having the issue of the admissibility of all evidence determined by the trial judge in the absence of the jury was required by Article 38 of the Constitution, since if such issues were determined as a preliminary matter by a jury there was a possibility of prejudice to the accused, as an inhibiting factor on the accused's counsel in conducting cross-examination on the *voir dire*, or on the effect on the jury in its determination as to whether the accused is guilty or not guilty or in assessing certain evidence on the *voir dire* without affecting the subsequent trial, since evidence given on the *voir dire* would not be admissible subsequently against the accused. Observations in *The People v Lynch* [1982] I.R. 64; [1981] ILRM 389 not followed. *The State v Treanor* [1924] 2 I.R. 193 followed. *Jackson v Denno* (1964) 378 US 368 and *The People v McGlynn* [1967] I.R. 232 discussed.

Per Henchy J: a jury informed of the circumstances and content of evidence which it determined to be inadmissible would be unfit to try the issue of guilt or innocence since it would lack the characteristic of impartiality, and the alternative of having separate juries determine the two issues would be inconsistent with the requirement of a unitary and unbroken trial with a jury guaranteed by Article 38.5 of the Constitution.

Per Walsh J (dissenting): the question of possible prejudice to the jury in determining the issue of admissibility could be overcome by having the jury determine the matter without being informed of the contents of the evidence in question and by the trial judge formulating specific questions requiring answer by the jury, and the requirements in relation to jury verdicts in section 24 of the Criminal Justice Act 1984 applied to such verdicts, and would not therefore involve the suggested anomaly of unanimous verdicts on admissibility.

(2) Once the appellant's counsel had indicated that his client would contest the legality of his detention on the basis that he did not feel free to leave the Garda station, the trial judge had erred in not requiring the State to establish either that his custody was lawful or that he was not in custody at the time, and in not permitting evidence to be adduced on that issue.

Per Walsh J: a person detained in garda custody may or may not have a constitutional right to be asked if he wished to have a solicitor, but where a person does ask for one he is entitled, on the basis of the obligation on the gardaí under Article 40.3 to observe fair procedures, to access to a solicitor. Provisions of section 4 of the Criminal Justice Act 1984 discussed in the context of the circumstances surrounding the taking of the statement from the appellant.

Per Henchy J: the trial judge's determination that a person detained by the police has no constitutional right to consult with a solicitor was in accordance with decided cases and should not be disturbed. *The People v Farrell* [1978] I.R. 13 and *The People v Shaw* [1982] I.R. 1 discussed.

Cases cited in the judgment of the Court of Criminal Appeal

The People v Farrell [1987] I.R. 13
The People v Lynch [1982] I.R. 64; [1981] ILRM 389

Cases cited in Supreme Court judgments
Attorney General v McCabe [1927] I.R. 129
Bartlett v Smith (1843) 11 M & W 483
Boyle v Wiseman (1856) 11 Ex 360
In re the Emergency Powers Bill 1976 [1977] I.R. 159; 111 I.L.T.R. 29
Jackson v Denno (1964) 378 U.S. 368
Jones v Fort (1828) Moo & M 196
Minter v Priest [1930] A.C. 558; [1930] All E.R. Rep 431
The People v Ainscough [1960] I.R. 136
The People v Cradden [1955] I.R. 130
The People v Farrell [1978] I.R. 13
The People v Lynch [1982] I.R. 64; [1981] ILRM 389
The People v McGlynn [1967] I.R. 232
The People v O'Brien [1965] I.R. 142
The People v Shaw [1982] I.R. 1
R v Basto (1954) 91 C.L.R. 628
R v Brinkley [1984] NI 48 (Note)
R v Chan Wei-Keung [1967] 2 A.C. 160; [1967] 2 W.L.R. 552; [1967] All E.R. 948
R v McAloon [1959] O.R. 441
R v McLaren [1949] 1 W.W.R. 529; [1949] 2 D.L.R. 682
R v Murray [1951] 1 K.B. 391; [1950] 2 All E.R. 925
R v Ng Chun-Kwan [1974] H.K.L.R. 319
R v Sparks [1964] A.C. 964; [1964] 2 W.L.R. 566; [1964] All E.R. 727
R v Wong Kam-ming [1980] A.C. 247; [1979] 2 W.L.R. 81; [1979] 1 All E.R. 939
The State v Treanor [1924] 2 I.R. 193
The State (Healy) v Donoghue [1976] I.R. 325; 110 I.L.T.R. 112; 112 I.L.T.R. 37

[1986] I.R. 460; [1988] ILRM 4

The People (Director of Public Prosecutions) v Francis Mulvey
[C.C.A. No. 75 of 1986]

Court of Criminal Appeal   16 March 1987

Criminal law – rape – corroboration – evidence relied on as corroboration – distress coincident with the complaint – whether distressed condition of complainant capable of constituting corroboration – judge's direction to jury

The applicant was convicted of rape. As corroboration of the complaint the prosecution tendered the evidence of certain witnesses to whom the prosecutrix complained, as to her distressed condition at the time that she made the complaint of rape.

The defence case was that the prosecutrix consented to sexual intercourse with the applicant and that her subsequent distress was due to the fact that she had lost her virginity unexpectedly and that this was not corroboration because, as the complaint was not corroborative of itself, the description of a distressed condition could not be treated as corroboration if it was part of the complaint or must be given so little weight as to be of no significance.

The trial judge left to the jury the question of whether or not the distressed condition constituted corroboration of the evidence of the prosecutrix, but did not state to the jury that the alleged corroboration was a description of a distressed condition apparent at the time of making a complaint of rape. On the applicant's application for leave to appeal against conviction and sentence it was

Held by the Court of Criminal Appeal (McCarthy, Gannon and Barr JJ) in dismissing the application:

(1) That the distressed condition of a complainant in a case of rape, might, depending on the circumstances, amount to corroboration of the offence but the jury should be wary of relying upon it.

(2) That the trial judge was bound to warn the jury of the need for corroboration, the weakness of evidence of a distressed condition as corroboration in cases of rape and the danger of convicting in the absence of corroboration. *Attorney General v Cradden* [1955] I.R. 130; *Attorney General v O'Sullivan* [1930] I.R. 552 and *Reg. v Knight* [1966] 1 W.L.R. 230 followed.

(3) That in the instant case the jury was told of its role in assessing what was corroboration and, in putting the defence case to the jury, the trial judge made it clear that the jury should consider the issue of whether or not there was corroboration in the light of the defence submissions as to the cause of the distress.

Cases cited in this report:

Attorney General v Lennon (Unreported, Court of Criminal Appeal, 5 May 1925) referred to in Sandes: Criminal Practice Procedure and Evidence in Éire, 2nd edition, p. 138.

Attorney General v Linehan [1929] I.R. 19; (1928) 63 I.L.T.R. 30

Attorney General v Levison [1932] I.R. 158

Attorney General v Corcoran and Donoghue (1929) 63 I.L.T.R. 145

Attorney General v O'Sullivan [1930] I.R. 552

R. v Redpath (1962) 46 Cr. App. R. 319
R. v Knight [1966] 1 W.L.R. 230; [1966] 1 All ER 647; (1966) 50 Cr. App. R. 122
James v R. (1971) 55 Cr. App. R. 299
R. v Wilson (1974) 58 Cr. App. R. 304
R. v Chauhan (1981) 73 Cr. App. R. 232
R. v Luise [1964] Crim. L.R. 605
R. v Suddens [1964] Crim. L.R. 606
R. v Ohoye [1964] Crim. L.R. 416
R. v Zielinski (1950) 34 Cr. App. R. 193
The People (Attorney General) v Cradden [1955] I.R. 130
Archbold: criminal Pleading Evidence and Practice, 42nd Ed., Ch. 16, p. 1142

[1987] I.R. 502

The People (Director of Public Prosecutions) v William McGinley
[C.C.A. No. 96 of 1985]

Court of Criminal Appeal   25 May 1987

Criminal law – evidence – accomplice – cross-examination – whether evidence from accomplice's previous trial relevant – whether going to motive or credit – test of admissibility – dangers of convicting on evidence of accomplice – whether trial judge's direction correct in law – procedure – defect in book of evidence – whether trial unsatisfactory

The appellant was charged with larceny of cattle. At his trial, the primary evidence tendered by the prosecution was that of an alleged accomplice of the appellant. The book of evidence contained a composite statement from the accomplice, who had made a number of statements to the Garda Síochána, but the composite statement did not include all the information disclosed by the accomplice. In addition, certain forensic evidence was not revealed until the trial was in progress. Counsel for the appellant referred to these gaps in evidence in the course of the trial. In the course of the cross-examination of the accomplice by counsel for the appellant, counsel attempted to introduce evidence of a newspaper account of the accomplice's own trial in relation to the same events as those involved in the appellant's trial. The trial judge ruled that such newspaper accounts were not admissible as evidence of what occurred during the accomplice's trial. He further ruled that only the official transcript of the trial would be admissible as evidence as to what occurred during the trial, and that evidence from a member of the Garda Síochána who was present at the accomplice's trial (and which the appellant's counsel wished to introduce) was also not admissible. The trial judge directed the jury on the dangers involved in convicting an accused on the evidence of an accomplice. The appellant was found guilty of the charges.

On the appellant's application for leave to appeal to the Court of Criminal Appeal (Finlay CJ, Costello and Barrington JJ), it was

Held in granting the application and ordering a re-trial:

(1) That although there had been some errors and omissions from the book of evidence as served on the appellant, in that not all evidence was revealed to the defence prior to the trial, effective use had been made by counsel for the appellant of these errors and omissions, and these errors did not constitute an unfair procedure, nor make the trial unsatisfactory.

(2) That the trial judge's direction to the jury on the danger of convicting on the evidence of an accomplice, which drew attention to the fact that an accomplice may have something to gain from giving evidence and that there was a danger of convicting without independent corroboration, was a full and correct direction to the jury.

(3) That although the trial judge was correct in ruling out the use of newspaper reports of the accomplice's trial, he was not correct in law in ruling that only the official transcript of that trial was admissible as to what occurred during that trial since the transcript was only of evidential value for the purposes of an appeal; and evidence of a member of the Garda Síochána who was present at the trial would have been admissible.

(4) That the line of questioning followed by counsel for the appellant as to what occurred at the accomplice's trial fell into the category of questioning which might lead to establish the accomplice's bias or partiality, as distinct from a general assertion of lack of credit; and the line of questioning was therefore one of the exceptions to the rule prohibiting contradiction of collateral matters.

Cases cited in this report:
Attorney General v Hitchcock (1847) 1 Exch. 91
Thomas v David (1836) 7 C. & P. 350
R. v Philips (1936) 26 Cr. App. R. 17
R. v Yousry (1914) 11 Cr. App. R. 13
R. v Treacy [1944] 2 All E.R. 229; (1944) 30 Cr. App. R. 93
R. v McCormick [1984] N.I. 50
R. v Baskerville [1916] 2 K.B. 658; [1916-17] All E.R. Rep. 38
R. v Shaw (188) 16 Cox's C.C. 503
R. v Turner (Bryan James) (1975) 61 Cr. App. R. 67
R. v Downer (1886) 14 Cox's C.C. 486
The People v Prunty [1986] ILRM 716
Hollington v Hewthorne & Co. Ltd [1943] K.B. 587; [1943] 2 All E.R. 35

The People (Director of Public Prosecutions) v Eamon Kelly
[C.C.A. No. 59 of 1986]

Court of Criminal Appeal   30 July 1987

Criminal law – evidence – character of witness – previous convictions of prosecution witness – record unknown to defence or prosecution – whether material to credibility of witness – extent of duty on prosecution to inform defence

The applicant was convicted, *inter alia*, of wounding with intent to do grievous bodily harm, contrary to section 18 of the Offences Against the Person Act, 1861. He denied the charged and denied being at the scene when the offences took place. The prosecution witness, who identified the applicant as being present at the scene, was not cross-examined as to his credibility however, unknown to both the prosecution and defence, he had a number of serious convictions recorded against him. It was argued on behalf of the applicant that there could have been a different verdict by the jury if this evidence had been available.

Held by the Court of Criminal Appeal (Finlay CJ, Lynch and Lardner JJ), in allowing the application and directing a new trial:
    (1) That, where the prosecution was aware of a previous conviction of a prosecution witness, they should so inform the defence before the trial.
    (2) That if the trial judge was satisfied that the conviction could go to the credit of that witness he could permit it to be put to him.
    (3) That the prosecution did not have a duty to make exhaustive or widespread enquiries about every prosecution witness so as to ascertain if convictions had been recorded against him or her.
    (4) That if, unknown to the prosecution and defence, there was a serious or significant conviction against a prosecution witness, and if this fact was discovered after the trial, the Court of Appeal may, upon being satisfied as to the fact of such conviction and being also satisfied that it was material to the credibility of the witness, allow an appeal and direct a new trial. *R. v Collister and Warhurst* (1955) 39 Cr. App. R. 100; *R. v Parks* [1961] 1 W.L.R. 1484 and *R. v Paraskeva* (1983) 76 Cr. App. R. 162 considered and applied.

Cases cited in this report:
    R. v Collister and Warhurst (1955) 39 Cr. App. R. 100
    R. v Parks [1961] 1 W.L.R. 1484; [1961] 3 All E.R. 633; 46 Cr. App. R. 29
    R. v Paraskeva (1982) 76 Cr. App. R. 162
    R. v Knightbridge Crown Court, ex parte Goonatilleke [1986] Q.B. 1; [1985] 3 W.L.R. 553; [1986] 2 All E.R. 498; 81 Cr. App. R. 31
    R. v Pestano (1981) Crim. L.R. 397
    Driscoll v R. (1977) 137 C.L.R. 517
    Practice Note 'Antecendent History of Accused and Convicted Persons' (1955) 39 Cr. App. R. 20

[1987] I.R. 596

The People (Director of Public Prosecutions) v James Carmody and Jeremiah Carmody
[C.C.A. Nos. 91 and 92 of 1986]

Court of Criminal Appeal   14 December 1987

Criminal law – sentence – habitual criminals – lengthy sentence imposed – whether amounting to preventative detention – whether attempt to reform by prevention appropriate basis for sentence – Prevention of Crime Act 1908 (8 Edw. 7, c.59), section 10

The applicants were habitual criminals, the first applicant having convictions beginning in 1968 and the second applicant having convictions dating back to 1961. Primarily the convictions were for burglary. They had served numerous terms of imprisonment imposed by the District Court, primarily for periods of up to 12 months. In the instant case, they were charged with burglary, and pleaded guilty to the charges in the Circuit Court. The trial judge (Judge Murphy) imposed a sentence of six years imprisonment on each applicant, stating that the applicants were 'not amenable in any manner to the ordinary constrictions of the society in which they live and they are preying on innocent people and my primary duty is to protect those people.' The applicants applied for leave to appeal against sentence.

Held by the Court of Criminal Appeal (McCarthy, Barron and Egan JJ) in allowing the application: The only justification for the radical departure by the trial judge from the previous measures of imprisonment which had been imposed on the applicants was an understandable attempt to procure reform by prevention, but in the absence of appropriate statutory provisions this was an unacceptable basis for the particular sentence, and a sentence of three years imprisonment would be substituted in respect of each of the applicants.

Per curiam: there are apparently no facilities in the State for preventative detention, as envisaged in section 10 of the Prevention of Crime Act 1908.

Cases cited in this judgment
The People v O'Callaghan [1966] I.R. 501; 104 I.L.T.R. 53
The People v O'Driscoll (1972) 1 Frewen 351

Additional cases cited in argument
King v Attorney General [1981] I.R. 233
R. v Ottewell [1970] A.C. 642; [1968] 3 W.L.R. 621; [1968] 3 All E.R. 153; 52 Cr. App. R. 679
The State (Stanbridge) v Mahon [1979] I.R. 214

[1988] ILRM 370

The People (Director of Public Prosecutions) v Anthony Hoey
[C.C.A. No. 47 of 1986]

Court of Criminal Appeal   29 June 1987

Supreme Court   16 December 1987

Criminal law – evidence – admissibility – statement of admission by accused in answer to question by member of an Garda Síochána – whether question an inducement or threat – effect of inducement – Offences Against the State Act 1939 (No. 13), section 30

The applicant was convicted before the Special Criminal Court of possession of firearms and ammunition contrary to section 15(a) of the Firearms Act 1925, as amended. The only evidence against the accused was a statement of admission of responsibility made by him to a member of an Garda Síochána while in custody. The applicant applied for leave to appeal against his conviction on the ground that his statement of admission was inadmissible as evidence because it was made as a result of a question asked by a member of an Garda Síochána which operated as an inducement to make the statement and therefore the statement was not voluntary.

Held by the Court of Criminal Appeal (Finlay CJ, Lynch and Egan JJ), in refusing the application for leave to appeal:

(1) That while the question asked by the detective inspector induced by the applicant to admit responsibility for the offence, the question was not a threat or an improper inducement by threat.

(2) That an interview with a prime suspect by the gardaí must involve an attempt to induce the suspect to make a statement in which he will either his guilt or establish his innocence. It is only an improper inducement which involves a threat or promise of temporal disadvantage or advantage which will render a statement thus obtained inadmissible.

(3) That for the gardaí to state that they may have to make further inquiries which may inconvenience or upset other persons, cannot in itself be regarded as a threat or an improper inducement by threat if it is a fact and not a threat to harass others whom the gardaí did not believe were involved. *Attorney General v Cleary* (1938) 72 I.L.T.R. 84 and *Attorney General v McCabe* [1927] I.R. 129 applied.

The Court of Criminal Appeal certified that its decision involved points of law of exceptional public importance and on appeal by the applicant it was

Held by the Supreme Court (Walsh, Henchy, Griffin, Hederman and McCarthy JJ), in allowing the appeal and setting aside the conviction:

(1) That the incriminating statement of the appellant had not been proved to have been free and voluntary and that therefore evidence of the statement ought not to have been received. The appellant was unwilling to make any form of admission until the question was put to him by the detective inspector and it was clear beyond all reasonable doubt that the effect of the question was to cause him to make the confession.

(2) That the onus was on the prosecution to prove that the statement was voluntary, the test being whether or not the question was calculated to induce the appellant to admit the

offence because of fear of prejudice or hope of advantage. The test was an objective one and it was irrelevant to consider the intention or motive of the person who posed the question.

(3) That the effect of the words used, irrespective of what they were intended to mean, was calculated to convey that the appellant's family would not be interrogated by the Garda Síochána if the appellant admitted responsibility. In the circumstances of the case, that amounted to an improper inducement which produced a confession.

Cases cited in this report:

The People (Attorney General) v O'Brien [1965] I.R. 142

Commissions of Customs and Excise v Harz and Power (1967) 51 Cr. App. R. 123

R. v Smith [1959] 2 Q.B. 35; [1959] 2 W.L.R. 623; [1959] 2 All E.R. 193; 42 Cr. App. R. 121

R. v Middleton [1975] Q.B. 191; [1974] 3 W.L.R. 335; [1974] 2 All E.R. 1190; 59 Cr. App. R. 18; [1974] Crim. L.R. 667

R. v Cleary (1963) 48 Cr. App. R. 116

The People (Attorney General) v Cleary (1938) 72 I.L.T.R. 84; [1934] L.J. Ir. 153

The People (Attorney General) v McCabe [1927] I.R. 129

The People (Attorney General) v Galvin [1964] I.R. 325

The People (Attorney General) v Flynn [1963] I.R. 255

The People (DPP) v Shaw [1982] I.R. 1

The People (DPP) v McNally 2 Frewen 43

R. v Thompson [1893] 2 Q.B. 12

Ibrahim v R. [1914] A.C. 599; [1914-15] All E.R. Rep. 874; 24 Cox C.C. 174

R. v Rennie [1982] 1 W.L.R. 64; [1982] 1 All E.R. 385; 74 Cr. App. R. 207

The People (Attorney General) v Cummins [1972] I.R. 312

DPP v Ping Lin [1976] A.C. 574; [1975] 3 W.L.R. 419; [1975] 3 All E.R. 175; 62 Cr. App. R. 14

[1987] I.R. 637

The People (Director of Public Prosecutions) v Jackie Kelly
[C.C.A. No. 115 of 1987]

Court of Criminal Appeal   16 May 1988

Criminal law – jury – majority verdict – minimum time limit which jury must spend in deliberation before trial judge can accept majority verdict – Whether time spent by jury attending to observations of trial judge constitutes deliberation – Criminal Justice Act 1984 (No. 22), section 25(3)

The appellant was convicted of indecent assault in October 1987 and was sentenced to three years imprisonment. The conviction was imposed by way of a majority verdict. This verdict was arrived at after the jury had retired for two hours and two minutes. However, approximately 12 minutes were spent in court in asking questions and in attending the observations of the trial judge. Therefore, the jury were unsupervised by the court for not more than one hour and 50 minutes. The appellant contended, *inter alia*, that the conviction was bad as not complying with section 25(3) of the Criminal Justice Act 1984 which prescribes a time limit of 'at least two hours for deliberation' which must be spent by a jury before a trial judge may accept a majority verdict.

Held by the Court of Criminal Appeal (McCarthy, Egan, Blayney JJ) in quashing the conviction:

(1) The minimum period of time which must be afforded to the jury for deliberation is at least two hours — No impairment, however small, of that period may be permitted.

(2) The time spent by a jury back in court listening to the further charge or charges of the trial judge cannot be considered as part of the two hours of deliberation. Whether the facts are clear this leaves no discretionary conclusion for the court of trial. *R. v Adams* not followed.

(3) On the facts disclosed in this case there was a patent failure to comply with the requirements of section 25(3) of the Criminal Justice Act 1984. Consequently, the application for leave to appeal must be granted, the hearing of the application treated as the hearing of the appeal, and the conviction quashed.

Cases cited in this judgment
R. v Adams and Hogan (1968) 52 Cr. App. R. 588
R. v Bateson (1969) 54 Cr. App. R. 373

[1989] ILRM 370

The People (Director of Public Prosecutions) v Sean Howley
[S.C. No. 156 of 1988]

Supreme Court   29 July 1988

Criminal Law – arrest – offences against the state – arrest in respect of scheduled offence – questioning in respect of non-scheduled offence – predominant motive for arrest – whether arrest a colourable device – validity of extension order for detention for further 24 hour period – Offences Against the State Act 1939 (No. 13), section 30

The appellant was arrested under section 30 of the Offences Against the State Act 1939, on suspicion of having committed the scheduled offence of cattle maiming. He was detained in Garda custody for a period of 24 hours during which time a Chief Superintendent authorised his detention for a further period of 24 hours. During this further period of detention the appellant made a statement confessing to a murder, which was subsequently admitted as evidence at his trial. The appellant was convicted of murder and on appeal to the Court of Criminal Appeal contended that at the time the admissions in question were made, his detention was unlawful and the statements made by him were therefore inadmissible as evidence. His appeal to the Court of Criminal Appeal was unsuccessful; however the Court certified two points of law for the consideration of the Supreme Court. These were as follows: (a) whether the arrest under section 30 was unlawful unless it was established that the predominant motive for the arrest was the desire to investigate the scheduled offence; (b) even if the arrest under section 30 was lawful, whether the extension order made by the Chief Superintendent was unlawful by reason of the fact that he was not informed by the Gardaí involved of their intention to interview the accused not only in respect of the scheduled offence but also in connection with the murder.

Held by the Supreme Court (Walsh, Henchy, Griffin, Hederman, McCarthy JJ):

(1) The trial judge was justified in concluding that the arrest in respect of the scheduled offence of cattle maiming was not in any sense a 'colourable device' to allow the Gardaí an opportunity to question the accused in relation to the alleged murder. *The People v. Quilligan* [1987] ILRM 606 approved. There is no requirement that an arrest under section 30 must be predominantly motivated by a desire to investigate a scheduled offence.

(2) There are no grounds for holding that the extension of the period of detention was unlawful. When the Garda officer empowered to make the extension order *bona fide* suspects the accused person of being involved in the offence for which he was originally arrested, the extended period of detention is lawful.

Cases cited in this judgment

Cassidy v Minister for Industry and Commerce [1978] IR 297
The People v Byrne [1987] IR 363; [1989] ILRM 629
The People v Kelly (No. 2) [1983] IR 1; [1983] ILRM 271
The People v Quilligan [1986] IR 495; [1987] ILRM 606
The People v Walsh [1986] IR 722; [1988] ILRM 137
Trimbole v Governor of Mountjoy Prison [1985] IR 550; [1985] ILRM 465
Webb v Minister for Housing and Local Government [1965] 1 WLR 755

[1989] ILRM 629

The People (Director of Public Prosecutions) v Michael Egan
[C.C.A. No. 54 of 1988]

Court of Criminal Appeal   27 July 1989

Criminal law – evidence – statement – admissibility – incriminating statement – Effect on accused of visits by members of his family – accused's wife informing gardaí in his presence of his involvement in the crime – whether statement voluntary

Criminal law – aiding and abetting – accused assisting principal – mens rea – Extent of accused's knowledge of crime – whether assistance rendered by accused made him an accessory before the fact – whether accused was an accessory after the fact – Accessories and Abettors Act, 1861 (24 & 25 Vict., c. 94) – Larceny Act, 1916 (6 & 7 Geo. V., c. 50), section 35

Section 35 of the Larceny Act 1916, provides:

> "Every person who knowingly and wilfully aids, abets, counsels, procures or commands the commission of an offence punishable under this Act shall be liable to be dealt with, indicted, tried and punished as a principal offender".

The applicant was charged with robbery and receiving stolen goods arising out of a theft of jewellery. He was convicted of robbery and sentenced to seven years imprisonment but was found not guilty of receiving stolen goods. The only evidence implicating the applicant in the robbery was his own written statement wherein he stated *inter alia* that he had a telephone call requesting permission for the caller to leave a van in his workshop and that he was aware that a "small stroke" was to take place and that he should be at his workshop door at an arranged time. The statement went on to say that the van arrived as arranged with a number of armed and masked men in it and a large number of sacks of jewellery, and that the men remained in the workshop for some time and left later that day. According to his statement the applicant found a bag containing a large amount of gold rings which had been left behind which he kept and later disposed of.

The applicant was arrested pursuant to section 30 of the Offences Against the State Act, 1939, and detained for questioning. On the evening of the first day of his interrogation he had a visit from his wife at his own request. She told the applicant that she had told the gardaí that he had been involved in the jewellery robbery and had also told them about the van in the workshop and the fact that he had brought jewellery into the house. The following day he saw his son, again at his request, and shortly after that visit the applicant made a written statement. During this interrogation the gardaí repeated to him an allegation of incest made against him.

It was argued on the applicant's behalf that his written statement was not voluntary, that he had been induced to make it because by that time his will had crumbled by the combination of his wife and son's visit and the allegation of incest. Furthermore, it was submitted that the applicant had been charged as a principal in the crime but that his part took place after the crime occurred which made him an accessory after the fact and was liable therefore to a term of imprisonment not exceeding two years, by virtue of section 4 of the Accessories and

Abettors Act, 1861. Furthermore, it was argued, the applicant had no knowledge of the serious armed robbery that was to take place and that the applicant's statement established him to be guilty of receiving stolen goods and not of robbery.

Held by the Court of Criminal Appeal (Finlay CJ, Costello and Johnson JJ), in dismissing the application and affirming the conviction:

(1) That the visit by the applicant's wife was at his own request and as it occurred twenty four hours before he made the written statement it was open to the trial judge at the trial within the trial to conclude that the allegations she made had not effect on the voluntary nature of the statement. The effect on the applicant of a visit by his son immediately before the statement was made was also a matter for the trial judge to assess. With regard to an allegation alleged to have been made by the gardaí to the applicant and he was guilty of incest, there was a conflict of evidence as to what was said and this was a matter also for the trial judge to resolve.

(2) That a person could aid and abet the commission of a crime without being present when the crime was committed, and accordingly be liable to be dealt with as a principal offender. *The People v Madden* [1977] I.R. 336 applied.

(3) That, in order to be convicted of the principal offence, it was not necessary for the prosecution to establish that a person who had aided and abetted the principal offender before the crime was committed had knowledge of the actual crime intended. It is sufficient that a person who gave assistance knew the nature of the intended crime.

(4) That, the applicant was an accessory before the fact of the crime committed by the principal offender because he knew that a crime was to be committed, that it involved the theft of goods and with this knowledge he assisted the principal offender when he agreed before the crime took place to make his workshop available to hide the stolen goods. *The People v Madden* [1977] I.R. 336 applied. *DPP for Northern Ireland v Maxwell* [1978] 1 W.L.R. 1350 followed.

Cases cited in this report:
　　The People (DPP) v McNally (1981) 2 Frewen 43
　　The People v Madden [1977] I.R. 336; (1976) 111 I.L.T.R. 117
　　DPP for Northern Ireland v Maxwell [1978] N.I. 42; [1978] 1 W.L.R. 1350; [1978] 3
　　All E.R. 1140; (1979) 68 Cr. App. R. 128
　　Reg. v Bainbridge [1960] 1 Q.B. 129; [1959] 3 W.L.R. 565; [1959] 3 All E.R. 200
　　The People (DPP) v Pringle (1981) 2 Frewen 57

[1989] I.R. 681

The People (Director of Public Prosecutions) v Mark Kenny
[S.C. No. 409 of 1989]

Supreme Court   20 March 1990

Consitution – evidence – whether evidence obtained in breach of constitutional rights is inadmissible – circumstances where such evidence may be admitted – rationale for exclusionary rule

Criminal Law – search warrant – nature of information required for issue of warrant – nature of determination to issue warrant – Misuse of Drugs Act 1977 (No. 12), s. 26(1)

Facts In the course of surveillance of premises at Rathmines, Dublin, on 2 October 1984, two members of An Garda Síochána observed activity which appeared to constitute trafficking in drugs. By wireless telephone, one of the gardaí requested a colleague to bring to him a search warrant obtained from a peace commissioner under s. 26(1) of the Misuse of Drugs Act 1977 as amended. The information upon which the warrant was issued stated the suspicion of the garda that controlled drugs were on the premises but did not include any facts from which the peace commissioner himself could be satisfied there were reasonable grounds for such suspicion. The peace commissioner made no enquiries beyond what was contained in the information to satisfy himself there were reasonable grounds for such suspicion. The form of information used on the application for the issue of the warrant was a standard form in use since the enactment of the 1977 Act. On procuring the warrant, the garda sought entry by demand, made a forcible entry through a window and found the accused with controlled drugs for which he took responsibility. That was the only evidence associating the accused with controlled drugs. The accused was convicted and sentenced to five years' imprisonment.

The Court of Criminal Appeal (McCarthy, O'Hanlon and Lardner JJ) rejected his appeal but certified a point of law of exceptional public importance for the determination of the Supreme Court pursuant to s. 29 of the Courts of Justice Act 1924 on 30 November 1989 namely whether the forcible entry of the accused's home by members of An Garda Síochána on foot of an invalid search warrant constituted a deliberate and conscious violation of the accused's constitutional rights such as to render any evidence obtained thereby inadmissible at the trial of the accused.

Held by the Supreme Court (Finlay CJ, Walsh and Hederman JJ; Griffith and Lynch JJ dissenting), in answering the question in the affirmative and quashing the accused's conviction,

(1) Evidence obtained by an invasion of the personal rights of a citizen protected by the Constition must be excluded in criminal proceedings unless a court is satisfied the act constituting a breach of constitutional rights was committed unintentionally or accidentally or is satisfied there are extraordinary excusing circumstances justifying its inclusion.

(2) When it is shown an act giving rise to a breach of the accused's constitutional rights was carried out consciously and deliberately, it is immaterial whether the person carrying out that act was aware it was illegal or that it amounted to a breach of the accused's constitutional rights in considering whether evidence obtained thereby was admissible at his trial. In deciding whether a given act constitutes an unintentional or accidental breach of

303

constitutional rights, the court must have regard to the knowledge and intention associated with the actual act or acts complained of and not upon any factual or imputed knowledge in the person committing those acts of the constitutional rights of the person involved.

(3) An information required to obtain a search warrant under s. 26(1) of the Misuse of Drugs Act 1977 as amended must state facts from which a district justice or peace commissioner could be satisfied there were reasonable grounds for the issue thereof. In the absence of an independent decision by a district justice or peace commissioner that a search warrant is justified beyond a suspicion by members of the Garda Síochána that controlled drugs are on a premises, there may be a failure to adequately protect the inviolability of the dwelling under Article 40.5 of the Constitution. *People (Attorney General) v O'Brien* [1965] IR 142; *People v Walsh* [1980] IR 294; *People (DPP) v Healy* [1990] ILRM 313 followed; *People v Shaw* [1982] IR 1 distinguished.

Per curiam: The duty of the Courts under Article 40.3.1° of the Constitution is to defend and vindicate the rights protected therein as far as practicable. As between two alternative principles governing the inclusion of evidence obtained as a result of the invasion of the personal rights of the citizen, a court has an obligation to choose a principle which is more likely to provide a stronger and more effective defence and vindication of the right concerned. To provide for the exclusion of any evidence obtained in breach of an accused's constitutional rights incorporates a positive encouragement to those in authority over the crime protection and detection services of the State to consider in detail the personal rights of the citizen protected by the Constitution and the effect of their powers of arrest, detention, search and questioning in relation to such rights.

Cases cited in this judgment

Byrne v Grey [1988] IR 31
People (Attorney General) v O'Brien [1965] IR 142
People (DPP) v Healy [1990] ILRM 313; [1990] 1 IR 388 (p. 188, above)
People v Lynch [1982] IR 64; [1981] ILRM 389
People v Madden [1977] IR 336; 111 ILTR 117
People v O'Loughlin [1979] IR 85; 113 ILTR 109
People (DPP) v Quilligan [1986] I.R. 495; [1987] ILRM 606
People v Shaw [1982] IR 1
People v Walsh [1980] IR 294
R. v Inland Revenue Commrs., ex parte Rossminster Ltd [1980] A.C. 952; [1880] 2 W.L.R. 1; [1979] 3 All E.R. 385
United States v Leon (1983) 468 US 897

The People (Director of Public Prosecutions) v Liam Towson
[C.C.A. No. 102 of 1977]

Court of Criminal Appeal   5 July 1978

Criminal Law – arrest – statutory power – emergency powers – motive – arrest in respect of scheduled offence – questioning in respect of non-scheduled offence – whether arrest lawful – whether arrest effected for spurious purpose unconnected with offence authorised by statutory power – whether sufficient reasons and explanation given for arrest – Emergency Powers Act 1976 (No. 33), section 2

Criminal Law – evidence – circumstantial – murder – statement of accused – whether sufficient to convict – absence of body of victim

Criminal Law – evidence – statement – admissibility – breach of judges' rules – discretion to exclude – whether discretion should be exercised to introduce – purpose of particular rule – Judges' Rules, rule 9

Facts The applicant had been arrested in relation to the murder of a person which had involved firearms, pursuant to section 2 of the Emergency Powers Act 1976. The arrest was made in respect of the firearms matter, which was authorised under section 2 of the Act, and he was questioned in relation to the murder, which was not an offence in respect of which an arrest could be made under section 2. The applicant made a verbal incriminating statement regarding the murder, and was charged with and convicted of the offence. On application for leave to appeal:

Held by the Court of Criminal Appeal (O'Higgins CJ, Finlay P and Costello J) in dismissing the application:
 (1) Since the suspicion that the applicant had been involved in the shooting in question also involved inevitably a suspicion that he had been involved in an offence of being in possession of a firearm with intent to endanger life, there had not been a spurious invention of an imagined offence, and since the correctly held suspicion arose direcly out of the matter being investigated, the arrest was lawful; and it could not be the case that in the investigation of a matter under section 2 where some other offence, in respect of which a common law arrest only could have been effected, was also discovered, only a common law arrest could be made; and in making an arrest under section 2 rights which would otherwise be protected could not be abrogated or set aside. *Christie v Leachinsky* [1947] AC 573 discussed.
 (2) There was no requirement that the applicant be informed of the precise length of his proposed detention under section 2 once he had been told that he was being arrested under that section in relation to a particular offence. *In re O Laighleis* [1960] IR 93 applied.
 (3) While the statement had not been recorded pursuant to rule 9 of the Judges' Rules, the trial court could, in the exercise of its discretion, admit the statement where there was a reasonable explanation of the failure to comply with rule 9, and in this light and the particular mischief which rule 9 was aimed at, namely the adducing of invented or planted oral statements, the trial court had correctly exercised its discretion.
 (4) The trial court was entitled to act on the statement made by the applicant, even in the absence of other evidence indicating that a killing had taken place.

Cases cited in this judgment
 Christie v Leachinsky [1947] AC 573; [1974] 1 All ER 567
 O Laighleis, In re [1960] IR 93; 95 ILTR 92

Subject Matter Index

(Compiled by Raymond Byrne and Eithne Casey)